W9-BRL-053

Advance Praise for
Fighter Pilot

"Reading Robin Olds's mesmerizing memoir is like sitting on his shoulder and physically experiencing his decades of flying, fighting, and defending America's freedoms and values. You will laugh, yell 'Oorah!' and maybe even shed a tear. If you ever wanted to fly a P-51 Mustang in combat over Germany or shoot down a MiG over North Vietnam flying your F-4 Phantom jet, reading this is the closest you can get without actually doing it. The man was bigger than life and reading his memoir will confirm all the amazing stories about this legendary fighter pilot. Olds's remarkable life experiences jump from the pages—in a book that is nearly impossible to put down."

   —David Hartman, aviation writer and original host of *Good Morning America*

"I just finished reading the draft. What a remarkable book—I was absolutely riveted! The fascinating details, the way it captured the true maverick spirit of General Olds . . . his blunt honesty and absolute integrity, his triumphs and tragedies . . . made for one terrific read! What an amazing man—and one of America's greatest warriors and leaders. I was incredibly honored to have known him and to have featured him in my TV series. This is a must-read for anyone who wants to get into the mind of a true fighter pilot and a brilliant leader. A truly remarkable book . . . I highly recommend it!"

   —Cynthia Harrison, Creator/Executive Producer of *Dogfights* for the History
      Channel

"This book is a must-read for all fighter pilots, history buffs, and patriots. The stories will fascinate the aviation veteran but will be just as interesting to the 'everyman.' General Olds was a legend, a leader, a hero, a role model, and a genuine Sierra Hotel character."

   —T. Allan McArtor, chairman of Airbus Americas and former FAA Administrator
      and fighter pilot

"If you like flying, or just talking or reading about flying, you'll love this great book, and at it's conclusion you will wish it could go on and on. *Fighter Pilot* presents a not-at-all-standard American hero, a wild and wooly, rock 'em and sock 'em, All-American football jock at West Point who went on to become a top fighter ace. He was our finest and no one should be surprised that he courted and won the hand of a stunning Hollywood movie star. What a great read."

   —Tom "Bear" Wilson, author of *Termite Hill* and *Black Serpent*

"My only personal contact with General Olds was as a new cadet at the Air Force Academy shortly before his assignment changed. I recall that we regarded him as a legend but didn't understand why . . . I do now. As a young F-4 fighter pilot, I knew that I wanted to be a Robin Olds–type fighter pilot, but I didn't know what that was . . . I do now. Having held a number of leadership positions, I've wanted to lead like Colonel Olds led a combat wing but didn't know how . . . I do now. The book is much more than a legend's memoirs; it's a lesson on how to be a man's man . . . in the best sense!"

—Terence "Tom" Henricks, former NASA astronaut and president of
Aviation Week

FIGHTER
PILOT

———————— ★ ————————

FIGHTER PILOT

★

The Memoirs of Legendary Ace
Robin Olds

ROBIN OLDS

with Christina Olds and Ed Rasimus

ST. MARTIN'S PRESS
New York

FIGHTER PILOT. Copyright © 2010 by Robin Olds with Christina Olds and Ed Rasimus.
All rights reserved. Printed in the United States of America. For information,
address St. Martin's Press, 175 Fifth Avenue, New York, N.Y. 10010.
Design by Kathryn Parise
LIBRARY OF CONGRESS CATALOGING-IN-PUBLICATION DATA
ISBN 978-0-312-56023-2
Printed in the U.S.A.

To the warriors who go forth to find and defeat our nation's enemies,
those I've shared the skies with, those I've known over the years,
and those who hopefully will follow the tradition in years to come:
American fighter pilots

Contents

★

Acknowledgments

★

I had the great joy and privilege of living with my father as he neared the end of his life. He spoke often about his unfinished memoirs and was adamant that no one would put words in his mouth. When I promised to compile his writings and complete his book, he pointed that famous Robin Olds lecture finger at me and asked if I knew what I was getting into. I innocently replied, "Of course!" Silly me. During the final weeks of his illness, I gathered multiple boxes of diaries, military documents, films, letters, interviews, articles, and photographs and brought them to a workspace around his old green leather recliner in the living room. We sat for hours on end talking about his life, what it had all meant to him, what he hoped he had given to the people who had given so much to him. To the stack of his written memoirs he added tales of events that he hadn't committed to paper. I took notes, asked questions, labeled photographs, and reminded him his favorite jokes wouldn't make it into print. We laughed a lot. The day after finally admitting he was tired, he died peacefully in my arms. There are no words to describe what a gift my father was to my life and what an honor it is to carry out his last orders.

Friends from all over the world rallied to Robin's side during his last months, and these same wonderful people continued as my guardian angels through the long year it took me to finish his memoirs. I am grateful to all of them. Without question, my deepest love and thanks go to Thomas Rex Ingram. His unwavering love, support, and belief in me enabled this book to be written. My father said Rex would have made a hell of a fighter pilot. He was right.

Offers of assistance and guidance came from dozens of people as I wove my way through the chronological events of Robin's incredible life. Right from the start, I knew I'd need expert help and was lucky beyond belief to find Ed Rasimus. Ed patiently kept me in formation and on target. Mission accomplished. For stories of Robin's childhood through West Point, Uncle Fred Olds, Margaret McNeil, and my dad's lifelong best friend, Benjamin B. Cassiday, provided invaluable insight. Woody Woodward introduced my father to my mother back in his P-80 days and I'm certain spared me half the stories. My sister Susan helped me reconstruct our lives as air force brats, my daughter Jennifer helped me whip boxes of loose papers into chronological order, Morgan Olds Hundley filled in gaps, Kate Sheldon assisted with transcription, and Candi Garrison held me together on weekly hikes. What a team!

General Bill Kirk was my go-to guy for Wheelus through Vietnam. J. B. Stone, Bob Pardo, Doc Broadway, Ruby Gilmore, Gerald Finton, Dave Waldrop, Joe Kittinger, and many others from 81st TFW, the 8th Tac Fighter Wing, and the River Rats kept me on track through Vietnam. Enduring thanks and admiration to each of them. Air Force Academy stories were contributed by Ed Eberhart, H. Ownby, John Young, Fred Strauss, Mike Dunn, Darrell Whitcomb, and Nino Balducci. May your high jinks remind USAFA cadets that all work and no play do not an air force officer make.

This manuscript would not have been possible without reading through many historic reports, biographies, squadron logs, magazine and newspaper articles, interviews, official reports, books, letters, meeting transcripts, speeches, and tributes to Robin written through the years by the likes of Walter Boyne, Bob Titus, J. B. Stone, Barrett Tillman, Scrappy Johnson, Lars Anderson, Ted Sturm, Mark Berent, Ralph Wetterhahn, Bob Ettinger, Ron Catton, Mike Faber, Lou Drendel, and so many, many more. What an education I've had. Special thanks go to History Channel producer Cynthia Harrison for capturing Robin's antics just in time, to General Bob "Earthquake" Titus for proofing and commenting along the way, and to the able staff of St. Martin's Press, especially Marc Resnick, for bringing my father's story back where he wanted it—with his fellow fighter pilots.

To my "brothers" Tom and Joe Abbott, Fred and Candi Garrison, Mike and Linda Curzon, I. J. and Carol Fisher, Jack and Anita McEncroe, Ron and Alice Lewis, Jack and Marit Perkins, Verne and Nancy Lundquist, Ron "Sluggo" Torgler, and the whole Aspenosium gang for taking good care of the old man of the mountain, an enormous THANK YOU. And to Tony "E. T." Murphy for pulling off the greatest missing-man formation anyone has ever seen, deepest thanks for taking Robin back up into the wild blue.

Lead is gone on the wings of love.

Christina Olds
December 2008

Preface

★

There is only one witness to a life. That is the person who lived it. No one else will ever know the totality of that life. A wife may bond completely with her spouse, but she sees only those portions of the man that they've shared. A family may think they know their siblings, but the thoughts within are the individual's alone. Close friends can sit comfortably in silence with each other, but the events past and the experiences outside the friendship can be understood only by the man himself. We show many different faces to the people around us.

Biographers inevitably fail if their objective is to tell the story of the whole man. We are fortunate in this instance because this isn't a biography. This is the chronicle of a life in the words of the man himself. Many of us knew Robin. Some knew him in childhood, some as classmates, others as military superiors or subordinates, still others as friends. Each saw a facet of the life, but without the writings and insights of Robin himself there would be no picture of the whole man.

I spoke with Robin several years ago, and we discussed his obligation to get his story from his own personal perspective into a book. I asked him if I could help him—edit his story, ghostwrite it if necessary, or simply help him to get it to a publisher. He was getting older and his story couldn't die with him. His reply to my overture was classic Robin.

"I've already written it. It's taken care of. I've done it already." Somehow I harbored doubts about that. I asked him if I could read it and help him to get it ready for publication. He confirmed my suspicions when he replied that it wasn't quite ready for that yet. To punctuate the conversation he gave me "the glare," which told me I'd best tread carefully, friend or not. "Nobody's going to put words in my mouth, either."

No doesn't always mean no, and the story was too important to let languish. Every time I encountered him, I brought up the book again. I spoke with other close friends of his, Bob Titus, Bill Sparks, Les Pritchard, Jack McEncroe, Stan Goldstein, about his memoir. Jack said he had seen parts of it, at least rough notes. He described it as a jumble of bits and pieces, scattered here and there, jotted down over the years. I asked him to prevail upon Robin to get it moving. The whole group agreed with me, but Robin continued to procrastinate. The story went that even Gen. Chuck Horner had come to Steamboat with Tom Clancy to try to convince Robin to let the famed author help him. It never came to pass.

When Robin fell ill it looked as though this book would never happen. During his final months his daughter Christina stayed with him, and he sought her pledge that she would follow through on the project. He left her an extensive collection of writings, photos, documents, and memorabilia to pave the way. He shared days with her telling her tales of his life, and when he left us, we had all that was necessary to bring this book together.

It was my very distinct honor to be able to help with this work. I hope we've done the man justice, and I hope that his wisdom and experience can offer us all some insight into how a great man lived a remarkable life.

Ed Rasimus
December 2008

1

★

Battle

I couldn't help but feel the excitement. My 479th Fighter Group was the lead, out in front of the two bomber groups and not tied to close escort or stuck at the back of the bomber stream hoping to sweep up the leftovers. Hub Zemke had gotten us where I knew we belonged, at the cutting edge. As a new flight commander, I was ready. I had two kills and wanted more. The weather was good, the sky was clear, we were at altitude and had gone into Zemke's fan formation, so we had a good chunk of the sky under our control. All we needed now was for Jerry to show up. There was no good reason why he wouldn't.

Since D-day, we had been taking the war to Hitler. It was payback time for the indiscriminate abuse he had rained on Britain. We were going deeper and deeper into Germany, and it felt good. With Zemke at the helm, the 479th was finally getting on the short list for the good missions from 8th Air Force. Strafing trains and supply convoys was fine. Bombing the occasional bridge or supply area was necessary. But it was air combat that we wanted. Bombers drop bombs. Fighter pilots fight. It was simply the way it was meant to be.

We hadn't expected any reaction over the North Sea, and we didn't see much going in over Holland. As the force turned southeastward, I edged Blue Flight out just a bit farther to the left. The flanks were the place to see the enemy first. With the 479th across the front of the bomber groups, and the 434th spread to the left, my flight was the farthest left of the leaders. I'd briefed my guys that we would edge away a bit to give ourselves every chance of first engagement. I looked over my left shoulder for Hollister, my wingman. He was forward of where he usually flew, and that wasn't a bad thing. He could always fall back during a fight, but it was damned hard to get back forward once you lagged.

It was cold at 28,000 feet, but I could feel my back damp with sweat against my flight jacket. I flexed my hands on the yoke and checked once again that my gun sight was up, my guns were armed, and my belts were tight. I pushed the vent for the puny cockpit heater down toward my knees. I didn't want a blast of warm air fogging the canopy at the wrong moment in a battle. I scanned the horizon, looking for contrails or telltale dots that simply didn't belong there. It was quiet. The only aircraft to be seen were the scattered fork-tails ahead of the spears of contrails from the bomber formations.

I checked Hollister again and caught the back of his head as he peered intently to the north. His wing rolled up slightly with the effort of his straining in the cockpit. It was good. He was doing his job. Radio discipline was good so far. Three squadrons on one frequency were never easy to deal with. It only got worse when the enemy showed up. Critical calls were hard to distinguish, call signs went out the window, knowing who was saying what was impossible. Fear, adrenaline, excitement, whatever. So far, so good.

The engines don't ever purr. They've got a rhythm, a beat that signals the minor differences in props and rpm and mixture. When it's constant and steady, you feel relaxed. When it is loud or too fast or too slow, it jangles the nerves. If it changes suddenly it stabs you instantly into action. It screams that something needs attention right now. The single-engine guys don't know about that pulse, but in the Lightning, you live with it all of the time. There's a continual tweaking, fiddling with the throttle quadrant, watching the gauges, adjusting the props to get just the right resonance between the pair. It's sort of like a team of high-stepping gaited horses staying on the right tempo. My left hand stays near the throttle quadrant, dancing a slow waltz between the power levers while my ears tell me what is getting better or worse. My eyes stay on the horizon.

There's always something that needs doing. The bomber guys have a committee to tell them what, when, and where. They've got manuals and checklists, and a cast of supporting actors to read them aloud and double-check that it all gets tended to. The fighter pilot is driver, navigator, gunner, bombardier, and flight engineer wrapped into one tense, high-strung package. If he's good, he covers it all. If he isn't, he misses some things. I've been pretty good, so far. I haven't missed the major things, and the minor ones haven't killed me. If I'm doing it right, I'll keep getting better. If I'm not, I won't be able to worry about it.

The radio crackles. Has someone seen something? There's no call to follow. Nothing. Just a crackle. I look back to my right and see that we've widened out spacing on Zemke's Bison Squadron. It doesn't bother me. I want to be out here on the edge of the package. I want to see the enemy first. Is that something? Are those aircraft out there coming from the east? I raise my goggles and check the canopy for smudges. One, two, four—there are more!

A dozen things happen at once. I push the props and mixture forward. The engines surge. I pull the yoke and roll left, climbing over Hollister's position. The radio starts to speak and the first word I hear is "Blue . . ." I know it's one of my guys and I know what he's going to say. These are my bogeys on our side of the formation, and I don't want to share. I mash on the TRANSMIT button, and the squeal of the two transmissions covers the rest. Hollister is inside my turn and drops below me. The rest of the group are now alerted, and they want to know what's going on.

We're closing fast, and I radio to Bison Lead that we've got a formation at our eleven o'clock and we're checking them. It's more than a formation! It's a damned armada. I've got forty, maybe fifty Me-109s and Focke-Wulf 190s ahead of us. As we get closer, the number keeps growing. The whole damned Luftwaffe is in front of me!

The guns, the sight, the engines, the radios, the flight . . . where's my flight? There's Hollister. I knew he'd hang on. Where's the element? Where's the damned element? They've lost us. Fuel! I've still got the drop tanks. I check that Hollister is clear and jettison the tanks. There's a pair of trailing Messerschmitts ahead. They haven't seen us. I'll have the first one before he knows we're here. Is this as good as life gets? I've got more than fifty enemy aircraft in front of me, and my wingman and I are the only ones here! I sure feel sorry for those bastards.

The sight reticle is full of gray-green aircraft. My finger wraps around the firing toggle. My right engine coughs, sputters, and quits. A split second and forty heartbeats—then the second one follows suit. Both engines are dead . . . silence . . . awww, shit!

2

★

My Early Years

My first memories are of sounds: the clang of a halyard on a flagpole, Liberty engines warming up on the flight line before dawn, my father singing with his Air Corps friends in the living room below. By the time I was five, I could name an airplane by the sound of its engine on takeoff or landing. My father sat with me on the front steps of our house at Langley Field, made me close my eyes and name them one by one. P-1s, P-5s, DH-4s, old Keystone bombers, P-6s through P-36s, all seared sounds of aviation into my heart.

At night I hid in my pajamas at the top of the stairs listening to laughter, tales of flying, and songs with incomprehensible words and unforgettable melodies floating up from the living room. I sat for hours on Saturday mornings watching P-12s in a Lufbery over the field pull up into a loop, then dive back through the circle again. My father brought glasses of lemonade and we watched together. He and his pursuit pilot buddies were gods to me, men of steel in planes of wood and cloth. I had to be a fighter pilot.

I was born in Honolulu at Luke Field Hospital on July 14, 1922, to Army Air Corps Captain Robert Olds and Eloise Wichman Olds. My mother came from a line of Hawaii landowners, my father from Virginians traced back to the Revolution, including Regiment Captain Return Jonathan Meigs, George Washington's aide-de-camp. Dad had been a pursuit pilot during the war in France before his assignment to Hawaii. When we returned to Washington he became aide to General Billy Mitchell, then moved to Langley, first as student, then as instructor and director of the Air Corps Tactical School.

When I was four, my mother died. I remember asking my father if she was in heaven with all the airplanes. He said yes. My father married again briefly after Mom's death, divorced, then gave us two baby brothers, Fred and Sterling, when he married Helen Sterling in 1933. I grew up surrounded by an extended family of loving adults in comfortable surroundings in Virginia.

There was always my father. He was a tough disciplinarian, a tender caretaker, an unquestioned leader, and a laughter-filled friend. People gravitated to him. My days were shaped by his intense energy and eagerness. He taught me to be tough yet a gentleman. Manners and courtesy were paramount. He took me for my first flight in an open-cockpit plane when I was eight.

The pulp-fiction heroes of *G-8 and His Battle Aces* were also the real men that moved through my daily life. My father's Air Corps buddies were famed pilots of the Great War. They were often joined by other aviation leaders of that period: Hap Arnold, Tooey Spaatz, Ira Eaker, Fiorello La Guardia, Harold George, Frank Andrews, Bob Williams, Ernst Udet, Roscoe Turner, Edward Mannock, Elliott White Springs, Jimmy Mattern, Beirne Lay, and more. All gathered in our home. I got to meet Eddie Rickenbacker but was too awed to say anything. The gatherings started with tales of flying and progressed to passionate discussions of current events and dreams for the future. They invariably ended in song, led by my father at the piano and Tooey Spaatz on guitar. The brotherhood of pilots impressed me as much as the thrill of flying itself.

As I grew I began to understand the dreams of these early pioneers. World War I made them determined to change things. If they could make air power prevail in future battles, the horror of trenches, endless stalemate, and thousands of casualties with no discernible gain could be prevented. Airplanes could carry the war to the enemy, attack his industrial base and his lines of communication, destroy his transportation system, and quickly erode his will to fight. All this could happen from the air, but with aircraft not yet built. Such was the dream uniting these pilots.

When publicly expressed, their vision met scorn and resistance. The Air Corps leaders were looked upon as lightweight, flamboyant flyboys whose limited capabilities were of no consequence in the grand scheme of land and sea warfare. Airmen could not occupy territory, or rule the sea. What good were they beyond providing eyes for the real fighting forces? What good was bombing or shooting from aircraft? It was laughingly admitted that the Air Corps could probably penetrate enemy territory, but not much farther than good artillery and certainly not as accurately. Billy Mitchell was court-martialed for his outspoken belief in the future of air power and for his criticism of those who denied that potential. My father was one of the men by his side during that trial. The outcome outraged Mitchell's followers and only encouraged them to greater effort. Mitchell died in 1936, but it would be World War II that vindicated his theories beyond any doubt.

In 1934, Roosevelt ordered the Army Air Corps to take over airmail, and Boeing began the development of a new bomber. After an epic struggle with battleship admirals, my father and his peers managed the development of the B-17 in 1935. The first prototypes, thirteen in all, were put under his charge at Langley. Lieutenant Colonel Robert Olds and his B-17s became standard fare in newspapers and newsreels around the world. He led flights on good-will trips to South America and made the Flying Fortress a household name, also breaking the military cross-country speed record when Howard Hughes held the civilian mark.

When Germany invaded Poland in 1939, the world was stunned. The shock reverberated through America. Our army and navy were seen to be living in the past. While Britain gallantly went it alone, America had time to build, yet we were still not ready when Japan struck Pearl Harbor. It took another two years before U.S. air power could be said to have a meaningful impact on the campaigns waged in Europe and the Pacific. As world war loomed, my father was tasked by Hap Arnold to build an organization to ferry new aircraft from factories to their operational units. The ferry system grew into the Air Transport Command, an invaluable player in the Berlin airlift after the war, and later the Military Airlift Command.

In high school at 6'2' and 190 pounds, I was a natural for football. I made the varsity and was chosen captain, followed by election to class president for three years. Hampton High won the Virginia state championship in 1937. Subsequently, full football scholarships were offered by Virginia Military Institute and famous coach Earl "Red" Blaik at Dartmouth at the end of my junior year. But I believed the only legitimate way to fly airplanes and not have to work for a living was to get a regular commission through the United States

Military Academy. I would earn my wings, join the Army Air Corps, and become a fighter pilot. Simple as that!

To pass the academy entrance exam I enrolled at Millard Military Prep when I graduated from Hampton High in '39. Studies kept us busy, but the radio kept us informed of world events. When news of Hitler's invasion of Poland hit I wanted to go after him myself. There had to be a way to get into battle right away, and not wait four more years! The next day I sneaked off campus in my prep uniform and went to the Canadian legation in Hampton, determined to join the Royal Air Force. I filled out an application and handed it over. The fellow in the office eyed me sharply and asked, "Son, how old are you?"

"Twenty, sir!"

He knew better. "Well, you need your parents' permission. Have them sign your application."

I went home to my startled father, who said, "What are you doing here? You're supposed to be in school!"

"Dad, please sign this paper. I want to join the RAF."

Nothing doing. He sent me back to Millard.

By March 1940, we found a congressman in Pennsylvania willing to appoint me to West Point. Only problem was I needed to live in his district to qualify. I headed to Uniontown and lived for ten weeks in a small, shared room at the YMCA, worked for an army recruiter, and swept a grocery store at night. The decaying town and grim faces of local mine workers made me more determined than ever to get into the air.

On June 1 my father delivered the news: I had passed the entrance exam and was accepted! We raced up the stairs to my room, gathered my belongings, and caught the last train to D.C. I was the first Olds to go to West Point, and the family was suitably proud. Millard Prep had given me a head start on plebe year at the academy, but I was determined to increase my preparation, rising before dawn to do push-ups and run laps around the parade ground at Langley. One month later I crammed with a bunch of other Point-bound boys into one compartment on the D.C. train to Penn Station. I think I saw a couple of girls dabbing at their eyes among the families waving good-bye, but mostly I saw my dad standing stoically behind the group. We locked eyes and he nodded to me.

Boyish chatter on the way to New York quickly turned to discussions of France's recent surrender to Germany. Roosevelt was already warning the American public that our nation wouldn't tolerate Hitler's suppression of free

Europe. Would we make it to the war in time? West Point would provide me with a commission, but would it adequately prepare me for what lay beyond? Carrying a rifle on the long gray line was not my ambition. The last hours before the Point seemed etched in slow motion. We walked from Penn Station to the ferry terminal, rode across the Hudson River, boarded the train from Weehawken, arrived at the spare gray West Point stop, and fell silent when we saw the grim faces of our reception committee. I stepped down from the train and my boyhood ended.

"You, mister! Stand up straight! Get your raggedy ass in line!" Uniformed, white-gloved upperclassmen screamed into our faces. "You are worms not fit to crawl on this earth! You only THINK you will be officers! By tonight, half of you lily-livered maggots will run home to Mommy! You're a disgrace!"

"Yes, sir!" we yelled back. I could hear confusion and panic in some of the nonmilitary kids.

"What did you say?"

"YES, SIR!" we roared. And that was that. They herded us into groups at the station, then marched us up the hill through the gray stone portals of West Point. As we emerged into the Quadrangle from the Plain my eyes stared straight ahead, chin jammed back tight and spine erect. No time for awestruck sightseeing; time only for the business of arrival. After uniforms were issued and heads shaved, we were marched back across the Plain to a spot above the river called Trophy Point. There, I raised my right hand with my fellows and swore allegiance to the United States. I was a U.S. Military Academy cadet in the class of 1944, a plebe, a beast. And, by God, this Beast was going to be a fighter pilot!

Plebe year was an intense grind with the rigors of locked-down cadet life and academics. I met Ben Cassiday my first day in Beast Barracks. Our parents had been close friends in Honolulu, and he and I had been stuck in the same playpens as babies while the grown-ups played gin rummy. We were better prepared for hazing, obeying orders, running an obstacle course, and bouncing quarters off our beds than half our classmates. Ben was the good student, while I excelled at military training and football. I suffered through classes by doodling caricatures. My Company A pals gave me way too much encouragement, and pranks were part of life. Several drawings disappeared only to reemerge on the faculty board. I caught immediate hell from a sour-faced history professor. Oh well, catching hell seemed almost as much fun as getting away with it.

West Point's varsity football team in the fall of 1940 had its most abysmal record in fifty years, a second consecutive losing season: 1-7-1. Our freshman squad wasn't much better in the beginning. We started with three losses but improved rapidly, ending the year 3-4-1. The low point for the corps came with Army's brutal loss to Navy in front of a sellout crowd in Philadelphia's Municipal Stadium. It was the rivalry's fiftieth anniversary. Army-Navy games had always galvanized football fans, but the battles raging in Europe really focused America's adoration on its military teams. Radios across the nation tuned in to the big game, including FDR's in the Oval Office. My freshman teammates and I were in the stands for that game, and I was overwhelmed by the crowd's patriotic fervor. Army lost 14–0, but it didn't matter. We didn't feel like losers. Our freshman squad would make a big difference next fall.

The Point's new superintendent, Major General Robert L. Eichelberger, knew that cadets and Army fans alike were demoralized by the losing streak. It simply wouldn't do. He courted America's best damn college football coach, and Dartmouth's Red Blaik came on as head coach when the squad started spring practice. I worked like hell under Blaik and made the starting lineup. By the first of May I was first-string offensive *and* defensive tackle.

Morale soared throughout the corps at the start of fall semester '41. Coach Blaik spurred the team to fame as the nation's newest darling, and West Point was an undefeated 4-0 by the time we met Notre Dame in Yankee Stadium on November 1. The game was played in a driving downpour before a capacity crowd of 76,000. It was a total mud bath. My right shoulder hurt like hell from a stupid late-summer swimming accident, but I played both offense and defense for the full sixty minutes. By the end of the first half we were so muddy nobody could tell numbers or uniforms apart. I was in physical agony, felt like a goddamn pig in a wallow, but God, it was fun! We battled the Irish to a stunning scoreless tie. It felt like a win and we went home heroes.

Surging national pride carried us like gladiators into the Army-Navy game on November 29. Tickets were sold out for months. A crowd of over 100,000 crammed into Municipal Stadium. Parking lots and city streets were jammed by groups of fans listening to their radios. All of America was tuned in. FDR's intention to attend the game was thwarted by the escalating situation in the Pacific. He was sequestered with advisers in a hotel but listening to the radio. The emotional roar of the crowd hit us like a tidal wave when we ran onto the field. We weren't two separate teams meeting to battle. There was only one team, united with the crowd, united with our country.

It was the most memorable football game of my life. Army lost to Navy 14–6, but it didn't seem to matter who won or lost. Fans rushed onto the field. Both teams were engulfed in a wild celebration. Spectators in the stands stood hugging and weeping. Both team alma maters were played. The national anthem was played again. Cadets and middies stood close together, all of us singing our hearts out.

One week later, Japan attacked Pearl Harbor. Roosevelt's address to Congress on December 8 was broadcast to the corps in the mess hall. Pandemonium broke loose. We stomped, cheered, whistled, and clapped until our hands were bruised. We were going to war! America's first troops would be on the ground in Britain in January. Pilots would follow by early July. Dear God, we thought, please wait for us!

Big news awaited the cadet corps in the spring of 1942. Europe's descent into the maelstrom of war had galvanized the nation into action. Roosevelt's commitment to ramp up military preparedness produced a stunning announcement: The class of 1943 would accelerate to graduate in January and the class of '44 would graduate in June 1943! By God, it was really happening. Better yet, everyone in the corps was asked to choose regular army or Army Air Corps as his service branch. To the great dismay of the old-time infantry and artillery guys who'd been running the Point for years, almost half the class chose AAC. This was it. I was on my way!

When classes ended in late May, we were routed to flight-training bases scattered across America. Qualification was determined through the neutral process of overall class standing. Thankfully, my military grades rescued my average academics! I was off to fly. Nothing else mattered.

The summer of 1942 was glorious. A group of us volunteered for the Spartan School of Aviation in Tulsa, Oklahoma, after Ben Cassiday suggested he had friends nearby, meaning girls! With sunburns from Virginia Beach and a few successful days around the swimming pool at the Army-Navy Club, Ben and I boarded the train to Tulsa with our group. Upon arrival we were met by an enormous man naturally called Tiny. He turned out to be jack-of-all-trades for the flight school and mentor to all aviation cadets, military and civilian. We noticed Tiny was trying to hide his laughter from us. It was our damned Jungle Jim helmets. Some sadistic wag at the academy had foisted them off on us as the prescribed cadet summer head covering. Where was my riding crop? We loved our khakis and hated those stupid hats. To our chagrin we became the laughingstock of the upperclassmen at flight school. We quickly found alternative headgear.

The first day we met our instructors. My primary instructor pilot (IP) was a solemn-faced guy named John Kostura, who turned out to be far less menacing than he looked. He gave us flight schedules and instructions with a fair bit of humor, a good sign. Flying would be mixed with ground-school courses on weather, aeronautics, flight regulations, engineering, some field training, emergency procedures, and blah, blah, blah.

Kostura was a thorough, patient instructor. His admonishments came in a steady, quiet voice, his guidance taking quick effect. I found myself liking the man almost as a father figure and did my best to learn as quickly as possible all he taught. In our barracks bull sessions I learned other cadets had instructors who believed fear was the best teacher. They shouted angrily and banged their students' knees with the control stick for emphasis. My IP's teaching style, on the other hand, greatly influenced my future. Our initial dual flights went well, and one sunny day, after I had amassed five and a half hours of flying time, Kostura got out, patted me on the shoulder, and said, "OK, Olds, take her up and give me four good landings."

I gulped. Take her up? Oh my God, by myself? I was shaking as I taxied to the takeoff end of the grass field. I was on my way to being a pilot! Despite the nervousness, I took off smoothly. Hot damn, I was solo! The landings were good and I knew it. Mr. Kostura's smile when I taxied in was one of the richest rewards of that period.

Days at Spartan passed swiftly. Most of us passed the challenges. A few washed out and returned to the academy or went on leave. In between having me march occasional punishment tours with a parachute on my back, Mr. Kostura spent extra time teaching me aerobatics. We looped, rolled, and spun daily out of sight of the airfield. Sometimes he'd point out an isolated shack and yell, "It's full of Japs! Strafe it!" I dove in, pretending my training plane was loaded with bombs and bullets. He laughed at what I thought were perfect attack passes. More solo flights were sheer joy. Being alone in the immense sky, master of plane and self, was beyond anything I had imagined. Practicing what I'd been taught, and experimenting further into the envelope of possibilities, worked a magic I can only describe as ecstasy. It was total exuberance, surrender and mastery all at once.

The day finally came for a last check ride with an Air Corps officer assigned to Spartan. This was it. Flunk and you were out. Pass, and you graduated from primary and went on to basic training. Mr. Kostura briefed his flight and told us not to worry. We'd be OK. Just do what he'd taught us. "Remember the importance of picking out two good objects for turning points in the pylon eight maneuver. Make sure they're ninety degrees to the prevailing wind. That'll make it easy to keep your wingtip pointed right at the pylon when you do your figure eights. And make sure you pick out a good emergency landing spot when the instructor suddenly cuts your engine," he added.

Pylon eights? What were those? I had never done one. When Kostura finished I rushed up to him. "Sir, we never did those pylon eight things, ever!"

Kostura looked blank for a moment; then the light dawned. He'd spent time with me playing, doing acrobatics beyond the normal curriculum, attacking storage sheds and other useful things. He shouted, "Hold it right there!" then went running down the hall. He returned quickly and told me to grab my parachute for a quick lesson on pylon eights. I was as twitchy as the proverbial cat on a hot stove, but I managed to pass the check ride and was declared ready for basic.

Everyone was authorized a ten-day leave before reporting back to West Point for fall semester. My father had a special treat in store. He sent a plane to carry me back up to Spokane, Washington, where he was commanding the 2nd Army Air Forces Bomb Wing as a new major general. Reaction on the Tulsa flight line was priceless when a huge B-24 arrived. Of course I milked it for all it was worth, sauntering casually out to the plane and turning with a final thumbs-up at the stunned crowd. The B-24 pilot turned out to be a West Point grad who would rise to be a four-star general, then president of Pan American Airways. After a lazy five days with my father and his delightful new bride, Nina Gore Auchincloss, I was flown back to Washington, D.C., in another B-24. I was twenty years old and completely full of myself. I was a pilot and a first-class cadet! Life was innocent. Life was good.

Those of our class in flight training knew we'd take basic and advanced at nearby Stewart Field during the compressed coming year, but how were we to fit it all in? Life was a frantic routine. Days were divided between classes and flying, alternating mornings and afternoons, plus football practice every afternoon. Study time was at a premium, and there were many nights in the johns after lights-out, just trying to keep up. Academics were intense, with two full years now compressed into one. All of us were graded each day in every subject, and the grades were posted. There was no such thing as a bell curve or getting off easy.

The daily schedule was not for the faint of heart. Half of us were bussed the seventeen miles to Stewart in the morning and did our flight training. We then went back to the Point and academic classes that afternoon. Those of us on the squad practiced football until chow. The next morning we had academics and then flew in the afternoon. This schedule rotated between the two halves of the class who were in flight training. By an arrangement through Coach Blaik, I was always scheduled for the afternoon's first flying and was sent back to football practice in a truck. All was OK until we entered the night flying phase. With that I was put back into a truck after football practice, went up to the field, and met the schedule for my night flight. Mind you, sometime during all of this I had to study for the next day of academics. There was no slack in the system. Flunk a course or two, and that was that. You were out. Gone. The pressure was enormous, but we faced it and grew used to the challenge. Very few, if any, of my classmates failed courses that year.

In the middle of this craziness, game schedules continued as usual through the season. Buoyed by cadet corps morale and national fervor, we faced Navy again. This encounter became the hardest, physically, of my football career. At the start of the second quarter, a middie smashed a deliberately vicious forearm into my face. I crashed to the ground, put my hand to my mouth, and felt gushing blood and a terrible gap. Where the hell were my goddamn teeth? I crawled around the grass searching for them. Red Blaik and my teammates yelled for a doctor. They hauled me off the field and laid me out in the locker room. I struggled to get up and back to the game. The team doctor sat on me, closed my gums and torn lip with thirty stitches, and ordered me done for the day. I jumped up howling at Blaik until he overruled the doc. With cotton stuffed up my nose, blood all over my uniform, and black stitches where my upper lip used to be, I emerged back onto the field to the roar of the crowd. Lined back up in front of that same middie, I smiled a toothless, bloody grin, and growled. At the snap I hit him hard and came down on him with one knee, then whispered, "How's that feel, asshole?" That guy got carted off with two broken ribs, out for the game. The game continued in a brutal back and forth, but Navy won 14–0. For some reason, my performance during our 6–3 season earned me All-American honors, but I never did get my goddamn teeth back.

At Stewart we called our flight instructor in basic "Military Bill." He was the only one who lined his flight up each day for inspection. He'd pace back and forth imparting orders. In the air his flight instruction had the same pompous bluster. Surely, no one flew an airplane better or knew more about one. We were to understand that clearly. The only problem was I quickly learned I could fly the BT-13 better than Military Bill. Unfortunately, he learned it, too. Sure enough, Mil Bill did what he could to cut me down to size. He announced that I was too big for fighters. He was going to see to it that I was sent to bombers. He did, and I was assigned to twin-engine advanced for the final phase of training the next semester. I was deeply disappointed to have my hopes for a fighter pilot career dashed by someone like Bill, but I would continue to do the best I could.

Basic training ended just before the short Christmas break. I went to my roommate Scat Davis's home in upstate New York for a visit. Scat had washed out of flight training before it even began, due to bad eyesight. He was beside himself about it. It seemed grossly unfair because he was just color-blind. I promised him he'd fly with me throughout my career. I vowed that his name would be painted on every aircraft I flew. Scat's parents made us comfortable for the holidays. It was the best Christmas vacation I'd have for the next several years.

We went back to the January grind, with June just a blink away, entering what was traditionally known as the Gloom Period at the Point. Football season was over, and I was aware that my glory days on the field were gone for good. I missed the exercise and team camaraderie. Life was getting serious. The dank winter weather deepened that mood. Gray granite walls dripped with black, icy water, and slushy snow piled up in every corner. The sun hid behind dark clouds and never showed its face for weeks. Academics were demanding and never ending. Our instructors were in nasty moods, probably from dealing with our own gloom. Day after day, hour after hour, we stood in our raincoats as the Tactical Department tried to think of something to improve the mood of assemblies. Marching didn't do it. Even roommates fell to quarreling with one another. I was lucky. My two roommates, Uncle Wilk and Scat, always had smiles on their faces and mischief up their sleeves. Our area in the barracks resounded with laughter as some poor soul found liquid shoe polish in his shoes, tried to clean his trashed room fifteen minutes before Saturday inspection, or found pages of a book glued together.

In the midst of Gloom Period antics, Ben and I went to New York City on weekend liberty in March. Just before returning on the evening train, I had one scotch and soda. That's all. When we headed for check-in at the Point, I was confronted by a guy who seemed to harbor a personal vendetta. He finally got me with the honor code by asking, "Did you drink?" I answered truthfully, "Yes." I was number eight in class military standing, but that was the end of my time as cadet brigade captain. My classmates went up in arms in my defense, to no avail. From cadet regimental staff, I got busted down to private, only the second cadet in the history of West Point to earn that dubious honor. The punishment included marching tours right up to graduation. One more thing to add to my schedule!

My multiengine instructor for the bomber lead-in, Lieutenant Hacker, didn't like the thought of having to fly two engines any better than I did, but our AT-10 was a decent aircraft. I learned to enjoy everything about it. He was good at his job and honed my abilities with enthusiasm; soon he admitted that I could land the bird better than he. Eventually the weather cleared and we took great glee in doing a few loops and barrel rolls, knowing we were breaking the rules for student bomber pilots, to say nothing of restrictions against doing such maneuvers in the good old AT-10. Another restriction prohibited us from penetrating any airspace near the FDR estate south of Poughkeepsie. That was too bad, I thought. Roosevelt might welcome the entertainment.

One day Lieutenant Hacker and I got crazy and flew under every bridge on the Hudson from Albany to New York City. That escapade implanted in me a love for pressing the limits of flight, a fascination that would piss off many bosses for the next thirty years. Lieutenant Hacker and I promised each other we wouldn't discuss our adventure with anyone, ever. Rumors abounded when calls came in from witnesses, but I faithfully kept that secret until long afterward. I don't know how he managed it, but that lieutenant convinced the powers-that-be that I should be sent to fly fighters. Military Bill got overruled. I probably owe Hacker my successes and possibly my life, considering the losses suffered by bomber people in the war.

Graduation was approaching when the saddest event of my young life blindsided me. I knew my father had taken ill with pneumonia and had been lying in a Tucson hospital for several weeks. Nina was constantly by his side, telephoning me with daily reports. His recovery seemed certain. She sent hopeful assurances. On the morning of Friday, April 23, my brother Stevan and I were fetched out of class and informed that Dad had suffered a heart attack the night before. He was asking for us. We flew immediately to be with him. As my beloved father lay dying I held his hand and told him I was going to be a fighter pilot. He smiled weakly at me and said, "Robbie, listen to me. I never once went up in the air without learning something new. Never, ever think you know it all." He died at noon the following Tuesday. His ashes were taken up in a B-24 and scattered over the mountains west of Tucson. I was devastated.

Life at the Point seemed trivial for the next month. Only a steely new determination got me through. My father's mother, Grandma Topsy, came up as my date for the graduation festivities. General Hap Arnold pinned on my class pilot wings May 30. I grimly marched my tours off through the night, completing the last one just an hour before graduation. On June 1, 1943, I received my diploma to thunderous applause from the cadet corps but without the one person who mattered most. As I repeated the words of the officer's oath and stepped into manhood, I dedicated my wings and my commission to the memory of my father. Then I stepped off the fields of West Point and into the wild blue yonder.

3

★

Pilot Training

With second lieutenant bars and shiny new pilot wings I joined seven West Point classmates with orders to Williams Field, Arizona, for training in the P-38 Lighting. Our group included a mixed bag of personalities, all good young men, but as different from one another as any such number could be.

Al Tucker, Lou Nesselbush, Charlie Waller, Hank Rosness, Buck Coursey, Don McClure, and Bob Orr went through the fighter training with me, and each of them played a role in showing me how individual personalities meet the stresses of war. I don't claim to have been aware of their impacts at the time, because life was too challenging, too much fun, too exciting, and too immediate for any of that. The lessons I learned took effect slowly and often weren't recognized until years later. Those of us who survived became wiser and more mature in many ways without realizing it.

We all became members of the 479th Fighter Group and went to war together. One was killed, two became POWs, one almost finished a tour but quietly disappeared, two finished and went home, and the remaining member went on to fly two tours, and became a twenty-two-year-old major and ultimately commander of the 434th Fighter Squadron. That was me.

Our train ride to Chandler, Arizona, was long, hot, and crowded. We had an appointment with the future and it included a raging world war. We felt it was the place we were supposed to be. In Chandler a truck picked us up for the twenty-minute drive to Willie airfield where we signed in and received a long list of offices to visit. The duty NCO gave us billeting assignments and orders to report to our training unit for duty the next morning. The rest of the day was spent wandering over the sprawling base finding the dozen important people who acted very bored as we signed paper after paper and listened to briefings concerning how we were to behave for the rest of our lives. These briefings were structured to make us feel we were the lowliest creatures God ever created, outranking no one and subservient to all.

We were disabused of our perceived valuable status as newly commissioned second lieutenants. However, after Beast Barracks at the Point, this was nothing. As a matter of fact, it was exhilarating! The next morning provided more of the same takedown treatment. Later we learned that this was a special treatment in response to the somewhat rambunctious attitude displayed by our predecessors in the January '43 class when they arrived at training. Lesson learned: Don't reveal your status as a West Point grad if it can be avoided. Have something to be proud of before you declare your value.

The P-38 would wait a bit in our training. First we had to fly the AT-9, a twin-engine of dubious performance. The intent was to introduce trainees to the rigors of twin-engine flight before meeting the P-38, sort of a training-wheels approach before being unleashed in the high-performance machinery. Fortunately, that phase passed quickly and the great day soon arrived. It wasn't a P-38 we were to fly, but a bird named the P-322. There were some major differences between the two, although they looked alike. For one thing, the props on the 322 rotated in the same direction, as opposed to the counterrotating engines on the P-38. That meant engine torque we wouldn't have to deal with in the Lightning. In addition, the oil and coolant flaps were manually controlled. You flew with one eye on the temperature gauges, constantly adjusting settings for every phase of flight by sliding levers back and forth to keep the values in the green. The P-322 lacked the turbo-superchargers of the 38, and its performance at altitude was pathetic. These particular aircraft had been built for the Brits, who wisely refused to accept them. The generally accepted belief was that the P-322 was a more dangerous airplane than the Lightning, at least for the pilot. Training was organized and we quickly got into the swing of things.

Late one afternoon, when I returned to my room, I found a note pinned to my door. I would report immediately to the base adjutant. I wondered what I had done to merit such individual attention. The adjutant was a crusty old first lieutenant whom I saluted smartly. He must have been in his late thirties, but he looked like Methuselah to me.

He fixed me with a hard stare, but I detected a hint of humor in it. He held my gaze for several seconds before saying, "Lieutenant Olds, there is a lady in that building across the street who would like very much to see you. Through the double doors, turn right, and she will be at the fourth desk on your right. Can you manage that?"

I saluted and left. What in hell was this all about? I heard the adjutant suppressing a chuckle as I left.

I found the woman easily and introduced myself. She was not as forbidding as I had expected. She smiled and asked me, "Lieutenant, are you independently wealthy?"

It was a strange question. I wondered what she was getting at. I assured her I was not at all wealthy. She began a stern lecture. "Lieutenant, whether you want it or not, and even whether or not you deserve it, Uncle Sam wants to pay you for serving in his Army Air Corps. In fact he will do so each and every month. All you have to do is go to the base finance office on the first of the month, sign your pay record, and collect whatever may be due for your sterling service. You seem unaware of this little fact."

It was obvious she was having a bit of fun at my expense. I blushed.

She then added, "Not only do we give you your basic pay as a second lieutenant; you get flying pay on top of that, plus any travel pay due, and you will even get what we call per diem occasionally. It tends to add up, and makes it possible for you to pay your officers' club dues, to buy things at the PX, to eat, and to cover all sorts of expenses that lieutenants seem to encounter every day. See that sergeant down the hall in his cage? He has lots of money and is anxious to share some of it with you. And he or someone like him will do so every month you wear that uniform. Now go, and it was nice meeting you."

Damn, no one told me about this at West Point. What else did I miss?

The sergeant counted out more money than I'd ever had in my life and smiled as he told me what trouble the finance office had encountered in trying to find the missing lieutenant. As I departed, obviously looking embarrassed, he said, "Don't neglect us again, Lieutenant—we might not find you twice." This was the most direct and enlightening education of my short career, and I was grateful to the people on the base for teaching me the financial facts of military life. I was going to be paid to fly!

Within a short time, the reality of this business hit our group of eight. Bob Orr was flying solo, crashed, and died. We never knew how it happened. It stunned us, but it was reality in the life of a pilot. We had lost five classmates back at the Point in training accidents before graduation, and wearing wings didn't keep it from happening now. I'd have to learn to deal with it. I was sorry to lose a good friend and squadron mate, but glad it wasn't me who had bought the farm.

Despite accidents our self-confidence soared, and we would often dogfight among ourselves. It wasn't exactly against regulations, but it couldn't be ignored when two of us jumped a stray P–322, which turned out to be our squadron CO's. That afternoon seven of us were lined up before the desk of a very livid major. We received a royal chewing out and wondered if this was the end of our fledgling careers. Finally, the major said he knew the "ambush" had been carried out by one of us and asked who had done it. He was astounded when Al Tucker and I stepped forward and confessed. He didn't know quite what to say. I guess he had never heard of the honor code. We had learned that officers do not lie, cheat, or steal, or tolerate those who do. We simply did what we'd been conditioned to do. He sputtered a bit, and I think he admonished us not to do it again. I was never certain whether he meant don't dogfight or don't jump him. It didn't much matter.

Our next step was gunnery training at Matagorda, Texas. We reported at the end of July for a month. The base was on a spit of land jutting into the Gulf of Mexico south of Victoria, Texas. It couldn't really qualify as a hellhole because any hole there would have been under water. Hell with humidity. We were there for training in aerial gunnery, and nothing else mattered, not the ovenlike heat, the lizards, the sandstorms, the wretched base food, or even the stinking, undrinkable water we were supposed to use. Whoever owned the Coca-Cola franchise for the base must have made a fortune. We even used the soda for brushing our teeth and shaving after a few people got sick from the water.

A lot of the June '43 class assigned to all types of fighters had converged for this phase. On top of great flying, we had a whopping good time together. We flew AT-6s, Texans, which had a .30 caliber machine gun pointing forward through the propeller, just like the ones used by our World War I heroes Elliot White Springs and Eddie Rickenbacker. No one seemed to care that those of us assigned to P-38s had never flown the AT-6 before. Don't worry, just fly it, we told ourselves. All of the aircraft were equipped with a 16 mm movie camera that recorded each firing pass at a towed target. We were taught to assess film of our gunnery passes, and most of us improved rapidly as the days went by. Understanding the physical and mathematical forces involved wasn't essential to success. Leading a target was subject to the laws of physics but also took a bit of luck, some Kentucky windage, and maybe some innate talent. Your speed, your target's speed, your angle-off, and the G forces involved all had to be taken into account. I got the big picture of all the factors in play and got pretty good at punching holes in the towed rag.

The P-38 class was sent from Willie to 4th Air Force headquarters in San Francisco to await orders. Then we were routed to Los Angeles. I wondered why we were sent to San Francisco first and then Los Angeles rather than directly to the final destination, but what did a lowly second lieutenant understand about the mysteries of the army? L.A. was just an enroute stop. More orders sent us on to our final training base.

The final leg of this circuitous journey was by train that headed up Cajon Pass east of L.A. At nightfall, we got off and found a place to sleep in a middle-of-nowhere high desert town called Barstow. At dawn we boarded another train that headed back northwest through the most desolate countryside I had ever seen. It was all rock and alkali basins, with only a few cacti and Joshua trees to break the monotony. At midafternoon the train wheezed to a halt and the conductor told us we had arrived. We debarked with our B-4 bags and stood on a platform attached to a deserted, weather-beaten building meant to be a train station. To our left was a water tank sort of leaning eastward above the horizon. It looked like it hadn't been used in forty years. Nothing much around but sand and rocks. An unlucky jackrabbit or rattlesnake would have been the only other living thing. A single-wire line of telephone poles marched south beside a single-lane dirt road. Both disappeared over a rise about a mile south. We looked at each other. Someone said, "Shit." That pretty much covered it all.

As the train pulled away, I went into the deserted station and found a telephone hanging on the wall. At least it didn't have a crank on one side. I picked it up. Without any operator responding, a voice asked how many of us were there. I told him seven and he said to hang on, a truck would come for us sooner or later. We sat in what shade we could find and waited. Sure enough, after about an hour, a truck trailing a cloud of dust came over the rise.

The corporal driver greeted us with a laugh and said, "Welcome to Muroc Field, oasis of the desert and garden spot of the Mojave. Climb on board, you lucky bastards, and I'll haul you to purgatory!" Off we went, bouncing down the dirt road at a pace that rattled our bones.

I knew about Muroc Dry Lake because my father was been involved with building a bombing target there in the late 1930s. It was still there. Considering the ongoing rivalry at that time with the admirals in the surface navy, it didn't surprise me that the target turned out to be a large wooden replica of a battleship.

At Muroc Field we went through the usual check-in process, were assigned to a squadron, and were given directions to our quarters. Quarters? Little more than tarpaper nailed to a two-by-four squad tent frame, but it was home. Oh, what the hell, it was the flying that counted. Besides, we wouldn't be here permanently, only as long as it took to complete this phase of training. Later, I thought of the permanent instructors at Muroc and felt a twinge of guilt comparing their situation to ours. Many of them had already completed a combat tour, and it must have been a tremendous letdown to be assigned to a base so far removed from anywhere just to train a bunch of green lieutenants.

Flying and ground school. Then more ground school, flying, and still more flying. The P-38s were incredible. Our days were filled with the wonder of the machines, even though the bulk of them were bent and battered, not even worthy of the distinguished status of "war wearies." There were D models and E models. There were even some earlier C models. Each was unique, with instruments never in the same location, the throttles, mixture, and rpm controls mixed around on the power quadrant, and switches all over the place. Each switch had a placard that hinted at a bewildering variety of functions, mostly mysteries to us, and I suspect also to our instructors, as they seldom mentioned them. The differences, however, could sometimes be quite frightening. On takeoff you'd be looking forward, reach to reduce the power and rpm, and suddenly realize you were pulling back the mixture controls, which of course could shut down the engines if inadvertently pulled back too far. At least the oil and engine coolant shutters on these fighters were automatic and required only an occasional cursory glance to be sure they were functioning.

Accidents were common. One morning we were outside the quarters playing jungle volleyball when two P-38s pitched out above us for landing. The game paused as usual, all pilots being in the habit of mentally criticizing another pilot's technique. We never knew who he was, but the second of the two rolled into his bank and kept right on rolling until he smashed into the ground not five hundred feet away. After the game, I flew my scheduled flight and then joined some others for a truck ride to the other side of the base for lunch. The road crossed the west end of the runway, where we had to stop for two birds taking off. One never got airborne. With smoking brakes he sailed right past our noses and on out into the desert. There, the nose gear collapsed; the pilot got out, turned, and waved to us that he was all right. Little did we know we hadn't seen anything yet. Coming back from lunch we found two more P-38s nose up off the same end of the runway. Let's see, that made four accidents so far. On the first flight of the afternoon there were two bailouts reported. Soon after that, someone tried to land with one engine out and botched it. He went bouncing off the east end of the runway and out onto the dry lakebed. There he stopped when the gear collapsed. Rumor had it he collapsed the gear on purpose, not wanting to face a longer walk back to his squadron. Finding humor in such situations was a macabre sort of pastime.

Toward late afternoon, two trainees had a midair collision. Neither survived. Flying for the rest of the day was canceled. Who could blame the instruction staff? Nine accidents in one day were going to be hard to explain to the higher-ups.

The remaining training days were a mixed bag of frustration and joy: frustration because we couldn't get an assignment to combat, and joy because there was plenty of flying available. Every few weeks we were moved to another base. I guess headquarters didn't know exactly what to do with this small batch of precious West Pointers. Finally, someone told us the Pentagon had ruled we would go overseas only as flight commanders. Fat chance of that! Then we heard that 4th Air Force headquarters decided future flight commanders in the units forming up could only be volunteers who had done a prior combat tour. What to do? Keep on flying, of course. Get as much time as we could beg, borrow, or steal.

We went from Muroc to Salinas on Monterey Bay. From there we split up. Al Tucker and I were sent to a place called Lomita Flight Strip. The flying was still great. We discovered that the desert north of the San Gabriel Mountains was a wonderful place to buzz, and we got quite good at it.

Our next stop was a strip right in the middle of the city of Glendale, for God's sake. The place had been camouflaged for some reason or other, and from the air the runway looked like the continuation of one of the city streets. This proved to be quite challenging at first, but once we located the building containing our favorite bar just across the field, lining up for landing was easy.

A few of the pilots from Muroc were now in Glendale. We teamed up for several evening forays into the dazzling lights of Hollywood Boulevard. As lieutenants we always seemed to run out of money by the middle of the month, so we pooled our resources, and selected one of our group to hold the cash and pay the bills. This usually stretched our cash for an extra week each month. Then we discovered we could always count on some old geezer in every bar who wanted to tell us he was too old to be in uniform but had done his stint back in World War I. As long as he fed us drinks we listened. I don't remember feeling guilty about those evenings. In fact, they were delightful. We got to hear some great war stories; maybe some were even true.

By December, we were all promoted to first lieutenant. This brought a pay increase, which was gladly accepted, but I worried that our exalted status would only make going to combat even more difficult.

All was great until one day Al Tucker and I were hauled into ops and yelled at by the flight commander.

"Olds, you and Tucker are grounded!"

Just like a thunderclap, there it was. Grounded. No more flying. Why, for God's sake?

The flight commander raged on. "4th Air Force found out you've been leading flights, teaching the replacements, and wasting valuable P-38 time allocated to this training squadron. You can't even fly the BT-13 anymore since those two knot-heads ran into Lake Arrowhead yesterday, so none of you guys get to fly that either. No flying. Nothing."

"But, sir . . ."

"No 'buts,' " he shouted. "That's an order!"

So here we were, almost eight long months out of West Point, past Willie Field for P-38 checkout; Matagorda, Texas, for gunnery; Muroc, California, for replacement training; Lomita for more training; Salinas, ditto; Grand Central in Glendale, more ditto; out to Ontario, and more ditto. Finished with gunnery, through all the phases of combat training (several times), stuck out here among the vineyards of Ontario, and screwed by conflicting rules from two different levels of command. All we wanted to do was go to war. Was that so bad? Or did the paper pushers behind their desks think us unfit because we actually agitated to go? The Pentagon had ordained that henceforth and forevermore, no precious little West Pointer would go off to war unless he was going to fill a flight commander's spot in a replacement unit. At least that's what we were told. With direct jurisdiction over units in California, 4th Air Force up in San Francisco made the rule that all flight commander positions in the future would be filled only with volunteers who had already completed a combat tour in P-38s somewhere overseas. I was living Catch-22 decades before Joseph Heller would write about it.

At this terrible news, Tuck and I looked at each other; anger on our faces and misery in our hearts. We had done our best. We hadn't asked to stay here. Tuck was an exceptional pilot, and I wasn't too bad either. In mock dogfights we had routinely waxed our instructors, all combat veterans. We flew better close formation, and stuck in there no matter what the instructor pilots tried to do. We understood and executed the combat formation and tactics we were taught (such as they were) better than they did. Those same instructors were the ones who had scheduled us to lead flights that were their responsibility. We did so gladly, while some of them didn't even come to work for days on end after Tuck and I took over.

What now? I could feel my stomach churning. My face felt hot. Tears of rage and frustration were close to the surface. I knew I was in no mood or condition to talk to the boss, but damn it all, what the hell did it matter now? Determined to do something, I marched down the hall to his open door, entered, and saluted.

The major looked up from his desk with a cold expression. "What do you want, Olds?"

I stared at a spot over his head. "Sir, I want to go on leave," I almost shouted.

"What?" His voice took on that menacing tone, the one adopted by squadron COs when sticky situations arose. "Where do you think you're going? Don't you know there's a war going on?"

"Sir, I'm going to Washington."

"And just what do you think you're going to do there?"

"Sir, I'm going to see General Arnold. He's a friend of my dad's. He'll listen—"

"Request denied." The major looked back down at his desk. That was the end of that.

I turned on my heel and went back down the hall and found Tuck at the ops desk. His face got grimmer as I told him my sad tale.

"Let's just go," he said.

"Where?" I asked, as we headed toward his old car.

"L.A. Fighter Wing headquarters," he replied.

Wondering what we could possibly do there, but knowing we had to try something, I climbed in, and off we went.

Wing headquarters was in downtown Los Angeles in an old requisitioned hotel building. I knew it rather well. A few months earlier, I had been caught buzzing and had received my first official punishment there in the general's office. It seems I had erred in my hopeful understanding that replacement trainees who committed flagrant flying violations were sent to war forthwith. I had heard the story of the guy who did the loop around the Golden Gate Bridge and was sent off to the South Pacific. That was supposed to be Dick Bong, who was racking up the victories. All I got for my effort was a royal chewing out, an Article 104, and a fine, which no one since then seemed interested in collecting. Anyway, Tuck and I marched into the building and looked for someone important. We wound up in the personnel section in front of a sergeant's desk. The sarge had a friendly face and seemed willing to listen to our tale of woe.

"You mean you really want to go to combat?" He seemed surprised.

"Damned right!" we replied together.

The sarge looked at us for a moment, shook his head, and asked, "You two finished training?"

"Yes, sir." (Well, he WAS a lot older than we were.)

"You're both crazy, but I'm not going to ask you why, just where. So where in hell do you lieutenants want to go?"

"England!" we chorused. I don't know about Tuck, but I could have kissed the man. Hope sprang like a flame.

The sergeant went over to a wall chart, stood a moment, and then came back to face us. "OK, there's a group forming up right now. Three squadrons: Lomita, Palmdale, and Santa Rosa. They aren't fully manned or trained yet, but they're going. I'm not allowed to say where, but you won't be disappointed. Any more of you in the same boat?"

"Yes, sir, there are." We named the five other classmates going through the same mess there in Southern California, and the good sarge started typing.

Tuck and I tried to look nonchalant as our savior worked away on his machine. I guess we were both worried some major or colonel would walk by and ask us what the hell we thought we were doing, but the sergeant seemed totally unconcerned. The fifteen minutes it took him to finish typing seemed like an eternity, but when he finished he went over to a mimeograph machine, and soon he handed over a stack of orders covering all seven of us in the unit. It hadn't occurred to us to ask the others whether or not they wanted to be included!

Which proves that if you want to cut red tape and get something done in this man's army, go to the NCOs.

The orders were well crafted. Tuck and I wound up back at Lomita Flight Strip near Long Beach, with the newly formed 434th Squadron. The others in our gang, Nesselbush, Coursey, Waller, Rosness, and McClure, went to the 435th and 436th, all a part of the 479th Fighter Group. The outfit was slated to ship out and was in the final stages of preparation. We weren't told where we were ultimately going, but it didn't matter—England, the Mediterranean, or the South Pacific. We didn't care, as long as it was to war. Personally, I was hoping for England, where I figured the best action would be.

Over the brief time before shipping out, we did a lot more flying but stayed humble when we were forced to do an army forced march up the hill in Palos Verdes, complete with pup tents and canteens. Our bosses suffered through a rash of POMs (preparation for overseas movement inspections), which were meant to determine whether or not we lesser troops were properly trained. We thought we were ready, but we didn't know how little we knew. Anyway, the three units, along with the group headquarters staff, gathered at Santa Maria base up north of Santa Barbara in late April. We went through more paperwork, more inspections, more delays, then a final squadron farewell party at a roadhouse out in the countryside. It was a hell of a party. In the morning we'd be off to war.

4

★

Off to War

Oh God, I didn't want to wake up. I didn't want to move. My tongue felt like a corncob, my stomach was heaving, and my head pounded. My leg felt like it was in a vice. Loud voices sounded in the hall, and then pounding feet, noises outside. . . . Where was I? What was going on?

Suddenly, it dawned on me. We were at the Santa Maria staging base. Early get up and muster for the ultimate roll call. Oh shit. We were to march to the railway siding and board a troop train for the East Coast and the port of embarkation. My God! What was I doing here on the floor? My eyes snapped open. The room was a shambles. The bunk bed was broken, the mattress was half over me, and my right leg was thrust through the paperboard wall into the next room. What happened? Hazy memories surfaced of the going-away party, too many drinks, going outside for air and falling backward into the tall grass by a tower of some kind, lying there wondering if someone would find me when the party broke up. Last conscious thought was, Can't miss that train! God, I can't miss that train.

I disentangled myself from the wreckage, got up, nearly fell back against the wall, grabbed my B-4 bag, threw my toilet kit into the middle, closed it, belted on my .45, and stumbled outside. The rest of the squadron was already lined up, so I fell into place in the rear. No one would speak to me or even look at me. Judging from my condition and the chaos in my barracks room, I could guess why.

Roll call completed, we marched off to the rail yard and the awaiting troop train. It was more like the retreat from Moscow than a military formation. We all carried one or two heavy bags. No one was in step, but I couldn't have done it anyway.

Our B-4s were collected and stowed in a freight car. I thought of my toothbrush and wished I had used it. Confusion reigned as we boarded in groups . . . by headquarters people, by squadron, by flight, by rail car. We found seats in what must have been a vintage 1910 day coach. I wondered dully where we were going to sleep. Maybe not at all. It didn't matter.

The general buzz of excitement didn't include me. I was deservedly miserable. A hammer pounded inside my head, focused somewhere behind my right eye. I don't know whether I slept or passed out. Time must have passed, for when I finally opened my eyes we were slowly rolling down the Pacific Coast. I wondered if this would be the last time I saw the Pacific and quickly buried the thought. Gradually my senses returned, my head stopped pounding, and I got caught up in the mood of my squadron mates. I asked Elmo Sears what in hell had happened last night. He looked at me sadly and shook his head. Others did the same. I was still in limbo, but enough of the story came out for me to realize I had resisted being put to bed by my caring mates. I'd thought it a great sport, but my rescuers hadn't shared my viewpoint. It explained my wake-up condition.

We rolled past the north end of a runway, and I recognized the training field at Van Nuys. P-38s were lined up on the west ramp, and a bird landed right over our heads as we passed. Then North Hollywood, Glendale, and Pasadena. As night fell, we headed up Cajon Pass and into the high desert.

Supper was announced and we lined up in the aisles to wait our turn in the dining car, which was more like a chow hall. That done, we sat for a while before being herded back one car to the berths, where it was two in the lower and one in the upper. Rank prevailed and lieutenants generally didn't get an upper. It didn't matter. Sleep came easily with the clickety-clack of the old train as it labored on through the night.

In the morning we were still in the desert, grinding our way slowly up a steep grade. One of our more creative guys suggested it would be good training to get some practice with our .45s. We filed through the cars to the head of the train, opened the door, dropped the boarding steps, and jumped off into the desert. We stood in a line popping away at cacti and rocks as the train crept past behind us. As the last car approached we jumped back aboard and repeated the exercise. It was on the third iteration that we were stopped by the group CO. He was upset. No, make that irate. How about boiling mad?

He confiscated the pistols and ammo with the indication that we would hear more about this incident. We wondered what would happen, but soon concluded he couldn't court-martial half his pilots en route to the war. We resumed the pattern of watching the desert, playing cards, and wondering when we would cross the Colorado River.

Past Albuquerque and across the Great Plains into the Midwest. On the third day we encountered fresh snow. It was April, but still cold enough for an overnight blanket to fall. At a routine water stop we were allowed off to stretch our legs a bit. That was a mistake. The ensuing snowball fight was remarkable for both size and intensity. We suffered no major casualties and were herded back aboard, red-faced and roaring with laughter as snow melted down our collars.

Eventually we chugged into Fort Dix, New Jersey. We were assigned to barracks and reunited with our bags. Here we trained for our ocean crossing. We got lectures, training films, and dry-land boat drills. We stood in line for everything: gas masks, infantry helmets, paperwork, and more. Were we ever going to get going?

On a train again, heading for the Hoboken docks. This was almost déjà vu. I can't say it was the same one, but we piled onto a ferryboat exactly like the one back on that 1940 summer day when a large number of brand-new plebes-to-be were ferried across from New York City to catch the train to West Point. God, that now seemed so long ago. This time I was going in the other direction, headed to war.

The ferry docked. We formed ranks, responded to roll call, then marched down the street toward the end of the pier. The baggage seemed lighter, and I remember we all tried to look military in spite of the damned duffels banging against our legs. Someone started singing "Jolly Sixpence," but it didn't catch. We turned onto the pier and halted. From the dock, we gazed up at what was the monstrous side of a huge ship. A gangplank slanted upward to an opening. As did all of the guys, when it came my turn I struggled up the gangway with my bag full of dirty laundry, my Class A uniform, shirts, a tie, an extra pair of shoes, socks, and a whole case of Rewco rye whiskey that some enterprising GI had foisted off on the more gullible of us before we left California. (That vile stuff would still be on the top shelf of the closet in the mess at Wattisham when I left England over a year later.)

We found our cabins and were told to assemble later on the A deck, wherever that was. Eight of us looked at the double-decked bunks squeezed in a cabin obviously meant for two in quieter times. No matter. We grabbed bunks, then headed topside. From the rail, we watched with fascination as the loading continued. The sun was low on the Jersey Heights when the hawsers were finally slipped and the USS *Argentina* slowly backed out into the Hudson. This was the best I had felt in a long time. I thought now I'd made it. It was really happening. I was on my way. All the training, waiting, and frustration were over. No one could jerk me back to an RTU now.

As the ship cleared the docks and busy tugs took up position to get her headed down harbor, a band positioned at the end of the pier played marching music . . . a nice gesture they had probably done routinely every day for the last three years. We got under way and slid outward past Manhattan and Governors Island.

We crowded the starboard rail as we passed the Statue of Liberty. The lady stood out in sharp profile against the evening sky, saying "Godspeed" to yet another shipload of young Americans headed to war. Several of us solemnly saluted.

After the initial lifeboat drill with another lecture about life jackets, emergency procedures, and the lot, we made our way to the mess deck for the evening meal. We were to be fed twice a day, and if we missed our appointed turn, that was just too bad. Fair enough. The hardworking cooks and kitchen detail could do no more.

The following morning was blue sky and open ocean. No land in sight and no other ships around. Suddenly someone shouted and pointed. There, right under our noses, a whale broke the surface and seemed to take forever to arc up and over as his back broke water, and an equally long time for his huge tail to flip skyward in what I fantasized was his wishing us good luck.

Second morning, like magic, there they were, ships from horizon to horizon, filling the sea in unbroken columns: freighters, tankers, troopships, destroyers, and, like a mother hen, a stately cruiser off our port side. She kept pace with the convoy between us and the flanking column far out on the edge of the sea. We had been a lonely ship last night, when every conceivable source of light on the *Argentina* had been secured for the blackout. Now here we were, early in the morning, one of an armada plowing slowly northeastward under a cloudless sky. We wondered how in the world the convoy had assembled in the dark, in proper formation, all headed in the same direction, and at the same speed.

After breakfast, a group of us sat on a cargo hatch on the topmost deck and enjoyed the spectacle. A destroyer came charging up on our port side. All eyes watched as she leaped through the seas like a terrier after a ball, her bow wave sparkling white against the gray of her hull, and her wake gleaming with the speed of her passage. As she passed the *Argentina* her Aldis light blinked out a rapid code. I noticed Bud Grenning busily taking notes, the bill of his ever-present leather cap pointed skyward and his tongue between his teeth in concentration. We were all trying to read the destroyer's message with our meager knowledge of the Morse code, and argued good-naturedly about our differing interpretations. Bud continued to scribble. Our squadron armament officer, Teddy Anastos, peered over Bud's shoulder and tried to read his notes. Turning his back, Bud shielded the pad against Teddy's curiosity.

"What's he saying, Bud?" asked Teddy.

Bud looked up in all seriousness and said, "I can't tell you, Ted. It's top secret. Besides, you really don't want to know."

That got Teddy's attention in a hurry. Ted was known to be a bit gullible, so we waited while Bud strung him out.

"Come on, Bud," he implored. "We're all in this together. I have a right to know. Whatever happens to one of us happens to all of us. Tell me."

"Look, Ted, I shouldn't do this. Remember all our lectures about keeping a zipped lip? About not starting or listening to rumors? About convoy security? You never know who's around. Maybe there's a spy right here on the *Argentina* with a radio and he's in touch with the German U-boats waiting for us up ahead."

Teddy's face fell and he twitched with worry. Bud had Teddy hooked. It was all the rest of us could do to keep straight faces. "Bud, you've got to tell me. It's not fair you pilots knowing and I don't. Maybe there's something I should be prepared for. Maybe the others in the squadron should know. . . ."

"All right Ted, all right, I'll tell you. But you've got to understand this is secret stuff and only the ship's captain should know. It's his responsibility and his alone whether or not the rest of us hear it. I'm sure he's got his crew working on the problem already, so there's no worry. Now, promise you won't breathe a word of this to anyone outside this group right here. Promise!"

"I promise," said Ted solemnly.

This was too much. Bud had us all hanging on: Ted to hear the awful news, the rest of us to learn what Bud had up his sleeve.

"OK, Ted, I'll read the message. I quote, 'SS *Argentina* from convoy flag. Urgent. Repeat, urgent. Top secret. Message follows: From transportation command Fort Hamilton. German saboteur apprehended last night. Confession indicates completion of his mission to wire your bilge pumps backward, repeat, backward. You are taking water in, not pumping out. Advise when situation under control and so on.' Unquote."

We looked at Ted. He looked at us. His face was a study in consternation. Someone snickered. We couldn't hold it. Then all hell broke loose. Old Ted turned out to be a good sport and finally joined in the laughter. But his was a nervous laugh, and I had the distinct impression Ted wasn't quite sure that it was just a joke.

Life on board assumed a steady routine. We got used to eating twice a day, and actually looked forward to the random lifeboat drills as a break in the monotony. Some of us were detailed to inspect the enlisted men's bunk areas and report any problems to the CO. I did so in my turn and found our 434th GIs crammed chest to back in six to eight tiered bunks. The guys seemed philosophical about the crowding, and I wasn't aware of any unusual bitching. The problem was, they had questions that I couldn't answer, like "How much longer? Where are we going? What about U-boats?" I don't know what anyone else said, but I pleaded ignorance. On the other hand, I didn't tell the CO how selfish I felt comparing the troop's living conditions to ours.

The third day out, late in the afternoon at the second meal, a tremendous thud shook the *Argentina*. We could feel it through our feet, up through our chairs, and into our bodies. It was quickly followed by another, even stronger bang. Most of us jumped up, thinking TORPEDO! Some made a dash for the mess hall doors. All were stopped by a loud shout from the Transportation Corps officer.

"Calm down, you greenhorns. They're only depth charges dropped by our escort. There's nothing to worry about. You'll get used to it. The ship acts like a drum when you're below the waterline. It's all noise. No problem."

We sat, feeling sheepish, but everyone thought, Depth charges? Sure. Below the waterline? Oh, yes, everything's just normal-normal. No problem.

What a relief. But I noticed one figure slipping out the door of the mess. It was Teddy Anastos. He reappeared about ten minutes later, wearing his life jacket. None of us said anything, not even later when it was apparent Ted slept in the damned thing.

About the sixth day out, we noticed that many of our companion ships had disappeared. The convoy had shrunk appreciably, including the number of escort vessels. We reasoned that we were close enough to our destination to have air coverage against the U-boats and would soon see land. Sure enough, later that day, a smudge on the horizon grew into dark green hills, and more seagulls joined the regulars that had followed us for the whole journey. Dark fell before we entered the harbor, and we went to sleep for our last night on board. Rumor told us we were approaching Scotland.

Just after dawn, the *Argentina*, aided by tugs, slowly made her way up a narrow inlet from the sea. We eagerly gathered on deck to see what came next. Low hills, brooding lushly green in the early-morning light, lined the waterway. Small villages crowded on the banks, each with a stone pier and moored fishing boats. The river, or inlet, narrowed as we proceeded inland, and I wondered how we could possibly be headed for a major seaport. But then, the channel opened into a harbor filled with anchored vessels of all descriptions. We jumped when our ship's anchor was released with a tremendous rattle and clank. The entire ship vibrated and rocked. It punctuated the end of our journey.

Tugs, barges, and lighters busily plied the waters. There was an air of purpose, of hustle, of constant motion, of no-nonsense activity. We could all feel the intensity, as though an epic scene were being enacted in the fast, jerky rhythm of an old silent film. This was so different from the impression I had experienced at dockside in New York that I couldn't define my reaction. I wondered if my imagination was heightened by excitement or by the knowledge that I was finally someplace where the war had dominated everything for over four years. Even the seagulls seemed caught up in the bustle. One sat on a stanchion close by squawking away as though he were directing traffic. We watched the activity wondering how and when we would be taken ashore. Rumors flew. Someone said we would be the first off because we were needed. Few of us believed that. Someone else said he had heard we would be stuck on board until the last debarkation. Another clairvoyant suggested our base wasn't ready; it had been bombed. Maybe our new aircraft had been sunk on the way over. None of us believed any of that. The harbor was Gourock. We were in Scotland. All of us believed that.

Breakfast was served, but I wasn't hungry—I was too excited. I went below to pack. We had lived out of our B-4 bags for at least a month. I felt like tossing everything out the porthole and starting over again, but of course I couldn't. There wasn't much to stuff into my bag, so now all that remained was the old army game of "hurry up and wait."

Finally, ship's loudspeakers squawked out, "479th Group personnel proceed to the main deck. Line up by squadrons. Personal gear hand carried. Debarkation in thirty minutes!"

We assembled on the main deck. The cargo doors had been opened and a gangplank stretched to a waiting barge. We quickly shuffled across the plank and stood shoulder to shoulder behind the railing, as all the available space below deck was already filled. The barge cast off from the *Argentina* and we were towed by a tug a short distance across the harbor to a railway dock.

A train waited, huffing and panting steam in the station building. We had just minutes to form up for roll call, and then we climbed aboard. The coach had an aisle down one side with sliding doors opening into compartments holding about eight people each. We scrambled into one and marveled at how everything was foreign and different from our American trains. The seats were incredibly comfortable; there were even curtains on the windows and little vases with artificial flowers on the wall!

It didn't take long to discover the outside compartment windows slid down. We crowded the opening with our heads poking out. Others up and down the length of the train had done the same. We sounded like a bunch of excited kids waiting to leave for summer camp shouting back and forth to one another. Come to think of it, I guess we were. After a shrill whistle, a cloud of steam, and a gentle bump, we were off.

The train moved smoothly out of the harbor area, passed slowly through a small town, then chugged through the outskirts of what must have been Glasgow. We picked up speed and emerged into the countryside. New impressions crowded my head: There was no clickety-clack from the train wheels (How did they do that?); farms, villages, crossings, streams, old houses, stone walls, manicured pastures, all were so different and wonderful. How neat everything appeared. Each quaint little train station had window boxes and pots full of flowers. There was no litter, no ugliness to be seen anywhere. It was the countryside of Arthur and Camelot, Robin Hood and Sherwood Forest. The dark side of Dickens wasn't anywhere in sight.

We had no idea where we were going or how long it would take. The train went on and on through the day. The countryside didn't change much. With the novelty wearing off, most of us made ourselves as comfortable as possible and dozed. We had some kind of meal, but I don't remember eating.

Night fell. Dark doesn't begin to describe it. Not a light showed anywhere, not from houses, towns, stations we passed through, not from the streets, not from vehicles. This was the British blackout. It brought home the grimmer side of the journey and, as if any of us needed it, reminded us of the reality. Now we were about to be thrust into the reality of what had only been impressions gleaned from Pathé newsreels and the idle chatter of instructor pilots, who had flown their combat tours in North Africa or the Pacific. All conversation in our railway compartment had ceased. We sat in the dark, each of us deep in thought, aware of our immediate future, and wondering how we would react. Would we face the dangers, the unknown, with courage and resolution? Perhaps some of us were worried, even frightened. In all truth, I wasn't. I can't explain why.

I thought back and tried to recall my feelings leading to this point in my life. I was excited and impatient. I wanted my turn at this war and I wanted it as soon as possible. It had taken us far too long to get here through all the red tape, seemingly foolish regulations, and insensitive and uncaring administrators in a huge war system far too big to care for any individual. Yet I was an individual and I did care. I cared a lot what happened to me. Why the hell did "they" think I went to West Point? To wear that ugly gray uniform with the black stripes on the blouse and trouser legs? To march around the parade ground with feathers sticking up out of the top of an excruciatingly uncomfortable thing called a shako? I really hadn't minded that part. It went with the territory, though all that pomp wasn't true military training, and we knew it. What combat training we did get the first two years had to do with shooting rifles and crawling about in the mud, neither of which I had any intention of doing after graduation. I suppose the West Point tactical officers thought we were being well prepared. Well, something must have been right. After all, West Point had been doing things that way since 1802. Look at Grant and Robert E. Lee, to say nothing of MacArthur and Eisenhower!

I must have fallen asleep, because I awoke with a start when the train stopped. Commands rang through this blackest of all nights. We were hustled out onto what must have been a station platform, told to hang on to the man in front of us, and ordered to step out. My God, it was dark! I had no idea what surrounded us or in which direction we were headed. We stopped only by bumping into the guy in front. I wondered who in hell was leading and how he knew where he was going. In spite of the dark, we found ourselves at the lowered tailgate of a large truck. We clambered up and found a bench running along each side under the canvas top and one running down the middle. I wondered when and if I would ever see that B-4 bag of mine again, but didn't really care.

The truck noisily ground off as soon as the tailgate was shut and the rear canvas was closed and tied. There wasn't much talking as we swayed with the turns and lurched into one another when the brakes were suddenly applied. If I couldn't even see to walk, how in the world did our driver know where he was going without headlights? It was so dark I couldn't tell who was sitting beside me.

After what seemed like an hour, we finally stopped for good and the rear canvas was opened. We piled out to find ourselves in front of a large building that could only dimly be seen. Three or four steps led up to an imposing double door. After going through the door, light struck us as blackout curtains parted and we were hustled into a large entry hall, complete with a picture of the king of England. I thought this must be a hotel where we'd bed down for the night. Not so. There stood Captain Horton and Lieutenant Thomas, our squadron intelligence officers. They had preceded us to England as part of the group's advance party.

Don Horton was all smiles as he proudly announced, "Welcome to RAF Station Wattisham, boys. This will be your new home. You 434th pilots follow Tommy down the hall. He'll show you to your rooms. But first, grab your bag from that pile over there."

I couldn't believe it. Where were the humble Quonset huts we'd expected? Who managed to get our personal luggage sorted out and brought here ahead of us? There were certainly no complaints as we made our startled way down the hall. We passed a bar on the left before coming to a cross-hallway. Wow!

Halfway down the corridor Tommy opened a door and said, "OK, Satch, here's where you, Robin, and Wally will bunk."

The room contained three beds, a couple of dressers, a closet, a regular sink, and two large windows with heavy blackout curtains drawn tightly shut. What a way to go to war. It didn't take long to decide who got which bed; it was always by rank, and Satch Turner was our D Flight commander. I threw my B-4 under a bed, flopped down, and zonked out.

The next day we explored our new home. It turned out to be one of the

RAF's prewar permanent stations. There were brick barracks buildings, three huge hangars, a headquarters building, squadron operation centers, a mess hall, supply buildings, maintenance facilities, the whole works, even a separated area containing family quarters. It was obvious the station had not been overlooked by the Luftwaffe. Only one of the hangars had a roof left and many of the buildings had been badly damaged. A 3,300-foot runway ran roughly east to west and was intersected by a longer PSP (pierced steel planking) northeast–southwest runway. A taxiway, called the perimeter track, or peri track, circled the entire landing field. Individual hardstands, each holding two aircraft, were clustered on either side of the taxiway. Brand-new P-38s sat on those hardstands, and we clamored to fly them right away. It was not to be. A great deal of local area knowledge had to be learned before we went barging off into the crowded skies over East Anglia.

We gathered at our separate squadron dispersal huts, where we received lengthy briefings on local customs, flight rules, the English monetary system (whew . . . farthings, pence, tuppence, bobs, shillings, half crowns, crowns, and pounds), and on and on. We were issued our flight gear: boots, jackets, parachutes, and Mae Wests. Sergeant Charlie Claybaugh opened up a dinghy and lectured us on its contents and use. We paid close attention when he explained that a downed pilot didn't have a chance of surviving the frigid waters of the English Channel unless he got into his dinghy quickly.

All that day, while we fidgeted in classrooms, a steady stream of aircraft buzzed our new home. We were being welcomed by the veterans from other bases: P-38s, Jugs, Mustangs, a Spitfire or two, B-24s, B-17s, and even some C-47 Gooney Birds. It was exciting and the days passed quickly. After a hot meal in our new mess hall, we gathered in the bar for an introduction to "arf an' arf" and mild and bitter. Somehow, cellar-temperature beer wasn't so bad after all. It wasn't as cold as American beer, but it wasn't as warm as we had anticipated. There was a bit of subdued chatter, befitting our status as new guys at the base. Certainly, no one admitted to nervousness. The barroom radio was tuned to the BBC and we listened up when Don Horton identified the announcer with the broad English accent as Lord Haw-Haw, the British turncoat speaking from Berlin.

Uneasiness turned to amazement when we realized what he was saying: ". . . and in closing this evening, I want to congratulate the 479th P-38 Group on a successful journey from California across the Pond and offer all of you a warm welcome to your new home, RAF Wattisham. We know you'll be comfortable there, and just to make sure you know we're thinking of you, we'll pay you a small visit very soon."

Not many moments later, a string of explosions went off somewhere nearby. Many of us instinctively ducked. It turned out that a lone JU-88 had dropped his payload on the depot base across the field from our location. No damage was done, and even better, no one was injured, but it sure got our attention. So much for the secrecy surrounding our overseas movement!

5

★

A Small Event Called D-day

We'd been at Wattisham since May 22. The base had beautiful quarters, good mess, adequate hangars, and brand-new airplanes. In fact, it was the best damned place I'd been stationed in the army. Even the English rain was refreshing. Mildew had yet to set in. I flew one of our new ships, a J15-LO, in the first week. God, they were sweet! It's unbelievable what an improvement they were over the older aircraft. Buzzing was almost expected here, so everyone did it. The Brits tolerated us as we dove at their fields, occasionally waving cheerily or maybe angrily when we spooked a plowing mule. One day I got the screwy notion to hop over and have a look at France. Didn't even have ammo. I started to climb, but then common sense prevailed. I knew I'd be seeing enough of it soon.

Until then the squadron had been focused on giving a few hours' "warm-up" time for each of us new guys before starting combat ops. A major from the 364th joined the 479th to coordinate our preparations and get us on the right track. We practiced missions daily. Soon our launch, assembly, and landing procedures were being executed with amazing smoothness. The major said he thought we were ready, and we knew we were. When I recalled the training we had received at 4th AF in the states, I shook my head. It had been inadequate, poorly planned and administered. It could have been much better preparation for combat. It proved to me that a war can't be fought effectively by armchair strategists. If those bird colonels had just come here first, observed the various fighter units, and then planned our training, we could have built a program with all the things that were so damned vital to combat flying. We were OK, but we could have been a whole lot better.

Mishaps weren't uncommon. Crazy Lieutenant Canella cheated death when he ran his plane into the ground at 400 mph, staggered back up into the air, dragged across the roof of a warehouse, plowed through a pile of bricks and tar barrels, and then walked away unscathed from a burning wreck. There wasn't enough left of the bird to cart away as scrap. Captain Walker, commander of the 436th, spun in on May 25. He had been test-firing his guns and when last seen was at 800 feet on a single engine and burning. It was a blow to his squadron.

My own airplane arrived that same afternoon: a spanking new P-38-J15-LO, just under twenty hours' flying time on her. It was a thrill to drink in the beauty of that living piece of machinery and realize it would be mine. It was my future, my survival or demise in this war. Sergeant Glen Wold, my crew chief, was enthusiastic. We had already plotted the myriad little tweaks and adjustments we would do to make number 28707 the best flying plane on the field, or for that matter in the whole theater. I thought we'd name it *SCAT II* for Scat Davis, my roommate at the Point. Even though he'd been disappointed when he couldn't fly because of his eyesight, Scat would at least be here symbolically. Wold took care of it that night, painting *SCAT II* on the nose for my first mission the next day.

My first combat was anticlimactic. I saw a few halfhearted puffs of flak but sure loved the hot-metal smell of my new P-38, the odors of oil, hydraulic fluid, ozone from the radio tubes, leather from the seat, and the faint whiff of residual perfume from the WASP pilot who had delivered it. The only thing missing was some cordite from the guns. On the second flight of the day we went on a patrol sweep over France and I damned near passed out from lack of oxygen. In debrief the major crawled all over me for not flying perfect formation. I doubt he could have flown perfect formation either without oxygen at 20,000 feet. It was one of those simple little mistakes that could get someone killed, and I had gotten away with it at least this time.

The next few days the first lieutenants got outranked. It really pissed us off. I figured that the captains and majors would be eager until things started getting hot, and then they'd remember their wives and kids back in the States and let the lieuts go on all the missions. Things always come out in the wash. We'd get our chance.

Missions got a bit more interesting with a bomber escort. God, those B-17s and B-24s! Box after box of them, columns for as far as the eye could see. There was lots of flak and I was quite certain that at least six bursts were aimed at me personally. We were diving as I watched the stuff in my mirror. It was fascinating. Big orange bursts with puffs of black smoke tracking directly in a line behind me. The same day we had yet another escort mission. I saw and called out eight or nine German cargo ships on the river, but got no reaction from lead. I vowed to go down lower the next opportunity I got. The following day was another escort deep into Germany. We picked up the bombers over the Zuider Zee and stayed with them to the target and back. We saw plenty of flak but still no German fighters.

I managed to worm my way into two more missions. The first was a patrol over the French coast between Calais and Le Havre. The bombers were obviously softening up the coast. It was a feint that didn't give away much, but I'm sure the Germans were getting worried. There was little enemy response. On the afternoon mission the group was assigned to various patrol points. We roamed all over occupied France but saw not a single fighter. The bombers blew the hell out of two airfields just as we were preparing to go down to strafe them. Had we been five minutes earlier we would have been in the impact area when they dropped.

I was frustrated by the lack of action. I slapped the release on the side of my oxygen mask to free up my mouth for a string of cussing at no one in particular. We'd been briefed on strict radio discipline for these missions. That meant shut up and don't say anything, no matter what we saw sitting or moving around down below. We passed trucks barreling down tree-lined roads, trains stopped in patches of woods with wisps of steam giving them away, deserted-looking airfields with small buildings backed up against surrounding forests, surely hiding something. There were large and small marshaling yards, sometimes with supply trains sitting there, just waiting. All of them begging, "Hit me! Please hit me!" There were plenty of lucrative, tempting targets, and our leader, "Highway," just kept sailing along as though we were over England. What was going on?

We all thought our squadron CO, Major Miller Herren, was a really good guy, although brand-new first lieutenants weren't very qualified to judge that. But our naive impressions were all positive. He worked long hours getting us organized before we shipped out. He trained us hard, and we liked that. He was direct and to the point. He didn't tolerate slackness, and he inspired us to do our best. We judged him to be fair and not intimidating, unlike some of the senior officers whom we'd dealt with in our short careers. Best of all, he flew the airplane well and more than once had proved himself with us.

But now it seemed that there was a problem. It wasn't that Major Herren was losing face by not leading us into battle the way we wanted and thought he should. It wasn't a case of beginning to think he was showing a timid streak by not getting at the enemy. It wasn't really that at all. I think we believed the boss was under some kind of pressure not to expose us to the wily Hun. We thought maybe he was getting the word from group or even higher up. For us, the situation was downright embarrassing. What were the men in the experienced groups over here thinking of the brand-new 479th? Our daily ops reports must have been embarrassing reading compared to theirs. I'd already made a habit of reviewing daily reports from other bases, and I admit I was sick with envy. Other squadrons were shooting up everything, even getting into aerial battles with the Krauts. We remained unblooded. It was a creeping, awful feeling to be left out, as though we'd been judged as pantywaists afraid to join the big boys.

I could just see it coming. "Daddy, what did you do in the big war?" Or from some veteran, "You say you were in the 479th back in '44? Wasn't that the chicken outfit that never shot its guns? Oh yeah, now I remember. Excuse me, pal, I see a buddy of mine down at the other end of the bar," and he'd walk away with a scornful sneer.

So on this fine June morning over Germany, the situation became intolerable for me, and, not for the first or last time in my life, the devil got behind me and gave a shove.

I broke radio silence and announced, "Newcross Lead, this is Newcross Blue Three. I've got a train at our eight o'clock! I'm going down. Will you cover me?"

"Roger, Blue Three," came the response.

I was already on my way, fangs out and trigger finger curled. After a quick check of the armament switches and a fast look around for other aircraft, I made a full-powered, shallow dive toward that bloody train, the train that was going to either get me into this damned war or get me court-martialed. Probably both.

I banked hard to the right to line up, then pulled the pipper through the length of the freight cars, put it a bit above my aim point to allow for range, rolled wings level, and made a pass, shooting in front of the train to stop it and to give the French engineer and fireman time to bail out. I jinked around again, stopped the sight on the engine's boiler, squeezed off a burst, saw the HEI sparkling all over the straining engine, and watched a fountain of smoke and steam burst out of the stack. I thought about the train crew and was glad I hadn't aimed at the engineer's cab. It wouldn't be nice to shoot up some poor Frenchmen forced to drive Hitler's freight around France in broad daylight, as these guys were doing.

I pulled up and reversed. The next pass I raked my .50 caliber along a part of the now-stalled train. It was easy to see the sparkles light up the freight cars, but kind of disappointing when nothing blew up. For more than a year Pathé News had been full of film clips of trains exploding during strafing passes—spectacular stuff for a twenty-one-year-old novice. Maybe they didn't always blow up.

As I pulled around for a third pass and checked over my shoulder for flak, the entire train was lit up from end to end! Then I saw that the whole damned squadron had come down to get in on the fun. My initiative had been too much for the rest of the troops to resist. I hadn't heard anything on the radio, so this was pure initiative by the individuals. Everyone got his chance. No frustrations were left in that bunch. They all banged away at what must surely have become the most shot-up train in the entire war.

Eventually, Newcross Lead took over and guilt set in. Major Herren's voice was like slivers of ice when he ordered us away. Then he fell silent, coldly silent. We formed, sorted ourselves out, and followed him back to England like docile sheep without a peep. His silence left us stewing and wondering. Had I gone too far? Was he angry, or just maintaining radio silence like the orders? Hell, he couldn't fire all of us, could he? Certainly I would be fair game. No doubt about that. But there was still the satisfaction of having finally fired my guns, and I thought of the happy looks I'd get from my crew chief and armorer when they saw the telltale powder marks on *Scat*'s nose.

It was a grim flight home. We had been out almost five hours and some of us were really sweating out the gas, since we carried only one tank. But our worries became insignificant when we passed over the coast just south of Dieppe and saw the bombers coming out about 15,000 feet above us. The flak they caught over Dieppe was the most vicious imaginable. One bomber caught it squarely, and I watched him fall in a huge ball of flame all the way to the ground. It was a horrible sight. One can't help admiring the courage of those bomber crews. That's no way to fight or fly, if you ask me, and a really horrible way to die. Here I was, stupidly worrying about a simple court-martial.

The truck ride back around the perimeter track as we headed for debriefing was not filled with exuberance. Someone tried to crow about our great contribution to Hitler's demise, but his remarks were halfhearted and no one was very talkative. It crossed my mind I should jump off the truck and head for the woods, but it was out of the question. Music was music, and the sooner faced the better.

Debriefing was intense to say the least. Old Mother Horton, our S-2, kept at us and stretched the whole process beyond belief. Finally it ended, and in the ensuing hush my name was spoken softly, quietly, and with great menace.

"Olds, come over here."

I went and stood in front of the boss at attention.

He started in on me with painful intensity. "You broke formation. You disobeyed regulations. You defied my authority. You exposed the squadron to unwarranted risk, and for all I know, you attacked an unauthorized target!" The major was really mad, angrier than any of us had ever seen him. His voice was low and steely and his eyes were blazing.

I had visions of steel bars and rock piles. It was going to be Leavenworth.

Major Herren went on with his tirade. As he warmed up, things grew even darker. The room shrank, the ceiling came down over my head, and my peripheral vision vanished. All I could see were those steely blue eyes of his boring into mine. I stood at attention and tried to stare back. I heard the major's words, but I concentrated mostly on keeping my eyeballs locked on his.

Finally he said, "Well, what have you got to say for yourself, Olds? Give me one good reason not to draw up court-martial charges right this minute!"

A ray of light broke through the dark and a glint of hope appeared in my well of despair. He actually wanted me to say something! He had given me an opening, right in front of the whole squadron, all of whom were at rapt attention. On the football field I had learned that aggressiveness often made up for size and sometimes a blind block carried the play.

"Sir," I replied in the steadiest voice I could muster, "I called you. I said, 'Newcross Lead, this is Newcross Blue Three. There's a train at eight o'clock.

I'm going down. Will you cover me?' and you said, 'Roger, Blue Three.' So I went down and attacked the train."

Major Herren glared at me. He clenched his fists, and his face turned red. He looked like he might explode. Now it was his turn to feel frustration. He opened his mouth but nothing came out. He tried again and only sputtered.

Finally he managed, "Goddamn you, Olds, I wasn't the one who said 'Roger'!"

It was chilly around the mess for a while after that, but the major was a fair man. Although he didn't say so, he knew he had been outmaneuvered. Of course, I never told anyone it was impossible not to recognize my wingman's way of saying 'Roger.' An Okie twang is an Okie twang, even over France.

We flew a few more bomber escorts, but at squadron level we realized we were just a small piece of the fabric of war, and not privy to the plans of head-quarters. Despite not being in on the Big Picture, all of us had a premonition that an invasion was imminent.

Our targets in May had disclosed the Allied intentions: bridges, rail yards, airfields, troop concentrations, and fuel dumps were all concentrated along the west coasts of France, Belgium, and Holland as though we were isolating the area, which of course we were. We wondered when and where the blow would fall or whether the Germans had already figured it out. A sense of pent-up excitement pervaded all of Britain, in the pubs, on the streets of London, and in every village and hamlet of the land. You could feel it, taste it, and sense it. All the dark years of facing the German onslaught alone, all the losses and frustrations, all the courage and sacrifice, the shortages, rationing, blackouts, bombing raids, destruction of glorious old buildings and entire rows of homes, everything the people had suffered, everything they had suffered with an unbelievable stoicism, that British "stiff upper lip" and endless dry wit—now, by God, and with His good grace, it was going to be THEIR turn! The emotion was electrifying.

The day the free world had longed for finally arrived. On June 5, Lieutenant Tommy Thomas routed us out of the sack at 0300 hours. We awoke to a dank, dismal, gray and cloudy day with a disagreeable wind. The 479th Group wasn't scheduled to fly until late afternoon. That didn't make much sense to us at the moment, but we didn't have time to care. We'd just seen our P-38s with hideous black and white stripes painted around the engine booms and encircling the wings. Someone said they were "invasion stripes" to make it easy for the ground forces to identify the friendly fighters. It had been a lot of furious, hard work all night long by our ground crews, we were told. This had to be it! In fact, the rumor was spreading that the invasion had started without us. Surely, someone on base knew what was happening, but not us.

Briefing was announced. We filed in, crowding the room with a rumble of excited chatter. Someone barked, "Attention!" and we snapped to as Colonel Kyle Riddle strode to the briefing platform. The room fell quiet as we took our seats. I won't accuse him of a bit of dramatic license, but his long pause and sweeping look at our eager faces was just right. I was holding my breath. Everyone must have been, for when he said, "Gentlemen, this is it!" the windows rattled. We were whooping and hollering, pumping our fists in the air, slapping one another on the back, punching the guys next to us, jumping on the chairs, clapping and whistling. It was an incredible scene!

After a few minutes, with order barely restored, the briefing continued. No, the big show hadn't passed us by. In fact, we were to play an important part late in the afternoon. The armada had left port, and because we were P-38s and easily recognizable by the navy gunners, we were to join other Lightning outfits providing escort as the invasion fleet steamed toward the Continent. We weren't shown the landing point or told much else, but who needed it? The show was on!

The rest of the briefing mostly concerned the weather and a lot of speculation about what was expected from the Luftwaffe. Old Stormy, our weather officer, turned out to have the right scoop. Just as he said, the weather stank. High winds with heavy low clouds persisted all the way across the Channel and throughout Normandy. I thought this would work against the German Luftwaffe, but wondered how General Eisenhower was going to fight the coming battle with thousands of seasick GIs. Well, as Caesar had noted, the die was now cast. As for us, we'd find out about the enemy air opposition when it happened.

In spite of the excitement and tension, the premission preparations got done and we headed to the airplanes, launched, and joined up in our group formations. To the confusion of many whose map sense wasn't too sharp, we headed a bit southwest to make our rendezvous with destiny. Then something odd happened. As we flew across the Thames estuary east of London, I swear I heard harp music, melodious and heavenly harp music on our VHF radio frequency, where such interference never happened. It couldn't, according to the signal people. It wasn't possible. But there it was. I heard it loud and clear. Was I the only one? Was someone or something sending me a signal? Surely I wasn't hallucinating, and I certainly wasn't going to break radio silence or risk the derision of every other pilot in the group.

Those weird thoughts were soon forgotten when we crossed the south coast of England, hugging the underside of the dark gray clouds in high winds. The turbulence was brutal. Visibility wasn't that bad, but we had to stay below 1,500 feet to avoid going completely on instruments. We found ourselves scudding through patches of low-hanging mist barely above whitecaps, staring ahead across an angry, wind-whipped expanse of empty sea. Suddenly, there was a ship ahead. No, it wasn't a ship. It was an object being towed by a large tugboat. As we hurried past, I saw that it was some kind of floating dock. What the hell was it doing out here? But then there was another and another and then, my God, there were ships, tens, hundreds, thousands of ships stretching to the horizons. All headed in the same direction. There were ships loaded with tanks and trucks, destroyers and gunboats, oilers, landing craft and supply freighters—every imaginable, and some unimaginable, kind of thing that could float. It was mind-boggling. Then, ahead, there was a cruiser, surrounded by escorts, and still more ships with more infantry, more vehicles. The heaving sea was black with objects, all moving inexorably toward France. I remember chills cascading down my spine, a feeling of utter awe and the soulful realization that we were part of what would become one of history's most unforgettable events.

Highway Lead finally called for a turn back the way we had come. We reversed to again pass the fleet along the coast of England near the Isle of Wight. There, we could see masses and columns of boats coming out of The Solent between the Isle of Wight and the Hampshire coast. As we paralleled the coast in our turn back toward the Channel, there were more ships converging from every direction, steaming to join that already unbelievable force headed for France. We tried to reach the head of the fleet, but I don't think we ever reached that point. We saw neither hide nor hair of the Luftwaffe. I couldn't believe it! Surely they knew by now. For God's sake, Sir Francis Drake and Admiral Frobisher had spotted the Spanish Armada approaching England in these very same waters 356 years before. Where were they? Why weren't they attacking? So much for the intelligence part of our briefing! The Luftwaffe was hunkered down waiting for the attack.

Dusk fell before we headed home to Wattisham. We landed after dark to find the base alive with excitement. My flight suit was soaked with sweat and my legs were weak when I climbed out. I tried to explain to my crew chief what we had seen but didn't have the words. It was too vast for rational comprehension. All I could think of were ships, ships, and more ships stretching from England to wherever, a bridge of ships, from island to Continent, streaming into battle to ignite an instant of history, to write in the annals of a dark war a glorious page of exultation and purpose.

The debriefings were raucous; everyone was yelling, a reaction to the emotional impact rather than the cold statistics of numbers and positions. Poor Horton must have done his best, but his intel report could only say, "SHIPS!" Things were quieter as we downed a beer or two before the usual evening mess of bangers and mash with grayish brussels sprouts. It wasn't totally silent at the tables, but I noticed that almost everyone who had flown was doing a bit of deep reflecting. Their thoughts, like mine, were on the troops headed for the battle. What awaited us in the morning? We thought of home and loved ones, wondering if we would see them again. The realization that this might be a last night on earth for many slowly sank in.

Sipping one last beer before turning in for the next morning's critical mission, someone muttered, "I heard harp music, bloody fucking harp music. Did anyone else hear it?" What a relief! We all admitted to hearing the same thing. There were chuckles as we confessed not wanting to be the first to talk about it. We never did figure out where it came from.

The sixth of June, 1944, was a day the world will never forget. The action was so vast, and so intensely important, that I think future historians will compare it to the battles of Marathon and Thermopylae, to the campaigns of Alexander and Caesar, to Charles Martel's battle against the Moors at Poitiers, to Napoleon's defeat in front of Moscow (which apparently hadn't made much of an impression on Hitler), to Trafalgar—to every decisive, turning-point battle in recorded history.

Those of us who had pleaded and fought to go on the first missions of D-day had front-row seats in the crowded briefing room that morning. Our mission was to fly top cover for the landing forces, to protect the ships from Luftwaffe attack. The weather and intelligence were the same as the day before: stinko and guesswork.

We took off at dawn in miserable weather then hurried to our rendezvous point off the coast of Normandy. There, the vast panoply of war was spread before us in a mind-numbing vista. Gunfire from cruisers and destroyers flashed in the gloom as they shelled the tops of the bluffs along the beaches. Strange bargelike craft spewed barrages of flaming rockets toward unseen targets ashore. Small craft crowded with men circled near their mother ships and then, as we arrived, set course for the beaches. Large, blunt-nosed landing craft stood off at sea, obviously waiting their turn. Columns of black smoke marked burning ships already hit by the German shore batteries. The sea around the small boats boiled and frothed with fountains of gunfire. Occasionally a boat erupted in flame and smoke, to disappear quickly in the roiling water. My stomach churned knowing that brave young men were dying even before reaching land.

We could see the initial waves of landing boats plow into the shallows. The front ramps dropped, and men splashed out into the water and struggled to wade ashore, some of them chest deep in the surf. Others sank out of sight in deeper water under the weight of their combat gear. Shells and machine-gun fire kicked up the water, and we could see red stains of blood spreading from floating bodies. Men surged up the beach toward the cliffs that rose a hundred yards ahead of them. My God, could they ever reach shore through that gunfire and then make it over the beach defenses extending ahead? They pushed on, some suddenly falling into total stillness. Dark forms lay in the shallows and on the sands. Other men followed, group after group, wave after wave, on and on through the surf. Vicious explosions erupted among them, explosions that could only be mines planted in the waters and on the sand. I wondered briefly about my West Point classmate and football teammate Harry Romanek. Harry had become an engineer for the army. He was assigned to the landing craft. I knew he was down there somewhere, and the thought of him in this turmoil sickened me. I saw the first of the figures reach the beach and run forward to the protection of the bluffs. They huddled there, gradually spreading out and arraying themselves in clumps. It seemed total confusion amid the smoke and shell bursts.

We orbited, watching from just off the shore. Our orders were to keep over the boats to protect them, but this was too much, too intense, too huge, and too personal to want to obey that order. Over and over, we had been admonished not to fire at anything on the ground. The planners had forecast the situation to be too confusing, and above all, we didn't have any air-ground communication to make sure we knew friend from foe. But, goddamn it, we could easily see the gray-uniformed German troops firing down on our GIs from the top of the cliffs. Christ, those cliff-tops were tempting! I knew we could make passes without endangering our own troops. I dutifully obeyed my orders.

Common sense and discipline prevailed. We had to believe that the commanders organizing this massive invasion knew what they were doing. If I went into the fray, I would more than likely be shooting blindly, get hit by our own artillery fire, or, worse, get in the way of the other fighter forces especially trained for close support. I couldn't see them, but I knew they had to be there. So along the beaches we flew, back and forth, over and over; as far as I could tell, the only people shooting at us the whole time were our own naval guys. Under the circumstances, it was hard to blame them, though later we wondered about the extent of their recognition training. I couldn't imagine anything in the air that looked friendlier than a P-38 with black and white stripes painted all over it.

The Luftwaffe never showed up. Our flailing back and forth off the beaches counted for nothing except perhaps adding a bit of noise to the din. We were part of the chorus without a speaking part. Finally, it was time for us to be relieved. We headed back to England, awed by the immensity of what we had witnessed and fully aware of the absolute necessity to keep those troops of ours safely on the beachhead.

We had ringside seats for one of the greatest events in history. Yet, for those of us flying over the carnage, smoke, and flame, the massive sweep of action lacked the reality of sound. Not even the largest of the thousands of shell bursts reached our ears. Our own engines blanked out all external noise, and we were so used to them as background noise that we heard them only if one of the Allisons coughed or sputtered. All we needed were subtitles to complete the sensation of watching a gigantic, silent epic war movie unfolding below us.

Everyone in the 479th made it home safely. Debriefing was far more solemn than the day before. Mental exhaustion set in as each pilot dealt personally with the scope and intensity of what he had witnessed.

The Allied invasion was successful, but that scarcely does justice to the event. Over 350,000 troops and millions of tons of supplies hit the beaches of Normandy between the mouth of the Seine and Cherbourg. Free French forces and Canadians were part of the ground invasion; paratroops and glider troops were inserted before dawn behind what were to be the impact points. The British army hit the beaches in front of the town of Caen at sectors code-named Sword and Gold. Air and naval support was provided by the Royal Australian Air Force, the Royal New Zealand Air Force, and the Royal Norwegian Navy. Canadians took Juno. There were contingents from Belgium, Czechoslovakia, Greece, and the Netherlands joining in the fight. Our troops landed to the west on beaches named Utah, Pointe du Hoc, and Omaha. The scope of the operation can barely be appreciated.

Throughout that day and the days that followed, our group patrolled over the invasion forces. We flew our missions over the beaches and farther inland as the troops advanced. Missions soon turned routine, and as time passed, we began to sneak still farther inland. The Luftwaffe never showed, but the battle became a personal thing. We identified with the ground troops as they clawed their way up the bluffs and fought their way through the hedgerows. Gunsmoke and artillery bursts marked their progress. It was remarkably sobering to see the hundreds of American and British gliders littering the fields and orchards. Some were intact, but many had run head-on into the hedgerows bordering every open space and lay there smashed in crunched-up heaps. Their invasion stripes stood out starkly against the green of the fields, and I felt a pang at the thought of the men on board those wrecks. I wondered how many of them had survived, but, all too quickly, our concern for their fates melded into the relentless routine of the war. Increasingly we knew that fate had little time for individuals.

Tons of supplies and ammunition, supporting tens of thousands more men, were poured onto the beaches during the next couple of weeks. By then we felt that nothing could stop our armies as they expanded the beachhead and moved inexorably inland. There was stubborn resistance by the German forces. The grind for the infantry and artillery troops was tough, field by field and hedgerow by hedgerow. With the beachhead established, two artificial Mulberry harbors were towed across the English Channel in pieces, then quickly assembled by June 9. One harbor at Arromanches was constructed by British forces and the other at Omaha Beach by Americans. The construction was fascinating to watch from the air. Severe storms destroyed Omaha harbor on June 19, and the landing of supplies stopped for several days, but by then the British and American forces combined had landed well over 600,000 men, 100,000 vehicles, and 200,000 tons of supplies.

Each of the pilots in the 479th Group flew ten to twelve missions over the Normandy beachhead in the two weeks following D-day. Exciting as the whole affair might have been, we still lacked personal involvement, for we still hadn't engaged the enemy air forces. Daily combat reports from the other 8th AF groups told of furious action, some air, mostly ground. Each day we were briefed on the progress the troops had made. The first major movement seemed to be a thrust by American forces that were fighting intensely on the roads to Cherbourg at the end of the Cotentin Peninsula. The Allies needed a deepwater port and needed it badly, but it would be almost two months before the port of Cherbourg became operational again.

We had only a glimpse of the Big Picture, but we were swept along with the tide of national emotion and felt it on a visceral level. We were able to keep up with the war news and follow the overall action from briefings in the squadron meeting room, through florid reports in the English tabloids, and through our own *Stars and Stripes* newspaper. In the fields of Normandy our troops fought slowly from town to town, facing stubborn resistance from the Germans dug into defensive positions behind every mound and sunken road. It was tough going but they persisted. We learned of their bravery through our favorite source of news: the great correspondent Ernie Pyle. As usual, Pyle was right there with the attacking units at the front line of the action. We all loved and respected the man for the way he kept the free world in touch with news of the individual fighting GI. He had done this throughout the African campaign, across Sicily, then on into Italy. Now he was in France and still at it. He wrote of big events in terms of the little guy who was making them work. Later, he went to the Pacific to cover the war and, sadly, was gunned down by a Japanese sniper on Ie Shima, a coastal island off Okinawa. It was a tragic loss.

After two weeks of providing beachhead cover, the 479th was released to join a bombing campaign designed to slow the movement of enemy supplies and reinforcements. We were thankful at being switched to interdiction missions throughout northern and central France. We loaded 500- and 1,000-pound bombs to hit bridges and rail yards. We dive-bombed supply dumps and troop concentrations. We strafed airfields and shot up truck convoys. It was wild, and though we suffered steady attrition, we didn't let up. We were hitting Hitler finally and it felt damned good. Anything remotely resembling enemy activity came under our guns and bombs. For the young, dumb, and eager, this was more like it! We were no longer the new guys on the block. It was a relief. Our missions were only a very small part of the war, but intensely meaningful to a group of young pilots just barely into our twenties.

Our losses were dispiriting yet not devastating. We dispelled sadness by lauding our fallen comrades over pints of beer. Old friends disappeared, replaced by a stream of new faces at the mess and briefings. Our CO wrote dispassionate daily reports of pilots lost, but always concluded with an optimistic "and we hope for their safe return." Time had little meaning. One day flowed into the next. Looking back, I can see how we changed individually and as a squadron. We were maturing as warriors, not necessarily as civilized men. What had been exciting a month ago became routine. Rather than flying willy-nilly into danger, we thought before we acted, acted quickly whenever we had to, yet still felt frustrated when the action passed us by and the older groups were given the more lucrative targets, or when operational reports told of aerial battles that we had missed.

Those of us who survived those days went on to fly and fight with an appreciation of life that can be known only by those who have been in combat. Laughter was as profound as sadness. Friendships deepened. Every moment of each day felt exactly right, and the edges of time seemed tinged by light.

6

★

The Heat of Many Battles

The third week of June started with a bang. Make that several. A B-17 bellied into a field about 500 yards from the officers' club. The crew escaped, except for the tail gunner, who didn't get out. We were in the club when the bomber hit, and we ran out to help. We were held back by the intensely burning fire and watched as the crash guys raced to put it out. Quite a crowd had gathered, but there were plenty of men on the job, so we stayed out of their way—until crewmen started running away from the aircraft toward where we were standing.

"Bombs!" one yelled as they streaked past us. "The fucker's loaded with bombs!"

We turned en masse and hightailed it back toward the shelter of the closest buildings, tripping over one another. I raced pell-mell into the club, barreled through the tables, and dove behind the bar.

"KABOOM!"

The concussion of the massive explosion blew out the facing windows of every building in the vicinity. The front of the officers' club was completely ventilated, several bottles of fine whiskey were sadly destroyed, and my ears rang for hours. Fortunately, no one was hurt beyond minor cuts from flying glass. We spent the rest of the day sweeping up shards covering every surface in the club.

News came that Lieutenants Kuentzel and Grdenich had failed to return from a mission. They'd been trapped atop an overcast topping out near 28,000 feet. When last seen, both aircraft were in a steep spiral headed for the ground near Rouen. Just three days later, more bad news. This time, four were lost, including my pal Al Tucker. He was hit by flak while returning home on one engine. Canella, Ilsley, and Lutz went down, too, lost forever; but it turned out that "Tuck's Luck" held, and Al survived to sit out the rest of the war in a Stalag Luft.

Bad weather kept us grounded until the Fourth of July. We were celebrating Independence Day the afternoon the squadron finally got airborne. Captain Jeffrey led us on a sweep of the area Saintes-Niort-Saumur-Nantes. We did everything we could to lure the elusive Luftwaffe out of its hiding place. No deal. We had to settle for taking out five locomotives and about a dozen supply vehicles. Lots of strafing but more frustration about never seeing any air-to-air combat.

Finally! Victory for the 479th at last! On the fifth, Jeffrey drew first blood from the enemy when he found an Fw-200 Condor taking off from the Château-Bernard Airdrome and shot it down before anyone else could get close. The O club scene that night was memorable! The following day, Lieutenant Tipps got the squadron on the board again by downing an Me-109. The rest of us were itching to continue the streak and were frustrated as hell by weather socking us in for four days. It had to be a joke.

Gleason and I got some jollies blasting an ammunition dump on the fifteenth but we both limped home with damaged ships. We were lucky. Both P-38s were full of holes, mine from flak and Gleason's from debris that was blown into the air when the dump went up. Sergeant Wold's face was the picture of misery when he saw his airplane, but it didn't stop him from running to get a camera before I'd even taxied to a stop. For him, even battle damage was a validation that his airplane was part of the war.

In mid-July I became a flight commander and was promoted to captain. Although the promotion wouldn't be official until August 1, the news mitigated some of my frustration over zero kills and formed a heady, make that headstrong, brew. I guess I decided to take it out on our intelligence officer,

Mother Horton, by stressing what I thought was an intelligent point. After all, he was the one who told us where the Nazis were and weren't, wasn't he?

I barged into the ops office one afternoon and said, "Hey, Don, you busy?"

Captain Horton looked up from his cluttered desk and gave me a welcoming smile. "What's up, Robin? You mad at someone or something this morning? Why don't you go work it off by drawing another cartoon."

By this time, almost everyone in the squadron knew that I spent a lot of time in meetings doodling what I was feeling on whatever piece of paper I could find. It seemed a more reasonable thing to do than react verbally to express my frustration. Maybe I was just bored. Horton, in his damned debriefings, had already been the subject of a few of these doodled caricatures, and unfortunately, he'd seen a couple of them.

I thought this might make it up to him. "Naw, Don, not mad, just thought if you had time we could go for a ride in the piggyback."

Horton's eyes lit up at that and I knew he was ready. He hadn't been flying yet, despite dispensing intelligence reports and debriefing us after missions. We'd been trying to schedule the two of us in the makeshift two-seater P-38 for a couple of weeks, and the right time had hit this morning. I'd already been out on the flight line conferring with the crew chief, and the aircraft was all set to go. I didn't bother to tell Don that the armorer had been asked to load and charge the four .50s and the 20 mm gun. That was going to be my little surprise. The weather was perfect for what I had in mind: a solid deck of clouds at 800 feet and almost 300 feet thick covered all of East Anglia, stretching across the North Sea and well out over the Continent.

I took Don into the parachute shop to fit him with a chute and helmet. Sergeant Claybaugh and I tried not to grin as Don bent his lanky frame into the chute straps before pulling the helmet down over his scraggly hair. With his long, lean body and his head jutting forward over a prominent Adam's apple, he looked like Ichabod Crane of Sleepy Hollow. The image was so acute, I often caught myself about to call him that. It's how he was portrayed in my doodles.

Claybaugh, nicknamed "Mudnuts," drove us out to the piggyback's hard-stand. I wasn't so sure the crew chief wouldn't give me away. No one had loaded ammunition into his guns before, and he seemed nervous as I performed a walk-around. I calmed him down by saying I was going to a practice range on the west side of the Wash (the North Sea), and promised I'd be careful not to hurt his bird. I suspected he was thinking about having to persuade someone to clean those guns later and didn't relish the thought.

Finally, Don asked, "Robin, where are we going? What are we going to do?"

"Tell you what, Don, how about going up north just below the Wash? The countryside up there looks a lot like Holland: windmills, canals, dikes, real flat, pretty farms and little villages. I think you'll be interested." Don agreed, and we set about getting him folded into the small space behind me where the radio normally sat. That put Don's head peering just over my shoulder when I strapped in.

Engine-start and takeoff went smoothly, and I turned north as we cleared the runway. I kept the bird in a climb, and we quickly entered the thick overcast. I leveled, made a sneaky turn east, then continued my climb. We burst into sunlight and hurtled up into a bright blue sky. I heard Don gasp and couldn't blame him, knowing he had just experienced that always-exciting moment for the first time. I know I never tired of it and was pleased he reacted as he did.

"Hey, Don," I asked, "how about a few maneuvers? OK?"

He shouted his approval, and I pulled the nose up to do a gentle barrel roll left, then right. I leveled, added power, pulled up almost vertically, and rolled inverted. I let the nose come through with the least g-force possible, and we sailed over the top, then down the other side of my loop. He gave several excited whoops. I pulled out of the loop gently, not wanting to slam Don with too many g's in his cramped position. I also didn't want him to park his breakfast on my shoulder!

I headed east and kept my eye on the clock as we did more gentle maneuvers. When I estimated we had crossed the North Sea I hollered, "I'm going down through the cloud deck. We should be just south of the Wash by now."

Don peered over my left shoulder as we descended. I knew he hadn't the slightest idea where we were.

As we broke out of the clouds, I made a couple of quick turns to get my bearings. Yep, we were over Holland all right. I turned away from the marshaling yards near Amsterdam before Don could see the city, then followed a canal running in a northwesterly direction. He paid rapt attention as I pointed out the canals and windmills. A truck convoy baited me as it barreled down a highway, and I was tempted. Targets like that don't happen every day. The Jerries probably had a flak truck or two mixed in the convoy, and that wouldn't do just now.

"Looks just like Holland, Don," I shouted.

He nodded and craned his neck as far as the canopy would allow as he took in the sights. "Just like I knew it would look," he yelled. "Wow, windmills in England, too."

We stooged around for a while, letting him soak in the sights. I was keeping my eyes peeled for any airfields or flak sites. Getting shot up wasn't part of the planned scenario.

Finally I spotted what I had been looking for and yelled to Don, "See that train down there at nine o'clock? Let me show you how we set up a strafe pass."

He didn't respond as I turned and dove at the locomotive. I had switched on the sight and guns a long time ago, so everything was in readiness. I pulled the sight up through the freight cars, and as it went forward of the engineer's cab, I pulled the trigger.

Four .50 caliber guns and a stream of 20 mm went roaring into the target. It was a good clean hit. The boiler blew with a huge plume of smoke and steam.

"What the fuck are you doing?" Don screamed. "What are you doing?"

"Strafing that train," I hollered back.

"But . . . but . . . that's not . . . but it's . . . holy shit! . . . YOU CAN'T!" Poor Don was choking on his words. A glance over my shoulder and I swear his eyeballs were about to pop out of his head.

Just at that moment a stream of tracers arced over the canopy, and I jerked the bird around violently in an evasive maneuver. More flak came at us from my right, and I rolled and yanked the nose down to get on the deck. We flashed across Rotterdam and really took some heavy stuff. This is no longer funny, I thought, and headed west just a few feet above the ground as fast as I could go. Fortunately, we didn't take any hits. I was damned glad to make it to the coast and head for home. I was soaked with sweat and breathing deep sighs of relief.

Don didn't speak to me all the way back across the North Sea to England. Of course he realized by then what I had done. It was reasonable to assume he was not amused. I felt a bit guilty and wondered if it had been worth it. I had to do something to make it come out all right with our esteemed squadron intel officer. Besides, he outranked me and had it in his power to make me darned remorseful. We landed, taxied in, and shut down without another word.

Don's expression was grim as we rode the jeep back to the 434th Squadron dispersal. After entering the door and dumping our flight gear, I turned to him and said, "OK, time for debriefing." That got his attention. Maybe he hadn't forgotten how we griped when he asked those scores of questions every day after our missions.

We entered his office. I grabbed the notepad he always used when grilling us and sat down in his chair behind his desk. I began, "OK, Don, let's get started. What was our takeoff time? Where did we cross out? At what time and where did we go feet dry on the Continent?"

Don shifted uneasily on the chair we pilots normally occupied when being debriefed.

"How many trucks were in that convoy we passed? Which way were they headed? What road were they on? Here, show me on the map. How many trains in that marshaling yard outside Amsterdam? Did we only get that locomotive or did we make a second pass on the supply cars?" I kept on as Don grew increasingly annoyed.

"Where did we pick up that flak? What kind was it? Did you count the guns? Was—"

He stopped me. "OK, Robin, you've made your point. I don't know any of that and probably never will. Now, thanks for the lesson. Get off my back and get the hell out of here!"

Believe me, I was damned glad to see him crack a smile as I hurried out. It occurred to me that this story might be better left untold for the time being. Damned shame. I thought it would go over well in the mess or at the pub. Maybe later when Don simmered down a bit and had a couple of beers. I realized I couldn't claim a locomotive, or even a mission, as I biked over to the officers' club for a pint of bitter. It turned out I couldn't tell anyone about this adventure without getting in more hot water with my squadron CO. I knew he wouldn't see any value in my prank, and I hoped Don would keep his own mouth shut. He did.

It occurred to me that I needed a break. It did seem a long damned time after arriving in May before I finally got a three-day pass in July. To be honest, up to then, I hadn't wanted one. I was afraid I might miss some of the action and couldn't bear the thought of anyone in the squadron getting into a hassle with some Jerry fighters while I was off gallivanting around England. It was past time for a couple of days off.

Guys had started going off to London in mid-June, but the most popular entertainment came in the form of a C-47 that landed once a week to drop off and pick up six pilots to head to Scotland for a six-day "rest cure." Judging by the way the returnees would stumble off the plane with wild tales of beautiful women, single malts, and Drambuie, then head straight for bed, it might as well have been a ten-day rest cure because it took them four more days to recover.

While Scotland was tempting, London was my first target. Exploring that great city had been a dream since boyhood. The possibility of maybe meeting up with one of the Red Cross girls from an O club party made it an easy choice. With my request for a pass approved, I threw a more-or-less clean shirt, pair of socks, two pairs of shorts, three oranges I had saved, and two fists full of pound notes into my musette bag, then caught the shuttle truck to the Ipswich train station.

I sat up front with the driver, a corporal who seemed about nineteen years old but acted remarkably knowledgeable in the ways of the British. He announced he'd been in the United Kingdom for almost a year, and it was apparent he thought that gave him seniority over any and all lieutenants, especially pilots. On our way to Ipswich I was subjected to a steady stream of yak about pubs, English chicks and how to catch one, pubs, girls, pubs, girls, and pubs. An occasional reference to "Limeys" made me uncomfortable, but I figured that word was supposed to reflect a certain "old-timer" status that was more of a put-on attitude than something actually felt.

In his way, the corporal represented the majority of the very young and brash American GIs in England. His attitude interested me as part of my own learning curve. Some might have resented him, but I enjoyed every minute of the ride. To my mind, the farms and small villages were like the illustrations in the wonderful ten-volume set of *Journeys Through Bookland* my father had given to me. The books, which proceeded from volume 1 nursery rhymes to the sophisticated essays of Pope and the letters of Chesterfield in volume 10, were old friends and had implanted an imagery that now matched reality.

Eventually I ignored the corporal's ceaseless babble and looked with fascination at the passing scenery. Aside from the old architecture, narrow winding roads, and driving on the left, I wondered why England looked so different from America; then I realized that the trees and fields, the buildings and barns, the small villages and narrow winding roads all fit together seamlessly, blended by time into a harmony. No one thing intruded on the other. Each fit the scene as though a natural process had ordained symmetry. Nothing jarred the eye; all was quiet beauty and neatness. There was no litter, nothing offensive to the senses. Every snug cottage had its garden, each shop a quaint window; there were no ugly signs. Even the lettering above the shop doors looked wonderfully ancient and elegant.

Dropping me off in the town square of Ipswich, the corporal shouted, "Don't do anything in London I wouldn't do, Lieutenant!" and leered at me as I climbed down to the cobblestone pavement.

I laughed, thanked him, and then asked, "How am I supposed to get back to the base?"

"Wattisham truck's here till the last train every night," he hollered, and meshed the gears as he pulled off.

Damned decent, I thought as I set off down the road to the train station. It looked like Ipswich had taken only a token bomb or two during the blitz, and I was fascinated to see the timber-fronted Tudor buildings still standing the way they must have been long before America was colonized. For a naive young fighter pilot, just turned twenty-two, being in this beautiful land was a constant adventure. I was enjoying myself tremendously.

The train station sat across the road at the bottom of the hill. It was a solid granite structure built with great care and attention to detail. Placards above the ticket windows proclaimed FIRST CLASS and THIRD CLASS. I hesitated, wondering where I fit into the class system. Might as well go first-class, I thought, and went up to that narrow barred window. The ticket agent looked at me quizzically and asked somewhat impatiently where I wanted to go. Feeling like a fool, I blurted out, "London."

"Righto," he said. "That will be a pound six." I pushed a £5 note through the wicket and he gave me a hard look. I could almost hear him thinking, "Bloody Yanks . . . over here, oversexed, and overpaid." That thought had become a standard music hall cliché.

I went outside and stood waiting on the platform for the train. No one checked my ticket or anyone else's as far as I could see. Well, I'll just follow the crowd, I decided; but which crowd? Some climbed a set of stairs going over to the platform on the far side of the tracks running through the station. Do the trains run on the left side like all the road traffic? And which is left as I stand here? My doubts vanished as the London train came whooshing into the station. The doors on the cars, or "carriages" as I learned they were called, were plainly marked with the class designation. I had to move toward the front of the train to enter an exterior door with a big 1ST on it. I found myself in an aisle with compartment doors the length of the carriage, just like on our original ride down from Scotland in May.

Each compartment had a sliding glass door with curtains partially covering my view of the seats. Those already having one or two occupants had closed the doors as if to discourage entry by newcomers. The people sitting within gave off distinct impressions of veiled hostility toward anyone foolish enough to enter their space. They hunkered down behind their morning papers, gave a quick glare of reproach, and turned a shoulder to my hesitant intrusion. I passed a few compartments before I finally gritted my teeth and entered one with an open seat next to the window. I congratulated myself on my good fortune a bit too quickly.

The train had just pulled out of the station when the well-dressed gentleman sitting in the center seat across from me cleared his throat and said, "Leftenant, I believe you are occupying a reserved accommodation."

My embarrassment must have touched him, for he then remarked in the kindest way, "The gentleman who will entrain at the next stop has had that seat for over twenty years. That being the case, I'm afraid you might possibly strain what he volubly and often proclaims to be our already delicate English-American relations. I should hate being witness to such an outburst on this fine morning. Might upset my kippers."

He smiled and patted the seat next to him. "Now, move over here. You'll find it quite comfortable enough."

I realized I was being teased a bit as I moved over, but my savior kept smiling and did not avoid eye contact. He introduced himself as Nigel Cartwright and asked my name and where I lived in the States. I realized he hadn't asked where I was based, or anything to do with my status as a young pilot. In fact, other than my name and my home, he asked nothing personal yet seemed sincerely intent on putting me at ease. We chatted away and soon all my impressions of distant, standoffish Englishmen were dispelled. Sure enough, the seat I had originally taken was occupied at the next stop. The two men nodded at each other, and the newcomer raised his eyebrows at me.

The hour passed quickly before the train slowed as we entered the suburbs of London. I was stunned as I looked out the window. My new acquaintance must have observed my distress at the devastation of more and more bombed row houses as we approached Liverpool Street Station. He explained, "Old Jerry went for the rail yards during the blitz. Couldn't always hit where he aimed. Poor blighters living here took a packet. No complaints though, those that survived, that is. Just hatred for Hitler and his bloody Luftwaffe."

There wasn't much I could say. The scene and his remarks brought home the awful consequences of the blitz. I could only wonder whether my own countrymen, under similar circumstances, would have shown the same courage and stoicism as the Brits. Cartwright changed the subject and to my surprise said, "I say, would you enjoy having a spot of lunch at my club? Nothing fancy really, rationing and all that, you know, but decent enough nevertheless."

I thanked him for his kindness and accepted. He told me the name of his club, but no location. I made a hard mental note of what he'd said, thinking I would just instruct a cabbie to take me there when the time came.

The carriages emptied with much hustle and bustle. Liverpool Station was just as I had seen it in the movies. The locomotive on the next track gave out one shrill hoot as it began to back out of the station. A glass ceiling supported by iron grillwork soared far above the platforms. There were many telltale holes in the glass. I could see a tall, grimy building past the access gates. Lettering on the facade proclaimed it to be the station hotel, and I wondered if anyone really stayed there. Of course, you dummy. This wasn't a movie. This was the real Liverpool Station. All I needed was Nigel Bruce, Charles Laughton, or maybe Dame Mae Whitty passing by to fulfill my fantasy.

The crowd moved purposefully through the gates, where our tickets were finally checked. I followed the flow and found myself on the plaza fronting the hotel. It was crowded with noisy lorries, blocky black taxis, and hundreds of people in an orderly tangle. Horns beeped, drivers shouted, and everyone seemed to be scrambling either for a taxi or moving toward a stairway marked UNDERGROUND.

Suddenly a harsh, growling, gut-wrenching noise split the air. It echoed off the surrounding buildings, filling my head with the pounding of muted explosions. I stopped in my tracks and searched the sky for the source of the terrible racket. The buildings limited my view and I could see nothing above as the noise reached an unbelievable crescendo. Then there it was! It hurtled overhead in a brief flash as it passed my field of view. It had stubby wings and a ridiculously small tail section. The fuselage was cylindrical with a bluntly rounded nose. It roared by, and then the noise suddenly stopped. I looked around to ask what the hell was going on and found the street completely deserted, not a soul in sight. The engine of a nearby lorry was still running. Where had they all gone? Why? Then it dawned on me. It was a V-1, the weapon our intelligence people had briefed us on with little detail, except that the Germans had started launching them in June. We had heard tales of pilots from the No. 150 RAF Wing chasing the things in their Tempests.

It all flashed through my mind in an instant as I hightailed it toward the nearest doorway. Those British must move like greased lightning. Who could blame them? Three years of this bombing crap and they were fully conditioned. I hadn't reached halfway to a nearby marked shelter when a huge explosion shook the ground and rattled the windows. Then silence again, broken only by the sound of tinkling glass. It had hit a block or two away. I worried about those under the impact point. The air-raid sirens started to wail. A little late, I thought. To my amazement, people started to emerge from wherever they had sheltered, and traffic began moving just as though nothing had happened. Talk about stubborn courage. Nothing and no one was going to defeat these people!

I ambled around Piccadilly Circus with hundreds of other Yanks for a while, then flagged a taxi and named the lunch club to the driver. He knew exactly where it was, and within minutes we arrived. I found my new friend inside the front entry, expecting me. Nothing was said about the "buzz bomb" except another grumbled curse for those bloody Huns. He sighed and offered, "I hope this doesn't upset your time in London, Leftenant. Come, let's go have a spot of dry sherry and see what the chef has in store today."

I heartily agreed with both suggestions. The lunch wasn't fancy, but it was the best meal I'd had in England, and it rested happily in my stomach, helped tremendously by two glasses of sherry beforehand. I hadn't told my host that I'd never tasted sherry before. My first day in London was being filled with new experiences. At lunch, the primary topic had been the V-1 buzz bombs the Germans were raining on the city. Mr. Cartwright and his friends had much to say about the barbarity of "the bloody Hun," and though I sympathized wholeheartedly, I couldn't help recalling newsreel shots of Hamburg and other cities burning under the wrath of the RAF Bomber Command's nightly raids. This was a vicious war. There was little civility or decency left in the world these days. The Allies had proclaimed it would be "unconditional surrender." The Germans were responding in kind.

I left the club to continue exploring. I hadn't the vaguest clue about London's geography. Naturally, I'd heard about Hyde Park and Piccadilly, Buckingham Palace, Parliament, and Trafalgar Square honoring Lord Nelson, but

they were all just schoolbook images. Where any of these places were in relation to one another, or to me as I left the club, was a complete mystery. I also
realized I hadn't a clue where the Red Cross building was. That was where
I'd be bedding down. At least I had the address in my pocket so that I could
hail a taxi when the time came. For a while I just wanted to walk and to see
what I could of London.

It didn't bother me much that the V–1s thundered overhead at odd times,
sometimes singly, sometimes two or three at once. Their guttural roar was
now punctuated by antiaircraft guns banging away from someplace in the city.
Before lunch I had seen some of the guns emplaced in a park nearby, so I
imagined they were doing the firing. Dodging the flying bombs became easy.
At first, I just followed the lead of the canny Londoners. They ducked. I
ducked. They ran. I ran. They dashed down some steps into a building and
I did the same. It was a macabre game, but certainly exciting. I couldn't help
wondering why the antiaircraft people shot at the damned things overhead.
They were going to come down anyway, but if one malfunctioned, kept on
going, and overshot the city, so much the better, it seemed to me.

I soon fell in love with London. The shops and hotels, the public buildings
and broad avenues, the narrow, crooked lanes with timbered pubs, all en-
chanted me. I found myself wandering in a residential district. Small shops
clustered on the corners: a greengrocer, a chemist's shop, a dry goods store,
and, naturally, pubs named the King's Arms or the Rose and Garter and proclaiming Watney's or Whitbread's and even one brand called Courage. Shop
display windows were pitiful in their bareness. Rationing dominated life;
there were no luxury items to be seen anywhere—certainly a grim reminder
of the privations the English were suffering.

Later in the afternoon, I came to an intersection where a sign proclaiming
OLDE ANTIQUE SHOPPE caught my eye. The bay window held an arrangement
of medieval armor. I didn't question whether or not the items were authentic.
They were magnificent! The breastplate, visored helmet, and crossed broad-
swords were right out of my treasured book *The Boy's King Arthur*. I had to
ask about them, so, screwing up my courage, I opened the shop door and
entered. A bell tinkled overhead. The place was dim. My eyes slowly accli-
mated to the darkness and I cautiously advanced through clutter barely seen.

A door in the rear opened and a shaft of light silhouetted an old man. He
approached slowly. I could see he was wearing a baggy sweater with elbow

patches and a long woolen scarf wound round his neck. Tiny spectacles perched halfway down his nose, and wisps of white hair peeked from below, of all things, a French beret. He had a thin mustache, and when he drew closer, I could see that his face and hands were like parchment. He was right out of Dickens.

The proprietor smiled as he approached and remarked with a chuckle, "Ah, an American. How nice to see you, Leftenant. How are you this fine day? What brings you to my little shop here in the wilds of north London?" He wasn't being condescending or patronizing; his greeting was genuine and his interest in me was open and friendly.

"Come in, come in," he beckoned. "Come in and tell me how you are taking the bombing," he asked, expressing his concern in what must have been the phraseology of the blitz. I hadn't thought of the V-1 attacks as bombing. To me, they seemed more like a shelling. The distinction was uselessly academic anyway.

"What may I show you in my humble shop?"

Looking about I had to say, "Everything, sir." This was in deference to his age and my growing respect for these Londoners.

"Well now," he exclaimed, rubbing his hands together, "I was just having a cuppa. Would you care to join me?"

I didn't know what a "cuppa" might be, but I thought I had interrupted something he wished to continue and said, "Sir, I would be delighted, if I'm not intruding."

"Not at all, not at all. Only too happy to have company. Oh, and by the way, my name is Warwick. Yours?"

"The name is Olds, sir," I replied, and followed Mr. Warwick toward the back of his shop. I had to turn sideways in places to avoid the haphazard stacking of old items. He opened a door and motioned me into what seemed to be the sitting room of his residence. A teapot and saucer sat on a small table near a tiny, unlit fireplace. I looked around as he filled a pot with water and placed it on a gas ring, which he then lit. Having put another cup and saucer on the table, he gestured about the room almost apologetically and said something about the war and no heating fuel. He sat down and asked if I would like a piece of the small morsel of pound cake left on a plate. I declined, saying I had enjoyed a fine lunch not long before. His hospitality was gracious, but I was reluctant to assume any of his meager ration. This was the second time in one day I had been befriended by a stranger.

The tea was excellent. Both the aroma and the taste fit the surroundings perfectly. A V-1 rumbled far away and my host muttered, "Bloody Huns!" That was his only comment and I just nodded. We finished our tea and Mr. Warwick asked, "What brought you to my shop this far from the more interesting center of the city?"

I told him of being in London for the first time and how, after lunch with a friend, I had relished every moment and each new experience just wandering about. I tried to explain my fascination with the knights of old, and how my childhood images of England and London had been delightfully confirmed. I went on to say that the longer I roamed the streets, the more affection I felt for this city and its people. When I came upon his shop window, I was drawn like a magnet to the display of armor. At that point in my babbling, I stopped. I wasn't sure how to go about asking if the pieces were for sale. They seemed to belong right where they were, precious statements of Mr. Warwick's understated yet genuine passion for history.

Warwick sensed my hesitation and explained, "Those pieces are truly authentic. Lots of cheap copies about, mostly in town in those posh places on Knightsbridge. Wouldn't go there if I were you. Are you interested in them? I happened upon that set long before the war at an estate auction. Some old duke in the Midlands died and his heirs didn't give a farthing for his treasures, only for his money. In any event, the duke's armory was a trove of ancestral history, and the heirs only wanted it cleaned out for a small price. My good fortune. Thought I could retire on my profit, but the normal trade in the old things has gone by the wayside for the duration, so I just let them sit and gather a bit of dust. They have very good papers, you know."

I was fascinated, but more than ever reluctant to ask the direct question. Would Mr. Warwick be annoyed or upset that a brash young Yank would have the audacity to want such an important part of England's history? If he intended to retire on the profit, as he had said, how in the world could a first lieutenant afford him that luxury? My interest seemed superficial under the circumstances.

Instead, I asked, "Is the helmet called a helm? Is it used for just tilting and jousting rather than warfare? Did it sport a feathered plume? How could the ancient smithies fashion such an intricate thing? Did they—"

"Hold on, Leftenant," Warwick interrupted, smiling, "one question at a time. I can tell you want to know a lot, but I'm old and there's a lot to tell."

Two hours passed as I listened to his detailed descriptions of the days of armor and knights. It was as though he had been a part of those times. I knew I had to have that armor, but by now was even further from how to broach the subject of the cost. I saw my host glance at the grandfather clock against a far wall. I hastily rose to leave.

"Thank you, sir. I've had the most wonderful time and deeply appreciate your hospitality. Would you mind if I came back to visit you in the morning? I would like to hear more of your stories, if it wouldn't be an intrusion."

He rose and shook my hand. "The pleasure would be mine, Leftenant. Not only are you the only American I've had in my shop, you're the first I've had the opportunity to chat with. Most interesting, I confess, and I look forward to your return."

I didn't know quite how to take that last bit, but assumed the best as he showed me out through his shop. He shook my hand again at the door and said, "Ta, young man. Take care. Can't win the war all by yourself, you know. I'd be pleased to offer another cuppa in the morning should you wander back."

The tentative nature of his invitation didn't escape me as I followed his directions to the nearby tube station. I supposed these war-weary people had learned long ago how totally final good-byes could be.

In the early hours of the evening, after checking in at the Red Cross hostelry, I was wandering the streets radiating from Piccadilly when a familiar figure suddenly approached. Of all the millions of people in London, here came Dick McChord, a classmate from West Point!

"Mac!" I shouted.

"Robin, I thought that was you!" We embraced with whacks on the back and a great pumping of hands. This brought a few stares from some bowler-topped, dark-suited Londoners. I could almost hear them thinking as Mac and I walked off together, *Crazy, loud Yanks. Rude blighters.*

"Where you stationed, Mac?"

"Lavenham, up near Ipswich. B-17s. Been there three months now. This is my first time in London. Boy, what a town!"

"My first, too," I replied, "and I agree. This city is everything I thought it would be and more. I'm at Wattisham, right next door to you. P-38s. Hell, we're neighbors, Mac. Let's go have a drink on that."

We turned off the Strand into the alleyway leading to the prestigious Savoy Hotel. The resplendent doorman with his green livery coat, gray trousers, and shiny top hat looked at us with an air of disdain but didn't offer to open the entry doors. Mac and I glanced at one another, grinned, then opened the door and walked in.

Once inside, I remarked, "Sure obvious he hasn't much use for Yanks. Must have had some bad experiences. Can't say I blame him."

"Oh well," Mac responded philosophically, "Maybe the barkeep will take our money."

We found a comfortable seat in an understated but elegantly appointed room overlooking the Thames. As we sat, another V-1 charged by not half a mile away. We watched silently as the thing, growling its ugly sound, flew left to right and then suddenly dove steeply out of sight, its impact marked a moment later by a column of rising smoke and debris. Seconds later came the explosion, a dull thud setting the plate-glass windows rattling. Mac and I talked of moving back from the glass, but then gave a what-the-hell shrug and called for another brandy.

Here was another first in a day of many firsts for me. Like the sherry at lunch, I'd never had brandy before, and though the bite of it was raw, the warm glow that soon followed in the pit of my stomach was agreeable. We believed the phlegmatic barkeep had palmed his cheapest off on us, but agreed that neither of us had the experience to question his choice. He'd probably done us a favor by not foisting the top-shelf premium stuff on a couple of poorly paid lieutenants.

Mac and I sat as dusk fell into night, jawing and recounting our experiences since graduation. It was a comfortable bond that reached between us as we shared our mutual impressions tinged with a bit of wartime fatalism. I had escorted Mac's bomb group more than once, watching from a distance as his ponderous formation of B-17s plowed into the flak on their bomb runs. Those guys flew into the bursting shrapnel with courage and determination. They paid a dear price in burning planes and blossoming chutes. Unlike fighter pilots, survival for the bomber guys was pure chance. You were either hit or you were not. There was nothing on earth you could do about it. Skill wasn't a player. The thought made me shiver, and I silently questioned whether or not I could have done what he did day after day.

We were both quiet for a minute, thinking about our friends, when I decided to cheer things up a bit. I told Mac about my encounter with Mr. Warwick and how I coveted that set of armor.

"Did you buy it?" he asked.

"No," I confessed, then tried to explain my feelings about it. "I just couldn't come to the point of asking, and besides, what in hell would I do with all that stuff here in London, and then how would I get it back to Wattisham, store it, and then get it back to the States?"

Mac grinned and replied, "Why don't you go back, put some money down, make a deal to pay on schedule, and have him hold the items till you figure out a way to handle them? I bet you'll regret it if you don't."

That made good sense to me and I vowed to give Mr. Warwick some money when I saw him in the morning.

We walked to the front of the hotel and parted company, to another wail of the all-clear siren. I wondered how they knew it was all clear with these buzz bombs. Flights of Luftwaffe bombers in the old blitz were easily tracked coming in, but these V-1s? They were random, one-way attacks and impossible to predict. A mystery.

As I made my way back to the Red Cross billet, I had to throw off a sense of gloom. I couldn't determine if the feeling was for Mac, for me, or just in general. Something felt wrong, very wrong, but the gloom dissipated when I saw Margaret waiting for me in front of the Red Cross building. We'd met at one of the Wattisham parties, and I had rung her up in hopes of meeting during my time in London. We shared a few drinks, talked a bit, then exchanged a few kisses before parting for the night.

The next morning, I returned by the Underground to Mr. Warwick's. I would follow Mac's advice and put some money down on that old armor, even if it took me years to pay it off. I climbed the steps out of the station, walked the half block toward his Olde Antique Shoppe, turned the corner, and stopped in horror. The block ahead of me was devastated. An ambulance, two small fire engines, and two police vans blocked the street. A white-helmeted group of bobbies along with other rescue workers dug at piles of rubble with pickaxes and shovels. A gaping hole in the ground was all that was left of the shop.

One of the bobbies muttered to me, "No survivors here, mate."

I felt an incredible loss. Losing people in airplanes wasn't easy, but it was a recognized part of fighter aviation. Losing comrades in war was difficult, yet we were doing what we all knew needed to be done. Here, these people, this kind old shopkeeper who had shared his meager horde of tea with me and quelled my curiosity about the armor and history, this entire nation that was subjected to this constant tragedy . . . they were changing me. I was maturing possibly or maybe altering my perspective. My anger at the enemy was deepened. My drive to win the war became greater than ever.

Less than a month later I returned to London to meet with some friends and maybe see Margaret again. It was a beautiful summer evening. I walked slowly through the streets, savoring London. The night seemed special. I was in a liquid well of time, each fluid moment poignant, every part of my being tuned to my surroundings, to the streets, the old buildings, and the sky in its rare clarity with a full moon shining down. All was a part of me and I felt immersed in an aura of belonging that was as palpable as anything I had ever felt.

Walking alone toward my destination, not hurrying or lagging, just walking, I was aware of having possibly earned the right to be a part of this proud city. I identified with its people, and I shared the agony and the defiant attitude of Londoners. It was an oddly ecstatic feeling. I had paid for my admission with over fifty missions to date. The savagery of aerial combat had graduated me into the ranks of the combat fatalists. What would happen would happen. We did our best and could control the outcome only slightly. The steady attrition of my comrades and close friends had edged me into the protective shell of knowing that only now exists. Forget yesterday, and to hell with tomorrow. Mr. Warwick remained etched in my mind.

The city lay quiet and tense awaiting the nightly onslaught. The blackout was betrayed by a moon so bright that lampposts cast shadows onto the street, and windows glittered like reflecting jewels. Air-raid sirens were quiet for the moment. Their moaning wail was a noise that had become a hallmark of the war here in England. I thought about what that rising and falling summons had meant to these people for so many years now. It governed their lives, dictated their days and nights, ruled their thoughts, and filled them with determination. Hitler had miscalculated. The more he bombed, the greater grew England's resolve. The more damage he wreaked, the more proud these people became of their resilience. They drew together in adversity, more stubborn in their support of Winnie and the war effort. These people on the home front fought and died just as their soldiers did in faraway battles. The British stood as one. Nothing could defeat them.

Every gaping hole where businesses had flourished and every shattered home where flowers had grown was a scar of battle on a grand and defiant old lady. The random attacks of the V-1s and V-2s were a form of war that was almost worse than the early savagery of the Battle of Britain. At least that, as horrible as it was, had been on a personal, even human level. The "Few" had now become the many.

I made my way along the streets. In the distance, an emergency vehicle wailed its distinctive warning. The sky glowed in places above random fires as the moon shone down with cold indifference. A faint familiar growl intensified as another buzz bomb flailed the night sky. Sirens began in warning. The noise of the bomb's approach became ominous. This one was going to be close. Like the Londoners, my ears were attuned to the nuances of these robot attacks. Every nerve responded to the ugly, rumbling blast of that ramjet engine. The damned machine was hideous in its mindless intensity. It wasn't aimed at a target. It was blind in its selection. The city itself and the people were its target. Only fate determined who would live and die. The Londoners had again taken to the deep shelters of their underground.

Time to duck! But where? That doorway there? Maybe not much better than out here on the pavement, but at least something. I dove quickly into my meager shelter as the robot's engine abruptly stilled and the inhuman monster nosed over in its final dive. There was an ear-shattering blast; concussion waves broke windows, then the ground heaved, slamming into my body. That was close, damned close. My ears rang. There was silence, then the patter of falling debris: lumps and pieces of bricks and boards thudding back to earth, ending with the last tinkle of glass and the rumble-slam of a falling wall. I came out of my doorway and resumed my journey as the sirens of the local rescue squad converged on the impact point only a block or so away.

Finally, my destination was ahead: the Wellington Bottle Club. I went down a flight of steps and rang the bell. The door cracked open, my club card was examined, and then the outer and inner blackout curtains were pulled aside to admit me. I entered a smoke-filled room jammed with people, most in uniform and mostly air force, both Brits and Americans.

The place was dimly lit. The crowd was standing still. There was no laughter, nor any voices. Two more distant explosions in quick succession were felt more than heard, and lent dramatic impact to the music holding the crowd mesmerized. Someone was playing the piano over in the far corner. Shivers rose up my spine as I recognized the piece. Never had the defiant and haunting melody of the Warsaw Concerto been more appropriate, and never had my response to a shared emotion sent tears streaming down my cheeks as they were at that moment. This was my family. I felt at home.

7

★

Victories—at Last!

By August we had all changed. Combat does that. It digs deep into your soul, searching to find the grit. For most, it isn't something you think about. It just happens. The world shrinks around you. Home, Mom, and apple pie become remote memories, and the mental image of your girlfriend back in the States is sexier than the rear view of Betty Grable. We learned to live one day at a time and to concentrate on survival. But to varying degrees we all developed a deep sense of frustration at our lack of real action. I needed something positive to make the empty beds of lost friends meaningful. There had to be more than just strafing trains, dropping bombs, losing people, fighting to come back home, then feeling like we hadn't really accomplished anything. It was part of the war effort, but the milk runs didn't fulfill the vision we held of a fighter pilot. Ground attack was part of the mission, but our focus always returned to aerial battles.

The group had made progress since our arrival in early May, but the price had been high. We'd lost three of our four flight commanders, both of my roommates had been shot down over Holland, and many pilots were KIA or

POW. Nearly half of the original 434th Squadron was gone. The other two squadrons in the group had suffered similar attrition. Our original group CO, Kyle Riddle, was lost to flak on May 10. No one was immune. We who survived had gotten smarter about combat.

Our salvation appeared with the arrival of Colonel Hubert "Hub" Zemke, who replaced Colonel Riddle as CO two days later. Hub was about to give us all some much-needed savvy in the art of aerial warfare, and we were ready. Zemke had loads of experience. He'd been an Air Corps pilot prior to the war and even flown a tour with the Soviet air force. As CO of the 56th Group at RAF Boxted, he had developed tactics in which his pilots rendezvoused at an easily found landmark in their bomber escort zone, then broke up into individual flights and fanned out in 180-degree arcs to respond to attacks on the bomber stream. The spread let his units cover a lot of airspace.

In May, both of Zemke's wingmen were shot down by Luftwaffe ace Günther Rall, who in turn was shot down by 56th Group ace Joe Powers in the same dogfight. After that, Zemke upgraded his "fan-out" tactic to the three full squadrons of the group instead of just flights. He jumped at the chance to command the 479th because he wanted to fly the new Mustangs. His 56th Group had P-47s, which were increasingly focusing on ground attack. He knew we were converting to P-51s when we heard only rumors. Hub was our kind of guy, aggressive, smart, relentless, and determined to hit the Luftwaffe where it hurt. He was already a triple ace and had created legends in the 56th, like Gabreski, Mahurin, and Johnson. We in the 479th knew about their exploits and were in awe of their skill and good fortune.

I'll admit we were a raggedy-assed bunch when he arrived. We had lots of desire but not much air-to-air experience. We never blamed Colonel Riddle for that. God knows he flew and led as many missions as anyone, but results count. For us Hub's fame as leader of his Wolfpack was nothing short of awesome. The new boss took over and rattled us right away. He taught, led, laid down the law, and put us on the right track. Things were going to be different. Although he put up a stern front, we quickly learned he cared about each of us. To tell the truth, we felt as though he had a hard time keeping a straight face at our bumbling eagerness. He had a great sense of humor, but we learned when it wasn't at the forefront.

On his first day at Wattisham, Hub put up a sign on the door of his office: KNOCK BEFORE YOU ENTER. I'M A BASTARD, TOO. LET'S SEE YOU SALUTE.

The young pilots got a huge charge out of that. Hell, we were in the habit of saluting everything anyhow, and wouldn't go near a colonel's sanctum unless under extreme duress. To be called before the boss meant trouble. Failing to knock would only have compounded whatever felony had brought us there in the first place, so we knew the sign wasn't about us. We watched and smirked as our immediate bosses and members of the group staff were seen outside that door, self-consciously tucking in shirttails, running hands over hair, buffing up the shoe shine on the back of each trouser leg, adjusting the tie, then knocking timidly, and nervously waiting for permission to enter. We knew and they learned.

When Hub arrived, a few of the pilots in the group had shot down an enemy aircraft or two, but I had yet to even see one. I was frustrated. Fighter pilots dream of victory in aerial combat; it's the be-all and end-all of the fighter profession. It was the price of admission, and I wanted to belong. Mission after mission since May, I had flown with my head on a swivel searching for enemy planes. Nothing. Nothing in that vast sky except bombers and flak, explosions and smoke trails spiraling down, anguished calls on the emergency frequency, parachutes and pieces, and the otherwise empty wild blue. No prey, no snarling little Messerschmitt 109s or Focke-Wulf 190s, just nightly mission reports telling us someone else had found them. Usually it was someone from Zemke's 56th Group. Gabreski had twenty-eight kills and I hadn't seen one enemy aircraft in flight.

The morning of August 14 finally offered something different: a predawn takeoff, a bridge over the river at Chalon-sur-Saône as the target. The German armies were in retreat, fighting for every mile, resisting fiercely as the Allies pushed through France toward Belgium and Holland. General Patton's 3rd Army was sweeping the southern flank. The bridges behind the Wehrmacht were important targets. Knocking them out would hinder movement and support Patton's intention of destroying everything in front of him.

Only 8th Air Force headquarters knew why the 479th FG was picked to hit this particular bridge. We certainly couldn't figure it out. Maybe they had greater faith with Zemke as our CO. I would ponder it for years yet never figure out the reasoning. We were in England, a couple of hours away from the target, and 9th Air Force was in France now, close to the ground action. They were veterans in providing the air support that had made Patton's dash possible. Perhaps all of the 9th squadrons were engaged in that truly close support in front of the troops, which none of us in the 8th were yet qualified to do. In any event, bombing bridges was something we'd been doing all summer, and I guess it didn't matter whose bombs did the job.

During the briefing there was a lot of stirring and nervous coughing. It wasn't the target or the opposition expected, nor even the anticipated flak, that made us nervous. The weather was good, in fact excellent for Europe. Group Lead Highway exuded confidence, the S-2 intel officer made the mission seem really important, our own airfield conditions were normal, and flight assignments stacked up well, so why the niggling feeling?

Christ almighty it was still black outside. It was obviously going to be black for takeoff, black for rendezvous, and black all the way into France. What kind of deal was this? We weren't bloody night fighters! We never had been, and you don't go fooling around when a man can't SEE. Somebody was going to realize the whole thing was starting about two hours too early and we'd all get another cup of coffee while ops replotted the timing. But, no, briefing ended with hearty encouragement from the podium and one small admonition not to forget our navigation lights.

No one wanted to ask the burning question, so it wasn't asked. There were a few sidelong glances, some shuffling about, furtive peeks at our hack watches, audible sighs, a few grumbles, but that was all. I guess we thought if we could do what we did every day, a little predawn action thrown in wouldn't hurt too much.

After the group briefing, I got D Flight together and tried to do some anticipating. I leaned forward at the table. "Look, guys, we all know it's tricky getting forty-eight P-38s in proper order out to the runway in broad daylight, let alone before dawn. I'll tell you what Newcross Blue is going to do. 435th and 436th are going first, 434th is last off, and our Blue will be the last flight in the parade, so I'm going to hold in the parking revetment until everyone passes on the perimeter track heading for runway 27. Then I'll flash my landing lights and fall in behind the gaggle. You stay wherever you're parked till you see my lights, and then follow me in order Two, Three, Four. Got it? Just stay clear of the rest of the mess. When we get airborne I won't do the standard join-up like the rest of the group. Instead of a left orbit, I'm going to climb straight ahead on a heading of 270. I'll throttle back and hold 150 at 800 feet. Two, you move over to my left wing as soon as its comfortable; Three, keep Four on your right wing and join on my right. If you don't see me, click your mike button three times and back off to 150. I'll start a slow left turn and click back three times. You start your turn and hold 500 feet. When we get around to the briefed departure heading I'll advance throttles to the normal climb power setting. You do the same. Watch for my lights. If you see me, click three times. I'll rock my wings. Then you'll know it's me. That should do it. We'll catch the rest of the gang over the Channel somewhere."

Yeah. Sure. Nice idea, Robin.

Everything went fine until half of Lakeside Squadron was airborne. Then some idiot got a wheel off the side of the taxiway and bogged down. With no way to taxi around him, the rest of us were ordered to do a 180 on the perimeter track then taxi all the way around the dark airfield for runway 09. Great! That put the remainder of the shooting match in inverse order for takeoff. The only good thing about it was that Newcross Blue Flight was now first in line for departure. That was great, except we were in reverse order on a narrow taxiway. I told Blue Four to pull into the first empty parking stub, Blue Three into the next, and Two wherever he could, then when I taxied past them, to come out in proper order behind me. This worked and we reached runway 09 in proper sequence. I lined up with Two on my right, made the usual pretakeoff checks, blinked my lights, and gave it the throttle. Two hung tight on my wing and we accelerated rapidly to liftoff speed. I hauled back on the yoke smoothly, accelerated, and waited for the bird to fly off the runway, thinking smugly how Two must be appreciating my technique.

Suddenly, my God! Right in front of me was a dim shape half on and half off the runway—the bare outline of a P-38, its wing right in my path. No room to swerve, no way to stop! I yelled and yanked back on the yoke. The airplane leaped straight up and off the runway. I snatched the gear handle up, then waited to settle back toward the runway, milking back pressure to keep the airplane from stalling and hoping to accelerate. There was only a slight bump, and then I was flying. I looked right for Two. He was nowhere to be seen. No time to call him.

I got on the horn and screamed at the gang that runway 09 was partially blocked. "Everyone rolling: STOP, STOP! Do single-ship takeoffs, right side of the runway, and look out for a stuck bird. For God's sake get a light on that thing before someone gets killed!"

There was pure bedlam on the radio. Everyone talked at once. Someone tried to organize things but only added to the confusion. I inwardly cringed at the thought of our new group CO's reaction to all this. Great way to impress Zemke. He'd have us all for lunch and bury the bones!

I set course for France at the briefed time. What the hell, at least I knew where I was, and maybe would soon catch up with whoever had managed to cling to Highway Lead after takeoff. I called Newcross Blue Two and was relieved to hear his bewildered voice announcing he hadn't a clue where I was. At least he had survived. Blue Three and Four were somewhere in that mess back on the ground, so I mentally wrote them off for the rest of the day. Blue would be a two-ship.

South across the dark Thames and southern England I looked for the flashing lights of the lead squadron as well as for Blue Two. Nothing doing. I could tell parts of Bison Squadron were somewhere airborne by an occasional radio transmission, but that was all. I just kept on the briefed course for our target area and headed out over the blackness of the Channel, my head on a swivel.

Dim white lines marching across the blackness below had to be waves breaking on the beaches below the cliffs at Fécamp on the Normandy coast. The minute hand on my watch confirmed my position. I was on course and on time as I crossed the coastline into France. The predawn black lightened as I flew steadily on toward Chartres, holding the briefed headings and speeds. The dim reflection of the Loire River flowing through Chartres was my first positive checkpoint, and I turned left 10 degrees to set course for Nevers on the banks of the Loire in Burgundy, about 85 miles and twenty minutes ahead.

Suddenly, a stream of tracers passed off my left wing. I jerked mechanically, and surprisingly enjoyed my first sight of flak in the dark. Someone else was on the predawn shift. I fantasized that the gunner, whoever and wherever he was, must have been in the last stages of his night watch. His effort seemed listless at best. Maybe he knew he'd catch hell from his section sergeant if his unit had heard me pass and he didn't react. No matter, I had expected to be fired at long before this. It was good to get the waiting over.

Soon, objects on the ground took shape and I could pick up the more prominent landmarks. There was the Loire, with the canal paralleling it, then Nevers, right where it should be. I turned to the east, about 105 degrees, and in three minutes there was our initial point, three little lakes shining in contrast to dark earth near a place called Le Creusot.

The sun wasn't yet over the horizon but there was enough light to see that the pale sky was empty. Where was everyone? Chatter soon broke out, a rather prolonged discussion about the location of the target in relation to Bison Flight's position. I knew damned well they weren't where they were supposed to be, because I was there. It was clear from their chatter that they didn't really know where they were in relation to anything except that they were over a river and the river was in France.

Bison Lead decided they would turn south to find the target. South? That seemed dead wrong. I had just corrected to the northeast a little to be on course. If Bison was north of the rendezvous point, he would be at or near the target. If he didn't see the target he had to be south of it. That assumed he and his people were reasonably close to course as they came in. The screwups just seemed to keep piling up.

Rechecking my armament switches, I pushed up full power and headed for Chalon-sur-Saône all by myself. Sure enough, there was the ribbon of the Saône River catching the first glow of dawn. It had to be the Saône. And there was the gray darkness of the town with the bridge clearly visible against the river's silver sheen. I lined up so I'd cross the target at about a 45-degree angle and came out of the west. My pass was shallow, more like a skip-bomb pass than a dive-bomb attack. The sight picture was good. Speed just right.

There was time to remind myself: Don't hit long, Robin, don't hit the town. I wanted to hit the center span of the bridge, so when the gun sight pipper came up to the release point, I pressed the pickle button under my right thumb. There was a thump as the pair of 1,000-pound bombs left the pylons. I broke hard left and stayed down low to make myself as difficult a target as possible. An orange flash in my canopy's rearview mirror told me the bombs had detonated. No flak. Must have caught the gunners sleeping late this morning.

Once I was clear of the target there was time to burn, and apparently I had the whole of this part of France to myself. Truthfully, finding the rest of the group didn't enter my mind. I stayed right down on the deck, as low as I dared, heading northwest. I throttled back, then tweaked the mixture and prop into auto-lean to save a bit of fuel. When the sun peeked over the horizon, I was paralleling a paved country road bordered by poplar trees and farmhouses set back behind hedges and stone walls. A ridge loomed ahead, running almost due north–south. The valley from my position, and all the way up the ridge, was totally covered with vineyards. Years later I would recognize it for what it was, the Beaune region: good Burgundy country. But not now. I was looking for something to shoot at, anything military: a convoy, a train, troops, anything.

After several minutes of this, two dark shapes suddenly flew across the road left to right about a mile ahead of me. They were just a little higher than I was. I turned right to cut them off, got right down on the grass, pushed the mixtures into auto-rich, rammed the props to high, and shoved the throttles to the wall. My P-38 leaped ahead as though kicked by a mule. The cutoff angle was good and I could see I would be coming in behind the bogeys in short order. I still didn't have a positive ID, but every instinct told me they had to be German. Instinct is no good when you're coming up behind a target with a 20 mm and four .50 caliber guns armed and ready to shoot. It is particularly no good when your adrenaline is pumping. Patience, patience.

I wanted those shadowy shapes to be Focke-Wulf 190s! My instincts told me they were Jerries, not a couple of Jugs out of 9th Air Force. Please, bogeys, please turn just a little. Give me an aspect where I can get a positive ID on you. I'm closing fast. There isn't much time left. I pressed rudder and slid the pipper onto the trailing aircraft's left wing. Another second and suddenly I could see the Iron Cross on the side of the lead plane's fuselage. No time left now. I squeezed the trigger. The wingman's bird lit up with strikes, spewed heavy smoke, rolled inverted, and hit the ground with a huge explosion. I had to get the other 190 before he gained an advantage on me. He made a violent left break the moment his wingman was hit. I followed, staying inside his turn, knowing my left wingtip was no more than 20 feet off the ground. The g-forces came on hard but I was scarcely aware of them. I flew the pipper slowly through his fuselage, pulling ahead, trying to get about a 100-mil lead. I pressed the trigger in a short burst and watched as strikes moved down his fuselage. Perfect! Another burst, more strikes, and he suddenly pulled straight up. The canopy separated and the pilot came out as though he had a spring in his seat. His chute opened immediately and he swung under it. I had pulled up with him and rolled inverted in time to see his aircraft hit in the middle of a farmer's field. I rolled into a hard left bank and watched through the top of my canopy as the Jerry landed close to his burning aircraft. He started running as I came around my circle to point my nose at him. I dove at him and he flopped onto his belly. He thought I was going to strafe him. No such thing! I buzzed him there in the mud and pulled up to do two victory rolls. I hoped he saw them. Then I felt like an ass doing such a silly, damned-fool, kid thing like that. Obviously I'd read too much of Hogan's *G-8 and His Battle Aces* and watched too much of *Wings* and *The Dawn Patrol*.

The flight home was uneventful, except for a mixed feeling of elation, disbelief, and nagging worry. I hoped my camera had worked. Confirmation couldn't stand on my word alone. That was a grim thought. The camera in the P-38 was mounted in the nose right under the 20 mm gun. It jiggered and bounced like crazy when the guns fired. Instead of getting a record of what was being shot at, it often quit, leaving kill claims unconfirmed. I also knew the circumstances would take some explaining. I didn't want to be too closely questioned on how hard I might have tried to find the others or what I was doing roaming around Burgundy alone. I even wondered if I should mention the bridge at Chalon-sur-Saône. I thought I had hit it but hadn't hung around to make sure. I never did join up with the rest of my flight. It was a lonely trip back with a lot of time to think.

Sure enough, my debriefing was met with obvious skepticism. I didn't press the point, just felt sick to my stomach. Then, Colonel Zemke walked into our squadron ready room. Uh-oh, I thought. Here it comes. All of us knew that Hub wasn't a man to be trifled with. His reputation as the leader of the famous Wolfpack had us totally in awe of him, to say nothing of the fact that he had more combat time than any of us had total flying time.

He came up to me as I snapped to attention, looked me in the eye, and said, "You don't know how lucky you are, Captain. I just got a call from the 355th Group. They were passing overhead and saw your engagement, the whole thing. Your two claims are confirmed."

I don't remember if I whooped out loud in the colonel's face, but I sure was whooping inside! I had kills. Two of them and confirmed. I was one lucky guy.

It turned out no one asked a lot of questions about the bridge. I guess there was a bit of embarrassment over that. It seems the rest of the gang flailed away at a bridge, the wrong one, and the less said the better.

What really got to me was learning how a pilot in one of the other squadrons had run off the side of runway 27 in the dark. His bird sank in the mud, so he just shut down the engines, climbed out, and made tracks. Obviously, two birds had become stuck, only no one knew about this second one till I almost hit it. When it was light out, the maintenance troops went to dig it out. They discovered a tire mark across the top of the wing that stuck out over the runway. The tire mark was mine. That had been the thump I'd felt. It took a while to calm down when I digested that one. Two P-38s loaded with gas and two 1,000-pound bombs each would have made a spectacular show. Someone told me they had a picture of that tire mark, but I've never seen it.

Years later, in 1949, I drove through France down toward Cap d'Antibes with my wife to show her the sights. I went out of our way to go to Chalon-sur-Saône. That bridge had been on my mind ever since that August morning five years before. It was still there, but one-third of it had been repaired by stringing one of the U.S. Army's Bailey bridges across a missing span. I took a picture, and then wondered who really cared. It certainly didn't matter anymore. At lunch in a charming café by the river I asked the old waiter what had happened to the bridge. When he understood my bad French he became excited and told me a P-38 had come by itself out of the east, blown up the bridge, then disappeared. The Germans (Bosche, he called them) had been very unhappy about it. They had stomped and screamed, then gone the longer way around on their journey back to the Fatherland. That made me feel good, but I didn't tell the old Frenchman I knew the pilot. I didn't think he would believe me. Besides, the Nuits St.-Georges wine was perfect with our lunch, and I didn't want to ruin the occasion by having my lovely wife disbelieve me, too.

Decades after those first two kills, someone asked me if I had been frightened during that initial aerial combat. I had certainly thought about that subject a lot. No, I was never truly frightened, either in combat or in other flying situations. Sure, there were times when whatever was going on was damned scary, but I didn't equate that with fright. I guess being momentarily scared, startled, or whatever is a natural reaction to danger. The old adrenaline pumps, your mouth turns dry, you pant, and if you don't watch it your voice goes up about an octave. That's a dead giveaway when you call out on the radio. You've just told the world you're in the "excited" mode, and usually your condition is contagious. Everyone within range is apt to tense up. Sometimes that's bad, sometimes it's good. Fortunately, experience overcomes these reactions, and the measure of the true veteran fighter pilot is his ability to stay calm, no matter what. Tom Wolfe would later identify that as "the Right Stuff," but I'm not sure he really understood where it comes from.

To me real fear is something in a man that grows and festers. It may start with a bad scare, but if you don't shake it off, it grows. It does not go away. It builds, day by day, hour by hour. It creeps into the soul, eats at his determination, and erodes his confidence and self-respect. I've seen it in many forms. One fellow may just simply go to pieces. He can't sleep, wears a haunted look, avoids his friends. Others come down with all sorts of maladies, some imagined and psychosomatic, but some truly serious. Some cope by trying to overcompensate. They try to play the he-man, tough-guy role; they do things to prove their guts and balls. Those individuals often prove dangerous not only to themselves, but to everyone around them. You never know what they're going to do in a given situation.

I didn't learn these things all at once. Initially, as I began to observe others and think about them in relation to my thoughts about fear, I tended to dismiss . . . no, that's not an honest word—I tended to look down on the men who didn't seem to match my youthful, simplistic impression of fighter pilots. I held an image of warriors as keen, fearless, steely-eyed gladiators of the wild blue. In my immaturity, I considered the few who did not measure up to be weaklings with annoying personality problems who were upsetting the unity of the squadron. But in combat, time is compressed, life passes swiftly, lessons are driven home, and regardless of your age or immaturity, your perspective on life evolves. Your understanding of what men do and what you are capable of changes. What you find easy, some may endure a mighty struggle before accepting. Apprehension conquered and mastered is quite different from fear that debilitates.

I learned another valuable lesson during our first two months of combat. I had two roommates, my flight lead, Satch Turner, and Wally Wallace. Wally was frightened. I'd hear him crying in his sleep, moaning and calling out his wife's name. I judged him something of a coward, and said so in the journal I kept. Then it dawned on me that Wally wasn't a coward at all. In fact, he was just the opposite. He was one of the bravest men I would ever meet. No matter what his mental state, Wally never failed or refused to fly. He never faltered during a mission. He performed as well as anyone else. Moreover, he did it despite the fear he was experiencing. Going on missions was easy for me. I looked forward to them and got on the schedule whenever I could, but who was I to judge another man? What I did wasn't brave. What Wally did took far more. He also taught me that somewhere deep inside there is a voice talking to each of us willing to listen. Sometimes that voice is extremely prescient, as in Wally's case: He died strafing an airfield in Holland.

Gradually, I came to realize that although no two men are alike, certain deep characteristics could indeed be generalized. One man can be self-assured. He's not the one who's going to get hurt. He has convinced himself nothing can touch him. He's type 1. The other guy has the unshakable premonition that he will not last out his combat tour. His apprehension often leads to fulfillment of the premonition. He's type 2. As it turned out, we lost both kinds. I guess getting shot down came as a surprise to type 1. Getting shot down only confirmed type 2's suspicions.

On August 25, eleven days after those first two kills, we were finally sent on a real, honest-to-God sweep out in front of the bomber force, clearing the way and daring Jerry to come up. The morning's briefing map revealed yarn lines showing the route of bombers in two segments, one to the north and the other farther south by a hundred miles or so. That wasn't unusual. What brought us to our feet was the red line depicting the 479th. We were between the two bomber raids, and OUT IN FRONT! We were the point of the spear. This was the position of honor and our first crack at the greatest of all distinctions for any fighter group in the 8th Air Force. At long last, we wouldn't be in the grind of close escort, just watching, weaving, and waiting, knowing that if our assigned bomber box got tapped by the Jerries, we'd already be at a disadvantage and damned lucky to down any Focke-Wulfs or Messerschmitts before they tore into our big friends like sharks into a school of tuna.

When Hub stepped onto the stage we settled down. He looked at us sternly for a moment and then started. "OK, you guys, here's the drill. I'll be leading Bison. Lakeside Squadron will be on my right, Newcross on the left. Copy down your numbers and we'll be sharp and crisp on the taxi, takeoff, and join-up. I'll do the standard three-circle orbit round the 'drome while you join up flights and squadrons in trail. I'll set course after the third go-round and start climbing. Squadrons, you fan right and left to your assigned positions. Hold close formation within your flights until I give the signal for combat spread. We'll set course for IJmuiden on the coast of Holland climbing to 28,000. I want us really spread out today, but don't lag. Keep it damn near line abreast right across the whole group. That way we'll cover the widest swath of sky and have the best chance of picking up the Jerries. Keep your eyes open and your mouths shut unless you really see something. The Hun has been coming up in large gaggles lately. That means we'll probably be outnumbered, but he'll be unwieldy and not as maneuverable as our combat formations. You wingmen, stick with your element lead. Check six o'clock and try to keep a mental picture of the general position of the aircraft around you. Remember, a midair collision kills you just as quickly as a burst of 20 mm. You've heard the weather. It couldn't be better all day, so no sweat there. No contrails though. That works both ways: We can't see them, but they can't find us as easily. Intelligence will brief the enemy order of battle and the known flak sites on our route. I'll keep us away from the bigger concentrations, but we can expect some attention from the odd marshaling yard or airfield we might overfly. As spread out as we'll be, we can't avoid all the gunners. Hell, shooting's what they're paid for anyhow."

He finished with a big grin. "Right, troops. This is your big chance. Let's give 'em HELL!"

A cheer greeted that, and we broke for our individual squadron briefing rooms. After a cup of bitter coffee and a piece of toast with real butter and some wonderful English jam, we tried to settle down for our squadron CO's short briefing. We could tell he was excited, too, but trying hard to hide it. His advice and admonitions were normal-normal, and I'm afraid we fidgeted and hardly paid attention.

On the way out I told Blue Flight I intended to sneak us out as far to the left of the rest of the squadron as I dared. I wanted us to spread out even farther than our normal combat formation, and we'd keep a sharp watch to our left front and out to the left side. Enough eyes would be looking straight ahead and to our right. We'd concentrate totally on our own piece of sky.

I reminded my guys to keep their eyes moving and not to let their focus fix on infinity. Look at the most distant airplane across the group, then sweep eyes back to our piece of sky. Look to the ground to refocus on every cycle. Always sweep. Remember, anything you see is bound to be enemy; no one else will be out there.

My wingman, the usually unflappable B. E. Hollister, was positively twitching. His eyes glittered with excitement. If any of my Blue Flight guys were nervous or apprehensive, it certainly didn't show. They reminded me of three six-month-old pups waiting for their master to throw the ball, tails wagging furiously, tongues out, prancing, waiting to be off. I don't suppose I looked or acted much different.

The takeoff drill went like clockwork. After the three orbits, Colonel Zemke rolled out on course for the North Sea and Holland. Lakeside and Newcross squadrons smoothly slid out to either side as we started our climb to 28,000 feet. We crossed the coast of East Angelia and headed out over the Channel. Highway called Colgate Control and announced, "Feet wet." Radio silence then settled over us, each in the cocoon of his cockpit with nothing but his thoughts. I looked down at the North Sea's relatively calm and peaceful surface and thought how deceptive it was. There were far too many burned and sunken ships and ditched airplanes, too many lives lost, too many years of agony and strife in those icy depths, to appreciate any beauty in it.

Hub's voice broke through. "Highway here. Go spread formation."

Each squadron moved slowly away from the other, and each flight, each element within the flight, then each individual, took spacing. Soon I could barely make out the farthermost flight of Lakeside Squadron, but I knew that Highway could see all of us from his central position leading Bison Squadron. What an absolutely wonderful sight from my cockpit: P-38s stretched as far as the eye could see off toward the right horizon, the morning sky deep blue and not a cloud anywhere. It was a great day to be a fighter pilot!

We crossed the coast of Holland and saw a few haphazard puffs of flak from IJmuiden burst below us. This was routine. We would have felt unwelcome if those particular gunners hadn't noticed our passage. We flew on across the Zuider Zee, and then the prominent peninsula on the eastern shore with the town of Urk at its tip slid beneath us.

Things tensed up as we flew over the patchwork fields and canals of central Holland. No flak. Everything was ominously quiet. Things were way too still. Then on into Germany, and my mind was working on two distinct levels: The predominant one was intensely alert, watching, analyzing, gauging, totally tuned to the sky, the land, and the aircraft around me. The subordinate part was more at ease, aware of the situation, yet free to enjoy the beauty, power, and serenity surrounding me.

Suddenly, there they were! Tiny specks way out in front moved right to left across our horizon. The hair on the back of my neck stood straight out. No problem of recognition—I knew they were the enemy. Many more of them were seen as a few seconds passed. I delayed a few seconds calling them out—a dirty trick on my part. My intentions were thwarted just as I started to call Highway. One of my flight members saw them and yelled out, "*Bogeys*. Eleven o'clock. Level!" I confess I mashed down on the mike button to block any further conversation, and then called, "Newcross Lead, Newcross Blue Lead here. Turning left to pursue and identify."

The air became a confusion of transmissions, most not decipherable, some broken: ". . . Say again direction . . . Blue, what's your heading? What's your heading? . . . I haven't got them yet. . . . Blue where are you?"

Blue knew exactly where he was. He was balls out, full throttle, max boost, full rich mixture, closing on the tail end of some forty-five to fifty Me-109s flying in a ragged formation of three big Vs of about fifteen aircraft each, with a few singles above and behind. These last ones bothered me. Common sense said to attack them first. Instinct told me to continue, keep an eye on them, but break off my attack only if they saw me and made a threatening move.

Suddenly, I remembered my drop tanks and hit the pickle button. Away they went with the usual thump, and I felt my P-38 surge forward from the reduced drag. I looked over my shoulders for my flight members. B.E. was right there with me, but the other two were far back, both trailing black smoke as their engines detonated under the strain of overboost. I knew they couldn't catch up and that the initial part of this fight was going to be two against the world.

"Newcross Blue Lead, Highway here. What's your position?" Zemke called.

That wasn't a question. It was a demand. How in hell did I know where I was? There was a huge lake just ahead and I blurted out, "I'm approaching a big lake, headed north, 28,000." That would surely merit an ass chewing when (or if) I got back. We were supposed to know where we were at all times under Hub's leadership. Then I remembered what I was supposed to be doing for the boss, and added, "I'm closing on a gaggle of bandits headed north, about fifty of them."

There were more confused shouts as the rest of the group tried to focus on the action. I had to ignore the bedlam and concentrate on my own situation. The few bandit trailers at my three o'clock hadn't noticed us yet, and I pressed on, zeroing in on the tail-end Charlie in the high Vick. He filled my gun sight with a slight angle off. Perfect. Just as I started to squeeze the trigger, both of my engines sputtered, chugged, burped, and quit. Good God, I had forgotten to switch to internal tanks after getting rid of the drops! I'm a glider!

No time to sort that out now. I clamped on the trigger. As I slowed and started to fall behind there were bright flashes along the fuselage of the 109; my bullets had struck home. A piece of cowling blew back in my face, black smoke spewed forth, and the 109 rolled slowly to the right and headed down. He was finished, and I had other problems. I dove away to my right, desperately working the tank switches, going through the start procedures and watching the high bandits all at the same time. The engines caught and I was back in business. It occurred to me that I was probably the first fighter pilot to shoot down an enemy while in the dead-stick mode, but fascinating as that realization was, there were some forty-nine other bandits out there.

Back under full power, I pulled around, climbing to go after them. The whole German formation started down to the left. I guessed the leader had decided the game was up, since they had been caught long before they closed on the bomber stream. Two of the stragglers were off to my two o'clock following the main bunch down. That put them crossing my path to the front, but I wasn't in position to go for them, and they kept me from continuing my attack on the main gaggle. I checked and there was B.E. off to my right like the good wingman he was. He was in perfect position to hit them. I hollered at B.E. to take the two in front of him and watched as he opened fire. He was on his game and nailed them both on the first pass.

I turned my attention to the main formation, closed on a tail-end Charlie, and fired. He, too, erupted smoke as the hail of bullets caught him. His 109 turned turtle and disappeared under my nose, going straight down.

This engagement had taken me away from the main bunch and I turned to pick them up again. There was absolutely nothing in sight. The sky was empty. It was as if the enemy planes had simply vanished. Then suddenly there, well below me, was an Me-109 with a P-51 chasing him. Where in hell did that Mustang come from? Then I saw another 109 closing on the P-51 and knew the Mustang pilot was unaware of the threat. He was in deep shit and without a wingman. I rolled inverted and pulled the nose almost straight down, diving to help him.

Airspeed built rapidly. Suddenly, my P-38 gave a shudder and the nose tucked farther down. I pulled back on the control yoke. Nothing. No feedback. No elevator response. Just looseness, and the nose tucked farther down. Damn it! It was compressibility, that dreaded phenomenon we had been warned about. Few pilots had ever recovered. None ever bailed out. There'd been smoking holes out in the Mojave Desert as mute testimony to the warning.

Down, down I went, the throttles in idle, prop pitch full forward, the aircraft shuddering and shaking as the shock wave tucked the nose and blanked my tail. Through 18,000 . . . no response, down . . . down . . . down . . . I held the yoke just on the point of burble and cranked a tiny bit of back trim on the elevators. Anything I could get might make a difference. The bird seemed to respond. Through 12,000 and the response increased a little. The nose slowly started to rotate from the vertical. Down, still down, too fast to think of bailing out. No time anyway. As the air grew denser, the control response increased, but the ground was coming up and I wasn't recovering. I kept milking the elevator back, back, and all of a sudden I had full bite.

The g-forces came on like a sledgehammer. Something exploded behind me with a horrible, rushing, tearing roar. I tightened my gut muscles and screamed to keep the blood from rushing from my head. The world turned gray. Looking down two dark tunnels as my eyesight went dark, I could barely see the ground. It was close, and I was going like the hammers of hell toward a huge brown plowed field. The nose came slowly up and then to the horizon. I had made it! I was dimly aware of the field furrows flashing just under my wing, scarcely 20 feet below. God, that was close. I was alive. My P-38 was flying but this boy had had enough for one day.

I tried to calm down as I got my bearings. My left canopy window was gone, blown out from the wrenching g-force of the pullout. That accounted for the continued noise and the buffeting I now felt on the elevators. In the P-38, anything that upset the airflow over the fuselage affected the elevators back between the twin booms. I knew I was one lucky bastard to be alive. I looked over my left shoulder to check for any damage, and there, not 300 yards away, was an Me-109 blazing away, his gun flashes bright against the dark line of his wings.

My God! The son of a bitch was trying to kill me!

I kicked left rudder, threw in hard left aileron, and hauled back on the yoke with all my might. My P-38 stood up on its left wing, turned broadside to the direction of flight, and abruptly slowed, taking the Jerry completely by surprise. He shot past and sailed out in front. I reversed, put the pipper on his fuselage, and pulled the trigger. The 109 shuddered under the impact of the five guns, rolled over, and dove into the ground. We never thought much about the other airplane as being occupied. The airplane was the target, not a man. It was a surprise when a body would suddenly come flying out of the stricken bird, arms and legs flailing, chute blossoming. I momentarily felt a pang of sympathy for the man. I couldn't dwell on the thought for long, because I was still some 400 miles from home plate, at low altitude, deep in enemy territory.

I stayed low and headed for the North Sea and England. After minutes that seemed like hours the coast of Holland lay ahead. I blundered just over the top of several coastal flak emplacements and jinked wildly as I flashed over the beach and out to sea. The flak followed and churned the water around me, but the firing dropped away behind and I was home free. My hands shook as I tried to light a cigarette as I flew on toward England. No way, not with the wind. Damn, I was fucking freezing!

Recovery was uneventful and I landed at Wattisham with a sigh of relief. Considering the unknown extent of damage to my bird, I had to forgo the time-honored victory roll. I taxied to my hardstand and Sergeant Wold waved me into my parking slot. When the engines shut down he climbed up on my wing and crouched just outside the cockpit. As I removed my helmet I could hear him clucking at me for having bent up his airplane. He wasn't serious but tried to sound exasperated at the carelessness of all pilots, particularly his. The sight and sound of him was wonderful, totally beautiful, and I scarcely heard what he was mumbling. He assured me everyone else had come home safely as far as he knew and then asked why I was so late.

I grinned at him and said, "It took a little longer to bag three 109s."

He smiled that shy grin of his and replied, "Well, I guess that explains it. And congratulations, you're the 479th's first ace."

That set me back all right. I hadn't even thought of it, but it really didn't matter at that moment. Life was sweet, I was alive, debriefing had to be endured, reports had to be written, and the bar would be open, hopefully with some of the rationed hard stuff left over after early returnees had made their usual assault on the place. As was normal in the bar, everything but the standard arf an' arf beer was gone by the time B.E. and I got there. No matter. Nothing could erase the feeling of complete aliveness coursing through my body, nor the exaltation in my soul. Tomorrow would be another day. This evening was here and now. Did anyone slap my back? I don't remember.

8

★

Mustangs and Mayhem

The rumor was true! Since mid-July we'd been hearing talk of conversion from P-38s to P-51s. The group adjutant hinted we might lose some maintenance people. The supply officers huddled together at one end of the bar, not exactly whispering, but looking like four conspirators. I tried to get my old buddy Captain Van Anderson, football teammate at Hampton High and now 434th maintenance officer, to fess up. His denials didn't fool me. It didn't take a genius to figure it out. We were getting Mustangs.

Of course, the pilots didn't have what headquarters called a "need to know." We were only going to fly them. No big deal. I wondered how long the checkout would take, hoping it would be nothing like the P-38 training tedium in California: engines, airframes, hydraulics, flight characteristics, control systems, gunners, skip and dive bombing, on and on. Eventually we knew the Lightnings inside and out, but how would the P-51 transition go? Formal schooling? Was there going to be a flying syllabus? Or would it be an ad hoc transition with some quick briefing from some experienced Mustang drivers?

Colonel Zemke made the official P-51 announcement on September 7. The news was ho-hum by then, but we sat up when he said the first batch of new fighters would arrive the next day. There were some mixed emotions. All of us had been weaned on the P-38. We loved it like a first love, maybe more. Hemingway had written about it. A pilot loves his first fighter and it is never replaced in his affection. As for me, as much as I loved the P-38, I couldn't wait to get into the Mustang. No more compressibility, better range, and some pilots claimed better maneuverability. We hoped so. In any event, it was coming and I was excited.

The 479th FG was overdue. P-51s had been introduced to the ETO in mid-1943, and their range and performance let the Allies reach out to bring the battle to the enemy's backyard. Compressibility didn't seem to hamper the Mustang. There was no beating it with the P-38. Like all aircraft, the faster it went, the more the airflow was accelerated over the curved surfaces. When it accelerated too much, portions of the airframe approached supersonic and a shock wave formed there that stood up perpendicular to the wing, canopy, or fuselage curves. In the P-38, that shock wave from the nose and leading edges blocked the airflow over the elevators. With no pitch control, there was little the pilot could do. At that point bailing out was impossible, and a pilot only got lucky if the denser air at low altitude and flat-blading the props caused enough drag to slow the aircraft down before he ran out of altitude. The P-51 with a new airfoil design they called laminar flow was supposed to help avoid the situation.

We were told all three squadrons would convert half a unit at a time, and that we'd be flying split missions, a couple of flights in P-38s, a couple in the new Mustangs. We glanced at one another at that news, but, what the hell, how about the training program? "Later," we were told. How much later could they get? The next morning, when the first new bird arrived?

Most of the group pilots were on the flight line the next day when the first flight of four sparkling, Merlin-growling P-51s entered the traffic pattern, pitched out, and executed impressive landing patterns. They taxied up to flight control like an acrobatic team. They swung around in unison, the engines shut down, and the canopies opened. Then came the shocker. The pilots pulled off their leather helmets and shook their heads, and long, feminine blond and brunette hair swirled in the breeze. We looked like a bunch of idiots with our mouths open and our eyes popping out. The female ferry pilots climbed out laughing and came over to us with big grins to shake our outstretched hands. It was obvious they'd done this at other bases, but that didn't detract a bit from the impression they made. I couldn't help wondering if the show had been deliberately planned for any of us who might've had doubts about flying the Mustang. Never mind. We were duly impressed, with most of the guys hoping the girls would stay overnight.

I went looking for Major Herren. "Sir, when do I get to fly one?"

Herren grinned at me and said, "Tell you what, Olds. You'll be among the first, just as soon as the engineers and crew chiefs have had a chance to look them over. Give it a week." Knowing I had never flown a single-engine fighter before, the good major added, "And watch out for the torque. Lots of rudder on takeoff."

Being among the first to fly was good news. Waiting for maintenance and crew chiefs was bad as far as I was concerned. A week seemed like an eternity, but I had an idea where I could focus my interests for at least the next eighteen hours. There were new girls on base and new airplanes on the flight line, and no one could fault a fighter pilot for wanting to talk about technique with the pilots who'd delivered the birds. Purely professional interest.

It felt like ages before the crew chiefs finished fussing and signaled that the birds were ready to go. In the meantime, I kept flying missions in my P-38 and passed my two-hundred-hour mark. Some other pilots got off in the P-51 before I did, and I urged my crew chief to hurry. Finally, Glen gave me the thumbs-up. I knew so little about the airplane that I didn't know how to mount the wing to get at the cockpit. The chief had to show me the kick step and recessed handgrip. Once shown, I clambered aboard quickly and buckled up.

What an office! Compared to the P-38s, this cockpit provided plenty of leg, shoulder, and headroom. All the knobs and switches were right at my fingertips. None of the instruments were hidden behind a control yoke. The Mustang had a proper stick grip. Everything in the cockpit felt just right. I was falling in love all over again with a new girl.

Not knowing what half of the switches were meant to do, I turned to the crew chief crouched on the left wing by the cockpit and asked, "How do you start this thing, chief?"

"OK, Captain. Put mixture in idle-cutoff. That's all the way up. No, you've got to squeeze the little latch on the mixture control handle to get it to move. Right, that's it. But don't move it yet, it's already in position. Now, prop control full increase, and crack the throttle just a bit, about an inch. Got that? Don't open it any more than that. Something happens in the carb and the engine will run away when you start her."

The chief continued, "OK, now look down here, behind the stick, right between your knees. See that? Fuel selector gauge. You start on the left main. Don't ask me why. See, you've got left and right mains, left and right drops, and fuselage tank. That's right behind you, and if you twist around over your left shoulder you can see the quantity gauge there on top. They told us not to fill it, so now it shows just a few gallons left over from the last flight."

He saw my face and laughed. "Here come the fuel guys now. Listen up, the main tank gauges are on the floor on either side of the cockpit just in front of your seat. See them? Radio's there, but we haven't had time to change the crystals to local, so you'll have to use button C to talk to the tower." While he pointed out things around the cockpit, the fuel guys had the hoses out and were pouring av-gas into the wing tanks.

"OK, one last thing. Like the 38, there's the engine primer switch, right next to the mag selector switch. Now we're ready to go. Here's the drill: We'll be starting with a battery cart, so leave the battery and generator switches off until you get her started. OK?"

OK already.

"What you'll do: Hold the primer for a few seconds, then hit the start switch. When the prop has turned over about six blades to build a bit of oil pressure, throw the mag switch to both and push the mixture down into auto-rich. She should fire up immediately. It'll be running on prime, just like the Lightning, so push the throttle over the detent to idle and you're good. We'll pull the battery cart and then you can flip on your battery and generator switches. The rest is up to you. Got all that?"

"Sure have, chief!"

Then he added, "Oh, they tell me the coolant temp is real critical. You gotta make sure she doesn't overtemp while you're taxiing. There's an override switch somewhere there on the right console. The cooler door is supposed to work automatically, but sometimes it doesn't, they say."

Gee, that was reassuring. "OK, let's give it a go."

The refueling finished, I felt a surge of excitement as I went through the start. The four-bladed prop turned, and suddenly those twelve Merlin cylinders popped, coughed, and caught again. I eased forward on the mixture control. As the engine settled into a popping rhythm the whole machine came to life with that distinctive Merlin roar. Unlike the P-38, which seemed a quiet lady by comparison, the Mustang began with a snarling earnestness, vibrating through my body and telling me, "I'm ready! You're ready! Let's go!"

We went. As I taxied I thought, Wow, this has been some checkout program! I fishtailed down the taxiway recalling the technique from my T-6 training days, stretching first left and then right to see alongside the huge nose cowling. Maybe I should have asked Major Herren what approach speed to shoot for, but then maybe he wouldn't know either, and I would have embarrassed him. Oh well, first things first. Some stalls to get the feel and a look at how she flies with gear and flaps, and then I'll know about approach speeds.

The takeoff was smooth. I didn't blast the throttle, so torque control with lots of right rudder was easy. The beautiful bird simply told me when to ease forward to get the tail up and then it flew off the runway when it was ready. Once I was up, I spent the next thirty minutes feeling out the stall, first clean and then with the garbage hanging. That gave what I needed for landing. Next, I pulled some g and was surprised to find I had to push forward a bit on the stick to keep the nose from tucking up under my chin during the turn. That's going to take some getting used to, I thought. The single engine created a need to constantly retrim the rudder as airspeed changed. Torque was no issue in the P-38, and the T-6 in training didn't show much in comparison to the Merlin. So far, so good. I loved it more every minute.

It was time to return to base. Someone else was chomping at the bit, waiting his turn, and I didn't want to be selfish. I flew the overhead pattern cautiously, got my airspeed just right, and came across the threshold perfectly. Finding the runway was a bit tricky compared to the P-38 because of the nose angle, but I managed to make a safe but sloppy landing. Getting back to tail dragging would take some concentration. Oh well, the next one would be better. I taxied in, giving Glen the thumbs-up. As Bogey had said, it looked like the start of a beautiful friendship.

More Mustangs arrived over the next few days, but I didn't get to fly one again until the rest of the squadron had their turns. Meanwhile, missions continued in the P-38. During the transition Glenn Miller and his band showed up to entertain us. He set up outside the hangar to the south of our main runway. As luck would have it, I was scheduled to get my second ride in the Mustang at the same hour. I felt sort of important as I taxied around past the gathering toward the takeoff end of the runway. A large crowd had assembled on the grass lining the taxiway to watch the band, and I got quite a bit of attention at the same time. I resisted the temptation to wave at a couple of pretty girls.

The second P-51 flight went better than the first. No surprises in my air work. Someone told us that stick-reversal trick would be corrected in the D model by adding bob weights somewhere in the elevator control system. No sweat there. I returned for landing full of what soon proved to be false confidence. Everything went well right up to the point of touchdown, but this time I couldn't quite find the surface of the runway. What the hell was the matter? I floated along, waiting for the little bird to sink quietly and perfectly onto the pavement.

It wasn't going to happen. Suddenly the left wing whipped down and struck the runway. I found myself at a horrible angle to the ground. I kicked right rudder and tried to lift the wing, but also gave the throttle a burst, trying to get some speed to regain control. Whoa, no! That was obviously the wrong thing to do. Torque from the engine and the blast across the rudder sent the bird up into an almost vertical left bank and veering off the runway onto the grass. I yanked the throttle back to idle and fought to get the right wing down where it belonged. The Mustang was living up to its name as we bucked and rolled along on the verge of disaster but, more critically, headed right for Glenn Miller and his band. The spectators could see me coming and scattered in every direction as I crossed the taxiway. In the midst of my gyrations I could see the band members bailing off the platform. The whole episode couldn't have lasted more than a few seconds, but it seemed like minutes before I managed to do a half ground loop and come to a stop in the middle of the spectator area.

I had made an entrance. There I sat, with the engine ticking over, my left wingtip bent up toward the sky, and grass draped across the nose of my bird as if she were some cow grazing. I taxied away without looking at any of the stunned faces glaring at me and just hoped the incident wouldn't end my flying career.

I'd learned some lessons. One, never think the Mustang was going to float into a landing like the P-38. You had to place the P-51 on the ground; otherwise, it would stay right where you leveled until it decided to quit flying, at which point you'd better be within a few inches of the surface. Two, never, never think you were going to pull out of a stall by blasting the throttle. Torque took over instantly, pulling you up and around to the left, and you were in deep shit.

The heavy-maintenance shop replaced the bent wingtip, but no one volunteered to fix my bent and broken pride. At least the guys understood how I felt and there was a minimum of teasing about my fall from grace. Some had done it and more would do it in the years to come. In any event, missions went on as usual. The gaggles were a mix of Mustangs and Lightnings, but we kept flying.

In a week or two I was assigned my own new bird! My last P-38 was named *SCAT III*, and now a P-51 was all prettied up with *SCAT IV* nose art by Fred Hayner, along with my name, five victory flags, and my crew chief Glen Wold's name stenciled boldly on the canopy rail. It was a thrill. I was on the schedule for the following morning's mission but just wanted to hang out with the bird on the hardstand. Glen was there, too, fussing around the two 100-gallon drop tanks I would be carrying for the first time. He mumbled something about not dropping them unless I really had to. He implied that he might demand my help in hanging replacements on the bird if necessary. I understood that.

He led me on a walk-around, showing me how things ought to look before flying: fluid levels, inspection plates, control movement, things like that. Nothing too complicated for a dumb pilot (Glen didn't say that). I really liked this quiet, somewhat reticent man. He had shepherded me through two P-38s, often coming to the club during those long summer evenings. He'd take me to our aircraft and show me how to help him pull inspections, check tires, change spark plugs, or some such task. To tell the truth, I really enjoyed getting my hands greasy, and Glen managed to teach me quite a bit in the process. The biggest lesson was that even the best pilot didn't go anywhere without maintainers. Teamwork won victories.

That afternoon I sat in the cockpit going over the starting drill and cockpit emergency procedures. Though I had made only two flights in the Mustang, I felt comfortable with it. God knows I had rehashed the proper landing technique a thousand times in my mind before drifting off to sleep. I wasn't going to make the same stupid mistakes again.

We flew bomber escort missions the first two weeks of September while the Jerries attempted to entertain us with daily buzz-bomb attacks near the field. We were getting the hang of the new Mustangs, all except for Pavlock, who was killed on a takeoff. In mid-September we got the chilling news that Hub Zemke and Lieutenants Gavrys, Matthews, Hendrix, and Rodgers hadn't returned from a mission. Later we heard that all but Gavrys had landed safely at Roye-Amy and were headed back to Wattisham. What a relief! Sleep was difficult that night as several V-1s impacted near the airfield. The bloody Bosche. I fell into the Brit vernacular regularly.

We went groggily to group briefing the next morning and listened to the standard information about times, checkpoints, rendezvous, altitudes, bomber call signs, and identifying tail markings. The weather both here and in the target area in Holland near the German border was excellent. Air opposition was briefed to be minimal, and the flak would be normal-normal, i.e., heavy and intense on the bomb run.

Field Marshal Montgomery was moving his army slowly up the one road toward Arnhem. We knew that. We had been briefed and had flown over that part of Belgium, Holland, and Germany almost daily in our Lightnings. The Germans had cut the dikes in their retreat to the homeland. The countryside was under water and only the road was passable. The 82nd and 101st Airborne had dropped to secure the bridges at Eindhoven and Nijmegen, thus paving the way for the Brits. But the British advance was slow.

We were told we were going to patrol an area to the northeast of Arnhem and were expected to wipe out anything that shot at us. Intel couldn't tell us what lay in the large forest we were to cover. He could say only that our time over target would be thirty minutes before the Brits dropped their paratroops on both sides of the Rhine just to the west of the town. Apparently, the idea was to capture the bridge crossing the Rhine, thus providing Monty with the privilege of being the first to invade the German homeland.

Now Lieutenant Colonel Herren led. We took four flights of four and set up orbits over our target area. Our idea was for the lead flight to draw flak so the following flights could spot it and strafe. It turned out the Germans weren't that dumb. Naturally, they shot only at the trailing flight, and we soon found ourselves in something resembling a trophy dash. No one wanted to be last! The tactic was a bust. We were taking hits without doing the enemy any damage. After five or six circuits we moved back toward Arnhem itself just in time to see the parachute force approaching from the west.

An impressive sight! The sky was black with Dakotas and Lancasters. Each smaller Dakota (C-47) towed a glider, and the British Lancasters pulled three each. Then the flak started, and the majestic scene turned into a nightmare. Bombers blew up or went spiraling down, often dragging their gliders. We watched as the battle raged. Then the sky erupted with thousands of parachutes on both sides of the Rhine near Arnhem itself. We watched in awe and wished the troopers well, but the Luftwaffe arrived and we got caught up in what turned out to be the biggest air battle to date for the 434th. When it was all over, the squadron had destroyed eighteen Me-109s and Fw-190s.

Over the next few days, Montgomery's plan fell apart. The army on the south side of the river failed to cross, and the troopers in the town of Arnhem fought a losing battle against a vastly superior German force. Intel had been unaware that there were two panzer divisions hidden in the woods we had been sent to patrol. They rolled on the Brits in Arnhem, and the rest is history. So much for Monty's race to the Rhine. He'd eventually be beaten across the following March when Patton crossed at Oppenheim.

By October, the 434th completed conversion to P-51s, with just one remaining P-38, the dear old piggyback. I was comfortable in the new airplane and one happy fighter pilot eager for some action. It wouldn't take long.

On October 6 the weather was beautiful, no clouds, unlimited visibility, and crystal-clear skies. Two unusual things were making me uneasy. Our bombers were at 31,000 feet, much higher than I had ever seen them fly, and there were no contrails, none at all. That wasn't good. Contrails were a big part of our being able to spot the enemy. We were already at a disadvantage. We had a hard time keeping track of our charges, the bombers, and an equally hard time picking up enemy attackers.

The mission went smoothly until we made the rendezvous with our box of B-24s and B-17s. We were on time and on course. We were fast approaching the target somewhere near Berlin and there'd been no sightings of enemy aircraft. The rest of the 2nd Air Division bomb groups were there, all turning precisely southward at the initial point . . . but our box wasn't among them. We frantically flew down the bomber stream, looking at tail codes for our assigned charges. No luck. Then, just as I started to turn my flight around the trailing box, I saw huge explosions at our altitude far up north. Those could only be bombers under heavy attack. Nothing else looked like that. God, what had happened?!

We tore up that way and arrived just in time to see waves of Me-109s and Fw-190s pouring down from six o'clock high on the hapless bombers. I managed to sandwich my wingman and me between the enemy waves, but it was practically useless. The Jerries hit so hard and so fast that there was little we could do. In singles and pairs, the squadron followed suit, and there was a chaotic parade: a wave of Fw-190s, a couple of P-51s, another wave of Germans, then more P-51s. Luftwaffe shooting at bombers and us shooting at Germans where we could. There was no way to estimate the number of stricken bombers or even make a wild guess at the number of Jerries. There was no time to count or worry about it. I had never seen such a melee, and I was hell-bent on getting some of those bastards.

The 190s split-S'd down as they completed each attack. We followed. The ensuing battle had all the charm of a dance in a junkyard. I maneuvered behind one Fw but he got lucky. The guns in my right wing jammed and the recoil from the three in my left slewed me sideways, spoiling my aim. The enemy plane fired his burst at a B-17 and the bomber lit up all along the fuselage and burst into flames. The 190 flipped over into a split-S and dove away with me right behind him. I tried to compensate for my aiming problem by walking the gun sight back and forth across the wingspan. That did it! I saw strikes and the canopy flew off, followed by several other large pieces. The Fw went into a violent skid, giving me a clear quartering shot. I hit the cockpit and flew over the Jerry as he plunged down, trailing smoke.

Just about that time I had to dodge the tail section of a B-17 falling straight for me. It was spinning like a maple leaf, and the poor tail gunner's chute must have caught in his escape hatch door. He was out at the end of his chute lines like a rock in a sling, still alive and trying desperately to free himself. We made eye contact for a split second as he fell close past my canopy. His face was grim with determination, not fear. That image burned itself into my mind.

Debris was falling through my piece of sky: parts of fuselages, stray bombs, half a wing, an engine, bodies, a whole plane flaming madly as it disintegrated on its way down. Above, I could see scores of chutes descending amid the mess. Suddenly tracers went past my canopy. I broke hard left and hollered for my wingman, "Newcross Blue Two, get this guy off my tail!"

"Just a minute," he responded, "I've got one cornered!"

I turned around in my seat looking for the bandit who was sniping away at me and saw, not the nose of a Focke-Wulf, but the silver spinner of a P-51, and yelled, "You idiot! Stop shooting! That's me you've got!" Needless to say, that guy never flew my wing again.

The trip home was grim. We had all seen bombers go down before. But this was different. This had been a total massacre—all those bombers, all those men. We picked up a few stragglers, some trailing smoke, some with tattered fuselages and feathered engines, all with damage, and, I presumed, most with on-board casualties. For what it mattered, our little group of surviving heavies made it back to the coast of England and our flight turned for Wattisham.

I don't remember my landing. I felt shattered and I fought a lump in my throat when I taxied in and shut down. Glen Wold sensed my dejection and didn't ask for details. I just told him it had been really bad and that I had to hurry to debrief.

The squadron ready room was quiet. Faces of the mission pilots were drawn, mouths tight, each man trying to deal with the horrific memories of what he had seen. The voices of the interrogating intelligence officers were brittle, knowing questions had to be asked and hating to have to do so.

Major Pillsbury, group intelligence chief, came into our midst. He stopped our proceedings and announced that someone from 2nd Air Division was on the phone. Headquarters wanted to find out what had happened, who was responsible, and why we fighter pilots hadn't stopped the attack on the bombers. The boss wanted a couple of pilots who took part in the action to report to 2nd Div immediately, right now, and to be quick about it. The tone of the request and the nature of the questions had an ominous ring. Someone wanted to hang somebody, and it would appear that the selected somebody might very well be a hapless fighter pilot. Before he could look around, I told Lieutenant Colonel Herren I would go, since I was the one who first spotted the bombers and was perhaps in the best position to provide factual data. Herren agreed (a little too quickly, I thought). Major Glover from the 435th Squadron was selected as the other victim. We grabbed our chutes and headed out to the flight line. Our transport to the 2nd Div was an AT-6, a trainer used for instrument instruction and general utility purposes. Since Glover was a major and I had just made captain, rank was invoked and I climbed into the backseat.

Our journey to Cambridge took about twenty minutes, and a waiting staff car whisked us to headquarters. There we were hustled into the presence of one very distraught and irate general. I don't remember his name, only his anger.

Once the location and timing of the forces involved were understood and plotted on the wall map, the general's anger faded. Those were his men and their terrible losses hurt deeply. The general realized the leader of this particular box of bombers had managed to get his formation far to the north of his planned course. Not only was he all alone out there with his escort vainly looking for him at the rendezvous point, but, as luck would have it, he had put himself squarely in the path of that large force of Me-109s, which happened to be headed south for the main bomber stream. The general dismissed us with a wave of the hand and a feeble "Thank you." The staff officer escorting us back to the airfield told us that at last count, the 2nd Div had lost forty-two bombers in that battle: over four hundred men.

Night fell before we took off back to Wattisham. I was dead tired and the drone of the engine faded into a lullaby. I dozed off in the backseat and must have slept for quite a while because when I awoke, something didn't feel right. Too much time had passed. We should have been in the traffic pattern at Wattisham by now. I glanced at the luminous dial of my issue watch and realized with a start that we had been airborne for over an hour. Was it possible the major was lost? Even in Britain's total blackout, the landmass of East Anglia could always be faintly discerned. You couldn't hide rivers or coastlines. And this wasn't the blackest of nights. The compass showed us headed north. That wasn't right. Wattisham was south of Cambridge! I peered hard toward the earth and could see absolutely nothing: no clouds obscuring vision, no mist, just Stygian blackness. It dawned on me. We were over the North Sea headed God knew where or how far out.

Now what? If I voiced my suspicions, or suggested my belief that he was lost, the major was sure to get pissed off. Hell, he knew he was lost. He didn't have to have some smart-assed junior officer tell him that. I'd be tactful, and give him an out.

I picked up the mike and said, "Beautiful black night, Major. Sorry, I dozed off back here. How much longer to that beer we spoke of?"

No answer. Uh-oh. What's your next move, Robin? Ask him if he's getting in a little night flying time? No, that was a bit snide, wouldn't do at all. I asked, "Uh, Major, could I ask a favor? I'm mighty behind on both my instrument time and my night hours. I sure would be grateful if you'd let me fly her for a while."

The stick shook and I grabbed it happily. I pretended to make some practice single-needle width turns, and gradually got us headed a little south of due west. Hell, we couldn't miss the whole of England and Scotland. To keep us on that heading without rousing the major's suspicions, I did a few controlled 300-foot-a-minute climbs and descents, coupled with 45-degree turns right and left. During one of the turns I caught the faint glow of surf on a beach. The setting looked familiar, and soon I picked up the sheen of the river we always used on low-visibility days as a pointer to the runway at home plate. The major hadn't been too badly lost. But if he had held his last heading, we might have made Norway in an hour or two, or maybe not.

October wore on, mostly with bad weather that kept us grounded for days at a time. Bud Grenning failed to return from a mission to Mannheim, and I was worried sick about my close friend. Then we heard he had landed safely in Brussels. He came back saying he would make all future emergency landings at Brussels and reported it was still a great city despite long German occupation.

I was out preflighting before takeoff, doing the usual walk-around to make sure both wings were on and the tail section was where it was supposed to be, the most important part of the ritual being the usual leak in the grass at the rear of the aircraft, when, just before climbing up on the wing, I noticed something had been done to my Mustang.

"Glen, what the hell is this window?" I asked, pointing to a small glass-covered opening on the left side of the fuselage just above the coolant radiator.

"It's a camera, sir. Some guys came into the hangar when I had the bird in for inspection and installed it."

"A camera? What the hell for?"

"They didn't say, but come here." Glen became all business and his voice was serious. "Take a look. See the lens? And over here; climb up on the left wing. See the two red lines painted on the left side of the canopy? Now look out at the wingtip. See the single red line painted out there? The guys told me that if you line up those marks, it's where the camera points. Then, all you have to do is turn the power on and hit this switch next to it over here on the right side of the cockpit, and you'll take pictures until you turn the switch off. The thing is automatic, they tell me. It'll keep on shooting all by itself till you tell it to stop."

I just shrugged. Take pictures of what? I thought. What's this about? I had a mission to fly, so I hopped in and promptly forgot all about the camera.

Two days later Don Horton and Tommy Thomas, our two squadron intel officers, took me aside before the early-morning group briefing. They had some glossy eight-by-tens lined up on a table and led me over there. "See these? Recognize what they are?"

"Sure," I replied. "What's the deal? That's a marshaling yard, a big one. Where is it?" I was beginning to get suspicious.

"Stuttgart," Don answered as he and Tommy exchanged nervous glances.

I was more than a little suspicious now. "Come on. Out with it. Is this today's target? Why all the personal attention? What's it got to do with me?" All of a sudden, I connected. The camera. Holy shit! What was going on?

Don became all business. "Robin, this is highly classified. Really secret stuff; 8th Air Force headquarters at Wycombe wants the pilot of L2-W— that's you—to take a sequence of photos of today's target before, during, and after. Down low, real, real low—"

I interrupted. "What the hell do you mean 'during' and 'down low'? That's crazy! You ever count the guns around that marshaling yard? You want me to zip across that place three times? Down low? During? During the bomb drop? AFTER? You've got to be shitting me!"

Don put on his sternest official look and assured me he was not.

I didn't like it one damned bit, but knowing I would do it anyway (what choice did I have?), my mind was already racing with half-baked ideas and a lot of questions. Most important, I sure wanted someone to know I thought the idea was totally stupid. Orders were orders, but I needed a plan to accomplish the task, so I hustled Don and Tommy over into a corner.

"OK, let's get busy," I barked. "What's the TOT? Will the lead bomber drop the usual smoke bombs? How long does it take for a load of 500-pounders to fall from, what is it, 28,000 feet? Am I going in alone or do I drop out of our escort and get up ahead in time to do this thing? Hell, let me see those pictures again. What's the weather forecast in the target? Will I be able to see the bomber stream from low altitude? How about the flak? Where are the guns relative to the target? You got any area blowups so I can pick a low-level run-in checkpoint? Jesus, Horton, whose fucking idea was this?"

Twenty minutes later I had it figured out. I had to forge ahead of everyone to set up for the photo runs. The configuration of that sighting procedure meant going in at about 300 feet and passing down the right side of the target, *three times!* The normal bomber force procedure was for the lead aircraft to drop some smoke markers. The rest of the bombardiers dropped on that smoke, or so we had been briefed. I would be able to see the smoke down on the deck where I intended to circle. OK, I had it: bomb drop time, first pass not too soon BEFORE (those three passes were now capitalized in my mind), then circle into position to see the bomber stream on their run-in, be so many seconds out so that I could pass down the right side of the target DURING the impacts, haul ass around to get the AFTER shot. Then head for home low, fast, alone, and hopefully alive. The second pass might be the real bitch, particularly if the bombers were ragged in their formation or didn't have the winds doped right. No telling where bombs might scatter while I was next to the target.

I didn't pay much attention to the regular briefing. Everything was normal, if you could call a huge bomber raid on a major German city normal. Weather was good. Flak anticipated as heavy, intense, and accurate over the target. Standard drill. Takeoff, rendezvous point, bomber tail markings, routes, altitudes, timing for everything, radio calls, winds aloft, safe course home, location of other fighter forces, latest intelligence info on the new German jets, emergency procedures, home-plate weather forecast, call sign and locations for the air-sea rescue people, our own aircraft assignments, taxi sequence, and so on.

Highway Lead gave his pitch about radio discipline and formation positions, issued a few cautions to the assembled group, and then said, "Newcross Blue Lead will be leaving formation prior to the initial point. Any questions?"

Questions? Hell yes! I thought. Is this necessary? Goddamned bomber people ought to take their own damned pictures. Grumble, grumble. I was in a snit.

"Hey, Robin, what the hell is that all about?" the guy sitting next to me asked. "What are you doing?"

A trifle dramatically, I replied, "I can't tell you. Ask Horton."

After the group briefing, the 434th Squadron ready room was in the usual turmoil: shouts for coffee, maps being drawn, individual flight briefings, people rushing about, tension in the air, lots of nervous banter. The squadron CO gave his standard briefing, followed as always by a mad dash for the johns, six hours being a long damned time to be strapped tight in a small cockpit. We used to wonder if the bomber boys, who had to fly almost twice as long, carried chamber pots. Soon we were off into Sergeant Charlie Claybaugh's domain to don our Mae Wests, pick up our helmets and chutes, then dump the contents of our pockets into our lockers. It wouldn't do to have old Jerry know anything about us if we got shot down. Heavens no, he only had a brochure and photographs on each of us since May, knew everything about us, probably more than each of us remembered about himself.

The churning in my stomach settled down as the jeep dropped me off at the hardstand where *SCAT V* made its home. Time for business. Sergeant Wold gave me his usual, calm "Good morning," but called me up onto the wing and went over the camera procedure again, somewhat unnecessarily, I thought. Then it occurred to me: How the hell did he know?

I asked him. "Glen, why are you giving me special attention this morning?"

"Well, Captain, this guy from group came by early and loaded up that camera with film, so I figured something was up today."

The mission proceeded normally, almost too precisely. The B-24s were right where they were supposed to be, on time and on course. The weather was great. Holland lay ahead and I could see across the coastal peninsula all the way to the eastern shore of the Zuider Zee. Everything was going according to plan, a somewhat unusual occurrence, leaving no need for makeshift adjustments.

With little to distract me, I couldn't help but think about the task ahead. I had to admit I was more than nervous, and I didn't like the feeling. This was the usual excitement but pumped by about 1,200 psi adrenaline flow. I never worried about flak or German fighters. Those always took care of themselves as they happened. Sometimes the local English weather ground at me. Hell, it bugged all of us. Those 200-foot ceilings with a half-mile visibility would bug anyone with as little instrument training and experience as any of us had. But now I had time to think about the guns and that marshaling yard. This wasn't impromptu. I knew my chances were good on the BEFORE pass. The Jerries would never suspect anyone to be dumb enough to come barreling across a target like that. Surely they'd be focused on the approaching bombers, or so I reasoned. Otherwise, how did those recce guys survive? But here was something that cut right across the grain. No sense at all. Old-timers and survivors all preached: "One pass and haul ass!" OK. Maybe I'd get by with the DURING pass. The bombs would be going off, confusion would reign supreme, and no one had ever been dumb enough to make a run like that *twice*. But the third pass? Waiting until the second box of heavies had dropped, maybe the third and fourth, then going in? Christ, the Germans would be raging mad, and rightly so. They'd remember that crazy lone Mustang pilot and probably be waiting, teeth clenched, eyes aflame, wanting to do something to get even. And I would be it. I really didn't give myself much of a chance to get within a mile of the target for that AFTER pass, let alone make a nice photo run. When hit, the best I could hope for would be to be able to pull up high enough to bail out. That is, assuming I wouldn't be a ball of fire like so many I had seen in the past.

Questions kept gnawing at me: how best to do this, how to survive, how to get it done? I even asked myself if I was scared. I had never been scared before. Well, not scared before doing something, but maybe a little afterward, when realizing how close I had come to "buying the farm." This was different, not like the time B.E. and I attacked some forty-odd Messerschmitts by ourselves. We just piled into them. No time to think, no time to weigh the odds or consider consequences. Just react, attack, fight, and think about it later. I finally decided I wasn't scared, just apprehensive and getting madder every moment. Whatever nameless lame-brain in some damned headquarters had dreamed up this idiot plan ought to be here, not me.

No more thinking about it. Time to DO it. OK, ease the nose down. Add some RPM and throttle. Get out front and down on the deck well short of the target. Have a quick glance at a well-memorized map for those vital checkpoints. All there: the bend in the river, the small town just beyond, that autobahn running parallel off to the right, Stuttgart ahead. I'm lined up almost perfectly. A small correction to the left, the target coming up, camera power ON, get down lower, quick glances at those red alignment markings to check the needed angle of bank, a few tracers and smoke trails of flak arcing over my canopy, then camera switch ON and . . . WHOOSH over the rail yard and on past. Surprisingly little flak. Must have caught them by surprise. So far, so good. Camera switch OFF and a hard left out to my holding point to time the DURING pass.

I watched the bomber stream approaching. That part was easy. The sky at their altitude was black with flak. A couple of B-17s were trailing smoke and falling from the formation. Poor bastards. I headed back west, still on the deck, and turned under the lead box to parallel their course back toward the target. My run had been timed so I'd arrive at the target just as the bombs were to hit, and I was in good position for the drop. The smoke bombs coming off the lead bomber stood out clearly, and I knew everyone else in the lead formation was releasing his bombs at almost the same instant. Now was the time to concentrate on my own run-in to the right of the target. Lineup was good. I was about a half mile off to the right of the marshaling yard. Ought to be close enough for good pictures but far enough away not to get mixed up with the explosions.

Things were getting tense. This time the flak gunners were really pissed; the sky was full of tracers and black bursts. It seemed forever for those bombs to fall, and I was practically on top of the rail yard with the camera running. Nothing had happened yet. Come on, bombs! Make this good. Come on! Opposite the target, no bombs, then, suddenly, WHAMMO, WHAMMO! The first bombs hit. They hit all right, just off my right wing! Ear-shattering, bone-crunching blasts, jarring my insides like a hammer, shock waves roiling the air, visible waves fast as thunder across the earth, tumbling my P-51 sidewise for an instant. Mind-crunching blasts of successive shock, noise like a thousand pile drivers hitting at once . . . WHAM. WHAM. WHAM. WHAM! And ALL of it happening off on my right side! My right side, for God's sake, not on the mar-shaling yard to the left, not where I was taking all those lovely pictures! The big boys had missed the damned target by a little over three-quarters of a mile, and I was almost in the middle of the bomb pattern, right next to the impact point.

Discretion got the better part of valor and I hightailed it out of there back toward England. No one had ever cleared a target area faster, lower, or an-grier.

Halfway home I got over my anger and started laughing. Hell, I was alive! Shaken up, yes, but perking right along with a healthy bird and plenty of gas. I even shot up a train on the way out, so the mission wasn't a total bust. The rest of the trip home was abnormally peaceful.

I buzzed across the Channel under a clear but cold blue sky. There was the black-and-white lighthouse standing on Orford Ness, as always, a welcome checkpoint and comforting sight. Then on up the river, a course of 265 from the fork, and give Heater a call, "Cleared for initial runway 27?" I made a low, fast break in a tight pattern, engine in idle all the way, exhaust popping and complaining, but letting it be known I wasn't adding power to make a correc-tion, then rolled out just above the runway for a good three-pointer, and tax-ied around the west side to my parking spot, where Sergeant Wold and his crew waited.

I grinned under my oxygen mask when I saw Horton and Thomas wait-ing with Glen. To my knowledge, they seldom ventured out onto the perim-eter track. Usually they were all geared up to ask their silly damned questions at the debriefing: where, when, what direction, what time, how many, etc., etc., but today, here they were, looking self-consciously nonchalant in their gar-rison wheel hats and shirt-and-tie uniforms.

I deliberately taxied into the hardstand the wrong way. Glen saw what was happening and moved away from the two intelligence officers. He flagged me in with a commendable flourish and grinned broadly as I swung my tail around with a blast of throttle, sending those wheel hats off their heads across the grass and blowing a couple of neckties straight out in the prop wash. It wasn't a nice thing to do to two good friends, now trying to keep their balance, but look what the hell they had done to me!

I took my time shutting down, unstrapping, filling out the forms, then taking an unnecessary leak behind the tail of my bird, and savoring the walk toward Don and Tommy with all the innocence I could muster as I buttoned my fly. Don was already headed toward me.

"What's up, Don?" I asked. "What're you two guys doing out here on the flight line? Something special?" Don didn't glare, but his look as a captain very much senior to me was certainly expressive. I could see Tommy suppressing a smile, so I knew I was in the driver's seat.

Don barked, "What about the pictures? Did you get them? Did the camera work? Are there—"

"Whoa!" I interrupted. "Let's go on into your office and I'll give you the whole report."

God, I felt smug. It was my turn, and it was going to please me to pull Don's leg just as far as I possibly could. He started to protest, but I was already climbing aboard the waiting jeep with my flight gear. I saw an unfamiliar sergeant removing what had to be the film from that special camera in my bird, and I tried not to laugh out loud thinking about what I was going to report for the benefit of all those staff people up the line.

We drove around the perimeter track as the rest of the group returned to base. Aircraft hit the traffic pattern in twos and fours and I was a little happy to see no victory rolls. That meant I hadn't missed anything interesting.

We entered Don's sanctum and I took a chair opposite his desk. Don was almost twittering with impatience. "Well, damn it, did you get the pictures or not?"

"I don't know, Don."

"What the hell do you mean, you don't know?"

"I mean I turned on the switches just like I was supposed to. The BEFORE pass was a snap and the DURING pass sure got my attention, but I can't know if that damned camera worked. That's your concern, and I guess you won't know till someone processes the film. Oh, incidentally, I made only the first two passes, the BEFORE and the DURING. I skipped the AFTER."

"Damn it!" he yelped. "They particularly wanted those AFTER pictures! Why didn't you get them? Why? My God, 8th will be furious!"

"Well, Don, you can tell the people at 8th Air Force headquarters that the

BEFORE pictures are all they really need to look at. The DURING and AFTER are exactly the same as the BEFORE. And while you are at it, please tell someone down there at Wycombe Abbey to kiss my ass!"

October 30 brought terrible disaster. Good weather over England, also forecast for Europe, turned deadly when the group encountered an immense front over Hamburg. Colonel Zemke, Lieutenant Colonel Herren, and Lieutenant Holmes all went down in the turbulence. They were last seen in the clouds in various stages of uncontrolled spins. One guy witnessed Zemke's wing being torn off. No one had news of any safe landings or parachutes. The pilots who made it home reported pulling 9 g's in recovery, and several of the planes were heavily damaged from the strain. All of us were stunned to know we had lost our group and squadron commanders in one day. Major Jeffrey quickly took over and tried to cheer us up, but we were devastated. We had to go on. There were still missions ahead. You can't survive as a fighter pilot if you dwell on your sorrow much past the first beer.

On November 2, I damaged an Me-109 on the ground, but Major Jeffrey didn't waste any time congratulating me in debriefing. He had other things on his mind when he hauled me into his office and announced, "Robin, you've just about flown out your tour here at Wattisham. Where do you want to go?"

"What? That can't be! Hell, Jeff, I haven't flown that much! I don't want to go home. How do those guys over at Debden and Steeple Morden and Boxted get to stay here for so long?"

Damn! What a fix this was! I hadn't even thought about finishing my sixty-five missions or 270 hours, whatever a tour was. I just assumed I could go on for as long as I wanted to, or perhaps more to the point, as long as they would have me. This was a hell of a piece of news. Here it was, November 1944, and though the war had really swung our way after the invasion, the Germans were a long way from throwing in the towel. How were the Allies going to whip the Third Reich without me?! Well, maybe they could manage—they had done all right before my arrival—but I still didn't want to miss the action. This was where I belonged and I knew it. I was absolutely certain.

The major smiled and told me I had a choice. I could sign on for twenty-five more missions, or go home on R&R for two months and then come back for another full tour. Something about that didn't feel right. Some of the guys in other groups had been over here for a couple of years, even more in some cases. Take Hub Zemke, our great group commander. He'd been over here with USAAFE since day one. Yes, he'd gone down in weather, but we happily learned he had survived and was a POW, so what the hell? Someone wasn't being fully honest with me, or perhaps no one in our outfit knew the ropes like the old-timers.

Colonel Riddle had reassumed group command, and I cornered him in the mess that evening with my problem. He repeated exactly what Jeffrey had told me, so I knew my situation had been discussed. It didn't take long to realize my best course of action was going home. But what home? I didn't have a home. Virginia was out because my dad was gone, stepmother Nina was out in Beverly Hills, and my dear aunt Kitty and uncle Phil were nearby in Van Nuys. California was too far to go. Brother Stevan was still at West Point and I knew I had to see him. He'd bust loose from the Point before Christmas and we could go down to D.C. together. OK, I didn't have a home, but at least I had a plan.

I also knew I'd be MIA as far as the squadron was concerned, and that didn't feel good. Over the previous seven months a deep-rooted camaraderie had developed among the surviving pilots. It wasn't something we talked about, or even consciously considered, but it was real enough. When someone went down, his absence was quickly dismissed after the first beer was raised to him that evening. He wasn't talked about other than a shake of the head and a sincere shrug of "Too bad." This reaction wasn't callous or emotionally self-protective. We had drawn into ourselves, both individually and as a group. Our daily existence was a shared mutuality of survival. Bad things happened, but not to you and not to those still around you. If someone was shot down, obviously he really didn't belong to the group anymore. Thoughts of him had no more relevance or meaning in our daily lives. His bad luck wasn't going to rub off on us.

Those thoughts extended also to pilots who had successfully finished a tour and were about to return to the land of the "Big PX." That individual no longer belonged. You felt it, and he knew it. So if you were one of the lucky ones and had those going-home orders in your pocket, the only thing to do was swallow any sentimental feelings and get the hell out of there as quickly and quietly as possible.

I flew the last eight missions of my first tour by the ninth of November, and did so without enthusiasm. The final mission was a milk run over Metz and my return to Wattisham completed 270 hours of combat time, but I landed with a heavy heart. Sure, I was coming back to the action in January, but somehow that didn't count for much. When I finished my last flight, I became a virtual outcast among my closest friends in the group and still had a week before leaving. It was like being invisible. The psychological impact was a real shocker. Sergeant Wold tried to express his good-byes and best wishes, but as much as I appreciated his thoughts, they didn't alleviate my sense of not belonging anymore. Oh well, time to swallow the blues and go home.

9

★

R&R, Second Tour, and Home

In short order I was on a C-54 headed for New York. The feeling of detachment persisted. The plane was full of returning crew members but we scarcely talked to one another. We were wrapped in our own memories. We seemed to be in a state of decompression. Each of us, whether he knew it or not, was significantly different from the guy who had started flying combat those long months ago.

After processing at Fort Hamilton in Brooklyn, I headed up the Hudson to see Stevan at the Point. West Point was still West Point. Nothing had changed. On the one hand, that was comforting; on the other, I looked at the plebes and wondered how running around with your chin tucked into your collar had ever been considered either character building or military training. Let it be. The strangest thing was the overwhelming sensation that I didn't belong here. The place was dull, dripping-gray dull, and it wasn't just upstate New York in mid-November. There wasn't that electricity in the air that I felt in Britain. The academy exuded an isolated atmosphere, as if nothing mattered beyond those Gothic walls. Not even the war existed. The cadets themselves seemed juvenile, though some of them were older than my twenty-two years. I checked in at the Thayer Hotel and tried talking to some of the officers at the bar. It was a wasted effort. We had nothing in common. I wasn't interested in them, and they certainly didn't give a rat's ass about me. The whole experience was upsetting. I didn't like being an outsider, feeling like a leper. I guess the one positive aspect of the experience was the realization that I was the one who had changed, not the Point. I had to ask myself what I expected of these others, and I came to realize the width of the gulf that existed between those who had been there and those who hadn't.

It was great to see Stevan. We spent as much time together as we could for two days, but I really disliked hanging around the Point during Stevan's classes, so I went up to Stewart Field to put in some flight time and found a haven there. Even if the people there weren't on the same frequency, at least they flew airplanes and I didn't feel so detached. Conveniently there were a few P-51s and P-47s on the ramp. Odd, but no one was too interested in flying them. I was! I had a ball.

I had an encounter at Stewart. I went into base operations after flying for a couple of hours to thank Lieutenant Colonel Benny Webster for the use of one of his birds. Colonel Webster had been a tactical officer during flight training before we graduated and was considered by the cadets to be a truly fine gentleman and officer. I enjoyed seeing him again. My visit was interrupted when I saw an all-too-familiar figure standing at the operations desk. It was Military Bill, my flight instructor from Stewart in the fall of '42, the man who had lined us up for inspection, the guy who had told me I was too big to fly fighters, and the guy who would personally assign me to bombers, IF I even graduated. So now, here we were, two years down the road.

I walked over and said casually, "Hi, Bill."

I watched his face as recognition dawned. He looked at me, checked my captain's bars, and tried hard not to notice the Silver Star, DFC, and Air Medals I wore. I was glad he noticed. The moment offered an opportunity for a bit of payback after the harassment all his students had endured.

"The name is Olds, Bill. Remember me?" The first-name business was an intentional reminder that we were no longer cadet and captain.

"Of course, Olds. Nice to see you again. What are you doing here?" he replied in a deliberately bored tone.

"Oh, just getting some flying time while on R&R. Say, I'll be going back to my outfit in England pretty soon. It's a fine unit: P-51s, great record, lots of action, but we've taken some bad hits these past weeks and are kinda short on pilots. We sure could use some guys with real flying experience. How about coming on over and giving us a hand? I'm slated to become squadron ops when I get back and I'm sure I could arrange it." (Squadron ops was true. The rest? Pure BS.)

"Well, Olds, that's a nice offer, but I figure what I'm doing here is far more important than anything I might contribute over there."

He was satisfied with his safe little slot there in the training business and had reached a point where he didn't even recognize how smug he was about it. I'm not proud of it, but his attitude revolted me. I couldn't possibly know it at the time, but he represented a whole class of air force pilots who were on one side of the fence, and to him, those of us who had been shot at were on the other side. I don't mean to imply that the differentiation was always of a man's own choosing, because many great guys tried and couldn't get to combat. Whether a man did or didn't want to go to combat wasn't the point. What mattered was whether he tried and couldn't, or avoided going and succeeded. Huge difference. It might be wrong to accuse Military Bill of combat reluctance. But I do.

I was the instigator. I pressed my point when I retorted, "Well, Bill, I'm not surprised. I guess I shouldn't have opened my mouth, remembering how you were. Please accept my apologies for making the offer." I'm a bit uncomfortable recalling the thinly veiled distaste I showed for him.

Christmas season arrived and I was back in D.C. Stevan came down for the holiday, and to my surprise we wound up on some kind of select social list. Party invitations piled high, often two a day. Though I couldn't figure out how people knew I was in town, it didn't matter. I guess it was because Stevan had gone to Western High when Dad was stationed here in D.C. just before the war. That had to be it. Though I had dated a few Washington girls when I was a cadet, I wondered if any of them or their friends were still around. Stevan and I plotted a schedule, borrowed a car, and made the rounds.

Some of the affairs were all right, some dull. My problem surfaced quickly. Though most of the young people were my age, I felt ill at ease with them. The girls were all beautiful, and either in college or doing their thing as debutantes. It didn't overcome the fact that they were superficial, self-centered, and dull. We had absolutely nothing in common, since I couldn't carry on the prattle of small talk and local gossip, and they couldn't imagine what to say to someone who must have seemed to be from Mars. I felt awkward and out of place, somehow socially inept, a bit of a misfit. What really ripped it for me was when one young lady turned from our conversation and started speaking French to some pimply-faced guy. I knew enough to catch the drift, and though my French had proved entirely adequate in the bistros of Montmartre after Paris was liberated, this was too much. Stevan was having a ball, so I played the good brother and wingman for the remainder of the evening.

I was bored, and as the holidays wound down I grabbed a train for Atlantic City to see if I could get back to Britain a bit quicker. I met a beautiful girl on the train and spent a few days with her in Philadelphia, so it wasn't a non-stop trip, but that's another story.

I was totally relaxed when I headed off again but ran into another slow-down. Processing in Atlantic City seemed to take forever. I was impatient and the center couldn't understand why I was there ahead of my scheduled time. I thought I was in serious trouble when one of the docs questioned me at length about my eagerness to get back to combat. He voiced a lot of "Hmms" and "I sees," all the while writing stuff I couldn't see down on a pad. It occurred to me he was the local shrink and wasn't sure what to make of me.

Apparently, after a while he judged me reasonably sane, and I was soon on a train headed for the now familiar staging area at Fort Hamilton. There I was assigned a shipment number, along with six other pilots in the same R&R category. The ranking man in our group was a full colonel. He impressed the hell out of us right away. We were standing in front of a Transportation Corps captain's desk and the colonel asked him when our ship was scheduled to sail. The captain squirmed and told us he couldn't divulge that information, what with the war and all, but if the colonel would look out the window over across the room, he would see our ship just now entering New York Harbor. He added that it usually took the *Queen Elizabeth* about six days to turn around.

The colonel fixed the captain with a stern glare and said, "Tell you what we're going to do. You're going to draw us all the usual gas masks and the rest of that useless crap you guys insist on having us carry. You're also going to fill out all the necessary paperwork on us. Meanwhile, we're going to proceed in good military order to the Biltmore Hotel and wait for our shipping date. When that arrives, you're going to give me a call. I'll be responsible for rounding up these troops, and you'll meet us with two staff cars in front of the hotel. You'll have all the paperwork with you, as well as the helmets and gas masks, and we'll proceed to the docks from there. Any questions?"

The poor captain was aghast. His jaw dropped and his eyes gaped. All he could do was nod dumbly as the colonel turned and marched out of the room. We fell into lockstep behind him. Momentarily I felt like kissing a senior officer! The feeling passed quickly.

The six days in New York were time well spent. I called the girl I had met on the train and she more or less moved in with me at the Biltmore. We did the town and each other with gusto. I saw my first Broadway show and loved Mary Martin in *One Touch of Venus*. She had a line, "the triumphant twang of the bedsprings." The days and nights passed with lightning speed. We danced to the big bands, strolled through Central Park at night, listened to Peggy Lee singing love songs, dined at El Morocco, and went to the top of the Empire State Building just for the hell of it. We window-shopped along Fifth Avenue, threw snowballs at each other, and laughed a lot. It was a wonderful time but destined to end quickly.

The call from the colonel finally came. "Get your butt in gear, Olds. It's time to go!" And he meant right NOW.

There wasn't much to pack, just rumpled clothes. Bills were paid, sad farewells made, and I was down at the curb within half an hour. Abiding by his instructions, the captain had arrived with the two staff cars. We all piled in for the short trip to the West Side dock where the *Queen Elizabeth* loomed. Her black hull was larger than a building and totally dominated the hustle and bustle of the loading operation.

The colonel thanked the Fort Hamilton captain and led us to the gangplank. Two military policemen stood there looking very officious, in spite of their youth. The buck sergeant tried to tell our colonel that he and his small group were out of order. This didn't faze the colonel. He pointed out that their duty was to keep people from leaving the ship. Since we obviously intended to board the ship, we neither fell under their authority nor were their responsibility. The perplexed MP stepped aside and we proceeded up the gangplank trying to stifle our laughter.

In the main salon a harried lieutenant colonel sat behind an overloaded desk with a sign proclaiming him to be the troop commander for the duration of our voyage. I wondered how things like that worked out, considering our friend the full colonel, but I was glad it wasn't my issue. I had another problem. To my surprise and emerging horror, I was appointed deputy troop commander for the forward third of this huge ship. The lieutenant colonel mumbled something about my responsibilities, which seemed to include the preservation of "discipline and good order." That didn't bother me until I was told there were roughly seventeen thousand brand-new infantry troops on board. One-third of them were to be my responsibility. My captain's bars suddenly felt mighty insignificant. Five thousand, six hundred and sixty-six combat-bound infantry replacements, and I was supposed to keep order? Holy crap!

The *QE* set sail in the late afternoon. I found a place on the crowded deck and watched in fascination as the New York skyline slipped past. Soon there was Lady Liberty saying good-bye to her youngsters once again. The familiar figure took on an added sentimentality as the ship drew abreast of Ellis Island. I thought of the many thousands she had welcomed, and of the many thousands to whom she had bid a final farewell. Her raised arm against the setting sun as we passed eastward was a personal, throat-tightening gesture. The normally raucous troops fell silent, and you could almost read each youngster's thoughts: Where am I going? Will I ever see home again? God, I miss it already.

The six of us with the colonel had learned we were the only ones on board who already had combat experience. I think that explained the feeling of detachment I felt from all those thousands of young infantrymen. My duties as assistant troop commander turned out to be nothing more than making the rounds. Deck after deck, down into the bowels of the ship, the troops were in eight-tiered bunks with scarcely room to pass down the aisles. Trying to make my way through the compartments, and literally climbing over piles of gear, I couldn't help wondering how anyone thought any of these kids would survive a torpedo attack. The *Queen* sailed alone in crossing after crossing; no convoy for her. She relied on her speed and random course changes to avoid the U-boats. Obviously, the tactic had worked, for here she was in January of 1945 still making her dash to England.

Our trip was mercifully brief, four days and a bit. It was a Sunday when we anchored in the harbor at Gourock, the same port as my first trip. I found the troop commander and asked when the six of us were scheduled to debark. He looked at a long, thick list and found our shipment number very near the end.

I swear he was smirking as he said, "Well, let's see. . . . Ah, here we are, Captain. You Air Corps flyboys will debark Tuesday afternoon. We hope." Whatever his problem might have been, I didn't envy him his job. I thanked him and turned away thinking I wasn't going to stay on this stinking hulk another three days, not for anybody or anything.

I went down to the cabin I had shared with seven others and packed a few things in my B-4 bag. I put on my trench coat, slung the gas mask across one shoulder and my musette bag over the other, donned the helmet, fastened the chin strap, and, feeling well disguised, went to find the nearest exit. Down on the main deck I joined a platoon of infantrymen as they shuffled off onto a barge tied alongside. No one questioned me or paid any attention as the barge filled and shoved off for the dockside railway station.

Once on dry land and fighting my sea legs a bit, I turned for the railway ticket office as the infantry troops were marched away to a waiting troop train. No troop train for me. I went up to the regular ticket window, pulled out a wad of pound notes, and bought myself a first-class ticket to London. I figured it might be wise to spend a few days in that wonderful city before reporting back for duty. Hell, I had come back early, hadn't I? What's more, I was ahead of schedule. I reasoned that the war could get along without me for one more day.

London was, thankfully, very much the same. It didn't take long to get reacquainted and feel back in the swim. But after one day and an evening, duty called, and the next day, January 15, I took the train from Liverpool Street Station for Ipswich and Wattisham. Soon I was enjoying the backslapping greetings of my squadron mates and listening to wildly embellished tales of derring-do in harrowing death-defying flights. All of these adventures, of course, had been heroically accomplished without any help from me. I was just their former buddy who had obviously deserted them and fled home to wallow in the fleshpots and hellholes of parties and sin. Admittedly I had, but I wasn't ready to feel too guilty about having left them to fight off Hitler's winter offensive alone.

I settled quickly into my new responsibilities as squadron ops officer as the days back in the U.S. quickly faded from memory. I flew as often as I reasonably could over the next week, but we were grounded for the entire week of January 21 to January 28 by weather. The weathermen said it was the worst winter in Europe in fifty years: icebox cold, nasty fronts, snow and sleet—wet, damp, freezing stuff. Our only consolation was that the Luftwaffe was grounded, too, but that relief was tempered by thoughts of Allied ground troops freezing their butts off. I gave silent thanks to my father for inspiring me to be a pilot. Grounded but grateful, we pilots threw a plethora of parties.

Word came that Major Jeffrey was being promoted to lieutenant colonel and would soon be moved to the 479th Group as deputy commander. Guess who was being promoted to major and rumored to take Jeff's place as squadron acting CO? Did these guys know what they were in for? They probably did.

On January 24 a slew of new pilots arrived for the 434th. Four of them were bomber guys and would take some training, but they were all good pilots. The 8th Air Force had offered some of their bravest and best bomber pilots an opportunity to transfer to fighters. All they had to do was fly and survive not just one, but two full operational tours in B-17s or B-24s. Once this was completed, they were granted their wish to become fighter pilots. Although we admired their spirit, we knew you didn't just step from two-dimensional to three-dimensional flying with the greatest of ease.

Bomber pilots were very special in their own right. It took barrels of guts to sit helplessly in those big birds plowing through fields of flak and persistent vicious fighter attacks. I probably could have, but no way in hell would I have wanted to. Despite their obvious expertise and experience flying the bombers, getting these men checked out in our Mustangs was a really scary deal. They proved they could take off and land without killing themselves or even bending the birds, but trying to get them to join up, fly close formation, follow the leader in a maneuvering rat race, loop and roll with confidence, and keep track of many aircraft in a roiling, three-dimensional mock dogfight was difficult. To get these pilots to do such things as second nature seemed an impossible task.

There were thousands of young men undergoing pilot and aircrew training at hundreds of bases in 1943 and 1944. It totally amazed me that in all that turmoil, and in those vast numbers, the process of selection functioned with commendable success. Somehow or other our instructor pilots seemed able to perceive a student's inherent capabilities and then to recommend what type aircraft he should fly after getting his wings. There is a marked difference between bomber and fighter pilot attitudes. In training and in combat, you don't just say, "I'm going to think this way or react that way." Your reactions have to be instinctive based on the situation around you. The selection process throughout flight training was as much about a man's attitude as about his flying skill. Men graduated and went on to fly bombers, transports, or fighters based on those instructor assessments. Yes, there were always exceptions, but the assessments usually worked.

We faced a difficult task in trying to bring our bomber converts up to speed as fighter pilots. Simply wanting to be a fighter pilot, even with hundreds of flying hours, isn't always enough. Those of us who had survived were only too aware of how little the normal fighter-trained replacements really knew. Reconditioning the crew-accustomed bomber guys was going to be something else. We had established a phase-in program we called "Clobber College." This involved a lot of local flying and many hours of ground school. We wanted to get the new guys comfortable with our procedures and to give them a running start at the demands of actual combat. The extra work for all of us was well worth the effort. That had been for incoming fighter-trained pilots, however; now we were facing a handful of men who had no fighter background at all, either physically or mentally. They literally had to start from scratch, and we had to convince them this was necessary. Their attitude going in was, "Hell, I'm a seasoned combat pilot, I know how to fly. Check me out in the Spam can and point me toward the enemy!"

I'm sorry to say that the conversion didn't work, at least not in our case.

A week later, I was flying back from some meeting or other and happened to pass over a bomber base near Wattisham that was being "beat up" by a P-51. I saw the fighter make a low pass down the perimeter track by the flight control building, then pull up, turn, and dive for another pass. Buzz jobs on bomber bases were old hat and hardly worth the effort. Besides, they were frowned on by headquarters. So what was this bird doing? It suddenly occurred to me that this might be one of the recently converted bomber boys showing off for his old buddies. I started to circle as the Mustang pilot pulled up at the perimeter of the airfield. He's going to roll, I thought, and, sure enough, there he went. Even at a distance I could see the nose way off line as the aircraft became inverted. The rest was like a slow-motion film. The P-51 stalled and snapped, and the nose went down. The bird spun through two turns and smashed to earth in front of a crowd of spectators. There was an explosion, parts flew in all directions, a brief fireball, and it was over.

I acted on my suspicions, turned, and landed quickly at that airfield. As I taxied on the grass toward flight control, an ambulance and several fire trucks were racing toward the scene of the crash. There didn't seem to be much for any of them to do. I didn't even have to get out of my airplane to learn what I wanted to know. A large piece of the fuselage from the smashed bird lay nearby, its tail number clearly identifying it as a P-51 from the 435th Squadron. What a waste, I thought as I took off back to Wattisham. The group bar would be a grim place that night. A bit of a lecture might be in order for the 434th fighter neophytes.

The weather was shit for a few days at the start of February, but once it cleared I was full of piss and vinegar and ready to get back at it. On February 3, I put my name on one truck with one trailer and shared a locomotive kill credit with Jenkins. Later that evening, I bagged one eager and beautiful British girl. No sharing there!

February 9 turned into quite a fine day. First thing in the morning, I pinned on shiny new oak-leaf clusters and officially became a major. Better yet, we ran into a flock of Me-109s and enjoyed reasonable success. By this period in the air war the group had settled into a daily routine of bomber escort. One squadron flew the close-escort effort as prescribed in the ops order, which meant staying close to the stream so the bomber crews knew someone cared about them. The bomber crews liked to see some friendly fighters around them. The second squadron flew area sweeps; their job was to rove within 15 or 20 miles of the bomber stream, hopefully putting themselves between the force and any attacking fighters.

The third squadron flew what we called "outlaw." That was the preferred mission. Take off any time you wanted, and catch the Luftwaffe force either forming up for their attack or trying to return to their bases afterward. This took experience, planning, and a bit of luck for those of us pulling this duty.

On this particular day, the 434th pulled close-escort duty and I was leading the flight. We took off as scheduled with a minimum package of twelve Mustangs and ground our way along with the big boys toward Stuttgart at 27,000 feet. The weather wasn't all that good. Broken clouds ranged in various decks right down to the ground, and off to the southeast a formidable front, like a gray wall, stretched away to the southwest.

I had just turned the 434th around the backside of our box of bombers and was heading parallel to their course on the right side of the stream, when I spotted a gaggle of shadowy contrails sneaking along the top of that cirrus bank and headed in the direction of our bombers. I was about to turn to intercept them when the 435th flight sailed past just to my right. I wondered what in hell they were doing so close to the bombers. By all rights those enemy fighters (and that's all they could have been) were their responsibility. I held my turn and watched the 435th go scurrying along out of sight. My God, a whole squadron, and it was obvious not one of them had spotted the enemy.

As soon as the 435th cleared, I dropped my externals, turned, and headed my bunch to intercept the rapidly closing bandits. Soon, the German leader saw us coming and, knowing the jig was up, broke off his attack. His formation turned into a gaggle of individual aircraft as we piled into them. All this time my outfit had uttered not a single word. We prided ourselves on radio discipline, and we fought that whole fight in silence. It was a weird one.

We ended up with the battle swirling along and then into the huge squall line. It was like flying into the proverbial milk bottle. I had managed to knock one Me-109 down quickly and went after another just as he entered the cloud. I concentrated on my adversary and hoped he was a good instrument pilot. Without a horizon, there was no up, no down, no left or right. There was also no "seat of the pants" to believe in. I closed on the 109, trying to get my gun sight on him, when everything went to hell at once. I could feel my bird staggering and shuddering, but wanted to get off at least one burst before I lost everything. To my amazement, the 109 snapped, and then spun straight up! Hell no, that wasn't up, it had to be down . . . and both of us must have been nearly inverted when we stalled. To hell with the German, Robin! Get your head in the cockpit. Get those gyrating instruments sorted out, and recover from this spin. I knew I had plenty of altitude, so I didn't rush things. Horror stories of pilots pulling the wings off in their haste to recover from similar situations flashed through my mind. I stayed cool as I sorted the situation, then recovered from the spin and pulled back to level flight.

So then why did I start shaking almost uncontrollably when I got the beast flying straight and level, headed more or less to the west? The whole incident had happened so quickly, was so intense and disorienting, that I'd had no time to be afraid. Adrenaline was pumping, and my reaction after the sudden return to the normalcy of the steady, soothing hum of the Mustang engine in the relative security of my snug cockpit made everything let go at once. I remember being glad to be alone in my plane, without a witness to my aftershock.

As was normal after an aerial battle, we straggled back to England in pairs or as singles. A few of us managed to join up over the North Sea to give the ground troops a victory roll or two when we entered the traffic pattern at Wattisham. I was enjoying the exuberance in the ready room when I was accosted by the major who had led the area support squadron. I won't say he was boiling, but he certainly wasn't in a very pleasant mood. More precisely, he was sputtering.

"What the hell were you doing down south of the bombers? Your mission was close support! How come you deserted your position next to the big friends? Why didn't you call out those bandits to me? We were the ones who should have intercepted. . . .!" Blah blah blah, he went on and on while I tried to keep a straight face. It wasn't easy, especially when I caught my guys smirking behind his back as they pretended not to listen to the major ranting and raving.

"Gee, Major, I'm sorry," I finally managed to blurt. "When you went sailing right across the front of that gaggle I thought you must have had a more threatening target in sight, so I had to head 'em off before they could get to the bombers. Did I do something wrong?"

"Yes, you damn well did, and you're going to pay for it."

I wasn't too worried because, despite what appeared to be my insubordination, by this time in the war we all knew that the term "pursuit pilot" had long gone out of use. We were FIGHTER pilots. We didn't pursue; we fought the enemy when we found him. It didn't take long before the guys actually doing the fighting stopped listening to the staff officers trying to run their lives from various headquarters. The poor bomber boys did as they were ordered. They really had no choice. Sure, there were several magnificent exceptions when an individual bomber crew or the leader of a formation of big friends managed to find some latitude to deviate in good cause from the prescribed routine, but such actions were rare. That latitude just didn't usually exist for them. On the other hand, as fighter pilots in small, fast aircraft, we had the maneuverability and the opportunity to pretty well do as we saw fit, particularly when we did so for the good of the bombers. Flying close escort was great for bomber morale but lousy for their protection. Imagine trying to stop a determined attack from six o'clock high by some hundred or so enemy fighters when you start from line abreast with their target. It wasn't your best place to be.

On February 14 I sent the Jerries a Valentine by blasting three enemy aircraft out of the sky southwest of Berlin. Two Me-109s and one Fw-190 bit the dust, and I gave each one the finger as he fell away. I got another one on the ground on the twentieth. The score was adding up! I was earning my keep as a fighter pilot!

That was why I was so stunned when, only a few days later, Jeff called me over and announced, "Robin, the military police have a warrant for your arrest."

"What?! What in hell are you talking about? Warrant for what?"

Jeff looked me right in the eye but couldn't quite hide a gleam of amusement at my distress. I caught that and relaxed somewhat, but not totally.

"You're wanted for desertion in the face of the enemy."

"Desertion in the face of the enemy? You have to be fucking kidding me! What the hell do they mean? Christ's sake, I just knocked down a couple of Jerries, been flying missions like mad, hitting stuff on the ground. . . ."

By now Jeff was openly laughing. "You left the *Queen Elizabeth* without proper orders and didn't show up at the replacement depot where you were supposed to be processed. No one knew where you were, so they figured you had deserted. I guess you know the penalty, usually a firing squad in time of war. Surely they taught you all about that at West Point."

"Jeff, shit, I just thought I'd go down to London for a day. . . ."

"Oh hell, Robin, relax! We told them you were here and scarcely in desertion considering the amount of flying you've done, let alone the fact that you've knocked down three Jerries in the past two weeks. Got your attention, though, didn't I?"

I had been had, again! Maybe I needed to lighten up.

March rolled around with sunshine for two consecutive days and everyone began shouting, "Spring is here at last!" But overcoats and woolies came out again almost immediately. Spring was, most definitely, not here yet. I led a bunch of bomber escort and patrol missions between the second and seventeenth but net kills were zero. The most fun during that dry stretch was my first encounter with the new German jets, the Me-262s.

We were over Magdeburg at 29,000 when I saw six little specks turning toward us from the northeast. They had to be German. No one else flew like that. None of our group, or anyone else escorting the bomber force, had reason to be out where those bogeys were. With full confidence in my identification, I called them out as bandits and turned into them. The whole squadron turned with me. The specks took form and came at us with amazing speed, nearly head-on. I focused on the bandit at my two o'clock and turned as hard as I could to get him in my sights before he came into range. Our closure was too fast and I realized I couldn't get my nose around in time to get a head-on shot. The aircraft looked like a greenish shark with a fuselage flat on the bottom and tapered to a rounded top. The nose jutted forward in a clean and beautiful sweep, and an engine pod hung under each wing. I saw all this in a flash as the jet swept past not 50 yards to my left, and I'll never know why he didn't fire. He had me dead to rights on that pass.

I turned to give chase, but by the time I got around, the jets were out of range in the distance. I could see Bison Squadron giving chase off to my left. They were somewhat ahead of my position, not having turned into the bandits as I had. Bison's contrails stood out sharply against the clean blue sky. Feeling certain the German leader had them in sight, I dropped down a few hundred feet to get below the contrail level and turned to the right of the Jerries' position. My only chance to close would come if the jet leader turned to his right, down and away from Bison Squadron. He did just that. I turned farther right to intercept them as they cut north across my flight path. Again, I couldn't match their speed, and the only shot I took was made in sheer frustration, totally out of range. The departing jets quickly disappeared.

Luckily, the jets didn't strike the bombers that day. There was some consolation in that, but I thought hard about how to deal with those beauties in the future. Anticipation would be our greatest asset—that, and following them to their home bases, hoping to catch them low on fuel and in the landing pattern. It meant we had some research to do in the intelligence files to find out what we could about these airplanes: where they were based, their flight duration, and what tactics these men had developed for their new machines.

Looking back, I can't help wondering why we weren't just given that information by the operations and intelligence people up at ETO Fighter Command. I needn't have wondered. Those of us flying against the defenses of North Vietnam twenty years later weren't informed either. It seems the vital information was so secret that only the North Vietnamese and the American intelligence people had a need to know. Those of us getting shot at weren't cleared for such highly secret stuff.

Encounters with the Me-262s became routine. We learned to insert ourselves between them and the bombers. This seemed to discourage them for the most part. I never did get a decent shot at one of them, but a few of the Newcross pilots did manage to get into their traffic pattern with some success. Major Jeffrey would get the first Me-262 kill for the group. By then we all knew the jets were faster but couldn't turn worth shit. We scornfully called them the "blow jobs."

Real action came again on the nineteenth, when I was leading sixteen guys on a bomber escort and fighter sweep. We sighted bogeys at 8,000 over the Münster area, a mixed bag of about eighteen Me-109s and Fw-190s flying a P-51 U.S.-style formation in elements of two. That really pissed me off, but I had to admit, these guys were exceptionally competent, aggressive, and fearless. We got into a hell of a tangle, with everyone split-S'ing all over the place. As good as they were, we were far better. The proof was in the final score: 434th Squadron got six, Germans zero. Two of them were mine, one Me-109 and one Fw-190. It was a very good day, and we earned an exceptionally memorable O club party that night.

I took official command of the squadron toward the end of March. We finished the month with a tally of twenty-five missions flown over Germany and many more kills for the group. Taking over the squadron meant taking over the CO's log, and I took great liberty in adding important and memorable events. A teletype was slipped anonymously under my door late one evening. No one knows who composed the epistle, but it was noteworthy:

CLAYBAUGH-COUCH
MOUSE OFFENSIVE . . . .
LATEST TELETYPE: H2020 25 MAR 45 . . . USING MT (QMMODELS)*
SGTS CLAYBAUGH AND COUCH IN TWO SWEEPS OVER THE LOCKER ROOM SCORED TWO DAMAGED AND TWO PROBABLES IN THE OPENING PHASES OF THE 434TH'S MOUSE OFFENSIVE THIS MORNING. ON A RECON MISSION HELD LATER IN THE DAY ONE OF THE PROBLEMS GOT AWAY. *MOUSE TRAPS, QUARTERMASTER MODELS.

26 MAR 45 CONTINUING WITH MOUSE OFFENSIVE SGT CLAYBAUGH GOT TWO CONFIRMED THIS MORNING, SGT COUCH ACTED AS TOP-COVER. LT PALMER ABORTED.

27 MAR 45 CHECK-UP OF ALL POINTS IN THE LOCKER ROOM REVEAL THAT MICE HAVE BEEN REDUCED TO CARRYING OUT SNEAK-RAIDS AT NIGHT. NO MISSION WAS CONDUCTED AS TWO MT'S WERE OUT FOR 100-HOUR INSPECTION. IN THE AFTERNOON'S MISSION SGT. COUCH GOT ONE MOUSE CONFIRMED AND ONE PROBABLE. SGT. CLAYBAUGH SIGHTED TWO BUT WAS TOO BUSY BITCHING ABOUT THE MICE BEING DEMOCRATS TO MAKE A KILL. LT. PALMER, AS USUAL, ABORTED.

LOCKER ROOM PERSONNEL, PILOTS AND VISITORS ARE CAUTIONED AGAINST NIBBLING ANY STRAY BITS OF CHEESE OR CANDY AS THESE MATERIALS ARE PART OF SECRET WEAPON. ANYONE HAVING A STRAY BRITISH BISCUIT PLEASE CONFER WITH SGT. CLAYBAUGH AS LATEST S-2 REPORTS CLAIM THAT ENGLISH MICE PREFER THEM FOR BAIT. 234567890- #@%^& OUT.

Finally spring weather arrived the first two weeks of April. Softball games erupted, and lots of pale skin emerged after the long dreary winter. We flew with enthusiasm as it became obvious that the war was winding down. We shot the shit out of airdromes all over Germany, strafing anything we could find. Our attacks were met by only light flak and small-arms fire. I downed one Me-109 in the air and also damaged an Me-262 and an Me-410. I destroyed six planes on the ground. Five of those were on the sixteenth, when we had great fun on a "freelance" mission to the Reichersberg, Kirchen, and Eferding airdromes. The squadron destroyed twenty-one aircraft and damaged seven at those 'dromes that day. Göring's Luftwaffe was largely crippled by this time. The mighty Huns had fallen to their knees under the daily Allied onslaught. By the end of the month, we knew it was all over.

10

★

Going Home

On May 8, Nazi Germany collapsed and gave herself up to the Allies. Words failed me for the squadron log that day and for many days after. Six long, bloody years were finally over for Europe. In celebration, everyone at Wattisham either went to bed or played in the sun. Churchill announced the end of hostilities over the wireless, and Colonel Riddle addressed the group, congratulating the officers and men on a year of good work by the 479th. Church bells in the villages were ringing wildly. Imagine the bells in London! That evening, we had parties at the Rocker Club, the Little Wheels Club, and the Red Cross. The celebration went on through the night; most of the men drank themselves silly, except for an unlucky few who had guard and KP the next day.

After V-E Day, things were strange. Now that the shooting had stopped, you'd think everyone would be anxious to get home. Not so. There were many of us who felt let down. It was a weird "now what do we do?" emptiness. Luckily, there was plenty to keep us occupied. My job was to tell the squadron what was next: our possible transfer to the South Pacific, and the training program ahead. We flew large formations all over Germany and the Low Countries. These were to emphasize the reality of the war's end before the ground occupation was established and some form of postwar government was in place. I had something else to think about. Immediately after the formal signing of the surrender terms, a telegram arrived at Wattisham. It was from USSTAF (U.S. Strategic Air Forces, which later became USAFE), and it ordered me to proceed immediately to headquarters just outside Paris. On arrival I was to report to General Carl A. "Tooey" Spaatz's office for further instructions.

Wow! Me, a lowly major way down on the totem pole, reporting to the four-star who commanded all of the Allied air power in Europe? Spaatz and my dad had been close friends and we had lived next door to each other at Langley Field when I was just a teenager. It still felt uncomfortable to be singled out. Regardless, I dug out my best uniform, grabbed my shaving kit, and took off in my Mustang for the Villacoublay Airdrome.

A staff car met me and delivered me to the front door of an imposing building, where I found my way to the commanding general's office. There, a master sergeant informed me I was expected at the general's château *"tout de suite."* After another short car ride, I was delivered to the château. I pulled the bell chain beside a massive ornate wooden door. After a long interval (enough to make me wonder if the driver had possibly made a mistake), the door opened and there stood Lieutenant Colonel Sally Bagby, known throughout the theater as the general's personal aide. The colonel informed me that I was early, the general was having a nap, the guests weren't due to arrive for another forty-five minutes, and I could find the bar in the corner of the main salon. Obviously, some kind of gathering was planned, and for an unknown reason, I was part of it.

I found the bar easily. Without asking, I poured myself a stiff scotch. Good stuff, too! The room was beautiful, with a high painted ceiling, dark oak paneling, oil paintings, antique fixtures, Oriental rugs, and comfortable-looking furniture, all dominated by the floor-to-ceiling windows overlooking a formal garden framed by trees. There was an almost unreal view of the Eiffel Tower in the far distance. The effect was like a sixteenth-century painting. I sipped my drink and leaned comfortably against the bar, not wanting to be seated when the rest of the crowd arrived.

The room gradually filled. I realized I was looking at men whose names and positions were known to the world: Eaker, Vandenberg, Stratemeyer,

Quesada, Norstadt, Doolittle, Patridge, Strothers, and more. I had never personally seen a three-star, let alone a four, and I felt as out of place as a pig at a party. I made plenty of room at the bar as some of the generals gave me a glare that said, "I don't give a damn, but who the hell are you?" Others simply ignored me completely, which was fine. I backed into the corner near the window and waited to see what would happen.

Voices rose as the room buzzed with excitement. There was loud laughter and a great deal of backslapping and hand shaking. It made me think of a locker room after a hard-fought football victory, but that was a really pallid comparison. These men had played large individual roles in achieving total victory over the German enemy. They were among their peers and seemed to let down some of the barriers of restraint and detachment usually exercised by men of their position.

Suddenly, there was a pause and everyone turned to the far end of the room. General Spaatz stood at the top of a broad flight of stairs. The crowd broke into cheers and there were cries of "Welcome back, boss!" as the ranking men expressed their unbridled respect for the leader they had followed to this victory.

General Spaatz acknowledged their greetings with self-deprecating waves of his hands as he came halfway down the stairs. He seemed to be looking over the crowd for someone. He stopped, looked right at me standing in the corner, waved, and shouted, "Hi, Robin! God it's good to see you. Glad you made it."

A murmur of disbelief followed him as he ignored everyone else and came across the room to my corner.

He put his arm around my shoulders and led me away, saying, "Come on, let's go into my poker room. We can't talk in here, and I have lots to tell you. Then I want to hear all about you."

Needless to say, I was flabbergasted, but the Old Man put me at ease as we entered the game room and sat at his green-covered poker table. An enlisted aide brought him a cocktail and asked if I wanted anything. I declined, thinking I'd better keep my wits about me.

After telling me my father would have been proud of me (which brought a lump to my throat), General Spaatz went on to relate his experiences at the surrender ceremony. He described how the Russians had toasted every signature with a shot of vodka, which naturally had to be answered in kind. By the time the envoy from Lithuania had his turn, his aides had to help him to the signing table. The general laughed and confessed he wasn't feeling too spry himself by that time and was glad his signature was one of the first. He went on to tell me of the new weapons of war the Germans had been developing: manned rocket interceptors, larger V-2s, better fighters, and a host of equipment that might well have prolonged the war by years. Apparently, the Allied crossing of the Rhine was not just timely, but extremely decisive.

I felt as though General Spaatz were my father. His manner was warm and personal, not at all military. He looked at me a moment and said, "Robin, I have some advice for you. You've told me you intend staying in the service. That's good and I'm glad. Now, I know advice is cheap and often suspect, but here goes. You've had a good start and there's a long road in front of you, but always remember this: Your most difficult problem will be the people. In the military, they mostly divide themselves into four major categories: There are the 'me-firsters,' the 'me-tooers,' the 'deadwood,' and the 'dedicated.' You are among the minority, the 'dedicated.' Stick with them, search them out, and work hard to be worthy of their company. You won't be popular with a lot of your bosses who act dedicated but really aren't, and that can make life difficult at times. Beware of the 'deadwood.' Most of them mean well and, in their own way, try hard, are loyal, and are even useful. But too often they'll botch things up and get you and your outfit in trouble.

"Watch out for the 'me-tooers.' These guys will tell you whatever they think you want to hear. They borrow thoughts and ideas from others and present them to you as though they were their own. They are the opportunists who look for every avenue to advance themselves, without sticking their own necks out. They ride someone's coattails and try to make themselves indispensible to the boss. Believe me, they are not to be trusted. You don't want yes-men around you, but you can't always avoid them."

Spaatz went on to warn, "The worst and most dangerous are the 'me-firsters.' Most of them are intelligent and totally ruthless. They use the service for their own gain and will not hesitate to stick a knife in your back at the slightest indication you might stand in their way. They seem arrogant, but don't be fooled. They are really completely lacking in true self-confidence. Do you understand all that?"

I nodded, knowing that if I didn't understand all of it in that moment, I sure as hell would remember and understand it in the future.

General Spaatz smiled and stood up. He reached out and shook my hand as he said, "Well, I've kept those great people out there waiting long enough."

He reached into the inside pocket of his Eisenhower jacket and pulled out a large bundle of francs neatly wrapped by a rubber band. "Here, Robin, take this. Those guys out there don't know their contributions at this poker table will be used to aid and abet the delinquency of a junior officer. Don't try to refuse. I've had Sally set up a driver and a staff car for you. It's out front. Get out of here and get lost in Paris. I'm sure you'll find lots to amuse yourself."

A general is not to be disobeyed. In Paris the money could buy a lot. I wound up with six bottles of champagne and three very affectionate girls who may have been professionals at this sort of thing. In the morning the girls were gone. So were my watch and wallet. My clothes, however, were cleaned, pressed, and neatly folded beside the bed. The hotel owner took pity on me, fed me for the remainder of my stay, and then had his wife drive me to the airdrome. I pondered General Spaatz's words during that flight home. In fact, I pondered his words for the rest of my career.

When I returned to Wattisham, six days past my authorized two-day leave, serious instruction and orientation for the South Pacific ensued. The men endured long lectures about mosquitoes, snakes, and lice, how to purify water, read maps, and avoid malaria and yellow fever, all while fighting the Asian enemy. We watched films on how to survive in the jungle, how to not get venereal diseases (far more interesting films than how to avoid bug bites), and a couple of shorts on Japan, reminding us why we were at war. Mixed in with this serious stuff were orders on increasing exercise. We all took that very seriously. Volleyball games became brutal. Men got hurt playing softball. Boxing matches drew blood. The enlisted men returned to the rifle range and remembered they were in the army. Pilots studied stacks of photos of Japanese aircraft and flew a few training missions. Best of all, some of our pilots who had been POWs came back for a quick visit before heading home. Imagine our happiness at seeing Hub Zemke, Al Tucker, Frank Keller, Tom Neeley, Ronald Maley, and Ossie Duval. Many pints of ale were downed and spilled as we greeted our missing pals.

June brought more training, more exercise, more inspections, longer showers, more pub crawling, three-day and longer passes, personnel transfers, and the establishment of the Wattisham Kennel Club for the many pampered dogs collected over the months. A station field day was held, involving three-legged races, bicycle obstacle races, volleyball tournaments, and even an air show put on by four of us. Major Pierce juiced up the performance by making a spectacular forced landing when his engine went out over the field. A picnic of fried chicken and ice cream was followed by a baseball game, dancing, beer, and quite probably the conception of a few children. Toward the end of the month came the official announcement that the group would leave England sometime in September. Based on May and June, how in the hell would we keep busy enough to stay out of trouble for two more months?

Life at Wattisham took on a form of normalcy for the rest of the summer. The news about going to the Pacific for the invasion of Japan was reinforced by the assignment of some fourteen brand-new P-47Ms to my squadron. Though no formal announcement was made, we were told to check ourselves out and do some training in these new birds, just in case. Since we still had more than a full complement of P-51s, about thirty of them, plus what we called "war wearies," and since none of us had anything else to do, we flew our butts off. Dogfights right above the base were a common occurrence as we sought to establish bragging rights in the different types of birds.

Part of our time was spent ferrying aircraft to Liverpool or to a base called Langford Lodge near Belfast. I took a P-38 over there one beautiful day. The bird had less than twenty hours' flying time on it and even smelled new. Before I had even finished signing all the transfer paperwork at Langford, a scruffy bunch of workers cut the tail booms off with acetylene torches and pushed it off to a trash heap. I nearly cried at the waste of a wonderful airplane.

The weeks wore on. We flew and we played volleyball. We went to London pubs and staggered back to base to fly some more. We partied at other bases and threw parties at ours. We weren't bored but, without making a big deal out of it, we missed the excitement and sense of danger that had anchored our existence for the previous year. I suppose it happens after every great conflict, but we found ourselves somehow adrift. We weren't unhappy; we just felt in limbo, impatient for direction and meaning.

August came, and with it screaming black headlines:

ATOMIC BOMB DROPPED ON JAPAN!

Then three days later: SECOND GIANT BOMB HITS NAGASAKI!

Then on September 2: JAPAN SURRENDERS. V-J DAY CELEBRATED AROUND THE WORLD!

Just as on V-E Day, we were confined to the base. It didn't make us feel too good to see the pictures in the British tabloids of celebrations in Times Square, Trafalgar Square, and Piccadilly Circus, women being mobbed by soldiers and sailors and a lot of vice versa. In the squadron ready room, someone muttered, "What's that goddamn sailor doing in Times Square? Why isn't he aboard ship somewhere?" To say we were jealous would be putting it mildly.

The rest of August following the bombing of Japan passed without fanfare. We continued to fly, but there was no enthusiasm in it. Those who had the tour points went home. There were celebrations, but no farewells. People I had fought alongside or had known in the squadron were there one day and gone the next.

As always, rumors abounded: The squadron was being sent to the occupation forces in Germany instead of the Pacific and volunteers were needed to stay on. I volunteered but couldn't find anyone to accept my offer. By the end of the month, morale had gone down the tubes. Everyone was now anxious to get on with it, whether that meant a new assignment or a long-awaited return to civilian life and a job at home.

At the end of August, the group adjutant called. "Come over to my office, Robin. Your orders have arrived."

I hustled over and Lieutenant Colonel Stenton handed me a TWX. I stared at it.

MAJOR ROBIN OLDS, USAAF, FR26046, WILL PROCEED ON OR ABOUT 010945 TO THE ZONE OF INTERIOR AND REPORT TO THE COMMAND-ING GENERAL OF THE PORT OF DEBARKATION FOR FURTHER OR-DERS. AIR TRANSPORTATION IS AUTHORIZED.

This was followed by the usual hieroglyphics spelling out travel and pay-ment authority for those who knew and cared about such things. There was no signature, and no further information.

I stared at the paper in disbelief. Hell, I didn't want to go home. Sure, the war was over here in Europe and in the Pacific, but life was good, the flying great, and I enjoyed being the CO of the 434th Fighter Squadron. Why go home? To what?

"Colonel, what's this about?" Obviously someone wanted me, but didn't want me to know anything until I returned Stateside. There had to be an an-swer.

"Beats me, Robin. You know as much as I do. See this? That symbol means the message came from the Pentagon. I figure somebody wants you real bad. Wish I could tell you more." He rose and shook my hand. "Good luck. Maybe we'll be seeing each other again someday, maybe not. In any event I wish you the best."

I found our group commander, Colonel Riddle, and tried to plead my case. Riddle looked at the paper, thought for a moment, and said, "Looks like they want you for something, Robin. Guess you're going to have to go."

That was the end of that. No more 434th, no more unrestricted flying and camaraderie, no more trips to London, just this new beginning, totally mysterious and unknown. Parting was too abrupt to allow time to feel emotional. I disappeared from the BOQ and Wattisham in the same invisible fashion as those before me.

Someone flew me up to Prestwick on the west coast of Scotland. There were a few hours spent processing paperwork, but still no clue about my final destination. There were several raised eyebrows at the form and wording of my orders, but what the hell, the war was over and everything was in turmoil. Everybody wanted to go home, and a single major's fate was about as important as a grain of sand on the beach. The next morning I was on a C-54 headed for the States.

The canvas seats lining the sides of the four-engine C-54 were not exactly the lap of luxury. They were designed for quick conversion to cargo or litters for wounded; but no invention of man except a sandpaper-covered toilet seat could have been more uncomfortable. It worked for airborne troops loaded with equipment and sitting on their parachutes. You felt as though your butt were drooped in a washbowl with the front edges cutting into the backs of your legs. A webbing of sorts provided no back support at all, and the ribs of the fuselage gouged if you leaned back.

Well, at least it's for only seventeen, maybe eighteen hours, I thought as I tried to squirm into a more comfortable position. After three or four hours of misery I gave up, took the thin seat cushion for a pillow, and stretched out on the metal flooring. Nearly everyone else followed suit, grabbed duffels as pillows and lay down on the floor, to the dismay of the loadmaster. The crusty old sergeant tried to enforce regulations and get us back into our seats. Finally, he got the aircraft commander involved. We told them both to go to hell. What were they going to do, throw us out? The pilot angrily slammed the door to the cockpit and the loadmaster shrugged. He'd done his duty and the problem had been successfully passed up the line in good GI fashion. His last avenue for discipline was to leave the cabin lights full bright. We didn't care. We were bone tired, war weary, physically and emotionally spent. This was the beginning of an adrenaline letdown and combat decompression.

Nothing much mattered. We were going home, strangers all, sharing the emotion without any talk. Each of us looked around, hoping to see a kindred soul, or at least someone who looked as though he had been in the same part of the war. You might have thought we'd be exuberant or excited. Not so. I think we were all too tired, immersed in our own thoughts, withdrawn. I lay on that metal floor and thought of the fate that had taken so many of my friends and left me physically unharmed yet emotionally drained. This last surprised me. I don't think any of us were aware of our psychological condition as long as we were together in the squadron. Perhaps it had been a holdover from those evenings when we didn't count the empty chairs, when death was something that happened to others, not you. Suppression of your emotions allows you to cope, but it isn't necessarily good for you.

The tension among us gradually disappeared as the plane flew on above the featureless North Atlantic. Most of the men slept fitfully. The hours passed slowly for those of us unable to sleep. The drone of the engines and the steady vibration of the aircraft faded into the background. I felt as though I were in a semihypnotic trance. There was nothing to do but stare up at the cabin ceiling and wait for this to end. I hadn't thought to bring a book. I couldn't get at the notepaper in my luggage, and conversation with my fellow passengers had ceased. I finally fell asleep, but awoke when I sensed a change in the engines' power settings. We were letting down into Keflavík, Iceland, a welcome break in the monotony of the flight. We were allowed off to stretch our legs. The place hadn't changed since December 1944. Once again, I thanked God I had never been stationed there.

The break was brief, and then we were back on board for the long final leg home. On we droned through a black night. After several hours, there was a stir of excitement as someone yelled, "Land!" We pulled ourselves up off the floor and seats to press our faces to the tiny windows on the starboard side of the ship. We were rewarded with a formless black mass, unpunctuated by any discernible features, not even a solitary light. We had to be over the northeast coast of Canada. Our journey was still far from over. In those monotonous hours, I grew to dislike that C–54 as though it were a living thing. Except for the fact that it hadn't fallen into the Atlantic, it had nothing to recommend it. I again gave silent thanks to the Fates for making me a fighter pilot.

Finally, as the dark faded into a gray gloom, we saw twinklings of the coast of New England and then the blazing lights of New York City. I remember trying to control a lump in my throat, not from elation, but from a sudden wave of gratitude at being alive mixed with sadness at the thought of the thousands and thousands of young Americans who would never return.

With an audible chirp of tires our big bird settled onto the runway at La-Guardia, taxied in, and stopped. We were home! The engines shut down and we all stood, preparing to disembark. Not so fast! We were told to sit. The door at the front of the plane opened and an officious-looking army captain entered. He carried a clipboard and literally quivered with self-importance as he made his way toward the rear of the cabin handing each of us a sheet of instructions. He returned to the front and announced that we had landed at LaGuardia. No shit? Then he gave us a lecture on the importance of the "in-processing" we would be receiving at Fort Hamilton. We were admonished that our behavior would be closely monitored by the military police, and we were advised that appointments and locations on our handout sheet should be scrupulously followed. His Good Conduct Medal fairly palpitated as we gave him a royal raspberry. I noted his newly created Victory Medal and kind of envied him. None of us had one yet.

We were herded off the plane in a sorry semblance of military order, all of us in tacit agreement to give the little prick a hard time. We knew we'd ultimately follow what was ordained, but there was no point in making life easy for him. To hell with that! Any semblance of order quickly disappeared as we spontaneously broke into a dead run for the soda fountain someone spotted at the end of the terminal. The soda jerk saw us coming and immediately lined his counter with bottles of milk. He knew the syndrome well. The milk in Europe had been taboo according to the docs, the powdered stuff was like paste, and we longed for the fresh American farm product. That fountain guy could have made a small fortune if he'd wanted to. I know I would have paid three times what he asked, without question.

Our milk cravings satisfied, we boarded the waiting bus in better humor. Somehow a dull spell had been cast aside, and there was laughter and shouting as the bus proceeded across Brooklyn to Fort Hamilton. Once there, we were ushered into an empty bay in a two-story barracks building, told to find a cot, pointed to the location of the latrine, and advised that reveille would be at 5:00 A.M. Reveille, for God's sake? None of us had been subjected to that horror since cadet days. If mission briefing was scheduled at 5:00 A.M. we'd be there. If we weren't flying that day, we slept in. Simple. But this? Reveille? Christ almighty.

Our Transportation Corps captain burst out laughing as he left us. It dawned on us that we had been had. Fair enough. He proved himself to be a decent sort and we had been foolish to play games with him on his home turf. Tomorrow would take care of itself. Twenty tired bodies happily hit the hay.

The next morning we were up well before six. Who could sleep? We were back home and raring to get cracking. Breakfast was a veritable feast: bacon, fresh eggs, sausage, good coffee, quarts of milk, as much as we could hold. I confess I missed the Hovis bread in England. It was great toasted and would have been wonderful with all that real butter and strawberry jam.

"In-processing" was as expected: long lines, shuffling forward to the finance window, signing papers for some corporal, rolling up the sleeves for more shots. God, the army must have stockpiled serum against the needs of the next century! Then dropping the pants for a short-arm inspection, all to be endured, all routine, all army.

I was getting impatient to learn what the commanding general had in store for me in those mysterious orders. Surely it was something important. I felt a little miffed that everyone else in my polyglot group seemed to know where he was headed. Not me. I got only blank stares when I tried to find out. Around two in the afternoon, I found myself standing before a chest-high counter with a bored-looking lieutenant wandering about behind it. Several enlisted aides sat at desks scattered about the room.

The lieutenant finally noticed me. "Orders," he barked, and tapped the countertop.

This hadn't started well. I glared at him as any good combat veteran with two rows of ribbons and major's leaves on his shoulders should and growled, "You speaking to me, Lieutenant?"

The lieutenant must have suffered from some misguided sense of power. "Orders!" he repeated, and tapped the counter again. This wasn't getting me anywhere so I slapped a copy of my TWX under his nose. He glanced at it with a sneer of contempt, pushed it back at me, and said, "OK, Major, what's this supposed to be? Where are your orders?"

"I don't know!" I snapped. "Those are my orders. I didn't write the goddamn thing but it got me here all right. Now where's this general I'm supposed to see?"

"The general?" he repeated.

"Look at the damned paper, Lieutenant! What's it say? Read it!" I didn't mean to shout, but this twerp had really pissed me off.

"I can't accept that piece of paper," he said. "It's not proper. Orders have to be validated. Any officer knows that. I ought to ask for your identification. Nobody comes here claiming something like that as orders. Where are your orders?" This lieutenant was quickly becoming a gold-plated son of a bitch. He was also getting damned close to a bloody nose.

"Look, goddamn it, that piece of paper was good enough to make me leave my squadron, it got me on an airplane all the way here to this stupid office, and it's going to be good enough to get me to whatever assignment your general has in mind. Now read it again and call the general, or somebody who's got some brains, and find out where the hell I'm supposed to go."

"For one thing, Major, we don't have a commanding general at Fort Hamilton. For another, you have no right to shout at me . . ."

Lose my temper? Damned right I did. It was becoming as hard to get home as it had been to get to war in the first place.

Just then a lieutenant colonel came out of a back office and stalked up to the counter, glaring at me. "What the hell's going on out here? What's the shouting about, Major?"

Both the lieutenant and I started talking at once. It didn't help my mood when the colonel told me to shut up and turned to the lieutenant. That SOB had long since surpassed my initial impression of him. Now I simply classified him as a world-class horse's ass. In my mind, the lieutenant colonel fared no better when he turned to me and demanded my proper orders. I tried to be calm, knowing I wasn't helping my case by resisting. These two bureaucrats had probably fought the entire war right here in Brooklyn, using the typewriter as a weapon, deriving great personal satisfaction from making life miserable for the hapless souls coming briefly under their jurisdiction. It suddenly occurred to me that I was experiencing a crystal-clear example of one of General Spaatz's basic types. These two barely qualified as deadwood.

"OK, Colonel, I apologize, but this man doubts these orders, and they're the only orders I have. He won't give me the time of day."

The colonel picked up the wire, read it, scratched his chin, and said, "Well, Major, I can't fault Lieutenant Andrews. I've never seen anything like this either."

"Look, sir, please just get hold of the general, like the orders say. He'll know what this is all about." I felt I was grasping at straws.

"Major, I can't call the general on this. You'll just have to—"

I interrupted. "Colonel, call the people in the Pentagon who sent the damned thing. My group adjutant in England said it came from Washington. Please call. This is getting ridiculous. Somebody wants me somewhere. I didn't dream this up and I sure didn't send myself to this place in Brooklyn. I'm sorry to cause a brouhaha, but—"

It was the colonel's turn to interrupt. "Major, let me put you straight. I'm not going to call Washington. You're not going to see the general. Hell, we don't even have a general here at Fort Hamilton. What you're going to do is tell me where you want to go for forty-five days of R&R and we'll tell you where to check in when that time is up. So where do you want to go?"

"You mean I can choose anyplace?"

"That's right, and we'll cut some proper orders to get you there!"

I stared hard at him and said through gritted teeth, "Colonel, send me to Los Angeles. That's as far away from this damned place as I can think of."

As it turned out later, the colonel at Fort Hamilton did me a big favor. The train trip back to Southern California was most pleasant.

The next thirty days passed quickly. I bought a 1939 Buick sedan, which was sort of a two-toned barnyard brown. I didn't mind the color. I was proud of it and learned quickly how to compete, cadge, hoard, and trade gasoline ration coupons just like everyone else.

I stayed with my aunt Kitty and uncle Phil. Being out of the military environment and part of a family was just what I needed to get my mind and body back to normal. Kitty played the piano for us in the evenings, and on the weekends I helped Phil around the yard. My stepmother, Nina, on the other hand, represented the high life. She had great fun dragging me to cocktail and dinner parties to show me off. It seemed as though she knew everyone who was anyone in Hollywood. During one evening with Nina I tried without success to strike up a conversation with a gorgeous young lady. She was leaning against a wall and just staring into space. I don't think she even knew I was there. Somewhat unnerved, I asked Nina what the matter was with her.

Nina laughed that throaty laugh of hers and said, "Robbie, you're funny. Don't you know who that is? That's Judy Garland, and as usual, she's stoned. Don't take it personally." Something new every day, I thought.

One evening a short time later, I spotted a fellow West Point graduate at one of the parties. He'd been an upperclassman and one hell of a good lacrosse player. He was a full colonel and his name was K. O. Desert. I went over and introduced myself, happy to have a fellow military guy to talk to. It turned out K.O. was the commanding officer at the replacement depot at Santa Ana, near Long Beach. I knew I was supposed to report there when my forty-five-day R&R expired. I mentioned my run-in with the people at Fort Hamilton and how I happened to be there in Southern California.

Colonel Desert asked if I had a copy of my TWX on me, and I dug it out of my wallet.

He said, "Let me have this. I'll give it back when you come down to the reppel-deppel (replacement depot) next month. Meanwhile, let me look into it. Where are you staying and what's your telephone number?"

The next morning he called me at Nina's house. "How'd you like to be a football coach?"

Football coach? Holy crap, what kind of joke was this? I was sort of stunned and didn't know how to respond to him.

Colonel Desert went on, "Your old coach, Red Blaik, wants you to be an assistant. You were supposed to have reported to West Point on the first of September. Since this is already the twenty-eighth it looks like you're a little late. You have a car? Well, pack it and get down here to Santa Ana. Report to my office, and I'll give you a priority run-through. You'll be on your way by midafternoon tomorrow. How's that?"

"Hello, Robin. Are you still there, Robin?"

"Yes, sir. I hear you. I'll be there as soon as possible. And thanks . . . I think."

Well, at least that damned lieutenant colonel at Fort Hamilton had really done me a favor. If he had made my requested call to that nonexistent general, I would never have had my R&R in California. I packed quickly and said my good-byes Kitty, Phil, and Nina. I got myself to Santa Ana and through the order processing.

It took four days driving the Buick across the country before I checked into a BOQ room in the lower floor of Cullum Hall at West Point.

It was less than 50 yards from my dorm to the West Point officers' mess. How could anyone get in trouble in such a short distance? It was seven in the morning on a beautiful, crisp October day. After the long drive from California and

a good night's sleep, I was looking forward to a hearty breakfast before reporting in. But here came trouble. I could sense it. The tall, skinny colonel coming
my way had an evil look and his gaze was fastened on me. What was the problem? Since I seemed to be the only moving object in sight, I had to assume the
colonel had me in mind.

I snapped him my best salute and continued on my way. I didn't get very
far.

"You, man! Halt!" he bellowed behind me.

Good grief. I hadn't been shouted at like that since plebe year. Did I look
like a cadet? Is this the way everyone still acts at this damned place? I certainly
hoped not as I turned around, saluted again for good measure, and stood at
relaxed attention, if there is such a posture.

Now what the hell? I wondered. My salute had been crisp, and my "Good
morning, sir" had had the appropriate degree of deferential respect. I looked
at him and saw a pair of beady eyes on either side of a hawk's nose. His lips
were two thin pursed lines radiating tiny wrinkles. His hat must have had an
iron grommet in it. Never had I seen anything looking more like a cloth-
covered manhole lid. His blouse fit like a glove, marred only by two ribbons,
the Administrator's Commendation Award and the American Defense Ribbon. He also wore a Sam Browne belt, something I hadn't seen since childhood at Langley Field.

The man glared at me as I stood there on the sidewalk. He was making
me feel foolish and I was getting annoyed.

"What's your name? Are you stationed here? What's your job? Where did
you come from?"

He paused and I attempted to enlighten him, "The name is Olds, sir."

"Let me tell you, mister," he expounded, "this is West Point. I don't know
where you've been, but we do things differently around here."

I thought to myself, Hell, I know where I am, but "mister"? Even this old
stick of a ground pounder with his stove-lid hat and his two little ribbons
ought to be able to see the major's leaves on my shoulders. I had to agree that
things were certainly done differently here if his treatment of me was any
indication. I didn't like being hazed. My annoyance deepened.

"Sir?" I asked somewhat churlishly.

The colonel started in, jabbing a long bony finger for emphasis, "That
object on your head is the most disreputable piece of military headgear it has
ever been my misfortune to see. It is an absolute disgrace. You need a haircut.

Your shirt collar is frayed. There are spots on that rag that's supposed to be a tie. Your blouse isn't pressed and your trousers look like they have never been cleaned. As for those shoes, I can't imagine where you got them—they're nonregulation and they're covered with grease."

He seemed to be warming up, and I found myself rather fascinated with his critique. To the colonel and to West Point, these matters were very important. I knew I had no excuses. I knew, from his standpoint, he was right on all counts.

What bothered me was: This was the only garrison hat I had ever owned. It had never had a grommet in it. It took me damned near six months of combat to get it to look right. I hadn't seen a barber for two weeks. The last one had been the head bopper in the barbershop at the Beverly Hills Hotel. For ten bucks he hadn't been about to give me a GI cut, but I sure smelled good afterward. I knew the collar was frayed. Yours would be, too, if it had been subjected to the soap used at the base laundry in England. Well, the tie was at least close to the color it was supposed to be, even if it was knit. I thought it was kind of sporty when I saw it on a rack at Harrods in London. As for the spots, to tell the truth, I really hadn't noticed. Give the old colonel top marks for an eagle eye. My blouse and trousers were the best I had. Too many dips in 100-octane avgas after particularly grueling trips to London. And, no, we didn't have dry-cleaning facilities at RAF Wattisham. My shoes? Now that really hurt. How long could a man walk around with holes under his metatarsals? With no cobblers handy in England, you bought the closest thing to regulation you could find, regulation shoes being something no decent person would want to wear around the base. I was fond of my Wellingtons, but had been really pissed at myself when I spilled some aircraft hydraulic fluid on them. They never could take a shine after that.

These thoughts didn't prevent me from hearing the old stick announce that he was the post adjutant, that I was to report to his office at 1500 hours properly attired for an army officer stationed at West Point, and that whatever future I thought I might have as an officer in the United States Army would abruptly terminate should I be even thirty seconds late.

I have to confess he got my attention. So much for football coaching this fine day. And so much for any importance I may have mistakenly attached to my recent activities fighting Germans. This was the REAL world.

The clothing sales store had a magnificent line of Lauterstein uniforms, plus shirts, ties, hats, and even shoes and socks. Fortunately, the post tailor shop wasn't too busy to handle some quick alteration. I appeared at the adjutant's office in the administration tower at precisely 1459, hoping neither he nor his secretary had seen me lurking outside the door with my watch under my nose. I passed muster without much else being said.

No one in Colonel Earl "Red" Blaik's coaching domain seemed to be interested or asked any questions about why I was so late on my first day or even why my "first" day was a month later than it should have been. I was assigned a corner desk in a back room, told to study a fistful of cards with Xs, Os, and arrows (confusing stuff for a simple former tackle), and informed that the B squad met at the south end of the practice field at 3:30. Obviously I was not intended to have anything to do with the varsity, at least not today. Fair enough. I didn't know what the hell I was supposed to be doing anyway, but I was determined to learn.

It turned out I was about as low on the coaching totem pole as a man could get. In this rarefied atmosphere of big-time collegiate football, military rank had nothing to do with the pecking order on the staff. Position determined authority. Colonel Blaik himself had come to the Point as a reserve officer and had not put on the uniform until after Pearl Harbor. Many of his civilian assistants had been commissioned at the same time, including some of the lowly B squad coaches. I worked for them now but I bitterly resented being treated like a gofer by some squirt wearing a first lieutenant's silver bars.

In the long run, there was much about the job that was interesting and fun. I enjoyed being at practice with the scrubs, I had plenty of time for myself, the football games were great, and I loved the flying I was able to do as a scout and recruiter. Once I became used to the idea, life at West Point as an assistant football coach was pretty good. I tried to take the job seriously, but felt myself at a dead loss with nothing to give these wonderful young guys they hadn't already picked up from Colonel Blaik's regular staff. Besides, I was assigned to the B squad, the junior varsity at most colleges. These youngsters were out there beating their brains out because they loved the game and not for any other reason. When I called them youngsters, I was taking advantage of the fact that I was a major and they were cadets. We got along just fine, and in many cases our ages were the same. I ran with them, helped them learn the plays of next week's adversary so they could scrimmage against the varsity on Tuesdays and Wednesdays, and generally tried to find something useful to do.

My real contribution seemed to be scouting, which I mixed with flying as I traveled to other venues. I sat in the stadiums with stacks of index cards, plotting the plays being used by teams we would meet in the future. My job was to keep track of what two or three individuals did on each series of downs, both offensive and defensive. The cards had Xs and Os for the opposing sides. I would watch what my guys did and plot their blocking or defensive moves on my card. God help me if I got behind. I confess I sometimes lost track and had to mark down what I would have done if I'd been down there playing, not what actually happened. No one on the varsity staff ever caught my bloopers.

What grated was the treatment by many junior officers on the coaching staff. "Olds, take this list down to equipment and bring up such-and such." This from some guy who had been hired by the colonel and given a wartime commission as a captain. He was no more a captain than I was a general, but the order of rank in the football office was based on what you coached and how long you had been there. After several missions from the fifth floor to the basement and back, I finally told one of those fellows to stuff it. If he wanted a runner, hire one.

They weren't all bad. Some were a real pleasure to work with. Andy Gustafson, Av Daniels, and Stu Holcum were all folks for whom I felt the deepest respect. Av had coached me when I was playing and there was a bond between us. My favorite was Herman Hickman, who coached the guards. Herman was about 5' 8", a yard wide, and must have weighed a good 240 pounds. He had played for the pros a bit after college but I forget where. He told me tales of the pro days before World War II, when he and his teammates had to drive their own cars between games with their football uniforms stashed in the trunk. In the shower room after practice, Herman would recite the classics, everything from Shakespeare to Byron. I never met another man in my life who was so well read and who could perform those classics with such total recall and feeling. He and I got along famously.

I remember a dinner at his house. The table groaned with heaping dishes of potatoes and vegetables, all complementing the main pork loin course. Herman kept heaping my plate as though I were a starving Armenian and I ate until my stomach hurt. His wife cleared most of the table, and I hoped I could find enough room in my stomach to tackle the dessert. Not so. The next thing I knew, Mrs. Hickman brought out a platter holding one of the biggest steaks I had ever seen. Herman proceeded to carve this into slices and ordered me to pass my plate. You guessed it: The meal had only just begun. There were four different kinds of pie, two cakes, and three flavors of ice cream. I still get stomach pains just remembering it all. In later years Herman went on to coach Yale, and if memory serves, Old Eli had some of its best teams during the years he was there.

Most of the original Blaik staff would progress to coach major teams. Stu Holcum went to Purdue, Av went to Pittsburgh, and Andy went to Miami or Florida State. After I left the academy, Colonel Blaik hired a new coach named Vince Lombardi. Red Blaik had a profound influence on the game of football in the forties and fifties. No one who loves sports can forget his national championship teams or the men who were inspired by his leadership and foresight. I hear that Lombardi guy did OK, too.

When the 1945 season ended with the Army-Navy game, I went around to the adjutant's office for the first time since my arrival. The old boy recognized me and I stood under his close scrutiny waiting permission to speak.

"Well, Olds, what do you want?"

"Sir, the football season's over and I would appreciate knowing where I am going next."

He stared at me as though I were some kind of dunce. "You're not going anywhere, Major. You're going to be here for a four-year tour, just like everyone else."

With that thunderbolt, he turned to some papers on his desk. I was dismissed. No sense arguing. Done deal. My fate decided. No choice in the matter. I was furious. I was missing everything going on out there in the air force, opportunities were being grabbed by others, new aircraft were being tested, the force was settling down in the aftermath of the war, and I stood a damned good chance of being totally forgotten over the next three years. I couldn't let that happen.

I went back to the BOQ, grabbed my toilet article kit, jumped in my Buick, and headed for Washington, D.C. Good Lord, was every new assignment going to be as difficult as going to war, getting back, and now this? It seemed as though I needed to be my own personnel officer or nothing good would ever happen.

Vast as the Pentagon was, it didn't take long to find the personnel section of the U.S. Army Air Forces. As though fate had ordained it, one of the first people I saw was Lieutenant Colonel Ham Bonham, a yearling when I had been a plebe. I remembered him well. He had been the first upperclassman in A Company to recognize me with a handshake long before June Week. We greeted each other warmly and stood there in the hall playing catch-up.

"What are you doing here in Washington, Robin?"

I explained my predicament, adding that I couldn't see wasting four years doing something for which I had little liking or any great talent. Ham made sympathetic noises and asked what I wanted to do. I suggested I be sent back to my squadron, or to one of the fighter units on occupation duty in Germany.

"You don't want to do that, Robin. That's no good right now. The whole place is in turmoil. People are coming and going. Nothing is really organized or permanent. Got anything else in mind?"

"Well, how about that new jet outfit in California?" I asked hopefully.

Ham looked at me thoughtfully for a moment and said, "Go down to my office two doors on the left. Our secretary will fix you a cup of coffee. I'll be back shortly."

The coffee was good and I scarcely had time to fidget before Ham came back and reported, "OK, you're on."

I could have kissed him. "You mean it? I'm going to California? When?"

"Quit jumping around waving your arms," Ham said, laughing. "Your orders are being cut right now. Give it a few minutes." Sure enough, a sergeant appeared about fifteen minutes later with a sheaf of papers that would send me on my way. I gave Ham a bear hug, thanked him, and turned to go.

"Wait a minute, Robin, don't think you can just leave here and drive back to March Field. Remember, you've got to check out at West Point."

Whew, was that all? I could do that in the blink of an eye.

I did the next day. A bit quietly, I might add. I was afraid someone would discover my good luck and pull some strings to have the whole deal canceled. I paid my mess bill, collected my pay record, packed my B-4 bag, loaded the trusty Buick, and waited until 1700 hours, when I knew the staff offices would be empty. It gave me great pleasure to sign out in the ledger book in the front hall of the admin building, and it was an even greater pleasure to place four copies of my orders on the center of the clean blotter on the adjutant's desk. I grinned, thinking how his face would look the next morning when he discovered I had skipped.

Not wanting to be anywhere nearby when that happened, I drove out the North Gate, turned left, and headed west in the gathering dusk. My only regret was not having had the courage to pay my respects to Colonel Blaik before sneaking away like that. I was afraid he'd cancel my orders. He had been a fine boss and I admired him tremendously. I also regretted not having said my good-byes to Herman, Andy, Av, and the other varsity coaches. But what the hell, the war was over, peace was peace, and good jobs were few and far between. I was off and running, singing lustily as I drove on through that night. It was the twenty-second of December and I had just wangled myself the Christmas present of a lifetime.

11

★

Life in the Fast Lane

I reported for duty at March Field in January of 1946. The 412th Group commander, Colonel Tex Hill, impressed me immediately. Even slouched forward with his elbows on his desk I could see the man was tall. He had on khakis, no tie, and an A-2 leather flight jacket. He wasn't smiling and his expression didn't exactly convey a warm welcome.

"Major Olds reporting for duty, sir!" I saluted smartly.

His return salute was more of a gesture of annoyance than anything military. I began to have grave doubts about my immediate future.

"Just how in hell did you get into this outfit, Major, uh, what's your name, Olds? Major Olds?"

The word "hell" was pronounced "hail," but beyond that the Texas drawl wasn't immediately apparent. I guess that the time the man had spent in China and Burma must have softened him a bit. I knew his reputation. What fighter pilot didn't? He was a top ace and was fighting the Japs before Pearl Harbor with the AVG "Flying Tigers" under Claire Chennault. He was right there with the Battle of Britain fighter pilots in my list of heroes during my first year at West Point.

"Sir, I used every bit of pull I could muster."

That told him his own personnel people hadn't screwed up, but it gave him a point to ponder. Pull? With whom? Fortunately he didn't ask or I would have had to confess it had been only a friendly lieutenant colonel in the Pentagon. He could have brushed me off easily with that knowledge.

His chair squeaked as he leaned back and fixed me with a pair of hard blue eyes. "Damn it, Olds, I got more majors running around here than the law allows, all of 'em trying to cram into that P-80, standin' on top of each other, gettin' under my feet, in my way, don't know what in hell I'm gonna do with y'all."

The words weren't threatening, just factual. And they came out in that distinctive Texas drawl. I decided that Tex, as he was referred to by one and all behind his back, was not a bad guy; he simply had a problem on his hands, and I was part of it. My mind raced as I waited for him to finish his assessment. The competition was going to be fierce, and I had to make some kind of positive move before the group personnel shop got into the act.

Colonel Hill sighed and told me, "Go on down to group ops. See if they can find something useful for you to do while my personnel guy sorts the problem. He'll let you know."

I was dismissed with a not unfriendly wave of the hand. Well, it was better than nothing. Now, to make myself useful but as unobtrusive as possible. For God's sake, don't screw up, Robin. That's all anyone would need to send me packing.

I went down the hall and walked into what I took to be group operations. A lieutenant colonel sat behind a GI desk reading the paper. He scarcely looked up when I saluted. "We don't do that indoors, Major," he said. "Who are you and what do you want?"

"Major Olds, sir, and I have a job in this office." That got his attention.

"And just who said so, Major?"

"Colonel Hill, sir."

Now the lieutenant colonel sat up. "That so? Well I guess you better find something to do. Take that empty desk over there. The guy who had it left yesterday. The lady there is Phyllis and she runs this shop. We do what she tells us and we fix our own coffee. Don't get on her wrong side or you'll find yourself in deep kimchi."

That expression identified the colonel as a Pacific war vet, most likely China-Burma. Not good, I thought, me coming from the ETO. There must be a majority of people from the Pacific in the outfit with pecking order already established, and all of them fighting to secure some kind of permanence in this pioneering jet unit.

The lieutenant colonel picked up his paper. Obviously, I was not someone of particular interest to him, so I went over to the assigned desk and sat down. Its gray surface was sticky with what must have been several years' worth of spilled coffee. Only two of the steel drawers had handles. When I opened the center drawer, it came all the way off its rails, and at least a basketful of trash cascaded to the floor. Phyllis's small smile and the colonel's chuckle told me I had been had, but that was all right. I laughed with them and cleaned up the mess.

"Well, I've got a lot to do," I said as I stood up after a while and walked out the door. "Save all my calls, please, Phyllis." She grinned and I felt I had broken a little ice.

What I had to do now was to find out where to store my flight gear and how to go about getting checked out in the jet, the P-80 "Shooting Star." Who would ever call it that? I walked over to a squadron operations lean-to in the hangar on the south end of the flight line. It was the home of the famous Hat-in-the-Ring 94th Squadron, Eddie Rickenbacker's outfit in World War I. A major was posting some names with a grease pencil on a scheduling board. He seemed to be the only one around who had a job, and I introduced myself.

"Hi, I'm Major Olds, group ops," I said in my most casual yet authoritative voice. "Came over to meet you guys and get checked out in the bird before getting stuck in the rat race."

The major looked at me with open hostility. It was very apparent the fight for survival started right here and my presence was a direct threat. As the new guy on the block, I was low man on the totem pole and would have to fight my way up.

"Well, I don't know about that. You'll have to get in line," he said as he tried to mount a smile, but failed. He hadn't figured out our relative status: where I fit in the pecking order, whose friend I was, what my date of rank might be, all very important stuff in this scramble for position.

"That's understandable," I replied pleasantly. "Put me down on your list, please, and give me a call when you have an opening."

That got his attention, all right. I figured I'd handle the situation as best as I could, if and when he made that call. I knew he'd contact somebody, trying to sort me out, but in the meantime, since no one here really knew me, I guessed I had gained some breathing space.

I went back to the chute shop, where I had already stowed my flight gear, put on my G suit, grabbed my helmet and a parachute, and wandered out onto the flight line. A staff sergeant was buttoning up one of the jets and I made for him just as though I had every reason to be there. The P-80 was absolutely beautiful: polished aluminum, smooth, different, big air scoops on each side of the fuselage, a small bubble canopy, a streamlined nose with four .50 caliber gun ports just visible, tricycle landing gear, and a big tailpipe sticking out the rear. I wondered what went on between the scoops and that tailpipe, but didn't want to display my ignorance to the crew chief.

"Morning, Sarge. That bird in commission?"

He looked at me kinda hard, but said deferentially enough, "Yes, sir. Uh, you new here, Major?"

"Been here awhile," I answered casually. Yep, almost all day now. "I haven't got much time in the 80 yet and I'd appreciate your help with the switches. I don't want to screw up the start procedure."

The sergeant was only too happy to oblige. I later found out I had said absolutely the right thing, because if a pilot did screw up the start, he usually ran the tailpipe temperature way up over the red line. That meant hours for the crew chief along with the hangar crew installing a new engine, a job none of them wanted to do.

I went up the ladder hanging from the left cockpit rail, climbed in, and wriggled my parachute into the seat. The sergeant stood on the ladder and helped me strap in. He then ran through the switches and gauges for me. The major differences seemed to be a thing called the I-16 pump and the large instrument that was calibrated in percent rather than rpm. There was also a large temperature gauge with a big red line somewhere around the 600 mark. There were two fuel gauges, one dial and one counter. I didn't want to display my ignorance, so I didn't ask about any of the strange equipment, hoping the crew chief would get to it all in his review. Most everything else was familiar: flap and gear handle, flight instruments, radio, throttle—pretty simple compared to the old P-38, I thought.

Sarge was good and his instructions were clear. He paid particular attention to that I-16 pump and I listened hard. As he explained it, hitting the start switch, advancing the throttle just the right amount out of cutoff, and flipping on that I-16 fuel pump were the critical actions. Too much throttle, early or late with the I-16, or leaving it on too long, and the engine would be flooded with kerosene, resulting in a blast of flame out the tailpipe and an impressive internal fire in the burner cans. With his guidance I got the hang of it, and we started the engine without trouble. Then he climbed down the ladder, pulled the chocks, and motioned me forward. A little throttle and I started rolling. Luckily, I had plenty of turning room, since steering was purely by the brakes, and you had to have some momentum to keep the nose gear from cocking sideways. The P-38 had the same problem, so I had no trouble and taxied out to the runway. The tower was cooperative. No one tried to stop me and I reached the takeoff position without a military police escort.

Naturally, I hadn't a clue about nose rotation speed on takeoff, to say nothing of flight characteristics or approach speed. I wasn't about to push the bird to its limits on this first ride anyhow, so away I went. The aircraft felt as if it could have flown itself. I applied a little back-pressure when the stick felt light, the nose rotated slightly, we skipped once, and lifted off the runway as smooth as silk. Good airspeed, raise the gear, milk up the flaps, a noticeable trim change, swift acceleration, an impressive climb out; we were off and flying.

It was a thing of joy. Effortless, three-dimensional maneuverability, light controls, honest stall characteristics, great cruise speed, impressive redline top speed, effective speed brakes (which were something new to me), and super visibility all around. I fell in love. The few snags seemed to be trivial. I quickly learned to keep one eye on the tailpipe temperature gauge and the engine percent gauge. Both were finicky. The engine speed, indicated by percent of rpm, increased as we climbed. I had to keep retarding the throttle to keep things in limits. That was no big deal, but something to remember. It took a while to find any kind of navigation gear. When I did, I realized the location of the radio range receiver meant I had to tune it by feel, and since I couldn't see the dial when I could reach the control knob, I knew that wouldn't work. OK, the Mustang didn't have much nav gear either, so what else?

I didn't want to return to base so soon, but the P-80 drank fuel like a thirsty elephant and it was time to head back to the field. Initial approach, overhead break, left downwind, boards down, gear and flaps down, turn to final, hold the airspeed at 125, throttle to idle short of the runway, and the bird settled down gently with scarcely a jolt.

The crew chief seemed somewhat agitated when I climbed down the ladder and complimented him on a good bird.

"Some major came out here and wanted to know who was flying 127. I told him I didn't know. What IS your name, Major?" he demanded.

"The name is Olds." I grinned at him. "No heat, Sarge. I'll straighten things out. I hope I get to fly your bird often, and I thank you for all your help." With that I went back into squadron ops and asked the major where he wanted me to post my flight time.

"What bird did you fly?"

"127."

"Hell, that 80 doesn't even belong to the 94th!"

"No sweat, Major. I'm from group and will be flying with your squadron often. Who wants my Form Five?" Might as well be aggressive, I thought. The major accepted things as they seemed to be and no one ever asked any embarrassing questions.

Later I was thankful nothing went wrong on that first flight. But then, we didn't much care about the niceties of emergency procedures in those immediate postwar days, nor did we pay much attention to a lot of bothersome flight regulations either. Life at March Field was going to be interesting.

Somehow I found enough to do in the office to justify my existence, and the threat of being transferred diminished. I knew I was still on the hook, but with each passing day, I felt more secure. The flying was terrific. It didn't take long to feel completely at home in the P–80. The only difficulty at all was the start, that I-16 pump being the culprit. It posed a real challenge with grave consequences should you screw up. Almost every day a deep rumble shaking windows across the base told of another hot start and another engine change for the hangar crews. Since the normal procedure in those early days was to change the tailpipe every twelve hours of flight and the engine every twenty-five, a hot start or so didn't seem all that important. The only thing for pilots to avoid was walking behind one of the birds when someone was attempting to get a start. One error, one missed switch, and a flame could shoot out the tailpipe, singeing your eyebrows if you were in the way.

A couple of weeks later, I received a call from Lieutenant Colonel John "Pappy" Herbst, commander of the 27th Squadron. He asked me to come over to his office to get briefed on a test he had been asked to run. Naturally curious, I hustled over, wondering how and why he had picked me, but delighted to be in on something. Pappy was the leading ace of the 14th Air Force with eighteen kills. He had an enviable reputation as a great pilot as well as a respected and admired commander. I walked in, saluted, and sat when invited.

Pappy got down to business. "They want two of us to take on the new navy plane, that single-place thing with a little jet in the rear and a conventional engine-driven prop up front. It's called the Ryan Firebee, or something like that."

"I think that's the Fireball, sir," I interjected.

He didn't seem to notice. "Anyhow, a flight of four of them will be coming out of Miramar. We'll intercept them down south of Lake Elsinore. They'll be in a navy fighting spread and we'll have a go at each other. I suggest we use the vertical as much as possible and don't even try to maintain our own flight integrity. In other words, I want the two of us to split up and keep them churning. I'll make a pass, take vertical spacing, call you when I'm clear, you come in, make your pass, take spacing, call, and so on. If we manage to keep each other in sight, which I think we'll be able to do, then the calls won't be necessary. The idea is, don't try to turn with them. I haven't any idea how well they perform, so let's not bleed off airspeed and get trapped. Our call sign will be Red One and Two, and we'll start engines at 1430. Any questions?"

All the time I was listening I was studying Pappy. He was soft-spoken, but his words had force and conviction. He had dark hair with keen, piercing eyes in a handsome, lean face. It occurred to me he was the spitting image of that new movie star Gregory Peck. Guys weren't supposed to think of another man as handsome, but I had to admit, he was all of that. He had a commanding presence without the need for posturing. Something about him exuded confidence. I liked him immediately.

Of course I had questions, but they weren't about the coming dogfight. I wanted to know why Pappy had picked me. I was pleased and flattered, but not so much as to ask some dumb question without an opening. Just to have been selected out of all the pilots in the group was enough.

Soon we were off and making our way south toward the rendezvous point. I flew a loose combat position, changing sides easily as Pappy made his turns. It was quickly apparent why he was highly regarded by everyone. He was smooth and flew with concern for his wingman.

I was determined to do my part to the best of my ability and kept position, scanning the sky ahead for the navy flight. Sure enough, there they were. Pappy and I blanked out each other's radio as we simultaneously called out the bogeys. The navy fighters were still coming at us, no split, no reaction. They hadn't spotted us, which was a plus for our gray color and small head-on profile. Pappy gave a slight wing rock and broke hard left. I went almost straight up and rolled inverted. The navy must have seen one or both of us at that instant because they split, two turning for Pappy and two continuing on toward me in a climb. As I closed, I watched Pappy pull up, roll inverted, and go for the two who had made the mistake of trying to climb for me. Had we been firing guns, there would have been at least two downed enemy in that brief ten seconds of the initial engagement. Instead, our gun camera film later confirmed our success. We made several more passes for the fun of it, then broke for home with a wing waggle of thanks.

"Good flight, Robin," Pappy said as we walked back to his office. "I don't think our jets will have much trouble with planes like that or anything with a prop, just so long as we keep our airspeed up and don't get to churning with them." I would remember this lesson clearly some twenty-odd years later over North Vietnam.

Our engagement with the navy must have broken the ice for me. It wasn't very long after that I was standing at the ops counter trying to convince the squadron operations officer that I absolutely, positively, unconditionally needed to fly. He wasn't impressed.

"Hell, Olds, you flew yesterday. You got more damn time than people who've been here twice as long. How'm I gonna tell those other guys you need that bird more'n they do?"

I was framing my answer when a familiar voice said, "Major Olds, how'd you like to be in my outfit?"

I turned to see Colonel Leon Gray standing beside me. I had been so intent on putting the bite on the ops officer I hadn't noticed him arriving. Neither had anyone else, for that matter. No one had called the room to attention when he, as senior officer, entered. Colonel Gray didn't seem to pay any attention to our breach of etiquette. He was looking at me with a serious, hard stare.

I had met him at Wattisham the previous summer, when he'd toured with a group of full colonels, but knew him more by reputation. He wasn't a big man in the sense of being tall, but he was solid, with a square jaw and intense, piercing eyes, a man not to be trifled with. He had served briefly in the Air Corps before the war and afterward flew for an airline. When Pearl Harbor was attacked, Leon reentered the service and, because of his experience, was assigned to the Ferry Command. In that assignment, he took aircraft across the Atlantic, over the Sahara, and all the way to Russia. Somewhere along the way, he managed to get out of Ferry Command and become a reconnaissance squadron commander working for Elliott Roosevelt in North Africa. He had earned the Distinguished Service Cross for his preinvasion pictures of the beaches of Anzio and Salerno, getting badly shot up in the process, and wound up in England as commander of the Reconnaissance Group at RAF Watton.

Now he was here at March, commanding a fourth squadron of P-80s. We junior officers couldn't figure that one out. Gray's squadron was a separate unit, not under the group commanded by Tex Hill. It turned out that the air force had put the best man in charge of pioneering a new age of photo reconnaissance, now to be done with jets.

I didn't hesitate for a second. "Yes, sir, I'd like that a lot. But, sir, I don't know anything about taking pictures." I could have bit my tongue. That hadn't come out the way I'd meant it, and I saw the colonel stiffen. I meant to be honest and confess I had no background in reconnaissance, except for that one time over the marshaling yards at Stuttgart, which surely didn't count.

"I'll take care of the picture taking, Major. I want someone to train my pilots and be my operations officer," he said with a bit of an edge to his voice.

Damn, I hope I haven't screwed this up, I thought. I didn't know much about Colonel Gray's outfit, only that it was a photo recce unit. They hadn't yet received their recce birds, so they were flying the P-80A like the rest of us, but they didn't belong to the 412th. Gray had a reputation as an aggressive leader and a great pilot. In addition, he wore the DSC, second only to the Medal of Honor. Tex Hill had the only other DSC at March Field.

Hoping to recover, I repeated, "Yes, sir, I'd like that a lot! When do I report?"

"This afternoon soon enough for you, Major?"

"Yes, sir, I'll be right there!" Whew . . . now things were really humming. Bless the man. He turned out to be the best boss I had for the rest of my thirty years and became one of my dearest lifelong friends.

I tried not to jump and shout, but inside, I was doing just that. Finally, a job! No more just hanging around and trying to "make work" as I had been doing for weeks. Assignment as the umpteenth assistant group ops officer didn't have much feeling of permanence about it. Not that I had minded scarfing up all the flying time I could beg, borrow, or steal, but I didn't like the lack of responsibility. The ax might fall at any time, and I'd be out looking for another job.

Running the paperwork for my transfer was a joy. It didn't take long. That same day I deposited my flight gear in my new locker and placed a pad and pencil on my new desk. Next, the important part: Get to know the people, get familiar with squadron procedures, and most of all, learn how Colonel Gray operated and what he expected of me.

Time passed swiftly. Colonel Gray was one smart operator. The squadron bustled, the people were happy, our jets were well maintained under the eagle eye of Warrant Officer Gruber, and we flew constantly, far more than the fighter squadrons down the flight line, much to their chagrin. The photo reconnaissance version of the P-80 wasn't yet off the production line. It didn't matter. We flew our butts off anyway.

Colonel Gray was an out-front, follow-me type. Under his leadership we took the new aircraft to the limits of its envelope, to say nothing of our own. We were the first to fly at night. People actually came down to the flight line that first night to see what they thought would be streaks of fire behind our tailpipes as we took off. Not to be so. Except for a dearth of nav gear the P-80 was a delight to fly in any and all conditions. Our main concern was the rate at which it burned fuel.

The fuel and range limitations of the new aircraft were an adjustment from what we were used to in aircraft like the Mustang and Lightning. A lot of people in the Air Corps asked questions about range and endurance, and some of them had enough clout to pose a menace to the future of jet aviation. However, we learned, sometimes the hard way with bent birds and lost pilots, but we learned. The higher you went, the thinner the air. That meant less drag, more fuel efficiency, higher ground speed, and more distance covered in the time airborne. That meant having to take off, climb immediately, and get to altitude, usually around 35,000 or 36,000 feet. For deep missions or on a long cross-country, as we burned down fuel and the bird became lighter, we would "cruise-climb," easing the jet higher still. On some flights we'd wind up around 42,000 feet. The new jet had been equipped with a cabin pressurization system, something new and not too reliable at that time. But when it worked, it was great, and allowed us to operate at those altitudes in comparative comfort. It was simply progress.

While I continued to serve officially as ops officer for Leon Gray's bunch throughout the rest of 1946, Pappy Herbst tapped me often to fly with him after our afternoon spent playing with the navy Fireballs. We were testing the new jets in every way we could, and, of course, in the true manner necessary to push the envelope, we engaged in some serious aerobatics. This tended to attract a lot of attention. Pretty soon, Pappy decided we should put on an official acrobatic show for the public. Local newspapers got hold of the news and the word spread announcing the date in mid-June for the first ever jet acrobatic show. We practiced and practiced, adding new variations of loops and rolls in each session. We'd put the jet through its paces for the audience.

Life in the evenings, and out of the P-80s, usually involved hanging around the officers' club bar at March. At that time the field was in the middle of nowhere. It was near Riverside, but it was too far from any interesting nightlife to tempt us off base very much.

One night in early June, about a week before the scheduled air show, my friend "Woody" Woodward and I were sitting in our usual places at the O club bar and idly chatting about nothing in particular, when the night turned into a different experience altogether. Woody was the club officer and we were both in Colonel Gray's P-80 squadron. We had become friends during the past months and shared many memories of our time in England during the war. Woody had flown bombers, two tours as a matter of fact, and had been rewarded for his effort by an opportunity to fly fighters in a special group of similarly experienced bomber guys. Their mission was to fly out in front of the bomber stream, checking the weather, especially over the target. To what end, I couldn't figure, but what the hell, they had certainly earned the right to act like fighters if they wanted to.

We were hashing over some finer points of flying bombers versus fighters, and savoring our beers, when "Ace" Hastings came over and joined us. He sat down, ordered a beer, and announced he had three hot girls over in Palm Springs eager to meet some real jet pilots. Problem was, he didn't have a car and knew that I did. Hmm, I confess I wasn't too eager to drive all that way at this hour, but after some persuasion, the three of us piled into my car and we set off through the Banning Pass toward Palm Springs.

Once we were there, Ace guided me to a motel. We parked and walked to the door of one of the rooms. Ace knocked. The door opened and we entered. There were the three ladies waiting for us. One was small and mousy, with an unfriendly look on her face. The next was good-looking, dark and tall, with a nice smile. The third—my God—was Ella Raines, the movie actress! I recognized her right away. We had seen her movie with John Wayne in the lounge at Wattisham, a flick called *Tall in the Saddle*, and had liked it so much we made the projectionist run it again. It turns out Ace had met her previously in New York and there seemed to be something going on between them. Woody immediately teamed up with Valerie, the tall, dark-haired girl.

She turned out to be Ella's stand-in. The little one was Ella's secretary, and by luck of the draw, she was my "date" for the night.

We went to dinner and I couldn't take my eyes off Ella. What man could? To me, she was ravishing. Perhaps it was my imagination or just hope, but I thought she seemed to be somewhat interested in me as well, for all the good that would do on this one evening. She was happy and laughing with Ace, and I found myself suddenly disliking him intensely.

The rest of the evening passed swiftly. Woody and I wound our weary way back to the base just as the sun came up, leaving that damned Ace with the girls.

What the hell. So much for that, I thought, but I couldn't get Ella off my mind. There was a spark to her quite beyond her striking beauty, and I was desperate to find a way to see her again. But how? Movie actresses didn't have listed telephone numbers. Studios were not about to reveal addresses. I was stumped. To this day, I don't know how he did it, but my friend Woody, with consummate resourcefulness, found Ella's telephone number and home address. I bought a bottle of champagne, jumped in my car just two days later, drove the sixty miles to Coldwater Canyon, and knocked on Ella's door. The secretary answered and announced Ella was not there.

I felt foolish, especially since the secretary had supposedly been my date, so I just blurted out, "This is a present for Father's Day," shoved the champagne into her hands, and left, driving back to March Field, cursing myself for being so stupid.

The formation acrobatic demonstration with Pappy was scheduled for a few days later at the main commercial airfield south of Los Angeles. I screwed up my courage, called Ella, and invited her to the air show. To my surprise, she readily accepted. I can't remember how it all worked out, but I picked her up and drove us down to the field that day. My jet was already there. Pappy and I did our thing, and then I drove Ella back to Beverly Hills after we finished.

The acrobatic show back in those magical days was incredible. There was little of the structure and oversight that would accompany such displays in later years. Pappy was in fine form, pushing me to my limits, as usual. Several times I thought, God, Pappy! You're going to scrape me off! It took everything I had to keep the right wingtip of his P-80 steady and still, right there about 4 feet up, 4 feet left, and 6 feet forward of my canopy. I was avoiding downwash from his wing. My own wing turbulence didn't affect Pappy at all. I had a reference line from his wingtip to the forward edge of his nose access panel. Any movement back or forward, up or down, from my position was obvious and easily correctable. Holding there also gave me enough peripheral vision to have some idea of what was happening in front of us. And what was happening right now wasn't all that reassuring. Pappy called, "We're going to loop!"

We started down to gain airspeed for the maneuver. I could sense our dive angle and acceleration. We were going like hell and still headed down as we crossed the north end of the flight line. We were already even with the tops of the hangars . . . and we still hadn't bottomed out? Now I could see the hangar windows. Oh God.

"Jesus! I'm four feet lower than you, Pappy! Give me some room!" I screamed over the radio as I eased up a foot or two and fought a bit of downwash from Pappy's wing. There was the grandstand itself. I could see the top of it, small as it was, across the top of Pappy's fuselage. And then came the g-forces, building rapidly—my G suit squeezing tight. It felt like a rock against my stomach. I was already tensing my stomach muscles as hard as I could and screaming silently into my oxygen mask. Now, everything seemed to be happening in slow motion. I fought to keep that wingtip where it belonged, but the world was growing dimmer by the second. Grayness closed in from all sides and my vision tunneled down to nothing but Pappy's wingtip. I was on the verge of blacking out completely when the forces relaxed slowly and my vision returned to normal.

What was this? Ten minutes later? Impossible! But that's what it felt like as we came to the top of our loop and started down the other side. Now a new thought. (You're thinking too much, Robin!) With all those g-forces as we went up the front side, did we gain enough altitude to complete the down side of this loop? This was the opening maneuver for our debut as the first jet acrobatic team in America. That we were first was an easy assumption. No one else in the United States had jets. Maybe we were the first in the world. I liked to think that was so but hadn't heard whether the Brits might have started something. We'd practiced several times, and Pappy's loops were a piece of cake. He was so damned smooth he made me look good hanging out there on his right wing.

But this was something different—a whole lot different! Even before we reached the vertical on the down side of our loop, I took a quick peek forward. One quick look, and all I could see was concrete. Hard, flat, gray concrete. With my nose pointed straight at it, and seemingly no room to finish our maneuver. No time to panic. Hang in there! This might turn out to be more spectacular than Pappy intended.

By now the g-forces were again peaking and the grayness started closing in. I fought the pressure with all my strength and concentrated fully on that wingtip as the world slipped again into darkness. The g's eased as we bottomed out. I saw the hangar roofs, then the windows, and then the viewing stand not 100 feet to our left. We had made it! I remember shouting in exultation as we pulled off, then wondering how I had generated so much drenching sweat in such a short time.

The rest of the show went well. Our formation roll, starting right from the deck and ending there, was an anticlimax compared to the loop. Pappy had one more surprise in store for the spectators . . . as well as for his wingman. I have forgotten all the other things we did that day, but I will never forget the initial loop or our finale.

As we turned back south toward the runway, Pappy said, "Let's give 'em a special landing pattern. Hang on!" As though I had any choice in the matter.

We were at almost full power as Pappy leveled over the north end of the runway and buzzed down toward the south. I gauged us to be about 20 feet and had plenty of time to wonder what was going to happen next. After that first loop, I didn't feel any particular concern; this final maneuver couldn't be too extreme. I mean, after all, Pappy was good. He was smooth. He knew what he was doing, and he obviously trusted me to hang in there no matter what.

When we reached the south end of the runway, Pappy started a pull up. This one was gentle, only about 2.5 to 3 g's, and I figured we were going for altitude. A flash of concern as I thought maybe he intended doing a reverse Cuban eight, but we continued on up and around. I could feel the airspeed bleeding down but couldn't peek at the instrument panel to see.

As we crested the top, Pappy called, "Idle power . . . gear down . . . full flaps . . . dive brakes . . . NOW!" I matched each configuration change with his aircraft as he made the calls.

Now what?" I muttered into my oxygen mask as we headed down the back side of whatever it was we were doing. I had time to glance through the top of the canopy and saw the earth coming up at us again. However, this time there was plenty of maneuver room due to the altitude Pappy had gained in the front side of the loop. We sailed down and bottomed out, having gained maybe 300 feet of altitude, and were doing perhaps 220 airspeed, still with everything hanging. Pappy kept pulling and soon we were headed back up some 30 degrees above the horizon. He let us coast on up at that angle, and our speed bled back down. I didn't dare glance at my altimeter. I really didn't want to know how high we were. It had dawned on me what Pappy was up to, and I just hoped his superb instincts had this one wired.

Sure enough, Pappy called, "OK, rolling left . . ."

With just enough airspeed to give me full controllability, I followed as we rolled inverted and started back down in a split-S maneuver. I hadn't split-S'd from this altitude since primary, when I had scared myself shitless in a PT-19 over Oklahoma. But here we were, in two of the Army Air Forces' jets, doing something I doubt had ever been done in one of them before. I mean, who would be dumb enough?

Again, there were a few seconds of uncertainty as the dirt off the end of the runway took on pebble-sized clarity. But then I realized we had about 200 feet of excess altitude—if 200 feet could ever be called "excess." Pappy eased off on the pull out, and we leveled, coasted up to the approach end of the runway, and touched down right on the threshold.

All I could think of as we taxied in was what a superb pilot Pappy was, and though there had been moments of gut-wrenching doubt, I was damned happy to have stuck in there during this first jet-powered formation acrobatic show.

All the dignitaries and guests gathered round our jets as we shut down. As I climbed out of the cockpit wondering what was going to happen next, I became acutely aware of my foul condition: sweaty and rank. I was embarrassed and wondered how I could avoid getting close to those pristine visitors. And there was Ella! I swore to myself to get my butt over to supply and draw another flight suit immediately. The chief of the Argentinean air force, General Duncan Rodriguez, must have been the consummate diplomat. He didn't even wrinkle his nose as he presented Pappy and me with a set of Argentinean pilot's wings as a token of appreciation.

Someone else must have flown my plane back to March Field. I can't recall. The details of the air show itself remain etched in my memory, but every moment with Ella was a blur. I guess that's because I was smitten and knew something really big was happening in my life. I must have been in a total daze, and when I look back, I'm astonished I even had the presence of mind that day to fly the way I did. Whatever I did, it impressed Ella, and we saw more of each other during the following months. I knew I was falling deeply in love not with the star, but with a wonderful woman. We were dancing at a club on the Sunset Strip one evening later in the summer when I whispered, "I love you."

To my amazement, she replied, "And I love you."

That did it. From that point on, we were hooked. We went to Tahoe with Val water-skiing. We went to New York for one of Ella's publicity appearances. She took me to endless parties. I often picked her up at the studio on a Friday evening when she was shooting a picture, and tired of my one tweed sport coat, she made me buy some decent civilian clothes. I hung out on her movie set out in the desert and got to know her pals and fellow actors. Over time, I became friends with John Wayne, Rod Cameron, director John Ford, Gabby Hayes, David Niven, and many more. Our life was a whirlwind of days spent in the sky for me, and nights spent at glittering parties or just at Ella's home in front of a fire.

One afternoon in particular, I drummed up my usual bravado and decided to buzz her movie set in my P-80. They were making a western, and I remember looking back over my shoulder as I pulled up fast and high from my low pass. All I could see was dust. Later that day, back at March, I learned that the noise and blast had terrified the horses and mules. Apparently, about two dozen went tearing off into the desert, snapping their reins. They weren't rounded up until the next day. Two mules pulled over the chuck wagon used to feed the actors, extras, stuntmen, and crew. A whole new one had to be made. Dust blew into all the camera lenses and shooting came to a complete halt for two days.

So it went with Ella, until one evening I asked her to marry me. I thought she might have the good sense to consider how totally different our lives were, but, no, she consented. We set the date for February 6, 1947.

I found out later that my gift of champagne for Father's Day had been translated into "Tell her I want to be a father." All I can say is it worked!

You could say our group at March helped usher in the jet age . . . showed the country a glimpse of the future, but for a while, especially in the summer of '46, it was routine to engage in a round of air shows, demonstration flights, and publicity stunts. We were sent on a mass cross-country flight in May, departing March Field around the fifteenth and returning on the twenty-seventh, sixteen of us, four jets from each squadron and a whole Gooney Bird full of supplies, support troops, and spare parts. We drew enormous attention from the general public across the country as we landed in different places.

The local newspapers and radio stations went wild, but for us, it was simply great flying.

When we left March on that first trip, we headed to Albuquerque. On departure the next morning, Captain "Honk" Hensley roared down the entire length of the north–south runway without getting airborne. With great flourish and a huge cloud of dust, he sailed off the end and down into a dry ravine. Scratch that bird! Fortunately, only Honk's pride was injured. The rest of the gaggle set course for Fort Worth, and from there, to Memphis. We didn't know who picked up the expenses for our stopovers, but we were given a warm welcome everywhere we landed.

The most unforgettable acro demonstration with Pappy took place at Del Mar Racetrack in California on the Fourth of July in 1946. What were we doing at Del Mar? Pappy and I had put on a number of shows all over the country, but never at a racetrack. This was really a throwback to the twenties and thirties, when barnstormers like Roscoe Turner and his Lion performed at county fairs. Guys flying old biplanes took brave customers up for $2 rides and that sort of thing. It wasn't really the place for a couple of jets. I guess someone knew someone who knew someone who had a friend in headquarters, so here we were.

Normally Pappy was smooth as silk, but not that day. I worked my butt off trying to keep in position as we went through our air show routine. I was drenched in sweat and kept thinking, God, I'll be glad when this is over, but I couldn't blame him. He had been married the day before and the previous night had survived a stag party to end all stag parties at Lake Arrowhead. Not only that, but the winds blowing in off the Pacific and over the low surrounding hills didn't help a bit. The flying was rough, the air was rough, everything was rough.

On the way to Del Mar before the show, Pappy and I landed at the marine airstrip at Camp Pendleton. Our own people from March left earlier with a refueling truck so we could take on a full load of fuel before the show. While that was going on, Pappy and I were driven to the racetrack to meet the crowd and to have a look at the place where we would perform. It didn't look inviting. The stands were backed onto some low hills. In front, perhaps for half a mile, there was some flat land, and then more hills to the north. Beyond the racetrack itself, a dry streambed ran westward through the shallow valley toward the ocean. We were glad to see there were no power lines or hills to the east. At least our maneuvers wouldn't be inhibited in that direction. I wondered at the time how Pappy intended to alter the routine, especially to avoid the small hills directly to the west of the racetrack. We drove back to Pendleton, climbed into our birds, and took off.

We were holding off to the north of the racetrack before our show. While we were being introduced to the crowd, two civilians were performing in a pair of yellow Stearmans. It looked as though they were making up their routine as they went along. They flew past us in close formation. The guy on the right did a barrel roll over the top and finished in close formation on Lead's left side. Then Lead barrel-rolled and wound up on number Two's left side, immediately doing the same maneuver back to his right. Now it was Two's turn, only Lead must have been in the rhythm of it, and when both of them rolled at once the two aircraft met with a terrible crash at the top of their rolls. Fortunately, both guys had parachutes. From their reaction, the crowd must have thought it was part of the performance.

Our show went reasonably well and our routine was nearly complete. I heaved a sigh of relief as we turned north to head out after going through our loop and split-S finale with a simulated landing. I wanted only to get back to home plate, grab a shower, drive down to Coldwater Canyon, and settle into the evening by wrapping myself around an ice-cold martini and Ella.

Pappy called, breaking my reverie. "Robin, let's go back and do that again."

God, no! I thought. Enough is enough! But a good wingman doesn't argue, and I tightened up close as we went around to gain speed for our simulated landing routine one more time. We came in from the west, dove over the low hills, and hit the deck in front of the stands, and Pappy pulled up into the loop. Everything went well until we completed the first part of the maneuver and, with gear, flaps, and speed brakes hanging, started back up for the split-S. All of a sudden, I knew something was wrong. We weren't gaining altitude as we normally did. The pull up was too shallow. Our speed bled off, and I was about to call out when Pappy said, "OK, rolling left!"

We were so close to the stalling point that I barely had enough aileron and rudder control to stay tucked in as we went inverted.

"Jesus, this is wrong!" I screamed. "Pull, Pappy, PULL!"

There was no way to escape, nothing to do but try to complete the split-S on my own. Nose through the horizon and down I went, milking the back pressure on the stick. Hanging on to the very edge of a stall, the aircraft shuddered and quivered each time I even breathed too hard. The ground was getting close, awfully close. Even when my nose was beyond the vertical, there wasn't enough room! I kept gently pulling. One mistake, one small pull too hard, and I would stall completely. It felt like minutes, but couldn't have been more than a few seconds. I was headed for the dry riverbed. The earth and gravel came at me as though it were my destiny to end everything right here.

"Lord, don't do this to me. Give me just a few more feet, just a little bit. Please, Lord," I begged.

My nose was now almost level and I had picked up a few knots of air-speed. Then I was into ground effect and the bird came through, skimming the far bank of the riverbed and throwing up a trail of dust from my exhaust. I kicked left rudder and looked back over my shoulder for Pappy just in time to see him hit nose low in a terrible smash against the bank. I knew immediately that no one could have survived anything like that.

Stunned, I banked away and pointed my bird for the airstrip at Pendleton. What else could I do? The lump in my throat was choking me and I fought to control my shaking and nausea. Even before I landed I was loosening my seat belt and shoulder harness and removing my oxygen mask. With only one of us returning, the ground crew knew something dreadful had happened. When I taxied up, they looked at me with stricken faces but asked no questions. I only shook my head and damned near broke down completely when Pappy's crew chief turned away to hide his tears. The turnaround went on in utter silence, except for the muttering of the tanker's fuel pump. There was no telephone available and no way I could call ahead.

With the refueling and quick check done, I took off for March, scarcely aware of what I was doing. The losses in the war, the ones in training, and the ones learning the new jet over the recent years should have hardened me to deaths, but this one really hurt. It hurt so deep down that I tried not to think about it, tried to get into that numb place deep inside and steel myself for what I realized lay just ahead. It didn't work.

The coastal clouds had moved inland and the late-afternoon skies were heavy and gray as I landed at March and taxied toward base operations. A small group was there, huddled together, watching and waiting. They couldn't know which one of us was down, which one was taxiing toward them. I wanted to go right past, down to the far end of the ramp, but I couldn't do that.

Pappy's bride of little more than twenty-four hours, Jeannie, was standing between two men, each of them holding an elbow. I followed the signals of the marshaler leading me to a spot right next to those faces. I kept my oxygen mask on, for no reason except I couldn't, and didn't, want to see their reactions when they realized it wasn't Pappy in this airplane. I had to shut down. I had to climb out. How? The jet engine whined to a stop, the ladder was placed for me. I leaned forward and removed my helmet, sat up straight, stood up straight in the cockpit, turned away, and backed down the ladder without looking in their direction.

On reaching the concrete, someone took me by the elbow and turned me around. I admit, tears were flowing down my face. I muttered, "I'm so sorry, so very sorry . . ."

No one said anything and I walked off without another word. What else was I supposed to say? How could I tell them? How could I say Pappy screwed up, that he was dead, that I was lucky and so grateful to be alive? How could I say anything to Jeannie that would help her in that moment? It was horrible beyond words, beyond thought. We were all devastated.

I don't remember much of that evening. I know I called Ella, then got in my car and headed to her house. All I know is that all the people who meant something to me in my life, those who were present and those who had passed on, came crowding into my mind as I drove. I know that I cried, but I know that my tears had dried by the time I pulled up to Ella's house. I knew that the door would open and I would have to help my sweetheart dry her own tears. And so I did.

When I think back on those days of flying the P-80s, I can't help wondering what the Army Air Forces really thought they were doing with those jets. Sure, we went faster and higher than anything else, and, yes, we had four .50 caliber guns in the nose, but the P-51 had six and the P-47 had eight. So what? As much fun as we were having learning to fly and maintain them, I wonder whether we had any real plan for determining what tactical advantage that jet gave us. We went out and tangled with the navy guys on several occasions, quickly learning what not to do, and sometimes we fired the guns at towed targets but never enough to sharpen our skills. I don't remember ever dropping a practice bomb from the P-80. As a matter of fact, the early production aircraft didn't have the capability to do so. What were we planning on doing with the jets that was useful?

In hindsight, everything that happens has an impact on the future, sometimes negatively, often for the good. Eventually we started to have fun racing each other, timing our laps around a course in the desert. We learned that we would be participating in the world famous Cleveland Air Races! The last race had been held in 1939; then the event was suspended for the duration of the war. On Labor Day 1946 the races were on again. Naturally we were excited! We were going to be the first jets to fly in the race, not just as part of the air show, but in the Bendix Trophy and Thompson Trophy races themselves.

Those of us chosen for the event went to work right away on our aircraft. I wanted to reduce weight and get as much thrust out of my jet as possible. With the connivance of the maintenance and armament people, we tweaked the engine, giving me more fuel flow, higher tailpipe temps, and a little more speed. Then we started working on reducing weight. Out went the four .50 caliber guns and the ammo boxes. We were working on the armor plate behind the pilot seats when we were told that any tampering with the birds would disqualify us. Apparently, this message was sent by the Pentagon but originated at AMC headquarters. It seemed strange that Air Material Command should worry about it, but since the Material Command was entering three birds in the race, most of us in the fighter group were damned suspicious.

We arrived in Cleveland before the Labor Day weekend races to squeeze in as much practice as we could. After I landed from a practice and taxied in, a fellow walked toward my bird. It was Tony LeVier, already a famous air race pilot from previous Cleveland events, but also currently the chief test pilot for Lockheed and the ultimate expert on the flight characteristics of the P-80.

After I climbed out of my cockpit and we introduced ourselves, Tony walked around my bird, scrutinizing it from every angle. He took one look at the wrinkles running diagonally down both sides of my P-80's fuselage and whistled. "Just how many g's did you pull, Robin?"

"Hell, Tony"—I shrugged—"I don't know. The g meter pegged out. I've been trying different ways to cut time around those pylons. Guess I overdid it."

"Yeah, I guess you did!" Tony shook his head and laughed. "Back at Lockheed we figured around eleven g's might do that to the 80, but no one up to now ever did it. I wouldn't stress that particular bird any more if I were you. Matter of fact, you might consider not even flying it again." Tony obviously knew what he was talking about, and I took him very seriously. In fact, all of us had him up on a pretty high pedestal in the pilots' world.

So I asked him, "What do you suggest, Tony?"

"Well, what has worked for the prop racers should work for jets, too. Aerodynamics are aerodynamics. Pull all those g-forces and you've increased your angle of attack drastically. Do that and you've loaded up enough drag to stop a train. And that will sure as hell slow you down. Since this is the first time any-one has ever raced jets around a closed course we have a lot to learn. But basic aerodynamics still apply. What I'd do is take those turns as smoothly as you can. Don't dive at the base of the pylons and jerk the bird around. Get enough spacing on your approach to each turn, rack up about 70 or 80 degrees of bank, dive a little bit, and cut around each pylon as closely as you can. I'm sure you'll find the speed you keep will more than offset the small extra distance you've taken. What do you have, two more practice sessions? OK, try it next time."

I did, and Tony was right. I gained precious seconds on each of the 18-mile legs of the racecourse. But there was something else to overcome.

We had been at Cleveland for several days before the participating aircraft from the AMC headquarters at Wright-Patterson showed up. Naturally curi-ous, and disguising my previously formed suspicions, I ambled over to have a look at them. To my astonishment and growing rage, I was barred from get-ting any closer than 50 yards from those competitors. Even at that distance some peculiarities could be seen: The air scoops on one of the P-80s were big-ger than normal, there were no gun ports in the nose, and the armor plate that stuck up behind the seat was very obviously not steel. It was more than likely made out of cardboard.

Once refueled, the Wright-Pat jets were trundled into a hangar and the doors were rolled shut. I was incensed but couldn't seem to find anyone who gave a damn. OK, we'll see. It occurred to me I might load a hundred or so rounds in the guns I would be carrying, but that might have been considered unsportsmanlike conduct. Besides, there was no place in Cleveland where I could get my hands on such ammunition.

Since we were fuel-limited, the jet division of the Thompson Trophy Race was cut to ten laps, as opposed to the twenty the propeller racers would fly. Even ten laps was cutting it close. I had other problems, too. Since my wrinkled bird was no longer usable, I had to borrow someone else's for prac-tice and for the race itself. No time to fiddle or twiddle, just polish the lead-ing edge and hope the borrowed bird was a good one. Fortunately, it turned out to be just that.

The morning of our race, we military pilots were called into a briefing room and given a stern lecture by some colonel we didn't know. We were told that we were there to represent the Army Air Forces, that the public and the press wanted to see our new jets, that we were expected to put on a polished and professional demonstration, that this wasn't a competition for our self-glorification, and that winning was not the object of the exercise. By the expressions on the other faces, I knew the rest of the pilots listening to the colonel wondered where in hell he was coming from. Not compete? Just whom did he think he was talking to—a group from the seminary? What BS.

Time dragged, but we were finally towed out to the parallel runways. There we were positioned into two groups, line abreast, wingtip to wingtip. I thought to myself, This ought to make that first turn around the pylon just off the southwest end of the runway pretty interesting, if not downright hairy.

Someone standing on the hood of a jeep waved a flag as the signal to start engines. For some reason it had been decided we would all make battery starts, not a good thing under any circumstance. My jet took forever to spool up. Glancing away from the tailpipe temperature and rpm gauges, I saw the rest of the guys signaling they were ready. I couldn't catch the starter's attention. Down went the flag.

My engine was only up to 96 percent rpm when away they all went! I felt like the tortoise in Aesop's fable. The other six jets left me fighting their exhaust turbulence and I was last off the ground. Actually, this turned out to be a good thing. As a matter of self-preservation the other six pilots had scattered out for that first turn. By the time I got airborne, my engine was really humming. I was pulling about 104 percent and the tailpipe temperature was just below the red line. OK. Good. Now, if the thing would just last for the next twenty-odd minutes, I'd be all right. I kept my bird down on the deck, about 20 feet off the ground, and sailed around the first pylon underneath several of the other jets.

When we completed a lap and a half I was right behind the leading jet. It was that special bird from Wright-Pat. The way things turned out, and thanks to Tony LeVier, I managed to gain on each of the turns, then had to watch in frustration as the lead guy pulled away on the straightaways. So it went: gain a little, lose a little, around and around. When I pulled the ninth piece of tape off my instrument panel showing I was on our last lap, I tried my best to smooth out each turn. It helped a bit, but even with the throttle practically bent over the quadrant and the temp stuck on the red line, I still went around the last pylon and crossed the finish line a scant second in trail.

At this point, my fuel counter, which I'd been trying to ignore, was showing fourteen gallons remaining. I yanked my throttle to idle and pulled up sharply, trading speed for altitude, setting myself up for a flameout landing just in case. Before I could request priority in the landing pattern, the Wright-Pat guy called a fuel emergency himself. OK, maybe he was pulling excess power the whole time . . . and maybe not.

My engine didn't quit and I landed behind him and then followed onto the taxiway and back to the ramp, unbuckling myself as I went. He was led to the winner's parking spot in front of the grandstands. I ignored my flagman and parked right next to him. On the pretext of offering my congratulations, I jumped out and hustled over to his bird just as the ground crew put up his ladder. Climbing up, I leaned into his cockpit and gave him a congratulatory handshake.

One glance at his fuel counter and I felt like hitting the son of a bitch. Mine had rolled down past zero. His read eighty gallons.

On one particular night in December, coming back from an air show in the Midwest, I thought, How lucky I am to be here in this moment, to be doing this and feeling for the umpteenth time that this is where I belong. My P-80 almost purred as we sped along at 38,000 feet toward California. It was a moonless night with millions of stars glistening over my canopy, so clear and close I felt I could reach out and touch them. Off to my right, several thunderstorms were putting on a magnificent display, lightning flashing from cloud to cloud and striking the earth below. With each flash the clouds nearby gleamed pure white for an instant, and before they returned to dull gray, another flash started the process somewhere else along the front. Of course, the spectacle was silent to me. The sound of thunder and ferocity of action within and beneath the clouds could only be imagined. At my altitude the air was calm, and with practically no headwind, each checkpoint ticked off within seconds of my planned estimates.

Ahead, the Rockies lay under a blanket of snow as they stretched north and south from horizon to horizon. Soon they were behind me, and only the scattered lights of lonely ranches and tiny towns told of people sleeping below. Grand Junction passed underneath. I could see the glow of the city lights of Phoenix off on the horizon to the southwest. The San Francisco Peaks of Arizona lay dead ahead, covered with their white winter's blanket. The small scattering of town lights along the south flanks of the mountain told me I was looking at Flagstaff.

As always, when passing this way, either flying or driving, I thought of the day back in April 1943 when I stood on the flight line at Davis-Monthan and watched the B-17 as it departed, carrying Dad's ashes to be scattered over those same peaks. It seemed very long ago, yet scarcely five years had passed—

five years filled with enough action and experience to last a lifetime: a war, jets, the loss of friends, and in another month, marriage. It was all happening so quickly.

When I crossed the Colorado River, gleaming like a silver ribbon, I knew I was back in California with the home runway only minutes ahead. A call to the last radio range station, instrument flight plan canceled, power back, and nose down started the long, gliding descent toward Riverside and March Field. A sleepy tower operator gave me landing information, and with an overhead pattern, flaps and gear down, a turn to final, and a slight bump, I was down.

I parked and rolled back the canopy. I sat for a few moments filling the forms for an OK flight, jotted down the takeoff and landing times, logged my night time, and listened to the metallic pinging as the engine cooled and the jet settled down until needed again.

On the way to squadron operations to stash my flight gear and change clothes, I thought of just getting into my car and continuing on to Beverly Hills and Ella. It was early Saturday morning and the weekend beckoned. Good judgment prevailed. I needed to get a few hours of sleep right here on base. The rest of the two days ahead could be taken care of with fresh energy . . . and I mean ENERGY!

Our wedding on February 6 in Beverly Hills was wonderful. My dad would have loved it. I missed him terribly that day. The crowd of photographers and people outside the church was really something. Ella and I headed off to ski at Sugar Bowl in Lake Tahoe for a quick honeymoon. It was my first time skiing and I terrorized that mountain. Ella was an old hand at it, having grown up in the mountains of Snoqualmie, Washington. I must say she was very patient with me. That honeymoon gave me a gift I'd enjoy the rest of my life. Skiing became a passion, not only for the sport and physical thrill of it, but because it was a great way to spend times with old friends and meet new ones. The après-ski appealed to me almost as much as the time on the mountain. It was also a grand thing to share with my wife.

We settled into Ella's house and I continued to drive back and forth to March Field. I was made operations officer of the 12th Recon Squadron. I enjoyed it, but, unfortunately, the experience didn't last long.

Not long after the wedding, Colonel Leon Gray was leading eight of us in a pass over the airfield. This wasn't showing off. It was being done for the benefit of the ground crews, who worked so hard to keep our jets in top shape. Leon had his flight in echelon to his right, with me and my flight in echelon on his left. That made a nice big V and looked good from the ground. After passing the north boundary, he started a gradual turn to the left. I eased the nose down, and as my three followed, I gave them the signal to go to right echelon. I never liked turning into an echelon. It was difficult for Three and Four, and seldom necessary. I wanted Leon to pass overhead as I kept going straight during the initial part of the changeover. When I knew my three guys were in trail, I started a gentle turn to the left to rejoin the colonel.

Something went horribly wrong. I couldn't see what happened, but while underneath me, number Four collided with Three and they both went down. Neither managed to bail. It was a bad day. Though I tried my best to give an accurate description in front of the accident board later, their findings made it look as though my actions caused the collision. I was finished as operations officer of the squadron, transferred to 12th Air Force headquarters, then made a personnel director, a task and position for which I had neither affinity nor training. I soon realized I was the one who selected who would go where as people arrived in the command. Moreover, requests for bodies to fulfill vacancies and to fill requisitions from other commands were also under my purview. It was interesting and made me realize how someone in that position might gain an exaggerated sense of importance in the overall scheme of things. I floated along with my new job and flew as often as I liked, which of course was most of the time.

Then one day a request came in for personnel to fill a quota for a new school just organized in Florida. It was called the Air Corps Tactical School. I was the one who would pick the attendees, and my name went on the top of the list. Sometimes even a bad assignment can have good results.

Ella and I laughed and sang as we drove east in my 1939 Buick sedan at the end of April. We were bound for Tyndall Field, located on the beaches of the Florida Panhandle near Panama City. We were excited and happy to be spending the next three months basically alone in a new spot, away from the bustle of Southern California. A new adventure lay ahead and my first headquarters job lay behind.

I returned to March from the tactical school at the end of September, but this time I was assigned to an operations job far more suitable to my experience. I confess those staff jobs didn't hurt me a bit. Whoever had me transferred out of the squadron in the first place really did me a favor. I'm not sure it was his original intent, but that's the way it worked out. It was during this last job at March that I was picked to be one of the escort officers for a flight of RAF fighters doing a tour of the East Coast. Those pilots had Vampire jets and put on shows at various fields, including Washington. They were marvelous fellows, with great skill as pilots and a delightful sense of humor about everything. I thoroughly enjoyed the month I spent with them. Later, when a request came through for someone from March to go on an exchange tour with the RAF for a year, I jumped at the assignment!

In October I was off to England again. Ella was finishing up her latest film assignment, so she'd be joining me in November. I was headed back to what had felt like home, despite the war just two years before, and I was happy!

12

★

Exchange with the RAF 1948

Tangmere was, as the RAF would say, pissing with rain on that late October day in 1948. Ragged gray clouds caught in the trees and blurred nearby buildings. And it was damp, thoroughly damp. Not your normal kind of rain-wet damp, but raw damp right through your clothes, down in your shoes, between your shoulder blades. It was the sort of damp that made mockery of a trench coat and made me wish for a fireplace and a hot glass of something. On top of that, it was cold, the kind of penetrating cold that drove the damp into your bones and made your nose water.

I trudged on toward the flight line and tried to work up some enthusiasm for the situation. It wasn't easy with wet pant legs flapping against my shins and a trickle of cold water trying to get inside my collar. Nor did it help my mood thinking of the night before, when I had spent hours trying to light a coal fire in my room in the officers' mess. I had given up and huddled for the rest of the night under soggy sheets and blankets. Most of all, it hadn't helped this morning facing a limp piece of toast upon which rested twelve evil-looking beans. That, together with a shot of canned grapefruit juice and a small cup of bitter black liquid meant to be coffee, had been breakfast, not just my own breakfast, but breakfast for everyone in the Tangmere mess. The hot sun of Southern California seemed remote and far, far away.

I had known it would be different when I finessed this assignment. I had wriggled my way out of a lousy desk job at March Field and back to a flying slot, a very special flying slot. I was assigned as an exchange officer with No. 1 Squadron of the Royal Air Force. The warriors of the RAF had been my inspiration and envy when I was a cadet at West Point. I grinned remembering how most of us back in 1940 worried the war would be over before we could get into it. The smile brought me back to the challenge of the present, and suddenly I didn't mind the water inside my shoes and dripping off the visor of my garrison cap.

How would No. 1 Squadron feel about having a Yank in their midst, especially a twenty-six-year-old major? Maybe my two Johnny-come-lately combat tours in the last year of the war in Europe and my British Distinguished Flying Cross would help. Time to prove myself would help most of all. I had been told I would find the boss in squadron ops, and the small, nondescript building just ahead had to be the place. Feeling every bit the new kid on the block, I squared my hat, gave a tug to my trench coat, opened the door, and entered the ops office. The room was full of men already. Even without his pips, anyone would have known the man over by a small table was Squadron Leader Tommy Burne, RAF, DFC, etc. A bit stiffly, and quite self-consciously, I snapped a salute, immediately wondering if the RAF saluted when inside. The CO seemed somewhat taken aback and returned the salute with a casual wave of the right hand. Lesson number one: Don't salute in the ops, at least not here in No. 1 Squadron. Lesson number two: Get here earlier in the future.

"Well, Major," Burne said, "welcome to 1 Squadron. Bit of a bother this damned weather, but I expect you'll soon get used to it."

Turning to the room in general, with a huff and a small cough that made his magnificent mustache tremble, Squadron Leader Burne announced, "Gentlemen, this is Major Olds of the United States Army Air Forces. Major, these are the chaps. That tiny one over there is Flight Leftenant Sammy Osborne, a thoroughly useless fellow. And over there, Keith Pearch, our Turk. Here we have Patterson, a colonial from some unlikely place out in the Pacific I think. This next chap is one of yours, another Yank. Goes by the name of Dean Jones. Decent enough, but doesn't seem to be able to leave the old RAF no matter how hard we try to send him packing. Jones, say hello to the major, and mind your manners, he's a big one, this Yank. Ought to do well at dining-in. The rest of these scruffy chaps are our other ranks. Volanthan, good head on him. Foster, silly man wants to be an officer. Young Barton here, and our resident socialist, Flight Warrant Officer Cover. You might smile a bit, Cover, we can't have our Yank thinking the current government of 'jolly old England' hasn't a sense of humor. And here we have the backbone of the old unit, Chiefy Frazier, and his second, Flight Sergeant Bader. These two chaps keep our kites fit and ready for flight."

Introductions made, the CO turned toward me. He was heavyset; "portly" was a better description. His florid face and full cheeks were ample and solid support for the sweeping handlebar mustache that all but hid his mouth. He had a pronounced limp, and I heard the same squeak that had accompanied the heavy thumping steps coming down the hall of our sleeping quarters early that morning. Obviously, he had a leg off and sported some kind of prosthesis. I wondered how he flew. My own air force would have retired him forthwith, intelligence and usefulness notwithstanding.

"That's it then, Major. I expect you'll want to buzz off to the adjutant's office and get read in on squadron bumph and all that sort of thing. But first have a look at what we call 'Pilots Notes.'"

The squadron leader handed over a booklet about the size of a *Reader's Digest*, but much thinner, perhaps no more than fifteen pages. A worn and dilapidated chair with the stuffing bunched all to one side sat empty in a corner. Going over, I thought of the rash of lessons so quickly evident. Squadron Leader Burne was a man to be reckoned with. He knew his people, and maintained a gruff, good-humored association with them. They respected him and did not resent his brand of understatement. I could tell he liked little Sammy, the Turk, Keith, and the New Zealander. He tolerated Jones and Barton. The two warrant pilots, Volanthan and Foster, were solid members of the squadron, but still "other ranks." You knew the CO was certainly not a socialist and didn't think much of the current government. You also knew he could barely tolerate Cover, but would never let that interfere with his sense of fair play and judgment in dealing with the man. Anyone with the squadron leader's impairment and in his position had to be a determined and resourceful individual. I knew I would enjoy working for him, but also I sensed I would quickly come to like him as a friend. Finally, I wondered what "bumph" was and why I had been identified as quite likely to do well at dining-in, whatever that might be. All in good time, I thought.

The cover of the booklet handed to me by the squadron leader simply said "Pilots Notes" and halfway down the page: "Meteor IV." The first page was a general description of the aircraft. A row of them could be seen through the rain-streaked window. They sat on the grass, gray in color and notable for their high, horizontal stabilizers. Twin engines were buried in wing pods on either side of the somewhat long fuselages. Gun ports were visible in the noses, and the RAF roundel with the station and squadron identifying letters gleamed on the fuselages midway between the trailing edge of the wing and tail section. None of this, nor the first page of the book, taught me much, but the impression was good. A general paragraph about the engine came next, and I was musing at what seemed to be the quaint spelling of a device called the "carburettor" when the CO stumped over.

"Righto, Major," said he, "let's go have a look at the kite." Having seen many a movie about my heroes, particularly David Niven in *The Dawn Patrol,* I knew immediately that "kite" meant the aircraft assigned to the squadron. Smart lad, I thought; that practically makes me a bona fide member of the RAF. Looking at the bird, er, kite, was a great idea and would make understanding the rest of the little booklet much easier. Chief Frazier joined us as we splashed out to the tarmac. The chief carried a big black umbrella and held it expertly over the CO. I trudged along behind in the rain.

At the aircraft, there was a wooden stand with stairs moved up against the fuselage next to the cockpit; for the CO, I thought. This proved to be right. Up he went, a step at a time, and motioned to me to join him. The first thing I saw in the cockpit was a parachute already placed in the seat. It looked to me as though it had been there for a long time. As I found when the CO invited me to climb in, both assumptions were entirely correct. I can't honestly say that water squirted out of the parachute in every direction as I sat, but I will testify that my bottom was instantly soaked and icy water ran down the backs of my legs.

The CO leaned over me in the cockpit. "Have a look round, Yank. All the usual stuff scattered about, as you can see. Throttles here, flap handle just there, and gear handle over there. All work as you might expect. That's the position indicator just there, and down between your feet: the compass. Damned thing wants to swing about but the boffins are working that out at present." I wondered, What's a "position indicator" and who are "boffins"?

"Oh, and here we have the . . . umm, ah . . . don't know what you Yanks call it, but it's quite useful." ("Quite useful" was sitting cattywampus within its case and occupied the center place of honor on the instrument panel.) "Belts are a bit different, you'll see. Parachute shoulder straps come over, leg straps come to the crotch and go under the loop, then all snap smartly into the quick release here on your chest. You then rotate the catch. Got that? Now, the shoulder restraints go over and into the lap belt device. Snap, and you're snugly in. Good chap."

The CO was warming to his task. Leaning forward, he pointed to a pair of buttons hidden on the upper left side of the instrument panel under the glare shield. All this time the rain continued, and the canopy was open, but who cared when you were having so much fun?

"Right you are, old boy! Advance the left throttle just past the idle stop. Good. Now, smartly press that left tit"—tit? I thought it was a button—"then reach back port side behind the seat and grasp the outboard lever, pushing down slowly, whilst watching that temp gauge over there."

I did as I was told and a whine grew in volume. Needles on a flock of gauges showed what I assumed to be rpm, temp, oil pressure, and fuel flow climbing. I had managed to start the left engine without blowing us up and felt satisfied that I would find the rest of my checkout easily accomplished after completing the ground training phase and successfully passing the expected written exam.

Not to be so.

"Now then, Yank, start the right. Same procedure, other hand, other side."

A horrible suspicion swept over me. The right engine started easily. I watched as the gauges settled down and the "quite useful" object in the center of the instrument panel came to sluggish life like a boat being tossed on a violent sea.

"Jolly good," said the CO as he handed me a leather helmet. Then he patted me on the shoulder and said happily, "Now then, old boy, off you go!"

Off I go to WHERE, for God's sake? Hell, I didn't even know where the runway might be, let alone how to close and lock the canopy, how to turn on the radio, what my call sign was, whom to call, what kind of clearance to get, at what speed to take off, where to fly in this soup, and more important, at what speed this critter landed. Most of all, how in the name of all that's holy was I ever going to find the field again in this stinking weather? The answer to these and a few other minor details didn't come immediately to mind, so I thought I might take a while finding out how to work the radio. Maybe if I took long enough I could run myself out of gas, er . . . petrol here on the ground.

It did cross my mind that the CO probably had some deep-seated aversion to Americans, and the son of a bitch was trying to kill me right then and there. Putting those thoughts aside and turning my attention to the radio, I soon found the lead wire that fastened to my helmet. I also found the oxygen hose connection. Not that I had any intention of going anyplace I might need oxygen, but old habits die hard, and the oxygen mask contained the microphone. Unfortunately, the radio was designed with morons in mind, and I realized my scheme to run out of fuel on the ground was no longer valid. A switch was clearly labeled ON-OFF. And it worked. I looked around the cockpit, trying to find any gauge telling me something was terribly awry, but that was no good, since I hadn't a clue as to what most of them meant anyway.

The radio was a four-button VHF set, very similar to those in the States. I pressed button A and listened to the familiar hum, then an open silence as the set cycled to that frequency. Not knowing who or what might be on the receiving end, I timidly said, "Hello?"

A cheery voice came back immediately. "That you, Yank? Tangmere Flying Control here. What can we do for you?"

What I wanted him to do for me was not printable or speakable, so instead I said, "Uh, what's the active runway?"

"Runway 27," said he. "QNH 29.87, ceiling 100, vis 500, light rain. You are clear to taxi."

Taxi where, I thought? And what in hell is QNH? Ceiling I can see, but vis 500? Five hundred feet or 500 yards? It sure as hell wasn't 500 miles! He must mean yards. I can see that, too. Holy mackerel, what am I doing? Make a plan—now!

"Uh, Tangmere Tower . . . I mean Control . . . uh, just where is the runway?" (Damn it, it's not my fault I sound so stupid!)

"Yank, this is Tangmere Flying Control. Turn left from your present position and taxi east. Further instructions to follow."

This was strange. Making a left turn put me out in the middle of the flying field. Nothing but grass. With rain puddles. And much splashing. Maybe one of the engines would suck up enough water to quit. Or maybe I could find a nice patch of mud and get stuck. Might be embarrassing, but I'd be alive tonight. No such luck. That expanse of macadam on my right . . . oops, starboard . . . was obviously the missing runway. I taxied on east till I saw the end, turned onto it, and held the brakes. A lot had happened during the past six minutes. I had taught myself to use the differential braking system connected to the rudder bar and operated by a hand lever on the stick grip. I had discovered "quite useful" was the RAF version of an attitude indicator. The horizon line had happily bounced up and down and waggled side to side as I lurched along on the grass. It was plain to see that the set of needles, one pointing more or less up and the other more or less down, was the British equivalent of the American needle and ball. I knew how to operate the radio and oxygen system. The engine instruments, though giving me indecipherable information, were at least telling me something as opposed to nothing. I had learned to close and lock the canopy. And I had told myself the rest of the gadgets didn't matter.

What did matter, and what I didn't know, was how to get this beast back on terra firma in such weather. Come to think of it, I hadn't flown instruments for a long, long time. It was back there in sunny Southern California. Was there a ground-controlled approach unit? I hoped so. There had to be. What was its radio frequency? At what speed did one fly the pattern? How slow or fast did you operate the gear and flaps? Those were minor considerations compared to the problem of getting back to the base. If I could just find the damned runway and get lined up, I felt sure I could get down in one piece.

Well, I thought, here goes nothing, and released the brakes.

"Tangmere, Yank is rolling."

"Righto, Yank, have a good flip." (Flip?)

I pushed the throttles forward, made sure I was aligned, glanced inside for the engine and oil gauges, couldn't find them, and peered through the heavy front glass at the runway ahead. The Meteor IV accelerated smoothly and the stick grip came alive. Experience told me when the elevators began to bite, and the nose rose easily with a slight aft stick movement. Now we skimmed along nose high, gaining speed rapidly. The jet felt eager to fly, and I no longer gave a damn about the rain smearing my windscreen and the dank clouds just feet above my head. The wheels left the earth and I immediately and instinctively pulled back the throttles, raised the gear, and lowered the nose. Not fast enough. We sailed up into the murk and I was in a dark gray bottle of milk. But things felt good, and "quite useful" was steady and level. I inched the power back a tad more and eased the stick forward very slightly. Keeping my eyes over the leading edge of the left wing, I watched for Mother Earth to reappear. Sure enough there she was, just where I had left her, trees and all. I settled into a very low and very slow cruise, and did a gentle 90-degree turn to my left, er . . . port. I knew that would bring me to the south coast near Bognor Regis, as I had done some map reading as soon as I knew of my assignment. After four minutes, more or less, houses appeared in the murk and I had to make a correction to avoid a large natural-gas storage tank in the town. Good landmark, I thought. A port turn paralleling the beach just above the waves and I was beginning to enjoy myself. I had time to wonder at the nature of a people who could enjoy a stroll on the esplanade in such weather, when it occurred to me they were probably thinking similar thoughts about the crazy pilot overhead. I guessed that made us even. Another ten minutes of this and it was time to tackle the hard part. I made a 45-degree turn to starboard and watched for the beach again. There it was! A 45 back to the west and soon enough, there was my storage tank. Turning around it and heading back north, I dallied along for about three minutes, put the gear and flaps down, slowed to a crawl, said a silent prayer, and watched over my starboard wing for the end of the runway. Suddenly, there it was! I didn't care that I was looking at the wrong end; a runway was a runway. And under these circumstances, any end would do. A hard, careful bank to line up, back on the throttles, and I made what would probably be my best landing for the entire rest of the year.

After that adventure, my taxi-in and shutdown were a breeze. I trudged up to squadron ops feeling somewhat proud of myself and secretly glad I hadn't had to bail out on my first sortie under RAF colors. I walked in, not knowing what to expect from my new squadron-mates, perhaps hoping someone might clap me on the back and remark joyfully on my return to the land of the living.

The place was empty. Flying had been canceled and they had all gone off to lunch.

The next morning I sat at breakfast with decidedly more confidence. Several members of the mess actually said a cheery good morning. This offset a noticeable rattling of newspapers in other quarters, a sound oddly conveying irritation. It made me remember those occasions during the war when I would settle into a seat in a first-class carriage on the Ipswich–London 810 train. All of us were aware of the Englishmen's opinion of Yanks. They looked upon us as very young, and very American. We were regularly described as oversexed, overpaid, and, worst of all, over there. Nothing personal was meant by this at Tangmere, but the hunching of the shoulders, the slight turn toward the window and, most of all, the rattle, clearly conveyed a message: "Don't crowd me, don't intrude on my morning routine, don't be rude by trying to speak to me." The reaction was one anybody feels when a stranger hogs the armrest at the movies or starts talking to him at a lunch counter, but there is something unique about the way an Englishman rattles his paper, especially when he feels put-upon. The action is totally eloquent and the message is clear.

Breakfast and the weather matched each other, equally depressing. I hoped the CO was right, that I would get used to it. He meant the weather and I meant both. I realized I was thinking selfishly, so I turned my mind to other matters.

After the previous day's flight the afternoon had been relatively busy and productive. Over in the Orderly Room, I had met the squadron adjutant, who turned out to be the New Zealander, Flight Lieutenant H. W. B. Patterson. He had duly "posted" me in, as it was called. I was then invited to sit at a table on which were lying what looked to be four large photograph albums. These were numbered and carried the squadron insignia and motto, "In omnibus princeps" (First in all things). Opening the first volume, I realized I was looking at the handwritten history of the unit. Patterson explained it was the adjutant's responsibility to enter events as they occurred and photos when they were available.

To tell the truth, I felt as though I were back in high school and our English teacher "Skinny" Lewis had just announced we were going to read Chaucer. I thought how my own air force unit histories were dry statistics and about as exciting and readable as legal notices. To my knowledge, no one outside some obscure person in the Air University had ever even glanced at one, but these RAF volumes turned out to be marvelous.

I saw how the squadron came into being in the second half of the 1800s as an observation balloon company. Proud men stood stiffly at attention next to their horse-drawn equipment. Pictures showed them going aloft in baskets, looking for all the world like those used later in World War I. But these fellows wore swords with cross-belts, epaulets, high collars, and shakos with chin straps. The penned entries told of daily events, of mishaps, of postings in and out. A record existed here of every man who had ever been in No. 1 Squadron. Not for the first time, I thought how wonderfully different was the British sense of history. I had always thought it unfortunate that our own American squadrons didn't have the same regard for their heritage.

Going on to the second volume, I found myself deep in the agony of the First World War. The book told of missions flown, of men lost, and of their aircraft. A scrap of doped linen with a bullet hole gave testament to the end of a German opponent. There were old photos with young faces, grim and fatalistic. It made me recall my dad and his friends talking of those times and how a new pilot had a life expectancy of something like six hours on operations.

Two hours passed quickly and I hadn't finished the third book. Leaving the squadron busily active in the Middle East in the late 1920s, I knew I would be back. Now I realized what the CO had meant by "bumph." It meant history, pride, and tradition; something to know and to feel; a basis for my own devotion to duty within the squadron.

Clothing supply turned into a bit of a problem. Only one flight suit came close to fitting. The corporal in charge kept shaking his head and muttering about overfed and oversized Yanks. Proper gloves and a leather helmet were easier.

Then it was time for tea. Somewhat reluctantly, I went over to the mess. Tea was for ladies, or so I thought. But I knew it would be rude if I didn't go. Besides, if I stayed away, I'd be the only one wandering about the base at that time of day. It turned out to be a wonderfully pleasant occasion. The tea was excellent and it was hot. With it we were served a slice of toast and a pat of real butter. That pat was each man's ration for the week. Luckily, I had hit the right day. Jars of peanut butter were within reach. Though it looked plentiful, I watched the others to see how they handled things. Keith Pearch sat across from me. His butter-spreading technique was masterful. I had to admire how he managed to get it evenly over the entire area of that piece of toast. Then came the peanut butter. This, too, was spread with concentration and deliberation. The reality of controlled rationing hit home. I gained a deeper respect for the men around me, and thought how they and their countrymen had been on strict rations since the start of the war. A sense of guilt at my own country's bountiful plenty struck hard. I pulled my knife away from the peanut butter with the determination to learn just a little more before helping myself.

Keith took a small bite, chewed slowly, had a sip of tea, and looked at me with his dark, brooding eyes. "Have a nice flight, Major?" he asked.

"Yes," I replied. "Good kite, the old Meteor." There, I thought, that bit of understatement ought to go over well.

Keith didn't stare, but I could tell he was reflecting on my answer. I thought it would be best to pull back from any further show of false bravado and added, "But I confess extreme happiness at seeing the runway once again." This brought a smile and a knowing nod. I had said the right thing.

People seemed to disappear after tea, so I went into the lounge and found a comfortable-looking armchair at the far end of the room. I didn't opt to settle too near the tempting fireplace for fear of taking someone's favorite seat. This, too, seemed a good decision. As the room filled, I couldn't tell if time on station or military rank determined nearness to the fire, but there was definitely an order of precedence. I found a magazine. It wasn't too old, about six months, and I tried to immerse myself in the social happenings in Cornwall and Middlesex. The room offered the first real warmth I had enjoyed for some time and I'm afraid I dozed. I awoke as the men were leaving. They moved as though they had a fixed destination, and I followed not knowing what else to do.

Lo and behold! Here was the bar! Pints of mild and bitter ale were had all around. Glasses clinked and voices echoed a chorus of salutations, the most frequent of which seemed to be the old standby, "Cheers!"

Squadron Leader Tommy Burne was holding forth at the center of the bar, pint in hand and mustache aquiver. He beckoned me over and made introductions with "And this is our new Yank." That certainly let me know my arrival had been the subject of some discussion. I accepted the proffered half-pint of "half and half" (normally pronounced "arf an' arf") and began to feel less a stranger among these RAF men.

It was apparent that two half-pints were the norm and no one drank hard liquor. As people started to drift off, Tommy turned to me and said, "A few of the lads are buzzing off to the old Unicorn for a bite to eat. Care to join us, Major? I don't suppose you have a motorcar as yet, so you might as well come along with me. Meet you out front in about twenty."

I wasn't aware of having been given a choice in the matter, but accepted eagerly, then looked for a clue as to whether or not we went as is, or changed into civvies. Civvies turned out to be the right decision. Sam Osborne met me at the front door of the mess. His baggy trousers, tweed jacket, old sweater, and RAF tie pronounced the height of casualness, so I quickly went back to my room and changed, then joined Sam out front.

Up drove Tommy in a prewar MG, which looked as though it had fought valiantly on the beaches at Dieppe. By any American standard, the thing was tiny. The torn and patched top sagged at the passenger side, and the hood (bonnet) was held down by a large leather strap. I was wondering how in the world the three of us were going to fit when Tommy said, "Righto, Osbourne, hop in the back."

Obviously, Sammy had done this before, and I watched in amazement as he wormed his way into a narrow space and sat cross-wise on what seemed to be a loose assortment of tools. I then scrunched down as much as I could and tried to slip backward into the left front seat. It didn't work. I turned and entered the other way, having to put my head practically across Tommy, turn, pull my legs in, turn again, put my feet as far up under the dash as I could, then sit with my knees drawn up near my chest and practically under my chin. I hoped the Unicorn was not too far.

Off we went with just a small lurch as Tommy hefted himself around, accommodating his game leg. As it was still pouring rain, I was beginning to wonder when he would start using the wipers when he reached up in front of the wheel and manually flipped a small handle back and forth. This very nicely worked the one and only wiper blade. After a bit, we reached an impressive speed on a very narrow and winding road. Moments of discomfort came when Tommy passed other cars as though he knew no one would dare appear around the next corner. Since he passed absolutely everything, my moments of discomfort turned into sheer and continuous terror. It was a huge relief to enter the town of Chichester and finally arrive in front of a two-story structure with a sign proclaiming it to be the Unicorn. Putting aside all thoughts of the return trip, I unfolded myself, stretched my cramped legs as unobtrusively as possible, and entered the "Old Uni" behind my two new friends.

It turned out the old pub had been a favorite hangout for the Battle of Britain pilots flying out of Sussex. The walls of the upstairs bar held photographs and marvelous drawings of young faces with dates and names. These men were already legends when I entered the war in 1944. I saw Sailor Malan, Cocky Dundas, Douglas Bader, Ginger Lacey, Stanford Tuck, and others, all heroes to me as a young cadet back in 1940. I had to admit, I still held them in awe.

Another half-pint, then a quick visit to the WC, and we settled down to a relatively excellent meal. I say "relatively," thinking of the two breakfasts I had experienced in the mess. I can't say the choice in the Unicorn was large. The menu offered a variety of lamb and mutton, a meat pie (contents unspecified), soup, and a dessert called "trifle" or something like that. I opted for the lamb and was glad I had done so. The mint sauce was tasty and the potatoes were filling. I don't know what the greens were and knew it didn't matter. Tommy and Sammy ate with appreciation. I had been given another subtle lesson. Things were still grim in jolly old England, but one absolutely did not speak of it, or even notice.

The evening was enjoyable and went quickly. Tomorrow would be another flying day and we did not tarry. The ride home was somewhat less terrifying, and I thought to myself how right Tommy was. Not only would I get used to the weather, I would get used to many things. I looked forward to them all.

A final and most blessed sign of my acceptance greeted me as I entered my room back in the quarters. A small coal fire glowed on the grate and the place was actually comfortable. Grateful for the thoughtfulness of the communal batman, I slept in peaceful warmth.

The next morning, Flying Officer Pearch and I walked over to squadron ops after breakfast. It was still gloomy and misting, but I saw the clouds had lifted somewhat. The ceiling seemed to be about 200 feet this morning and the visibility was a good mile. There were about 350 questions I wanted to ask Keith about instrument procedures here at Tangmere and in the UK in general. Somehow or other, it didn't seem the time for that. Keith was musing about generalities. I knew he was avoiding discussing the very normal questions any pilot would be asking. There must have been a reason, so I hunched my shoulders and trod on.

Chief Frazier was busy filling out some forms when we arrived. I guessed it to be the aircraft lineup for the morning. Flight Lieutenant Sam Osborne was at a small table scribbling something with a pen in a large logbook. The CO arrived, threw his RAF trench coat on a peg, and stumped over to the logbook. He glanced over Sammy's shoulder, pointed, mumbled something, and beckoned to me.

Well, I thought, perhaps now I'll get to hear a flight brief for a training mission under these weather conditions. Not to be.

Tommy pointed to the logbook and explained, "Here we have the day's lineup, old chap. Fellow just has to have a peek to know what's up." I peeked.

There, quite plainly, was a flight of five with aircraft identifying letters, a takeoff time, and pilot names. My name was opposite number Five.

Number Five? I thought. Then I saw the word "Cinegun" under the column labeled "Mission." Cinegun? What in hell is that? I asked myself.

Tommy explained. "Command's laid on a Lanc. Be at twenty-two. Mock attacks for the lads, with film, y'know. Taxi out in twenty."

Oh, OK. Sure, I thought to myself.

I watched the other pilots as I struggled into my flight suit. All took leather helmets and gloves and a Mae West, some took a neck scarf, and each went over to another small table and picked up a 16 mm film pack, just like those we'd used in our P-51s some time ago. I picked up mine, scribbled my name and flight number on it, and followed the flight members out to the tarmac.

Not one word had been said about formation, radio frequencies, join-up, climb-out headings, attack parameters, fuel minimums, recovery procedures, emergency procedures, alternate bases, weather forecasts, or anything like that. Well, the CO had said, "All in good time," but I couldn't help thinking this time was as good as any.

I climbed in my assigned bird (KITE, damn it!), and a ground crewman helped me strap in. The gun camera was right in front of my face, so it was easy to load the film. Since I didn't know if the guns were loaded and armed, it was a bit of a panic to figure out the armament switches so I made sure I learned how to pull the trigger and squirt film instead of 20 mm shells. That done and the radio on, I turned and watched the CO. He soon waggled a finger over his head, and I almost gave a nervous giggle, thinking of *The Dawn Patrol*. The start procedure went easily and the CO taxied forward. Each of the others followed in order and I fell in behind like the smallest duckling.

As we taxied out to the active runway, I made a momentous decision. Number Four was going to have a Siamese twin. I would shadow him like glue. He was going to be my support to home plate. If he landed safely, so would I. If he goofed and ran us into the English Channel, I'd splash right behind him.

The flight lined up two and two on the runway. There was no room for me beside either Three or four. OK, so be it. I stuck the nose of my Meteor right between the two of them 20 feet aft and held the brakes.

Flight Lead called Flying Control and was cleared for takeoff. With a great spray of water kicked up by their twin exhausts, Lead and Two accelerated away. Three and Four ran up their engines and, covered with blinding water, so did I. When I saw them move I let go the brakes and stayed not 30 feet behind. Aside from the water, and the fact that I could barely see the two aircraft so close ahead, it was really not too difficult. Three, with Four close on his right wing, cleared the ground. I kept my bird rolling for just a fraction longer in order to have room to slide over beneath Four. As his gear and flaps retracted, so did mine. But my timing was not that good. Before I could get close enough in trail, Four disappeared into the soup.

There went my ticket home. This was the moment of truth, as they say. If I lost him, I hadn't a clue how to get back on the ground in one piece. I knew this with certainty. What the hell, press on! Since my last perception of him was a good steady closure with a safe vertical clearance, I held what I had. After what seemed an eternity, but in reality was only a few seconds, Four loomed ahead of me and slightly above. His misty image in the thick cloud was one of the prettiest things I had ever seen. It was a great relief to move right up underneath his tail and just below his tailpipes.

We climbed quickly. As the clouds grew brighter I could see that Three had latched onto the lead aircraft's right wing. I wondered if he had used the same closure technique as I had. Damn, I sure had a lot to learn. These lads could teach me a thing or two about formation instrument flying.

We burst out of the clouds and into a bright blue sky. The CO, who had been working the radio for some time and obeying ground control instructions, now made a turn to the north. Gaining more height and following the calm voice coming from some radar center far below, he soon called out a tallyho on the Lancaster bomber, which was our cinegun target. It was on a reciprocal heading, 1,000 feet below us, about 3 miles out and at our ten o'clock position. Even tucked under number Four, I could see we had been vectored into perfect position for our mock attack.

Chalk up one for the pros, I thought as the CO reminded us to check proper switch positions and follow him down and to the left for a high-side attack.

Two, Three, and Four took interval as they followed the CO down the chute. Not Five. By God, Four was my ticket home, and I wasn't going to let him get more than 50 yards away from me.

So it went. The rest of the flight made half a dozen or more practice attacks, keeping an interval allowing each to close and fire off film as though he were actually attacking. Somewhere in this aerial ballet, the CO called, "I say, number Five, move it out a bit, old boy." I pretended complete language barrier syndrome and possible radio failure and kept sticking close to Four.

Eventually the CO waggled his wings, signaling join-up, and started a shallow left turn, allowing the rest of the flight to cut the corner and move into close formation. This was no concern of mine. I was already as close to Four as I could get.

Now comes the fun part, I thought. Let's see how we get home.

At his signal, we changed radio frequencies with the CO. "Tangmere Control," he called, "Red Flight requesting a steer and a QGH."

"Right you are, Red Flight, pick up a heading of 150 and descend to angels 20. Oranges are sour but vis has picked up a bit. Should be no bother." I was delighted to hear that bit of news.

Tommy responded with, "Tangmere, Red Leader here. Heading 150, letting down through 24 to angels 20. Airspeed 350 slowing. Three and Four are on my right wing." (Hey, what about Five?)

"Red Leader, turn left 145, level at angels 20."

"Roger, Tangmere Control. Steady at 145, airspeed 250, and leveling at angels 20."

Obviously, Control was taking a fix on the CO's transmissions and was vectoring us toward home plate. We stayed at angels 20.

A few more transmissions and responses and Tangmere announced, "Red Leader, you're overhead. Turn right to a heading of 240. Hold angels 20 and 200 airspeed."

A moment or two, then, "Red Leader, start your descent. Heading 240, airspeed 200."

I reduced throttles when Four did and held my position under his tail. Down we went and soon entered the soup. All the while, Tangmere Control verified our headings and the CO responded with altitude, heading, and airspeed. When we reached 10,000 feet, Tangmere Control ordered a descending left turn to a heading of 005, to descend to and maintain an altitude of 3,000 feet.

So far so good; I could tell what was going on, and holding my position on Four was easy. I didn't have to glance at the instrument panel to feel us level off. Throttles were not advanced and I knew we were bleeding the airspeed down to a point below 200.

A few minor heading corrections after verifying altitude and speed and Control turned us over to GCA.

A new voice came on the air. "Red Three and Four turn right 095. Descend to one thousand five and maintain."

Red Three banked smoothly right to the new heading and let down. We were still in the soup. Thirty seconds later GCA ordered Red Lead and his wingman to turn to the same heading and to maintain the same altitude. We were now two elements on parallel courses on the downwind leg of our GCA pattern. Soon the controller turned Red Lead left to a heading of 005. Seconds later the three of us in the second element were turned to the same heading. The turn onto the final approach heading was accomplished in the same fashion. This put the Lead element directly ahead of the three of us with about a 2-mile separation.

A new voice came on the air. "Red Lead, Final Controller here. How do you read?"

"Loud and clear, Control."

"Righto, Lead. Gear should be down. You are approaching the glide path. Turn right 278 and begin descent."

The rest was routine. Control efficiently and smoothly brought all of us down the chute. For me, it was a breeze. When Four's gear started down, so did mine. Same with the flaps.

We broke out of the clouds at about 300 feet. I could see the end of the runway dead ahead under Four's belly. I pulled back on my throttles and concentrated on landing in the first few feet so that Red Four would touch down well ahead of me. It worked and we all rolled down the runway together, slowing to taxi speed before turning off onto the perimeter track.

As we walked into ops, the CO turned to me and grinned. "Good show, Yank."

What greater praise could a man want? I grinned back.

My entire year with No. 1 Squadron in England was a dream. Many adventures were had and new friends were made. Much time was spent in various pubs and roaming the countryside in my own little MG. Visits were made to theatres in London. It was a pleasure to wander on the streets at night under brightly lit streetlamps and to see the graceful old city rebuilding itself. How different this experience was from a mere four years earlier! Over several decades after this great assignment, No. 1 Squadron mates continued to keep in touch, and we visited each other often.

Although Ella had film projects often taking her back to California, we managed to rent a wonderful old, drafty stone house near the base, which we enjoyed immensely during her visits. The plumbing never worked correctly and the peat fires we set in the fireplace often smoked up the whole house, but bottles of ale, dinners at the pub, and all the good men of the RAF made this a magical year. Had I known what lay ahead, I would have enjoyed it even more.

13

★

F-86s at March Field, the Pitts, and Stewart

The trip back from England to California was a grind. Military transports were still four-engine piston jobs and a journey across the Pond to the West Coast took a couple of days, not hours. It was good to get home, and Ella was waiting for me in Coldwater Canyon with chilled champagne and a warm bed.

I reported to the 1st Fighter Group at March AFB, where I was assigned as operations officer for the 94th Fighter Squadron, Eddie Rickenbacker's "Hat-in-the Ring" outfit. It was Nieuport 28s and SPADs for Eddie and new jets for us. It was a thrill for me in a lot of ways: I was finally stationed close to my beautiful wife, the challenge of the F-86 kept me hopping, and the honor of serving in Rickenbacker's old unit made me intensely proud. Eddie was a good pal of my dad as I grew up, but in my eyes he had been a superhero. As a kid I sat at the dining table in total awe of the two of them.

March had changed drastically during my year at Tangmere. The primary organization was now the 1st Fighter Group, which had the 27th, 71st, and 94th squadrons; all had served with distinction during World War II.

The 27th was commanded by Lieutenant Colonel Jack Bradley and the 71st by Major Jack Hayes, and my boss in the 94th was Major James Lemmon. Lemmon was a tolerant man, which was fortunate, as he put up with our often differing opinions with great patience. The three squadrons were filled with strong personalities, almost all with extensive experience in the recent war. One didn't so much command men like these as persuade them that your way was better. It was a challenge.

In the previous year the 94th had transitioned from the P-80 into the new F-86A-1. We referred to them as Dash Ones because they were the first of their breed. Modifications in succeeding Dash models would be incorporated on the assembly line as lessons were learned from these originals. The Sabre was a huge leap forward in aviation technology. She was a single-seat, single-engine beauty with swept wings and six .50 caliber machine guns in the nose. The leading edges of the wings featured movable slats designed to increase lift and reduce speed during takeoff and landing. The engine itself was an axial-flow design, much sleeker and more efficient than the old centrifugal-flow engines. The air entered the nose intake, went through a twelve-stage compressor, and then through the burner cans. There, jet fuel ignited, causing the compressed air to expand. The expansion gave a lot of thrust and was much more responsive than the old-style engines. Along the way the blast of superhot air passed over a turbine, which drove the compressor section up front. All of this sounded complicated, but in truth those engines were far simpler than pistons. The process entailed two simple laws of physics. Newton told us that actions had reactions, and Boyle explained that when you raise the temperature and pressure of a gas it accelerates. Get it all expanding and pushing in sequence and you go fast.

The new fighters had a lot of glitches, however, some of which were downright dangerous. For one thing, the leading edge slats had to be manually locked in the retracted position after takeoff. This was supposed to happen when our speed reached a point at which the air pressure pushed the slats flush against the wing. Then the pilot pushed a handle to lock the devices. We soon learned that that procedure was not to be trusted. It looked as though things were securely locked, but sometimes they weren't. Later, when we pulled g's in maneuvering or slowed down rapidly, one of the slats would release and bang forward. This caused huge drag on one side, slewing the aircraft sideways. The result was exciting, to say the least. A violent roll coupled with a pitching moment was always disconcerting but could be disastrous too close to the ground. We dealt with the problem by humping the jet into half a negative g just after liftoff. That banged the slats back against the wing, and we quickly hit the locking handle before releasing the negative g.

Another problem was the control system. The ailerons and elevators were fully hydraulically boosted. That was fine unless you lost hydraulic pressure through engine flameout or failure in the hydraulic system. We were supposed to be able to fly the bird without boost, but that wasn't always so. I was lucky and never encountered that one.

There were some difficulties with pitch control. These first-generation aircraft had conventional elevators on the horizontal stabilizer. At high Mach numbers they were prone to stresses the engineers hadn't anticipated. Failure of an elevator on one side made for an interesting ride home, sometimes by nylon or else by the grace of God. Later models would have a full flying tail plane or slab rather than fixed and movable sections.

Major Hayes of the 71st FIS Squadron was reassigned and I was given command of the squadron. It was sad leaving the 94th, but squadron command was a new challenge. I soon found the morale low and attitude poor within all ranks of the squadron. I guess I shouldn't have been surprised. My limited contacts with Major Hayes had left a sour taste in my mouth, and the conditions in his squadron tended to back up my opinion of the man. Fortunately, the unit had some great guys, so it didn't take long to get things running smoothly.

The squadrons tended to be measured by the amount of flying time racked up each month. It didn't seem to matter to anyone if training was actually accomplished; it was the total hours that mattered. I thought the practice wasteful and was determined to change things in my squadron. At a meeting with the maintenance, armament, and supply sections, along with the squadron ops officer, I announced my plan.

"OK, troops, we've got eighteen aircraft assigned. I want only five aircraft on the first scheduled flight each day. Four will fly the mission and then an hour later I want five more. If the fifth plane isn't used as a spare on the first go, it can be used to fill in the second go, and so on and so forth during each flying day, initially for six such flights a day. Ops will publish a daily order and you will know how to configure the birds for the training mission to be flown. There will be no trolling around the sky building up useless time. Each flight will have an assigned mission and each flight will do just that. When we need to schedule more than one flight at the same takeoff time, for whatever reason, you will be advised days ahead of that requirement.

"Now, to get started, we are going to work the pilots' butts off out at the Dry Lake Gunnery Ranges. I want each flight loaded with exactly 110 rounds of color-coded ball ammo. Note the color in the aircraft form and make sure no two aircraft in the same flight carry the same color. We will start with strafing. Squadron pilots will rotate as the range duty officer for five days. That duty will be rotated. The range officer will assure the strafe targets are up and range time is available for each scheduled flight. We will phone to let him know the lineup. He will score the targets and call the results back to us, so by the time the flight lands we will have everyone's scores.

"I emphasize, I do not want you men to produce a flight line full of in-commission birds by eight o'clock each morning and then spend the rest of the day playing catch-up. Every man in the squadron will know exactly what we plan to achieve each day, with what resources, and when. If you maintenance troops have five birds ready to go at six in the evening, they go on the next day's schedule. And you guys go to the club or go home. No working late into the night to see how many birds you can put out on the line the next morning. I want only those five. GOT IT?" They got it.

We quickly settled into this new routine, and it was gratifying to see the squadron pull itself together. Our missions were productive, there was no wasted time, and, without even trying, we were so far ahead of the other two squadrons in both useful and total flying time it wasn't even a contest. Best of all, our aircraft were better maintained, their availability soared, the troops were happy and proud of the squadron. Even group headquarters took notice.

So did the 27th Squadron, which then doubled its schedule in an effort to outdo the 71st. I suspected they were indulging in a bit of time padding and sent one of my people up to the control tower for a couple of days to log their actual takeoff and landing times. We then checked the times the squadron turned in officially. Surprise! As an example, one of their planes took off and landed after an hour and forty minutes of actual flight. What was the pilot doing during that time? He logged two hours and fifteen minutes. That wasn't the worst case. One pilot went on a weekend cross-country and came back Sunday evening. He logged forty hours in three flying days, and without drop tanks. In my view, that might have been funny if it weren't downright criminal.

I understood that competition was the breath of life among fighter pilots and that many things were done in the name of one-upmanship and unit esprit. Unfortunately, the rivalry got out of hand. Many commanders fostered and actually encouraged it, while the duty of serious training and efficient operations took a back seat to squabbling in the sandbox. It took a long time for the practice to be stamped out.

Our group commander moved on and Lieutenant Colonel Jack Bradley took over the outfit. One day it was announced that all three squadrons would put up twelve aircraft each and he would lead us in an out-and-back cross-country. He would lead the 27th, his old outfit; I had the 71st on the left, and the 94th was on the right. The plan was deceptively simple. We would line up all thirty-six aircraft on the runway in flights of four. Each would follow the flight ahead as closely as possible, which meant almost half the gaggle would be on the roll before the lead flight became airborne. That also meant we would be eating one another's exhaust and fighting the jet wash of all the birds in front. Then Lead would circle the field just once while the three squadrons formed up in the positions briefed. The whole mass would then climb out on a heading for Las Vegas to the northeast while maintaining close formation. I had deep misgivings about the whole scheme.

The J-47 engines on the F-86s gave off black smoke at full power. Thirty-six of them all together created a dense, choking black cloud. We could not see anything ahead with any certainty. The smoke coupled with the turbulence produced by all those in front made for one of the hairiest formation takeoffs any of us had ever experienced.

Once off the runway, we struggled to play catch-up to Lead. I kept the 71st flights of four in trail position and stayed down low during this maneuver. That was comfortable for my guys and had the added benefit of keeping us down where we could cut across his circle for join-up. It also placed us in a position where he couldn't see us and offer some caustic advice on how to fly our aircraft.

Once in position, we climbed out over Cajon Pass, crossed Victorville, and sailed out over the Mojave on our way to Vegas. We kept climbing, still in close formation. The F-86 was a great little fighter, but a pilot had to be on his toes to keep it happy at extreme altitudes. We reached reasonable cruising altitude and still climbed. I think we leveled at 44,000, each of us struggling to hold position. None of us dared gaze around to enjoy the view. Keeping formation took total attention and a delicate hand on both stick and throttles.

My sense of time told me we ought to be just about over Vegas when Lead suddenly made a hard turn to his left. There was immediate pandemonium! Twenty-four aircraft were turning into my squadron. There was no way I could pull the power back far enough to stay in position. I pushed the nose down as smoothly as I could just in time to have the 94th Squadron sail right over our heads from their position on the right. It took a good twenty-five minutes to catch Lead as he headed back the way we had come. I still remember his angry orders for me to get my unit back into formation.

When we approached Cajon Pass, headed southwest, we were still at 44,000 feet. Lead announced we were going to make a pass across the home airfield and suddenly pushed his nose down sharply. March Field was only some 30 miles ahead at that point. All thirty-six of us, still in close formation, tried to follow suit. The dive angle was steep and our birds began to shudder as we approached the F-86's limiting Mach.

Each of these early Sabres had its own little peculiarities of engine and airframe. Over time each pilot had developed his own techniques to cope. I don't know what the hell he thought he was doing, but my number Two suddenly lurched past me; his aircraft porpoised once or twice, then snap-rolled violently as he passed right over me. I felt a bang but my bird seemed OK. I lost sight of number Two. Aircraft everywhere were pulling up and out of the melee. I did my best to keep Lead in sight but admit I pulled the power back a tad to avoid losing what control I had. I could see March over my nose and watched in fascination as Lead, with his wingman in tow, crossed the field at an extreme rate of speed and then pulled up to avoid the low hills across the way at old Camp Hahn. His wingman actually blew dust during this pullout. I still followed at a respectable altitude and distance and went up as Lead rose in a steep climb. Up and up he went, then did a wing over and came right back down at me.

For God's sake! Suppose the whole group had been able to stay with him? Did he think they had? Did he ever look over his shoulder for a wingman?

Debriefing was grim. All of us got our butts chewed for failing to maintain formation. We weren't worthy of calling ourselves fighter pilots, and on and on. I looked around and saw that no one else was going to speak, so I stood up.

"Yeah, Olds, what do you want?"

"Sir, perhaps given today's performance, we should fly combat formation."

"Combat formation? Ah, what do you 8th Air Force guys know about combat formation? Anyone else have anything to say?"

That ended the meeting. My number Two had dented the top of my vertical stabilizer when his bird went out of control. He had lost part of his elevators. We were lucky that day. No one was lost and all had landed safely, if somewhat shakily. There were lessons learned by all of us except possibly Bradley.

On June 25, 1950, North Korea stormed across the 38th parallel and invaded the South with a massive force of ninety thousand troops. The news was a bombshell. By 1950, the United States already had army and air force units stationed in South Korea to support the ROK military, and the massive blow put our own troops in direct contact with the invading forces. It took only a day or two for America to take action against the North Koreans, and our intentions were sanctioned by a unanimous vote of the United Nations Security Council. The Russians made the grave error of walking out on the debate, and the vote was taken without them.

The war that followed was grim. The North pushed down to the southern tip of the peninsula. We held on to a small bit of territory surrounding a place called Pusan, mounted an invasion at Inchon, and pushed back. Our troops went almost to the Yalu River separating Korea from China. Then China entered the fray and pushed us back to the 38th. At that point both sides dug in and faced each other. U.S. forces would spend the next three years attacking and counterattacking, up one mountain and down in battle after battle. It proved futile and costly in human lives. We lost over thirty-six thousand Americans. Washington would not call it "war" but referred to it as a "police action." Whatever Korea was, I would miss it completely.

At March, the 1st Fighter Group was ordered to move all three squadrons to Victorville and reopen George Air Force Base. We did it in mid-July. All of us thought we would be deployed to Japan or Korea to take part in the intense fighting, but it was not to be. To my disappointment, in September the 71st and 27th squadrons were ordered to Griffiss AFB near Rome, New York. There, we would become part of the Eastern Air Defense Force.

Air defense against what, for God's sake? Russian bombers over the North

Pole? There was a war in Asia and we were patrolling the extreme northeast U.S. Worst of all, we deployed baggage, furniture, kids, and wives to the East Coast while the Pentagon sent the 4th Group out of Langley all the way from the East Coast to Japan. The 71st stayed at Griffiss for just three months, August through October, before we were transferred again to what we soon called the "armpit of America," Greater Pittsburgh Airport. The conflict with Korea created a sudden demand for pilots, and my experienced troops were drained off quickly. I put my own name at the top of every list, only to have it removed by someone at higher headquarters. I was furious and frustrated. I tried repeatedly without results.

I was made base commander for the unit at Pittsburgh. I don't know if that was meant to pacify me or to punish me for my repeated requests for combat assignment. Suddenly, my job entailed herding a bunch of engineers and command administrators through the design and construction of new base facilities. The construction part was interesting. The office hours were not. I wanted the roar of engines, not the sound of clacking typewriters, an inside view of a heavy overcast, not a mountain of papers. I was a fighter pilot, not a paper pusher.

Ella had been warned when I proposed to her in 1946 that I was and always would be a fighter pilot. She seemed comfortable with that and we were so in love that nothing could have kept us from getting married. Now here I was, an honest-to-God desk driver, barely a pilot and certainly not a fighter pilot. My poor wife. Our move from California impeded her acting career in Hollywood because she started commuting from Los Angeles to New York as soon as I got to Griffiss. She kept her house in Coldwater Canyon while she fulfilled her contract obligations to Universal Studios for two more movies. She rented an apartment on Park Avenue in Manhattan in order to be near me, and we spent as much time there as we could. Television was emerging and the National Broadcasting Company's headquarters were in New York City. One thing naturally led to another and Ella immediately started appearing in TV shows, including the premiere of the *Pulitzer Prize Playhouse* with Charles Coburn in October. We made the most of that apartment and had great fun mingling in the glamorous high society of the city.

At one party, I ran into Eddie Rickenbacker and was stunned that he remembered me as a boy from Langley. He seemed to know all about my exploits at Wattisham during the war. By then he had been running Eastern

Airlines for several years. His early vision was to turn the former mail and transport carrier into America's first commercial airline, and he did it with the generous financial investment of one of his greatest fans, Laurance Rockefeller, son of John D. Rockefeller. Laurance was an aviation nut, a pilot himself who spent endless hours engrossed by Rickenbacker's tales of combat. After a brief chitchat, Eddie dragged me across the room to meet Laurance, and a friendship was born that would last the rest of our lives. Larry was a gem of a guy, witty, down-to-earth, easygoing, deeply intelligent, and unusually kind. I liked him right away. My friendship with him took on many permutations over the years. I introduced him to Ella at the party that night. I had no clue what impact that meeting would have on the rest of my life.

On the home front, Ella was feeling my frustration. I know it affected her television work and her moods. She suffered an entire month of ghastly illness in December, and there was little I could do to help her from Pittsburgh. The phone rang one cold afternoon in my office. It was Ella's doctor in New York telling me she had suffered a miscarriage. I took two days' emergency leave and rushed to the city. We'd had no idea she was pregnant. It was a sad two days, but I had to get back to work. Ella did, too, and appeared in a few shows on the new series *Robert Montgomery Presents*. We were both committed to our jobs.

Back in Pittsburgh, I returned to training pilots for Korea. I kept putting my name at the top of all lists headed in that direction. My group boss chided me endlessly, saying, "Olds, I can't get to Korea, and if I can't go, you're not going." It made me mad. Was he really taking my name off the combat lists as they passed his desk? What right did he have to do that? That man became a pariah to me, and I blamed him for the next fifty years. Of course, if I had gone to Korea, I would never have made it to Vietnam. Fate plays a strong role in our lives.

It also brought me my first child. Ella thrived during her next pregnancy in 1951. The doctors put her on a simulated estrogen therapy called DES to prevent miscarriage, and she gave birth on January 5, 1952, in Manhattan to a squalling, healthy girl. We named her Christina Eloise after my mother. Ella hired a nurse and settled her into the apartment with our baby, then got back to the business of regaining her health and svelte form for television and film work.

I kept grinding away at my 71st Squadron CO job and flew often from

Greater Pittsburgh Airport to visit Ella and baby Chris in New York City. The flight to Mitchell Field on Long Island was a simple one and I knew the route by heart. I also knew all the radio range station frequencies, flight times, headings, altitudes on the airways, reporting sequences, and fuel-consumption data for every type of aircraft I flew on that route: the F-86, the T-33, the twin Beech AT-11, and even the old Gooney Bird C-47. The route was boring but each visit with my wife and baby daughter made the trip worthwhile.

I gave up trying to get to Korea in June of '52 after being offered a job as a civilian test pilot at North American. I submitted my resignation. Damn it all. My boss, Major General Freddy Smith, commanding officer of the EADF, easily persuaded me to tear up that resignation. He and I both knew I didn't really want to leave the air force, and as some sort of compensation for not getting to Korea, I was reassigned to Smith's headquarters at Stewart as a staff officer. That assignment was the low point of my thirty years of service.

It wouldn't be until 1998 that I learned the truth about why I never made it to Korea. I heard it from a colonel who had been stationed in the Pentagon in 1950. Ella and her TV producers persuaded Laurance Rockefeller to use his considerable political influence at the Pentagon level to get my name off the list every time it came up. The show had to go on, and a worried and distracted air force wife was not a good investment. It was hard to be pissed at that point, because of the track my career took, but I was sure surprised. More than anything, I felt like a heel for blaming my group CO all that time.

When I moved to Stewart from Griffiss, Ella and I rented a lovely country house on the north face of Storm King Mountain in Cornwall on Hudson, New York. I was actually able to come home for dinner. Cornwall was only about seven miles from New Windsor, and life settled into a comfortable routine. Little Chrissie was tearing around the house chasing our two English spaniels; we had a nice German couple working for us doing cooking, cleaning, nanny duties, and house and grounds maintenance; and a beautiful second daughter came along on March 12, 1953. We named her Susan Bird Olds after Ella's mother, Bird Zachary Raines. Our family felt complete and life was full.

The staff job at EADF headquarters at Stewart was chief of the Programs Division. I was unhappy with the desk job yet slightly ambivalent about it. The early 1950s were a time of great change for America's armed forces, and I found the position as a programming officer somewhat challenging. We were entering the Cold War and building a military force based on deterrence and nuclear weapons with an underlying philosophy of massive retaliation and mutual destruction. It was going to be a huge economic drain to support a force that would by definition be a failure if it was ever used.

The Air Defense Command grew to sixty-four interceptor squadrons based at some fifty airfields. Our airplanes were F-86Ds, F-89 Scorpions, and F-94 interceptors, all armed with 2.75" air-to-air rockets. There was even acquisition of a nuclear air-to-air missile for some of these units. Integrated with this, the army manned surface-to-air antiaircraft missile sites in defense of major cities. Fascinating as all of this was, I developed an aversion to the whole mess. I was convinced that the system lacked any true capability against a determined assault. To me the only positive part was that the ADC created assignments for experienced fighter pilots returning from Korea.

In May 1954 I was moved to Operations as director of Ops and Unit Training at Pittsburgh, and then promoted to full colonel at the age of thirty-three. Many, including me, thought it might be a bit premature, but what the hell, I was determined to do my best. Things perked along at a steady pace, but I was antsy.

Ella had gone right back to television work after Susie was born and she started her own production company, Cornwall Productions, with Joan Harrison. They produced a series called *Janet Dean, Registered Nurse,* which ran for a year. Ella starred in the leading role as a nurse back from the war who employed her detective abilities to solve military medical cases. Some of the plot ideas came from my Wattisham tales, and those were, of course, the best shows in my opinion. Ella was happy, and, given that she wasn't the most natural of mothers, we were both grateful for the good care given our daughters by the German governess.

Then things sort of fell apart. Ella decided she wanted to live in New York City again and bought a co-op apartment in a building at 1075 Park Avenue. Off she went with the girls. Her mom, whom I liked, moved into a small cottage with me up on that mountain. None of this was exactly what I had bargained for. The situation went on for more than a year, and then I received

Robin's father, Captain Robert Olds, 1920.
(Olds Family Collection)

Robin's mother, Eloise Wichman Olds,
1920. *(Olds Family Collection)*

Captain Robert Olds *(seated, front row, middle)* with fellow pursuit pilots at Langley
Field, 1919. *(U.S. Army Air Corps)*

Robin *(crouching left)* at pilot training in Oklahoma between semesters at West Point in 1942. *(U.S. Army Air Corps)*

Robin next to a battle-scarred P-38 Lightning with the 434th Squadron at Wattisham, England. *(Photo by Colonel Leon Gray)*

Major Robin Olds in a P-51 Mustang at Wattisham, England. *(U.S. Air Force Photo)*

Major Robin Olds on the wing of his P-51 Mustang, *SCAT VI*, at Wattisham, England, in 1945. *(U.S. Army Air Corps)*

The first jet aerobatic team on a one-day cross-country publicity junket in 1946: breakfast in Los Angeles, lunch in Washington, D.C., and dinner back in L.A. *(Left to right)* Lieutenant Jack Richardson, Major Leon Gray, Lieutenant Jack DeMoss, and Major Robin Olds. *(U.S. Air Force Photo)*

P-80 Shooting Star jet cross-country team in 1946: Jack DeMoss, Red Burdett, Robin Olds, Leon Gray, and Harold Moffat. *(U.S. Air Force Photo)*

Beverly Hills wedding to Ella Raines in 1947. *(Universal Pictures Company Photo)*

No. 1 Squadron—Royal Air Force, Tangmere, Sussex, England. Olds *(far left front)* Meteor IVs behind. *(Royal Air Force Photo)*

Ella, Susan, Robin, and Christina in Manhattan, New York, home in 1954. *(Allied Photo Service, N.Y.C.)*

Colonel Robin Olds, wing commander, 81st TFW, addressing his wing in front of an F-101 at Bentwaters and Wood-bridge Royal Air Bases, England. *(U.S. Air Force Photo)*

Colonel Olds *(left)* and Captain John B. Stone *(right)* after Bolo operation January 2, 1967. *(U.S. Air Force Photo)*

First Tactics Conference, December 1966, Ubon Royal Thai AFB. *(U.S. Air Force Photo)*

Colonel Olds *(right)* and Captain Stone *(left)* meeting with Brigadier General Edward McGough *(center)* the evening of the successful Bolo mission. *(U.S. Air Force Photo)*

Colonel Olds meeting with the Thai forces T-28 squadron commander, Lieutenant Colonel Salukiat, at Ubon Royal Thai AFB. *(U.S. Air Force Photo)*

Colonel Olds *(first row, third from left)* with the 8th TFW Satan's Angels squadron. *(U.S. Air Force Photo)*

Colonel Olds with an 8th TFW crewman, Ubon, Thailand. *(U.S. Air Force Photo)*

After downing a MiG, Colonel Olds with the May 4, 1967 mission flight members *(top, left to right)* Colonel Olds, Lieutenant Bill Lafever, Major Bill Kirk, *(bottom, left to right)* Captain Norm Wells, Captain Dick Pascoe, and Lieutenant Bodahl. *(U.S. Air Force Photo)*

Colonel Olds preparing for his final mission, supposedly number 100 but really mission number 152. *(U.S. Air Force Photo)*

Final mission prep with ground crew. *(U.S. Air Force Photo)*

Colonel Olds in the cockpit of an F-4 Phantom II, *SCAT XXVII*, on his last flight out of Ubon as the wing commander. *(U.S. Air Force Photo)*

Colonel Olds and Lieutenant Steve Croker after their final mission. *(U.S. Air Force Photo)*

The final-mission portrait. *(U.S. Air Force Photo)*

Colonel Olds carried on the shoulders of his men after his final mission as they bore him to the officers–club party. Olds was hoping that no one saw the tears streaming down his face. *(U.S. Air Force Photo)*

Colonel Olds waving to the troops after his final mission, September 1967. *(U.S. Air Force Photo)*

The famous Robin Olds "finger" at the final mission celebration in the Ubon officers club. *(U.S. Air Force Photo)*

Meeting with President Lyndon B. Johnson the day after returning from Vietnam. Olds told LBJ to "get us out of this GD war!" When LBJ asked how, Olds replied, "It's simple, sir— just win it!" *(White House Photo)*

Debriefing the Chiefs of Staff after the meeting with LBJ. *(Department of Defense Photo)*

First day as commandant at the U.S. Air Force Academy. Four red stars depicting his four MiG aerial victories had been painted on the chair before his arrival. *(U.S. Air Force Academy Photo))*

Robin promoted to brigadier general. *(U.S. Air Force Academy Photo: commandant, official portrait, 1968)*

Chappie James joins Robin for the USAFA Class of 1969 dining-in, leading the cadets in the traditional fighter pilot songs, which were censored for the more sensitive public. *(U.S. Air Force Academy Photo)*

Christmas vacation with Ella and daughters at the Sugar Bowl ski resort, Lake Tahoe, in 1970. *(Photo by William S. Young for the San Francisco Chronicle)*

Retirement in Steamboat Springs, Colorado, 1988. *(Olds Family Collection)*

Robin and Morgan Olds in 1986. *(Olds Family Collection)*

Robin gleefully hooking into a twenty-five-inch rainbow trout in Alaska. *(Photo by Eric Newman)*

Robin in the cockpit of his original P-51 Mustang, *SCAT VII*, after restoration by Jim Shuttleworth. *(Photo by Leslie Hicks)*

SCAT XXVII comes home to rest at the National Air Force Museum in 1998, its battle scars honorably intact. Robin insisted the museum not repaint or clean his Phantom. *(Air Force Museum Photo)*

Fighter Aces reunion *(from left to right)* Tex Hill, Joe Foss, Robin Olds, Gabby Gabreski, Bob Hoover, and Skip Lehman. *(American Fighter Aces Photo)*

Robin *(right)* and his lifelong best friend, USAF Brigadier General (Ret.) Benjamin B. Cassiday *(left)* at the Air Force Academy–Army football game in October 2005. *(U.S. Air Force Academy Photo)*

Susan, Robin, and Christina July 4, 2006. *(Photo by Tommie Stone—Mrs. J. B. Stone)*

Lead is Gone! Number 1 pulls up for the missing man ceremony over the USAFA cemetery June 30, 2007. It was stunning because it's normal for the number 3 man to pull up. Pilot E. T. Murphy asked Christina's permission to pull a "Robin" maneuver the day before the funeral. *(Photo by TSgt. Rollan "Yoke" Yocum, USAF [Ret.])*

A 1996 lithograph, *Phantom Strike,* by Robert Taylor depicts the March 30, 1967, low-level strike on the steel mills at Thai Nguyen. *(Military Gallery Publishing Photo)*

orders to Germany. I was assigned to command an interceptor group at a place called Landstuhl.

Now it was Ella's turn to be pissed off. In so many words, she said "OK, I'll rent out my New York apartment and take the girls to London. You can find me there." And off she went.

14

★

Landstuhl to Libya

In the middle of July 1955 I found my way to Landstuhl after stopping in London to see the family. Ella and the girls were ensconced in a lovely old town house in the Wilton Row Mews of London, near Hyde Park. I had to admit it was more her style than an officer's house on an air force base in Germany, or for that matter on any base. Ella was already working on a movie being filmed at Beaconfield Studios in Buckinghamshire. *The Man in the Road* would be her last film. She called me her "Man in the Sky" when I left for Germany. It wasn't offered endearingly.

The CO at Landstuhl fixed me with a watery sort of stare when I showed up in his office, and proceeded to give me my welcoming briefing. There I was, a wet-behind-the-ears, brand-new full-bull colonel, just arrived, facing the senior colonel who was my wing commander. I had heard of the man before but little was exceptionally positive or negative. My elation at being assigned as the 86th Interceptor Group commander began to waver.

"The 86th has been in Germany on occupation duty since the end of the war," announced the colonel with clearly discernible disdain. "Its reputation leaves much to be desired, particularly the off-duty behavior of the pilots. I will not tolerate the situation any longer. For your information, the two Georges [previous 86th Group commanders Bickle and Simler] did nothing to stop the custom of breaking all the bar glasses in the officers' club every Friday beer call. As the group commander I expect you to put an immediate stop to that habit, and I mean RIGHT NOW!"

"Yes, sir," I answered. Holy shit, I thought. Ten years of tradition, and all of a sudden I should stop it? If it pisses you off so damned much, Colonel, what have you done about it? Obviously the ball was in my court, and whatever happened next would be my doing, not his.

I signed in at group headquarters and was shown to my office. I was in no mood to appreciate the decor or to acquaint myself with the pictures of my predecessors. I had to think about this new setup and try to grasp my position in the pecking order. The air force had recently reorganized into operational wings, as opposed to the old system of groups. The flying group had always consisted of three or four squadrons, at least in my experience. A full colonel normally commanded a group, and a lieutenant colonel or sometimes a major commanded a squadron. Apparently the 86th was the last of the old system, with a wing headquarters grafted on top of it. Back in World War II, a wing contained as many as six groups. Guys at squadron level didn't even bother to try to understand organization changes. Headquarters seemed to reorganize just to have something to do. Nothing much changed. Responsibilities remained the same. Maybe the shuffle meant the air force could justify more colonels and generals. It didn't much matter.

It occurred to me that my boss had resisted eliminating the group level of command with pernicious intent. He would place some feckless junior colonel in the position of solving what he considered a serious disciplinary problem, namely the glass-breaking tradition. I knew this to be a weak conjecture, but it suited the moment and gave me resolve to play the game, MY way.

I called in the deputy group CO, my assistant, and asked him to have all four squadron commanders in my office at four o'clock that afternoon. He understood that "ask" was tantamount to an order, and left to go about doing whatever deputy group commanders do. I spent the rest of the day roaming around the base, learning where everything was, meeting the supply, maintenance, and administrative people, and generally getting acquainted. Just before four o'clock I reentered my office and found the squadron commanders assembled. Their expressions were blank when I introduced myself. I knew each was wondering who the hell I was, what I was like, and what I wanted. They were soon to find out.

"Gentlemen," I began, "this morning I was given a direct order by the wing commander that I would be responsible for stopping all glass breaking in the O club. I suspect that directive has been tried officially and unofficially several times in the past, obviously without effect. Since I am obligated to carry out the orders of my superior, I intend to put an end to this unit's old tradition. Today is Thursday. Tomorrow is beer call. I expect every officer under your command to attend beer call. No excuses accepted. And if one of your troops breaks one damned glass, you are fired! That's all. Dismissed."

I'm grateful looks can't kill, because I would have been dead on the spot.

The club was packed after work on Friday. I was grateful the squadron COs had taken me seriously, even though the chill in the room was palpable. I pretended not to notice and went around introducing myself. My welcome was less than lukewarm. Every now and then I noticed a hand going up, armed with a glass and aimed at the fireplace. Another hand would grab the arm and there would be a slight scuffle.

When I sensed the mood was right I got up on a chair and whistled for attention. There was immediate silence. Everyone wanted to know what was coming next from this new asshole CO.

I pointed to two of the larger young pilots and ordered, "You two, look around. One of you pick eight of your friends, the other pick nine. Then line up over here. The rest of you make way. We are going to play an RAF game. It's called 'high-cock-a-lorum' or 'buck-buck.' I'm sure you'll think of your own name for it. I'll join the eight guys. The other team is the down team. OK. Now, each of the down team, line up single file facing your team captain. Good. Now bend over and stick your head between the legs of the guy in front of you. Hang on to his thighs. The team captain serves as the end post, standing facing the guys bent over. A member from the other team will take a running jump at the down team and land on someone's back. All will jump one at a time in similar fashion. If the down team breaks, the other team gets to jump again. If, once atop the down team, the jumping team so much as touches a foot to the floor, the teams will change position, and the down team becomes the jumpers. You and you, station yourselves on either side. You are the judges. If a jump team foot touches the floor, you are to raise your arm and the sides will change. Should one of your decisions be questioned and the audience agrees with the petition, you will have a pitcher of beer poured over your head. That's it. Now let's get on with it."

By midnight there wasn't a rug, piece of furniture, or fixture remaining intact. It turned out to be one hell of a beer call.

As can be imagined, I faced an angry wing commander on Saturday morning. He was livid. My chewing out was classic, although I felt he lacked the vocabulary to win that honor in more serious competition. After much shouting, sputtering, arm waving, and foot stomping, he screamed, "What was that about? What do you think you're doing? The club is in ruins! Headquarters has already called wanting to know what happened. What am I supposed to tell them? TELL ME!"

"Sir," I answered politely. "I suggest you tell them the club has not been redecorated since it was first opened. The fixtures were already beyond repair. A collection has been taken and the squadrons are footing the replacement costs, as should be, but most important, in compliance with your order, not one glass was broken the entire evening."

It was an auspicious start.

Landstuhl was an interesting assignment, despite its undesirable identification with Air Defense. The 86th Fighter Intercept Group was there as part of USAFE's role as NATO's air defense. The nations of Europe, along with Canada, Iceland, and the United States, organized a common defense structure to protect Europe and counterbalance the Soviet and Eastern Bloc threats. We were just one cog in the wheel.

Tactical air power and USAFE were beefed up again to help defend Western Europe. Landstuhl Air Base was an old Luftwaffe command airdrome complete with runways, control tower, ramps, and other flight-related facilities. It would serve while French engineered and designed Ramstein Air Base was under construction by German contractors just three miles away. Ramstein was the location for higher-echelon headquarters, family housing, schools, and base support departments. Both Landstuhl and Ramstein were operated by the U.S. Air Force. To describe the whole setup as complicated would be a vast understatement. The bottom line was a lot clearer. We were there to keep an eye on the Russians.

Headquarters 12th Air Force had been reactivated in early 1951 and assigned to USAFE. It became the first USAFE unit to be committed to NATO and was transferred to newly opened Wiesbaden Air Base. Landstuhl had been equipped with the F-84F Thunderstreak before my arrival. In August 1954 we became the 86th Fighter Interceptor Wing to reflect our new mission, and we flew the F-86D Sabre. Our mission was air defense of Western Europe and if necessary delivery of tactical and strategic nuclear response to Soviet aggression. The concept was "massive retaliation." I called it a big fucking mess. But the flying was great and the O club was the center of all the best action.

I got to London as often as I could on my off-duty days, and Ella brought the girls to Landstuhl with their German governess from time to time. In true Ella style, we had to rent a small house off-base in a charming nearby village, so once again, I wasn't allowed to live in housing on base close to my men. Juggling family and fighter pilots was not my idea of how to run a unit. We should all have been together but Ella's refusal to live on bases where I was assigned was an ongoing struggle between us. After seven years of marriage, mostly good and always interesting, I envied the guys with supportive wives. It takes a special woman to be an air force wife. Ella was certainly special, but her talent wasn't geared toward being a happy part of the Officers' Wives Club. The tension created by our vastly different careers came to a boil in 1956, when she lost an important film tryout to an English actress. And it didn't help a bit when I told her I was being transferred to Libya.

I thought it would help plead my case if I told her from a hospital bed. At least my being flat on my back recovering from a horrendous surgery I'd just endured might elicit some sympathy or pity. I had visions of my beautiful dark-haired wife bending over me and looking at me tenderly with those green eyes as I explained that I was merely a pawn being moved around by the air force machinery. The hospitalization was due to a horrible case of what we termed the "fighter pilot's complaint," too many hours, and too many g's. The radical hemorrhoidectomy to cure the problem caused the greatest physical agony of my life, before or since. Without exaggeration I must say I was one sick puppy. I languished in that hospital for forty days and forty nights, well taken care of but not healing well, and running a high fever for weeks. The joke was that when I got out of the hospital I would finally be a perfect asshole.

On one of those miserable days, when my fever was still over the 100 mark, Colonel Dean Loring came to visit. He didn't know me and I didn't know him, so I figured the visit was more than a social "how're you doing?" thing. Turned out I was right. Loring hemmed and hawed a bit and finally asked how long I thought I would be in the hospital. Good grief, how did I know? He then announced that the people in USAFE headquarters wanted me to take over the training unit at Wheelus, our big base in Libya. For some time all the fighter units in Europe had been sending flights or entire squadrons there for weapons training on a gunnery range at a place called Tarhuna. Did I want the job? Hell yes! But could it hold until I got out of this place? I told him I was his man, but to please be patient.

With a conspiratorial air Loring informed me that I would be chief of the Weapons Proficiency Center, would take charge of weapons-range scheduling, would have the opportunity to organize the training curricula—in fact, I was to be the boss of all the units deployed. He then asked if I wanted to be directly under USAFE for operational and administrative control. I thought about it for a moment and replied that I felt my unit should be in the normal chain of command under the wing/base setup at Wheelus, and therefore under the 17th Air Force, which at that time was located in Morocco and due to move soon to Wheelus. Then I gave him a caveat. I wanted a direct communication link back across the Mediterranean surfacing at the desk of a good contact in the headquarters at Wiesbaden. That way if I needed extra pull for something, I could get directly to USAFE HQ and bypass the 17th. It wouldn't be routine, but it was an emergency backup to get the job done. Loring thought about that and agreed. I knew he would have to get my request approved higher up, so I thanked him for everything and said I looked forward to working with him in the future. In spite of my current misery I had some challenging things to think about. I was happy.

Ella was not. She gave it to me straight in that hospital room. No way in hell was she going to Africa, of all places, nor would she bring our two little girls down there. But I have to give Ella credit. I was sent to her house in London to recuperate and she took good care of me through two more unexpected operations in the military hospital at Ruislip. Her nursing was responsible for my eventual recovery. Once I recovered, she packed her clothes, prepared the girls, and left for California. I wasn't sure when we'd meet again, but her choice had been made and time would tell.

With mixed feelings, I closed up the London house and my quarters at Landstuhl, tucked our little dog, Mr. Magoo, into an open flight bag, grabbed a T-33, and left for Tripoli.

OK, Robin, look around! What's here? What needs doing? Whom have I got working for me? How have things been organized? What is the relationship of my organization with the base wing? Where do I go to get materials, funding, tools for my ground crews, flight gear for my chase pilots, housing, etc.? And how do I gain a modicum of control over range scheduling? Wheelus was every bit the challenge I thought it would be. OK, just tackle one or two things at a time.

First, go check out the British-built ground gunnery range at Tarhuna. Clearly it was far too small for our current needs, let alone for the modernizing forces from units in England and Europe. Next, see the El Watia nuclear target area that was out in the desert, 80 miles down the coast and far inland. Its 23,000 acres consisted of a long, straight path bulldozed due south and ending in a target of two old steam boilers painted in black and white checks, filled with sand, mounted vertically on a mound. There were absolutely no support facilities whatsoever. Nothing. No spotting towers, no telephone capability, no bathrooms, just sand. It was nothing, but it was perfect for the task of catching simulated nuclear weapons slung off of fast-moving jets.

Wheelus was a big base seven miles east of Tripoli, perched at the edge of the Mediterranean. It had been built by the Italians during their attempted conquest of North Africa in 1911. They consolidated this crumbling vestige of the Ottoman Empire into a nascent state called Libya and, in 1923, established the Mehalla Air Base near Tripoli. The Germans joined with the Italian forces when World War II broke out, and the base was used by the Luftwaffe until early 1943. Montgomery's famous "Desert Rats" captured it as they pursued Rommel across North Africa toward Tunis.

At the end of the war, the Allies remained in Libya and the Americans took over Mehalla, renamed it Wheelus, and immediately began air operations. Libya was desperately poor, and the Allies struck a deal that would prove to be a mutually useful relationship for eighteen years to come, paying millions to the ruling family as "rent" for the base. Unfortunately, as in most third world countries, the money flowed right to the richest families instead of finding its way to the poor, and the discovery of oil later in 1959 made that situation worse, instantly transforming Libya into one of Africa's wealthiest nations.

Wheelus's location and clear weather were ideal for the aerial training that ensued. Except for the *ghiblis*, choking dust storms that roared through with temperatures soaring above 110 degrees, the climate was generally tolerable and pleasant, a lot like Southern California. USAFE took over in 1951 and established the 7272nd Air Base Wing, which later became the Fighter Training Wing as the host unit. Also operating out of the base were several tenant units, including the 7235th Support Squadron and the 431st Fighter Interceptor Squadron "Red Devils" flying F-86D and F models. My command was the new 7272nd Air Weapons Group and, as I had requested, we were under the 17th Air Force. USAFE was quickly modernizing the base; the runway and facilities were being expanded, schools and medical buildings were being erected, and a large housing complex was being built for the assigned troops. The housing was mostly trailers, not very glamorous, but comfortable and efficient. Only a few, choice high-ranking base officers received free-standing houses.

Wheelus's primary mission had been "post-strike Recovery," meaning if the balloon went up, the site would serve as a recovery base for our long-range bombers. When the fighter units started deploying for their weapons training, life on the base changed radically. For one thing, the constant noise of arriving and departing jets soon upset the apple cart. There was more than a little friction between the base permanent contingent and the rotational fighter units. Schedules had to be adjusted on many levels, and flying operations had to cease all noise according to the premandated orders of the muezzin calling Muslims to prayer from the minaret of his mosque.

The rotational units, both pilots and ground crews, lived in tents with common latrine facilities away from base housing. They had to go clear around the north end of the field to eat and relax in the messes. Always creative, the fighter guys "relaxed" in the isolated atmosphere on the air base side of the field. They were not appreciated for their rowdiness and were frowned upon by the permanent staff. Of course, that only induced the fighter guys to make their antics all the more objectionable, and of course I had no hand whatsoever in influencing any rowdy behavior. I pleaded innocent.

Shortly after I arrived at Wheelus I paid the customary visit to the wing CO, a man named Colonel Kane. He seemed nice enough but apparently didn't much care for the fighter units. After a few pleasantries I was informed it would be my responsibility to stop the fighter pilots from painting their squadron numbers on the base water tower. It was an old custom from the first rotations, and I had to agree the tower was indeed a mess. But why hadn't he stopped the custom himself? Oh well, another welcome to a new command. It seemed part of routine in-processing for me to be asked to quell the pranks of the aircrews for the resident commander.

A couple of weeks later Colonel Kane called me into his office and asked what I had done about the water tower problem. "Sir," I replied, "I hung a bucket of red paint and a bucket of white paint on the bottom of the ladder, along with some brushes. I figure it will take about another week for the white squares to be red and the red squares to be white. Then I'll have the base civil engineer cut off the bottom twenty feet of the ladder. That ought to discourage any further disfigurement of government property."

The colonel was not amused. I didn't think it necessary to tell him I had threatened each of the fighter squadron commanders with no range time if his number appeared on that damned tower in the future.

After my arrival the fighter-bombers made much greater use of the El Watia bombing range. We used the airspace overhead for training in air-to-air combat, and the targets for air-to-ground gunnery with conventional and nuclear ordnance delivery. My guys provided the ranges, towed aerial targets for the fighters, and flew the chase aircraft for the interceptor units doing airborne radar training. That had to be done because the interceptor pilots flew under the hood and made their firing passes using their onboard radar and without visual reference. The chase pilot had to make sure the interceptor guy wasn't locked on to the tow aircraft. The group I had commanded at Landstuhl was the only USAFE unit equipped with all-weather fighter squadrons, so I was familiar with the capabilities of the F-86Ds assigned and didn't trust either the equipment or the pilots to always sort out the tow ship from the target on a firing pass. Our all-weather capabilities were primitive at that time, and I had several run-ins with HQ over what constituted acceptable weather conditions for training.

To get anything done efficiently, I often made use of the "Link Across the Mediterranean" contact I'd been promised in my hospital bed when I first agreed to change Wheelus from a gunnery camp to a mini weapons center. Colonel Robert Worley was my go-to guy and we met often at some point halfway between USAFE HQ at Wiesbaden and my post at Wheelus. More often than not, it was a base just outside Marseille or Capodichino in Naples. We'd each grab a T-33, he'd come south out of Germany, I'd fly north across the Med, and we'd lunch somewhere near the base and get a lot done. I'd give him status and progress reports, future plans, and lists of things I was having trouble getting. We talked money a lot, too. My boss, General Richard O'Keefe at the 17th, used to wonder how in hell I managed to get bucks for the weapon center so fast, but I never told him until after he retired.

Bob Worley was great fun because he was always a little on the gullible side—a dangerous weakness around pranksters like me. General Gabe Disosway at the 12th Air Force was also a prankster. He teased his staff a lot and pulled a memorable trick on his guys, including Bob, on one of his trips to Wheelus. He did it as much to tweak General O'Keefe as to put one over on his own staff. One night before General Gabe was to depart for a visit to Incirlik Air Base in Turkey, we had dinner at O'Keefe's Wheelus base quarters. General Gabe asked me quietly if we ever checked shot records on crew members and passengers departing for the Middle East. I confessed I didn't know and said I'd sure find out right away. General Gabe smiled and said he thought it might be a good idea, since he'd overheard Worley and Ben Davis [Gen. Benjamin O. Davis, chief of staff, 12th AF] worrying about it on the flight down. Bob and Ben both knew they were way overdue for those shots. I got the hint loud and clear, got up from the table, went into the kitchen, and called the base hospital commander. Understandably, the hospital CO needed lots of convincing, but he agreed to go along when I insisted it was a direct request from General Disosway. I returned to the dining room and quietly told General Gabe the plan was a go. He grinned and told me to keep it quiet.

The next morning at six o'clock there was consternation and mass confusion out on the departure ramp. The hospital commander was as good as his word. O'Keefe turned brick red (an easy trick for an Irishman) when he got his first look at the medics standing by a white-clothed table complete with autoclave and poised needles. He started to issue some kind of order, but General Gabe interrupted him by saying how much he'd enjoyed the visit and asked him to relay his appreciation to Louise O'Keefe for the excellent dinner. Disosway then pulled out his shot record, went up to the table, rolled up his sleeve, and took his needed shot. After bounding up the ladder into his waiting C-54, he kept poking his head out of the door hollering at his guys to "Hurry it up!"

There was no way for me to keep a straight face as I watched the aircraft crew, the passengers, and Gabe's staff jostling for last place in line and fumbling for wallets revealing a lot of overdue injections. Jesus, some of them took a lot of shots! Bob Worley and some brigadier needed five apiece. When they finally departed for Incirlik, I was left on the ramp with a sputtering, nearly apoplectic two-star Irishman. He whirled on me, knowing I was probably the only one in his entire command who could have been involved in the situation.

"What in hell do you mean pulling a stunt like that on Disosway?" O'Keefe thundered. It wasn't a question. I tried to look contrite instead of amused. It didn't work. The Old Man went to work on me and thrust his fiery red face at mine. He reminded me of a first classman on Beast Detail during Plebe Summer at West Point. It dawned on me that I hadn't handled the situation with a great degree of tact. I knew I was caught between the two generals, as different from each other as any two men could be. One, Gabe, was affable, full of humor, self-confident, hard-nosed, highly respected, and popular throughout the 12th Air Force. The other, General O'Keefe, was also highly respected, but for entirely different reasons. His modus operandi and personality fit his temperament, and his anger was not always the most reasonable trait he possessed. His staff feared him. The more ambitious of them were prime examples of the "me too" staff officer syndrome, forever feeding the Old Man information that satisfied his perceptions rather than reflecting the truth. I didn't know whether that obsequious form of staff work fooled or flattered O'Keefe, but the 17th Air Force managed to get the job done.

I didn't dare take my eyes off the general as he vented his anger. Behind his head I could see members of his own staff gathered in a knot, looking around the airfield as if not connected with the scene going on in front of them and obviously pleased that the tirade wasn't directed at one of them. O'Keefe finally gave me an opportunity to answer his question. I tried to explain that General Disosway had told me not to give away his joke. He didn't want Worley and Davis to catch on before the morning. I knew my words were lame. Realizing General O'Keefe's position I felt embarrassed and at least a bit contrite. I guess General Gabe figured I was a big boy and could take the consequences of his joke. Things were understandably tense around the Wheelus Wing HQ for a while, but returned to normal in due course.

I felt I had to return the favor for that memorable ass chewing, so, waiting for General Gabe to be out of reach for any kind of prankish retaliation, I looked for an opportunity to get revenge on some member of equal rank on General Gabe's ops staff.

The victim turned out to be gullible Bob Worley, and the opportunity came a few weeks later during one of our lunches at Capodichino. Bob and I had finished our meeting and were in base ops filing our flight plans and Form 21s for the flights home. I saw Bob struggling with his 21, checking frequencies and stuff, so I walked over and said casually, "Hey, Bob, you don't have to go through all that bullshit. Here's a 21 I used just four days ago from here to Wiesbaden. All the frequencies are good, and the fuel data worked out to the gallon. I've already looked at the winds aloft and they're the same. Go ahead and use it. Save yourself all that hassle."

Bob took the card gratefully. I said good-bye, filed my clearance for Tripoli, and went out to my bird. As I taxied past ops I saw Bob climbing into his T-33 and knew he'd be right behind me when I took off. As soon as I was airborne, I switched frequencies and called Rome Control. Everyone over there knew that Rome Control never answered a position report or check-in. We didn't know what the hell they were doing in their control room, but it didn't involve giving a shit about USAFE pilots on their airways. I stayed on Rome's frequency and waited for Bob to check in as I turned south for Wheelus.

I was climbing through at about 8,000 when I heard his voice on channel ten. "Hello, Rome Control. This is Air Force 4578. Departed Capodichino 1420, passing 2,000 for 25,000." All this was spoken in a monotone, knowing Rome wouldn't answer or even be listening.

I mashed the transmit button and said in my best Italian accent, "Allo, Aira Forsa foura five sevena eight, thees issa Roma Control. Roger you departa froma Capodichino. Pleeza you giva me you esteemat abeama Civitavecchia. O-vair."

I could hear the surprise in Bob's voice—"Aah, Roger Rome Control"—then a long pause . . . "Uh, say again your request?"

"Oh-kay, Aira Forsa sevena eight, thees issa Roma Control. What ees you esteemat abeama Civitavecchia? O-vair," I repeated, trying to keep from laughing. I knew Bob didn't have a clue where Civitavecchia was, and I could picture him madly unfolding maps while trying to keep his bird upright with the stick between his knees.

He came on the air with, "Uh, Rome Control, this is seven eight. I estimate abeam Ponza at 48. Over." I knew he took that off the Form 21 I had given him and he sounded kind of wistful, like he was asking Rome to accept a substitute.

"Roger sevena eight, thees issa Roma Control, we hava you estimate abeama Ponza, butta what issa you estimate abeama Civitavecchia?" I voiced this with a tone of exasperation and a small flare of appropriate Latin anger.

"Uh, stand by, Rome . . . ," and Bob's voice trailed off.

I waited a few moments and came back with, "Aira Forsa sevena eight, this issa Roma Control, eef you no giva me you esteemat abeama Civitavecchia, I'm-a gone putta you five-a thousa feeta ana I'm-a gonna leafa you there!"

Enough was enough. I was already feeling guilty and began hoping Bob would never find out who Roma Control really was. I changed channels and went on past Malta and Pantelleria hoping I hadn't misjudged his sense of humor.

Two weeks later I was in Wiesbaden and poked my head into his office. He looked up from a mountain of papers and waved me in. I declined his offer of coffee and said, "Christ, Bob, I was on channel ten when Rome answered you. What a ration of crap that was! They sure didn't answer MY call. Matter of fact, that's the first time in two years I've ever heard them on the air."

"Yeah," Bob growled, "all this time over here and I've never heard those bastards answer, not once, not ever. Jesus Christ, you'd think they'd get with the program. I've a good mind to write the sons a bitches up the next time they don't respond. Hell, we've done nothing but cooperate all this time, helping set up this European air control system, and they're out drinking vino or something."

He was getting pretty worked up and I wondered if my little joke hadn't backfired a bit, so I asked in my best dialect, "Aira Forsa sevena eight, did-a you ever finda Civitavecchia?"

Bob looked at me for a moment, then exploded. "Robin, you son of a bitch!"

Bob Worley was a hell of a guy and a great friend, but he came to a sad end ten years later. He had made major general and was vice commander to General "Spike" Momyer at the 7th Air Force in Saigon. He was on a recce flight over some damned place in South Vietnam and took a golden BB. His F-4 caught fire, and instead of immediately punching out, he tried to get back to base. It didn't work; it seldom does. The backseater ejected and survived, but they had used the wrong ejection sequence. A chase pilot flying formation on them watched Bob overcome by flames as the rear canopy departed. He had no chance to pull the ejection handle and went in with the bird.

Life at Wheelus turned out to be wonderful in many ways. I finally convinced Ella to join me in the desert of North Africa by promising the rental of a big house on the outskirts of Tripoli. I also talked up the allure of the beach and great social high life. Much of it was British based, so it was quite civilized and just to her taste. We also had some really good long-standing friends stationed there with their children. My family arrived in late October and quickly settled in. The house was a walled villa, complete with gardens full of tropical flowers, date palms, the requisite flowering cacti, and a raised concrete pond with lilies and voracious catfish. Little Chris and Susie, ages four and three when they arrived, had the run of the garden and the compound, watched over closely by their nanny. We were attended by several Libyan houseboys, part of the staff inherited from the previous tenants.

Ella was quite the picture out on the veranda in the evenings, dressed in white linen (including a white Hollywood-style turban) and large dark sunglasses. The incongruity of the scene never escaped me. I would leave the modern facilities at the base, the noise of jets, smell of jet fuel, sight of personnel in sweaty uniforms, and drive out the east gate through the dusty squalor of huts, garbage, cooking fires, herds of goats, groups of brown children running happily in rags accompanied by their squadrons of flies, and then turn through the high gates of our compound, immediately entering a clean, calm, green and white world. I would find my wife waiting regally for me with chilled crystal martini glasses ready on the veranda, Muhammad standing close by and holding a silver tray bearing a silver martini shaker. I admit, I enjoyed the juxtaposition of our little world to the other worlds outside.

The better part of off-duty time was spent at the beach with our friends. We'd gather up the children, load the cars with scuba-diving equipment, blankets, umbrellas, picnic baskets, and ice chests, then head to the coast in a caravan to relax at our favorite spot. Arab children jumped on the running boards of the cars and reached through the windows to beg whenever we slowed down. The local men knew the routine and were always ready at the turnoff to push our cars down the long, sandy road to the beach, happy for their rewards of cigarettes and root beer. The wives would set up the blankets and umbrellas at the perfect spot to supervise the children playing in the shallow tide pools while we men outfitted ourselves in scuba gear to explore the coastline.

These excursions into the Med weren't just to look at fish. We quickly learned that a veritable treasure trove of artifacts from ancient ships sunk off the coast lay scattered on the sandy bottom. One day my friend Grumpy Steele and I found an old barnacle-encrusted cannon half buried in the sand. It was much too heavy to lift, so we pushed and dragged it along the bottom as far as we could toward the beach before abandoning the effort. Over the course of a few weekends, Grumpy and I moved that thing bit by bit until we got it all the way out of the water. It became the centerpiece of a great party under the beach umbrellas that day, but for the life of me, I can't remember what became of it. No doubt it's still somewhere in Tripoli, maybe in a museum but more likely in some sheikh's courtyard.

Those were happy days for my family. We were all as brown as berries. Chris and Susie learned to swim in the Med, and my marriage was thriving. Ella became pregnant again. The girls were still too young to attend the base school, but they went with other Wheelus children to a nursery school near the compound, where they sat on woven mats and piles of straw to learn the alphabet from an Arab teacher fluent in English. Those classes were also attended by local boys wandering in to learn some English and accompanied by their small herds of goats. This naturally translated into the girls begging for goats as pets, so one was added to the compound garden. Our dog and cat were not amused. Ella was not amused either when the goat took up residence in the kitchen. Chrissie came home from those classes speaking Arabic with the fluency of a five-year-old and became our translator with the house staff. After Tripoli, her memory of the language naturally faded, but far into their teen years Susie would often wake Chris up to stop her from babbling loudly in Arabic in her sleep.

Both girls couldn't understand why Ella wouldn't open the compound gates and allow the little Arab children to come in and play. So one day, with Chris as the ringleader, they took matters into their own hands. Ella was pretty vocal about the precious value of the family silverware stored in the dining room chest, so the girls emptied it, dumping all of it out of a window over the street. They believed the Arab children could sell the silver and buy clean new clothes, which would qualify them to be invited by Ella into the compound to play. The happy result of this "grand theft" was the appearance at the front gate the next morning of the dignified elder tribesman bearing a large basket of silver. Every single piece was returned. The sad news is that Ella taught Chris and Susie the lesson of a lifetime by throwing all of their toys into the street and issuing orders for the Arab children to keep them.

More unhappily, Ella was at full term with our third child when things went horribly wrong in her labor. The baby was stillborn. It was a boy. Once home from the hospital, and blaming me for forcing her to live in the wretched unsanitary and backward conditions of Libya, Ella retreated to her room for two weeks. I had tiny Robert Ernest Olds cremated, and a few days later I drove to the beach by myself, donned my scuba gear, swam far out from shore, dove down, and released the ashes of my son into the water of the Mediterranean.

Two months later, July '58, I was reassigned to the Pentagon and was once again in the Air Defense Command, USAF HQ. This unwelcome bit of news prompted me to write several letters to an old West Point classmate of mine, Colonel Paul "Pat" Hurley, who was in the Colonel's Assignment Branch deep in those very headquarters. I'd been doing my level best since 1951 to live down the stigma of any connection to the Air Defense Command, and there was no way in hell I was going to go quietly. I recognized intercepting nuclear bombers as a necessary evil but had no use for the basic concept of their defensive mission. In my opinion, there was only one thing that counted in air power and that was offense. Offense was delivered in only two ways, SAC and fighter-bomber wings scattered around the perimeter of the Soviet Union. My hard work of the past two years had helped build combat capability within the tactical forces of USAFE. When would HQ USAF realize that it would be at least ten years before we could rely on the effective performance of missiles in either defense or response? Until that time came, the tactical fighter troops would have to carry the burden of taking the war to an enemy. When a missile was ready to take over my job, I'd be ready to take up hog ranching. Fifteen years herding fighter pilots in the air force left me eminently qualified for that occupation.

My pleas to avoid the Pentagon fell on sympathetic but deaf ears. All I could do was beg not to work in ADC, but my assignment as dep chief Air Defense Division, USAF HQ, was written in stone. If the air force was going to throw away pilots, drain away fighting capability, and relegate this fighter pilot to desk jockey status, then I would have to make the most of it. Shit, I felt like a Christian entering the Colosseum, not knowing whether I'd be burned at the stake, stoned by Romans, eaten by lions, or raped by ravenous Amazons. Abandoning hope upon entering seemed natural.

At least part of the family was happy with the news. Ella, of course, was ecstatic. Washington social circles would be her cup of tea. I didn't have a clue how to break it to the dog or the cat, let alone the goat.

15

★

Pentagon to Shaw

The family enjoyed the return from Naples to New York on the newly commissioned USS *Independence*. This mode of transport was normally only due general officers and their families, but, once again, Ella batted her movie star eyelashes at her connections and pulled some rank. I had to thank her for this one. We relaxed the whole way back, although it felt like I was leaving heel marks all across the Atlantic. Ella was the happiest I'd seen her in four years, and I had hopes this move back to civilization would smooth our troubles. Once disembarked in New York on September 1, she moved into an apartment at the Carlyle Hotel, put the girls into a nearby school, and set about selling her Manhattan flat. I reported to the Pentagon and started looking for a house in the D.C. area. Whether or not I wanted the ops job in the Air Defense Division was no longer important. I was determined to make the best of things and devote whatever skills I had to flying a desk.

My first stop was to visit an old friend who had an office somewhere deep in the Pentagon subbasement. When I found his cubbyhole there was a small sign hanging out over the corridor: AFOOP/I. Jesus, only in this damned madhouse. It didn't help my mood to recognize what the sign meant. The Installations (Bases) and Units Sections of the Directorate of Operations in the Office of the Deputy Chief of Staff Operations, Headquarters, United States Air Force. It was to be my new home. It wasn't a corner office with a Potomac view.

Our job wasn't really improving the war fighting of the USAF. We simply worked for a chief whose job it was to convince Congress that the air force needed money to operate. By law, the chief didn't command anything; he donned his Joint Chiefs hat for occasional appearances. Sure, he put out policies and doctrines; controlled force structure; made overall operational, matériel, and personnel plans; had the last say on promotions in the colonel and general ranks; and had the respect of the major command warlords, but that last was more military courtesy than anything else. Command of the war fighting was done through the Joint Chiefs, not the service chief of staff. The air staff in the Pentagon wrangled over roles and missions, fought over dollars, and spent hundreds of thousands of man-hours responding to the bullshit coming off Capitol Hill, to say nothing of the doctrinal battles with the navy and army.

Within a few weeks at the Pentagon I felt defiled, as though everything I had ever done, everything I had ever believed in and given my loyalty to from the time I was a small Air Corps brat at Langley, was suddenly of no consequence. I'd been bitching about getting stuck in the air defense business since 1950, and all my discomfort came to a clear, sharp focus with the new job. I'd never been able to make myself believe in the air defense mission, as much as I was involved for the preceding eight years. I began seriously questioning what was really going on rather than giving blind obedience to the system. My dad and his buddies after World War I had fought for air power against all odds, against infantry and artillery generals and battleship admirals. Despite Billy Mitchell's court-martial, my father stuck by his beliefs. They believed in themselves and in the mission of air power. They weren't afraid to speak their mind, and many of them put their careers on the line fighting for their convictions. It was in my genes. I could follow my upbringing or go along with the pack.

At Landstuhl and Wheelus I'd had time to think. I began to realize that the infantry and artillery generals my dad had argued against still existed, but they had evolved into bomber generals, who had taken control of the USAF after World War II. The new bunch were just as arbitrary and thickheaded as the stuffy old bastards my dad had fought. I was damned if I was going to give in to their system even though my own beliefs were not yet clearly focused. I realized Wheelus had been a foundation for my thinking on tactical air training. I knew what needed to be done to build a fighting force, and I determined to be the missionary for those concepts. I had managed to get us out of an inadequate bombing range at Tarhuna and had moved the whole works to El Watia. I knew what it took to get into the desert and haggle with the local sheikhs to get their agreement to use thousands of acres to build a huge tactical target complex, with dummy airfields, convoys, bridges, supply dumps, and all the stuff fighter guys needed to see to get in some honest training under realistic conditions. I had been planning to have air opposition and dummy flak to liven things up, but when I went to USAFE for the money to do that, I was turned down. Washington had told USAFE that the air force didn't need to spend much money on conventional training. The fighter role in Europe was nuclear strike and that was it. We would focus on what we had been doing and downplay the conventional tactical mission. I found another way.

The base civil engineer at Wheelus was a friend and turned his head when I raided his supply yards. We loaded stuff on trucks and headed 150 miles west to Sabrata, then south to El Watia. We laid out the dive, skip, and strafe targets, built the spotting towers, put up the radio masts, erected a cinder block mess hall and a crude barracks building, moved in power generators, and built a first-class range complex. With some reluctant volunteers to run the place, do the cooking, and score targets, we were in business. Bob Worley, in Wiesbaden, couldn't approve what was happening in the Libyan Desert, but he didn't object. In fact, Worley went to bat, telling quite a few of the USAFE staff to sit down and shut up. But the monkey was on my back. I had an ally fighting the system and I was getting the job done. I felt I knew what it would take.

It was a blow to the plan when my assignment to the Pentagon came. I was yanked back into the air defense business, screwing with mountains of paperwork and knowing that less than 25 percent of anyone's sweat and long hours amounted to one-half of bloody fuck-all for the guys in the field.

There are ninety-two steps from the subbasement of the Pentagon up to the E Ring on the fourth floor. I know. I counted the damned things, routinely at five thirty or six o'clock on Friday afternoons, and countless more times during the normal working hours of the week.

Fridays were special to normal people in one way and to many denizens of the Pentagon in quite another. Working America anticipated Friday as the best day of the week. TGIF! Time to enjoy a breather, time to spend with your kids, go to that dinner party, do some work in the garden, maybe even polish the car. But here in the damned Pentagon, Friday meant "What will the big man up in the E Ring have in store for us this weekend?" TGIF meant The General Is Fucking with us. It had become an irritating fact of life, an unpleasant certainty, to get that dreaded Friday call late in the day: "Come up. I've got something for you. Bring Al." Sure, boss, right away, boss.

One, two, three, four, five steps . . . there goes another weekend . . . twelve, thirteen, fourteen . . . always something generated by the rampant hysteria of Cold War in the late fifties . . . twenty-nine, thirty . . . hysteria fanned, of course, by that paragon of virtue, that holier-than-thou asshole, that scaremonger and hate spreader who must have been elected by an enclave of mass paranoia somewhere, a senator named McCarthy . . . fifty-six, fifty-seven, fifty-eight, hell, only thirty-four to go. Not only did McCarthy manage to provide the basis for the expenditure of untold billions for defense against the THREAT, the son of a bitch managed to dominate and ruin MY weekends. Of course, he wasn't alone; he had a lot of expert help from the E Ring. . . . Seventy-three, seventy-four . . . and its vaunted inhabitants in a hallowed realm of windows and broad vistas, relatively fresh air, desks, chairs, and carpeting the size and thickness of which signified your relative importance in the heights of power. What combination of past egos had dictated that those physical things be considered the very manifestation of wisdom and position of rank and glory? Ninety, ninety-one, ninety-two. Open the door, three, four.

We existed in that underground, windowless rabbit warren called the Directorate of Operations, United States Air Force. Hundreds of us worked in cubicles where the original designers of what was then the largest office complex in the world had intended files to be stored, prisoners to be interrogated, cars to be parked, supplies to be forgotten, janitors to make out, and mice and rats to multiply. It was a natural place to put the operational guys, the pilots who loved the wild blue yonder, whose souls swung and soared in the footless halls of air, who had flung their eager crafts up, up the delirious blue, chased the shouting winds along, and done a hundred things. We were the guys stuck in the basement without even a piece of sky to view. We occupied dank corridors and fetid cubicles, where even the air conditioners gave up. God knows the circulatory system installed in 1942 tried hard to keep the brass comfortable. Even that was marginal. So it's not difficult to imagine how little fresh air reached the trolls in the subbasement. Of course, everyone smoked in those days. I won't try to describe the stink that clung to the walls, reeked in corridors, and permeated our clothes. Most everyone had a raging head-ache by ten each morning.

We toiled in mindless, soul-searing, thankless, and mostly unproductive drudgery. When you had to tell someone up "above" how to find your office, the main physical landmark was a ludicrous purple water fountain. It sat at the bottom of the only stairwell that strangers from "above" could understand how to find. All directions to our rat holes referred to that device. Find the purple water fountain, then make so many left turns, so many rights, past this many doorways, to a door marked AFOOP/AD/NA/YUCK.

I had been unhappy to leave Wheelus for an assignment in the Squirrel Cage, but once I accepted my fate I was determined to do my best for God and country. It hadn't taken long to realize that three-quarters of the droning hours of every day were a total waste of time and that productive moments were devoted to rationalization and justification to Congress for a budget slice. We colonels were the peons. Brigadier generals were the file clerks and horse holders. Major generals, God help them, were the personal aides and boosters for the three-stars, who were lords of the E Ring, who huffed, puffed, and made loud noises as though they knew what air power was all about. These, in turn, convinced the four-stars that data gathered by cap-tains, put together by majors, massaged by lieutenant colonels, fed to colo-nels, presented to panels, torn apart by boards, rewritten by majors, remassaged by lieutenant colonels, refed to colonels, who recoordinated all over the world (the world, naturally, being that five-sided sorry slab), pre-sented to and finally approved by a board of generals in a form scarcely re-sembling the original directive, and passed to the poor four-star who had an appointment before the House Armed Services Committee, would justify spending another billion to, once again, restructure the Air Defense Com-mand, which couldn't possibly keep up with the demise of the vacuum tube and the rapidly expanding capability of the silicon chip in the first place. All that money, amounts beyond comprehension, to do what, against whom, to what end? I got used to referring to one and a half *billion* as simply 1.5 on briefing charts.

Soon I stopped trying to do all the stuff that came across my desk and started looking around with open eyes. General Bob Petit was there. He was a hell of a guy and a damned fine commander. We'd been together at March Field in '46. He showed me the project he had been working on: counting up our bomb and bullet supplies all over the world. Bob came to the conclusion that we couldn't fight a conventional war for more than four months. I don't remember his exact figures, but they sure as hell impressed me. It was what was behind those figures that got my attention, so I started looking into it. First thing I did within a month of my arrival at the Pentagon was see Colonel Gordie Graham in the TAC Division. I asked him what we had on the drawing board or in production for a replacement fighter for the old F-100. Gordie showed me the specs on the F-105. That was it. The 105's figures were impressive, but Christ almighty, the damned thing had a bomb bay! It carried a one-megaton nuke in there. The 105 was supposed to take off from a 10,000-foot strip, go 1,000 nautical miles at night on the deck, and deliver that bomb in a driving thunderstorm against some target in Russia. It sure would be a great replacement for the F-100 in that role, but was it a tactical fighter? Could it deal with the most likely form of warfare I was convinced we were still going to fight for years ahead: with bullets and iron bombs? The F-105 proved itself a great fighter-bomber in Southeast Asia a few years later, but at that time the fighter capability seemed minimal.

I went back to Bob Petit with my questions. What kind of R&D is in the works for conventional weapons and delivery systems? Is there any money allocated to build up our munitions reserves? All of his answers were negative or unknowable. For my efforts I was put on some panel or other tasked with future plans. The talk was strictly missiles and nuke delivery requirements, who would hold the bag, and who'd get the lion's share of the budget. It was clear to me that any system devoted to nukes was a weapon system meant never to be used. If we ever pressed the button and sent a Minuteman into the wild blue yonder, the damned missile wouldn't have served its real purpose, which was not to be used in the first place. "Peace is our profession" had become the motto of SAC, the strategic air command tall dogs. Seemingly BS, this military stance worked far better than the well-intended efforts of the antinuke soapbox orators and the left-wing liberals. Nuclear warfare did not occur. Holding a mighty big stick was marginally better than disarming yourself, yet it seemed a damned expensive way not to fight.

I started looking into our training programs and found that TAC, under bomber general Walt Sweeny, had cut out all but the merest suggestion of conventional training for fighters. That explained why Gabby Gabreski and his wing were totally unprepared when they were sent to Turkey for the Syrian crisis. At the time Gabby had flown down to Wheelus and, after explaining the situation he faced in Turkey, asked me for help from some of my weapons-training guys. I had said sure, and sent a couple of really sharp captains to Incirlik to show Gabby's weapons guys how to mix na-palm, hang rockets, and set fuses for skip- and dive-bombing . . . stuff like that. It wasn't Gabby's fault. He and his troops hadn't been allowed to do any of that during their training in the U.S. Yet there they were, sent off to make our presence known in a purely conventional warfare situation. To me, something needed to change. I guess those were the events that started my evolution from a fun-loving young fighter pilot into a worried adult fighter pilot.

Everywhere I looked in the rat hole of the Pentagon convinced me we had damn little conventional capability. The fact that we didn't was a deliberate course set by the bomber guys who ran things. Yes, we were keeping the Soviet nuclear bear at bay. I don't deny that. The troops sitting alert all over the world in missile silos and navy guys in subs were doing a superb job, along with all the support people, but the most likely physical threat remained conventional. The need to fight with real bombs and real bullets was staring down our throats. The nuclear threat was real, but the conventional threat was at least as real and a lot more probable. Korea had certainly demonstrated that. Yet here we sat in that goddamn moldy basement breathing the goddamn stale air and doing practically nothing about it.

By early fall of 1959 I was fed up with my lot in the Pentagon. I received an invitation from superintendent Major General William Stone to become the athletic director at the new Air Force Academy in Colorado Springs. It was tempting. I wanted to run for those hills—anything to escape ADC and the Pentagon. I didn't care if it meant the end of my career as a fighter pilot. By then, it seemed there was no future left for fighter pilots anyway. Ella was at the end of her rope. After two miscarriages, a stillbirth, and the death of her mother, she was in a severe depression, drinking heavily, and under the care of a psychiatrist. She told me in no uncertain terms that I'd go to Colo-rado alone. She was staying in Washington with our children. Divorce was imminent. My heart broke but my love for little Chris and Susie and the shreds of my deep love for Ella left me no option. The letter I wrote back to the general at the USAFA explaining why I had to decline his offer was the hardest letter of my life. I would serve my sentence at the Pentagon.

It was a late-November afternoon in 1959. The telephone rang just like clockwork at five o'clock. I picked it up. "Yes, sir, Colonel Olds here."

"Olds, you and Shiely come up here."

"Be right there, sir." I looked over at Al as he was preparing to leave. "Hey, Al, take off that coat. It's Friday! Guess who needs us where, and it's not the Russians. It's the E Ring. Boss's office." Al groaned, and we gathered our notepads and set out to climb those fucking stairs.

This time, it was General Howell Estes. He lost no time getting to the point. He paced back and forth as Al and I made notes of his instructions for the weekend. Shit, there went the sailboat I had rented for the Chesapeake! This wouldn't be just another Pentagon weekend assignment. Hell no. Finished with his orders, the general waved us away.

It was less tiring going down the ninety-four steps than going up, but the task before us weighed heavily. When we got back to our desks, we looked at each other without a word and picked up our respective phones to start calling the troops back to work. As they straggled in, Al and I considered our instructions and how we could go about it. We knew it would take coordination from almost every section of the air staff, just for starters, and then approval would have to be secured from every echelon upward along the way. The general hadn't given us a deadline but he wanted answers as fast as they could be formulated.

Our task? Change the entire programming for the Air Defense Command for the next six to eight years, drawing the command down from sixty-four squadrons to perhaps five: close bases, transfer people, cancel support actions, close aircraft production lines, transfer mission responsibility to National Guard and Reserve units, and then convince Congress the actions were necessary and worthy of budget approval. We weren't told how much programmed money we were to generate, but it didn't take a genius to figure out it would be a bunch. Naturally, we weren't told what this was all about, but it seemed a tad stronger than the usual, daily Washington drills of "what if?"

Before setting to work on the problem, we placed phone calls to our aggravated wives. Don't hold dinner. Cancel weekend plans. Sorry, honey. Then each man was assigned the tasks befitting his position on the air staff and told to get to work. I didn't get home to Georgetown until after midnight, and I lived a lot closer than most of the troops. We were back at it on Saturday morning and continued working, with only Christmas Day off, until the end of March, when we gave our last briefing to Congress. Our group generated a $6.5 billion fund pool, part of which we learned went into the Minuteman missile program, but where the remaining $4 billion went, we had no clue. Five years later, I found it had gone to the SR-71 Blackbird and considered it money well spent.

After all the endless nights and weekends in the Pentagon, the general never thanked us. I guess it wasn't in his nature. I was glad we never worked together in a flying situation. A year after this, when I was assigned to a position on the Joint Staff, I passed him in the hall in the E Ring. He was walking in the other direction and, without breaking stride, started giving me orders for another job. I turned, interrupted him, and announced that I no longer worked for him. I didn't say where and I guess he didn't give a damn. He just uttered a loud "Harrumph!" and walked away. I was utterly relieved to be moving on.

I worked for then–major general Maurice Preston, who was in charge of operations in the office of the deputy chief of staff of the USAF. Two or three visits to General Preston's office left me unable to tell if the Old Man was always chewing me out or giving me fatherly advice. It was hard not to stare at his missileer badge as he constantly told me I was living in the past. When I last visited his office, armed with statistics to prove my point, the Old Man finally blew. He told me I just wanted to put on my leather jacket and white scarf, pull down my goggles, and go out and do battle with the Red Baron. He explained things weren't that way anymore. This was the modern age. No more iron bombs and .50 caliber bullets. No more dogfighting. He told me my studies trying to prove we didn't have any conventional capability left in our United States Air Force were a waste of time. He claimed we didn't need bombs and bullets and conventional training programs for fighter pilots. He said we didn't need to make formation takeoffs and overhead landing breaks, and we didn't need to pay too much attention to the close air support mission I was harping about. Then he looked right at me and pointed his finger. He told me to get it through my head and understand we would never fight a conventional war again. Never! Then he ordered me to get back to my desk to take care of matters that concerned my job. If the director of operations of the United States Air Force was saying that, what was coming from topside?

But I knew damned well what was happening. Who had been the chief since Vandenberg? Who was sitting in the front offices on the E Ring? Who had plans, operations, personnel, installations, and the budget? Who was running the air force? It was the B-17, B-24, and B-29 guys that carpet-bombed Europe and dropped the nukes on Japan and who had parlayed themselves to the top at the expense of the navy, the army, the marines, and our AF tactical forces. It was hard to argue against success. No one had dropped nukes since '45 and the whole world appreciated it, but we had enough warheads to destroy the world three times over. How dead is dead? The only real fighting we'd done since '45 had been in Korea with bombs, bullets, and airlift. How could that be ignored? We were no longer ready to fight like that, and no one seemed to notice.

One memorable Joint Chiefs morning in 1961, I trudged upstairs with my colonel boss for yet another important meeting. The colonel was a nice fellow: a phlegmatic, unflappable, pipe-smoking, slightly chubby, uninspiring type of staff officer who sailed through the tensions and demands of each day without visible upset. He looked a little like a dieting Oliver Hardy, complete with a scrap of a mustache. He was a good guy to all of us. I liked him and had the gall to think I understood him. I guess he knew that enough crap came floating down from above to keep the rest of us docile and downtrodden, so he ran the air defense shop with a steady, quiet hand.

I smiled to myself thinking of the briefing papers I held under my arm as the two of us plodded up those hated stairs. Today was going to be something new and totally different. I was going to take my far-out thoughts before the high and mighty, and I wasn't at all sure of the reception I would get. Neither was my boss. He was already projecting an attitude of detachment, one that would convey the impression he was with me only because he was my boss and his presence didn't necessarily mean he endorsed the ideas I was presenting. Well, OK. That was par for the course.

Some weeks previously, a small group of us had been charged to perform a study on the future structure of North American Air Defense. At least that's what we thought. Al Shiely and Marty Martin, two West Point classmates, plus some other officers under the benign and bemused guidance of a fine general named Randy Holzapple, had met, scratched our collective heads, floundered around, sought to get a grip on the real threat to the United States that the air force was charged to defend, and wondered whether to simply build or to destroy current forces.

To me, the obvious threat was simple: nuclear weapons in the hundreds.

Deadly, hulking, menacing weapons controlled by pawns in the world power struggle. The nukes created mass paranoia. They were proliferating everywhere: burrowing into the earth, sliding under the seas, clustered in bomb bays, and slung under fighter wings sitting on alert pads around the globe. They were restrained and chained, but ready to respond to the superegos of a handful of evil vodka-fueled men holding court in an onion-towered fortress, men who held power through fear, who used their hatred of other nations to control people and divert attention from their own miserable existence. It was a caricature surely, but it couldn't be far from reality.

There had to be a way to obviate the nuke horror, something that would break the stalemate and give America an undeniable edge in the mutuality of deterrence, of massive retaliation, of graduated response, of the "first strike" option, and in the ridiculous international game: "I have more nukes than you have." "Oh no you don't! Mine are hidden in the mountains and under the plains." "Well, you don't know about the ones I have under the ice cap." "Yes I do. And my attack subs will wipe them out the minute I say GO." And so on, like schoolchildren playing with loaded pistols, only in this case with the whole of civilization at stake.

Once started, there seemed no way to reverse the trend. It was a fact of life. The only way to ban the bomb was to have more and better nukes than the bad guys, to be ready to use them at a moment's notice, but to have them under absolutely airtight control so that no one individual or group of individuals could possibly break security and launch one of the damned things. Of course, all of those procedures were highly classified. But oddly enough, we had to make sure the Russians knew of those measures and had as much confidence in them as we did. Otherwise, they might get nervous and figure they'd better launch first before someone on our side went berserk and punched the button. Naturally, the reverse was true, but no one had ever reassured me about it. Maybe that was why the Big Boys had such large desks and thick rugs. Someone had to know.

No soapbox oratory, no unilateral disarmament, no tricky antimissile missiles (like outfielders trying to shag a hundred fly balls all at once), none of that seemed to me to be the answer. My thinking was that the only way to make the threat go away would be to catch the enemy missiles on the rise and their aircraft on the runway. That concept presupposed not just the means to do so, but the existence of a technology demonstrating that the idea itself was feasible and worthy of development. It meant using space as the medium. It would be necessary to sit above, and to shoot down a missile the moment the silo doors opened, to catch the threat on launch. It meant both having the capability to do this and making sure the enemy knew we would do it. It also meant we would control the use of space for whatever reason someone wanted to launch anything. It was a Buck Rogers, science-fiction, block-'em-from-space kind of idea, but why not? Stranger things had been conceived and done.

So I did what research I could, checked the archives, asked questions, sought to find out if anything along my line of thought had been considered. I found nothing. Taking the bull by the horns, I decided to attempt to write a national doctrine for the military use of space. I convinced our Air Defense study group that was the way to go and was assigned the task of creating the document. Some of my contemporaries thought I had lost my mind. Yet NASA had recently introduced the Mercury astronauts, and our space capabilities seemed on the verge of serious development. We would have to start somewhere, so I wrote a paper rather grandly titled "A National Strategy for the Military Use of Space."

Briefing the brass on this idea was my mission that morning as we climbed those bloody stairs. No wonder my boss seemed bemused and a trifle distant. I couldn't blame him for wanting to avoid any of my wild thoughts rubbing off on him before he determined what the reception would be on the E Ring.

I knew the colonel sensed my thoughts when he stopped on the third-floor landing and said, "Robin, I confess I had thought of you as a lightweight flyboy. My opinion sure has changed. This briefing of yours shows a lot of deep and original thought. I'm impressed."

So was I, not knowing if I was being damned by faint praise or being humored in my madness.

The briefing was given, eyes glazed over, heads nodded, and I was sent on to the next large desk for further briefing and seed sowing. After a week or so of being shunted from office to office, and trying to worm my way onto the thickest carpets before the largest desks, I had to give up. I hadn't expected anyone to jump up and shout, "That's the way to go! We'll run with it!" The needed technology was too far in the future and hadn't even been imagined. The idea fell on deaf ears.

Years later, we had "Star Wars." It didn't go far, as the threat changed and the technology never quite met the challenge. At least my version of "Star Wars" hadn't cost the taxpayers anything but my salary.

Life at home swung through ups and downs that resembled life in the Pentagon. Which world was more real, and how did they manage to coexist in the same time frame? Nuclear holocaust or connubial crisis? Ella, Chris, Susie, and I lived in a nice townhome on P Street in Georgetown, with all the amenities of Washington, D.C., social life close at hand. I had a workshed-garage out in back of our long, high-walled garden and spent hours there working on projects. Little Chris was often by my side. Together we built birdhouses and shelves. I let Chris hammer away at things and asked her to take measurements. This was a sly way of grilling her on her math homework. It kept her occupied and also meant she wasn't climbing trees or walking along the top of the brick garden wall. Susie was often in the garden, too, and the girls devised a playhouse under a tall holly tree. Truth be told, all three of us were out of the house together as often as possible. I even started going to Christ Church just two blocks away. I'd walk my daughters to their Sunday school class, then sit through the service. It was a refuge for me, though not a religious one. After church, we'd walk slowly home, always stopping at the corner drugstore for ice cream or the comic books forbidden by Ella. Both girls promised they wouldn't divulge our secret. I took them to nearby Rock Creek Park, to the Georgetown Public Library, or to walk the path along the Potomac Canal. I read to them at night and got them off to school in the morning. I made breakfast while Ella slept in. Pancakes, scrambled eggs, and raspberry jam smeared on the morning funny papers—that was our happy routine.

Ella and I often had cocktail parties. Mixing my military cronies, her Hollywood pals like Jack Benny and Jimmy Stewart, our D.C. socialite friends, and the requisite New York psychiatrist often provided hilarious results. Ella also liked formal dinners. I dreaded them, but admitted they gave beneficial table-manners training to the children. Sunday nights were sacred and the only real time we spent together as a family. It was meat loaf and macaroni in front of the TV in my den watching *Lassie, Bonanza, Walt Disney's Wonderful World of Color*, and *The Ed Sullivan Show*. Comfort food and comfort TV.

We had one old dog and a collection of Siamese cats regularly entertaining us. During one of those formal school-night dinners, one of the cats tore across the top of the dining room table foaming at the mouth, scattering silverware, wineglasses, and women in all directions. Ella screamed, "Rabies, rabies!" and dragged the girls out of the room. I went for the barbecue gloves and chased that damned frothing cat all over the house. I could hear the drama unfolding in the upstairs bathroom as Ella poured bottles of French perfume over the girls to decontaminate them. Chris was pleading, "Wait, Mommy, wait, don't let Daddy kill my cat! Please, no!" I finally cornered our hissing, foaming feline, stuffed it into a pillowcase, and took off for the vet hospital. When I phoned home to call off the alarm and report the foam was just toothpaste, Ella replied that Chris had brushed the cat's teeth. Ella was furious. I laughed. Better than nukes any day.

The family escaped from Washington, D.C., each summer to stay at Laurance Rockefeller's ranch in the Tetons of Wyoming. Those were languid days of fishing, horseback riding, pack trips, and water-skiing followed by pleasant evenings at the main lodge with good friends. Larry and his wife, Mary, were the sweetest people in the world, and gracious hosts. There was always a passel of children visiting with their parents, so all the kids ran off to play while the adults spent relaxing evenings together. The time was magical for all of us, albeit short for me. One week at a time was all I could manage away from the Pentagon, but the girls stayed on. Those summer visits seemed to heal and soothe our various ills in a special way.

I was assigned to the Joint Staff and spent two more years in the Pentagon fussing against the system but content to at least be where a man got to do something meaningful. JFK put his name on the Bay of Pigs during that time and the Cuban missile crisis the following year. I was in the thick of things at work while my children were practicing how to "duck and cover" beneath their desks at school.

My final year in Washington was spent at the prestigious National War College at Fort McNair, where the seminars with army colonels and navy captains kept us philosophically arguing with one another for ten months. The man who made the most sense in the whole school was George Viney, a U.S. Army lieutenant colonel, who stoutly maintained we could fight a war in Europe without involving nukes. I wasn't sure I could swallow that, but everything George said about the need to keep our conventional swords sharp was in total agreement with what I had been thinking.

Finally, toward the middle of 1963, my name was plucked for a prime assignment: wing commander of the 81st Tactical Fighter Wing at RAF Bentwaters, England. Flying again! Never mind that it was still in a "defense" posture. The air force had really ratcheted back on training fighter pilots, so I looked with a great deal of envy at the navy. Boy, they really had their shit together in training elite guys for combat. There was something very wrong with that picture. The navy was training fighter pilots and the air force was planting bombs in missile silos. Shouldn't weapons in or on the ground be controlled by the army?

Leaving Washington wouldn't be well received by Ella. This time it would be harder to uproot the girls, now ten and eleven, from established friendships and familiar classmates, but the promise of living in the land where some long-haired band called the Beatles dwelt persuaded them that it might be tolerable. We sailed to England on the *Queen Elizabeth II* and then settled, for our first time together, into officers quarters on base. Ella wasn't happy, but I was wing commander and she relented to take a stab at being an air force wife. Colonel Daniel "Chappie" James was my deputy commander for ops, and his family lived just across the street. Chappie and I became good friends. Little did we know how our lives would later intertwine.

The 81st TFW had changed in the late fifties from fighter-interceptor to fighter-bomber operations, carrying both conventional and nuclear weapons on F-101C "Voodoos." We operated three squadrons, the 78th, 91st, and 92nd TFS, in support of USAFE and NATO. The mission was clear: Train pilots for low-altitude delivery of nuclear weapons on a Soviet or Eastern European target. Our nuclear reach was significantly extended, but it was understood that it was likely to be a one-way mission. Our guys were being trained extensively in escape and evasion techniques once they ejected behind enemy lines. The prognosis seemed to be escape and evade capture but succumb to radiation. It was a hell of a scenario and I didn't like it one damned bit. Yet the job itself was demanding and challenging and the guys were a great bunch. RAF stations Bentwaters and Woodbridge were neighboring bases with many shared facilities, so there were double the number of good folks making the fighter business run for me and my next-door counterpart. I thrived on the smell of jet fuel and pilot camaraderie.

Our daughters were happy with their gang of subteen friends on base but unhappy with a brief stint at Ella's insistence in an English school in nearby Ipswich. They switched to the RAF Bentwaters-Woodbridge public middle school. Susie did well, but Chris, at twelve, had started pushing back at Ella, expressing teenage independence. The fights raging through our house were horrific. It didn't take long for me to realize that everyone's sanity rested on separating the two. We made the decision to put Chris into an English boarding school in High Wycombe. I drove my weeping child to Wycombe Abbey, and it did no good to reassure her she'd be safe and happy with the possibility of meeting Robin Hood, or maybe Friar Tuck. It wasn't quite being banished to a nunnery, but it may have seemed so to the twelve-year-old. The imposing old buildings and grounds had served as the headquarters of the 8th AF when I was at Wattisham. The familiar location was reassuring and comfortable only to me.

On November 22, 1963, the "red" phone in my home office rang while we were having dinner. Not a good sign. I answered it and returned to the table with the terrible news of President Kennedy's assassination. Chris was the only American in a school of three hundred English girls, and we brought her home for a few days. Sadness enveloped the base, and all of us felt very far from home, but I had to do my job. Grim times.

The 81st continued its mission with pilots routinely rotating to Wheelus for weapons training. The F-101s stood alert, weapons loaded and ready for nuclear war. Each day that passed without the nuclear balloon going up was counted as a silent victory. By 1965, things were running well. All was quiet. The 81st had passed all the latest wing inspections, the aircraft in-commission rate was where it should be, our maintenance schedule was flowing, the flying training was proceeding without any hitches, and my people at both bases were pleased with themselves, proud of the wing and proud of one another. So what was bugging me?

It was a war, a growing fracas on the other side of the world in a place called Vietnam. I had missed Korea, and I'd be damned if I was going to miss this one. Reports drifting in told us the action was heating up; our fighter squadrons were striking targets around Hanoi and there was heavy opposition. I sat comfortably in England with the best assignment an air force colonel could hope for, and I wanted to be somewhere else. I wanted a piece of the action. Rotation was coming up in August. Maybe something would happen.

The phone rang in May. It was an acquaintance calling from the Pentagon. He got right down to business and whispered, "Don't say anything to anyone, and don't say who told you, but you're on the List."

"Oh God," I gulped, "Er, ah, thanks for warning me. No, I don't mean that, thanks for the alert. Damn, that doesn't sound right either. How about just 'Thanks'?" We hung up and I leaned back bitterly. That blew it for sure. A general. Who wanted to be a general? Generals didn't fight, not since Custer anyway, but that was a brevet rank and he reverted to lieutenant colonel for his most noteworthy battle. What was I to do? What could I do? If I told the air force I didn't want to be a general they'd say, "Fine. What retirement date would suit you?" Hell, that wasn't what I wanted either.

An idea suddenly popped into my head. I had to make my boss in London so mad at me that he'd take my name off that promotion list. Something bad enough to get noticed, but not so bad as to have General Disosway at Wiesbaden want to court-martial me; not too hot, not too cold, just right. So what to do? Hmmm. All right, I'd lead a formation acrobatic show for the upcoming Open House Day. Since every American flying base in the UK would be open to the public, there'd be press coverage. The boss would see a write-up about the air show at Bentwaters, and if I knew him, he'd blow his stack because I didn't ask his permission. I had time to form a team and get in some practice. Boy oh boy. No one had ever done such a thing in F-101s. I guess no one was ever dumb enough to think of it. The bird was wonderful to fly, but acrobatic? No way! One look at the tiny wings would tell even a Piper Cub pilot that close-in acrobatics would be out of the question. Reading the flight manuals and more than a few accident reports on the airplane would reinforce that high-g maneuvering was dicey in almost all situations. I wondered what we could demo that wouldn't get anybody killed while still getting me in just enough hot water.

From my own evaluations of talent plus a lot of help from the squadrons, I picked C. R. Morgan, Ski Fantaski, and Tom Hirsch to be my team. Ski would be Four and fly the slot. Our first practice went well until I called for the bomb-burst maneuver. We burst all right, but it took quite a while to find one another afterward. I screwed up the countdown for the recovery, and deeply ingrained fighter pilot survival instincts of each guy took over. Then I called Bentwaters tower for permission to make the high-speed, low-altitude pass, and went right down the runway at Woodbridge. Wrong airfield! OK, so that's why you practice. The debrief was bloody, with everyone contributing to the critique in order to get it done right the next time.

On the Saturday of the show we took our turn for a programmed Open House pass over nearby RAF Mildenhall. Our timing was thrown off by the parachute demonstration, but we did a nice, safe formation barrel roll down the runway and headed for the real show back at home. Our rolls and loops there went as smooth as glass, not a bobble. For the finale, the bomb-burst maneuver was perfect. At its finish we met simultaneously head-on as we crossed the center of the runway from four different directions, 100 feet off the deck. After landing, I looked at Ski's vertical stabilizer and saw it was black from my exhaust smoke, just as a slot man's rudder should be. What a job those three had done! If memory serves, no one else ever had the gall to put on such a show in the F-101 Voodoo. The spectators, including my family, were all thrilled. No one had a clue it was a no-no.

My transgression produced the desire effect. That same day, an angry two-star general called me at home. He had watched the show at Mildenhall and was suitably pissed!

"Olds, you were late for your pass! You were too high! And you did an unauthorized barrel roll! What have you got to say for yourself? That was a crass exhibition of irresponsibility. I can't believe your incompetence. . . ." And he ranted on at me.

Oh boy, I thought. Wait till he hears about the show at Bentwaters! Then the shit will really hit the fan. When the general saw the London papers on Sunday, his telephone call was classic. I really felt a bit guilty and hoped he wouldn't have too severe a heart attack as he thundered at me. The culmination of the chewing out was an order to appear in his office the following day, before he slammed the receiver down.

I headed to London by train and spent the time penciling an outline of the bawling out I knew was coming. It turned out I was right on track. I sat on a couch in the general's office, facing his desk. My head was lower than his and I watched as he theatrically read me the riot act. He waved his finger and waggled his wattles as he warmed to the task. After the initial verbiage, he opened the right-hand drawer of his desk and pulled out my Effectiveness Report. As he waved it at me I could see most of the X marks were over on the wrong side of the paper, a sign in those days tantamount to the kiss of death for any aspiring officer. I marveled that the general had even had time to prepare it. Maybe some staff officer had done his bidding. The general then pulled another paper from his desk and told me it was the Legion of Merit I was to have been presented on my departure from Bentwaters. I had to admire his dramatic flourish as he tore it in two and threw the pieces to the floor, but the pièce de résistance was the next paper he waved at me. It was small and I didn't recognize it.

"This, Olds, is a 505 Form, which all general officers fill out on the colonels working for them. I'm forbidden to show it to you, but I'll tell you this. It says you will NEVER be promoted! NEVER!" His face grew red and his voice shook. His finger punctuated every exclamation. Then came the shocker.

He bellowed, "And you, Olds, you're exactly the kind of officer who should be in Southeast Asia!"

With that I rose, saluted smartly, and said, "Thank you, sir. I was hoping you'd say that, sir!" He was still shouting at me as I did an about-face and walked out. To tell the truth, I've never been proud of my actions at that time, but what the hell, I didn't get promoted. They shipped me off to 9th AF headquarters at Shaw in Sumter, South Carolina, two months later. In a way, it was a punishment and I knew it. I also knew I was going to Southeast Asia right from Shaw. I'd got what I'd wanted in the first place.

The assistant deputy ops assignment at the 9th went well, and the year passed quickly and quietly. Ella lived in D.C. again. Chris spent her eighth-grade year as a boarding student at Holton-Arms in Bethesda. Susie lived with me and went to seventh grade at the Shaw AFB school. We had a great time and gave each other lots of freedom. I took up golf. Life at home was casual and stress-free: simple cooking, favorite TV shows, a cat, friends over, base picnics, swimming at Myrtle Beach. Chris visited during school vacations. Ella and I talked on the phone and exchanged some letters. I was flying. Who could complain?

The job was interesting. The 9th AF had control over all fighter squadrons in the eastern United States, and we shuffled pilots through the pipeline of combat training before heading them off to Nam. My boss and I dealt with a challenging problem. HQ got a message announcing a new policy for air force fighter pilots. Every aircrew member would go to SEA once before anybody would have to go twice. It was the dumbest thing we'd ever heard; there were navy guys on carriers in the Gulf of Tonkin who had rotated through three or four times. The CO and I sat down one night to figure out how long it would take to run through every fighter pilot in the tactical forces: PACAF, USAFE, and TAC. Each guy was given a year and we'd allow six months for the one-hundred-mission tour, the "counter" thing for missions over North Vietnam. How long would it be before we ran completely out of pilots, figuring two to an F-4 cockpit? Just two and a half years! Maybe less. How could we use up our talent like that? That meant SAC and MAC guys would have to be trained to do the job of fighter pilots to fill in, and we were sorely behind even on that task. TAC guys were volunteering for another tour, but it certainly took a real hard-nosed guy to come home to his wife and say, "Well, honey, I just volunteered to go back." Guys didn't want to do that! It's just not good psychology on the home front. Yes, it's a lot easier to go home and say, "Gee, the bastards just ordered me back!" Then he looks like the helpless good guy to his wife, but he gets to go fly. Lots of pilots were willing to go, but the air force didn't have the guts to order them.

I spent the year wondering what the hell I'd find when I finally went to war.

16

★

The Phantom and the War

I got my orders to the 8th TFW at Ubon Royal Thai AFB in Thailand with a stop en route to get a quickie checkout in the F-4. Chappie James was deputy commander for operations for the 4453rd Combat Crew Training Wing at Davis-Monthan AFB in Arizona, so I gave him a call. An excellent pilot and close friend, Major Bill Kirk, was also at D-M as an instructor pilot. Chappie called Bill right away. "Bill, the boss is coming. He needs to get checked out and only has a week to do it!" It didn't seem a problem to me. So what if I had only five days to learn the F-4 after all the different birds I'd flown in my life. How hard could it be?

I packed up the household goods at Shaw, shipped a footlocker and my personal gear to Thailand, and sent Susie to live with Ella and Chris in Washington, D.C. Both the girls would be in the same school for the first time in four years, Ella was happy and seemed content with the D.C. social scene, so the family was OK. I was headed to the war at last, but there was a lot to think about.

I knew that the war was not proceeding very well and wondered how I'd cope with the Washington bureaucracy pulling the military strings. In the Cuban missile crisis of '62, when I was buried in the Pentagon, they concluded that a determined but carefully controlled American response was what faced down the Soviets. As a result, the Washington bigwigs and think-tank guys did a good job of convincing everyone in real power that the true objective in combat was not to destroy the enemy but to convince him it was in his best interest to settle the matter by conceding instead of facing escalation and defeat. Persuasion would work rather than the threat of overwhelming defeat.

The air strikes against North Vietnam in early 1965 and the first Rolling Thunder missions were intended to warn Hanoi of worse things to come. The concept was of gradual escalation rolling toward serious consequences. President Johnson, SecDef Robert McNamara, and adviser McGeorge Bundy all believed these early strikes would influence Hanoi's attitude by focusing on LOC (lines of communication) in the southern part of North Vietnam, the panhandle above the DMZ. The attacks seemed useful for hampering the movement of matériel south, but they didn't seem to be putting sufficient pressure on Hanoi. America was moving ground troops into South Vietnam, and a significant portion of our air power was diverted to supporting that effort. The Rolling Thunder campaign was handled from the bases in Thailand and the carriers on Yankee Station. LBJ thought that Hanoi would come to the bargaining table under this gradual "pressure." Rolling Thunder was one part of a four-part strategy intended to bend the will of the Communists: First, stepped-up operations on the ground in South Vietnam; second, civil, political, and economic programs in the South; third, Rolling Thunder bombing of the North; and fourth, offers of negotiations and aid in postwar economic development.

The decision not to apply our military force decisively was balanced by concern that South Vietnam was so weak politically that it could collapse, especially if heavier bombing caused Hanoi to increase its infiltration and direct military involvement. The greatest fear was of provoking Chinese intervention or Soviet retaliation. Finally, Washington was reluctant to risk punishing North Vietnamese civilians the way they had once attacked the cities of Germany and Japan. On paper this looked fine and made sense, but in the battlefields our loss of American lives in a limited war seemed a waste of good men. It was frustrating. I wanted to go in and win the damn thing. Spare everybody the suffering!

Hanoi was already exploiting the escalated bombing with a worldwide PR campaign it knew was triggering growing antiwar sentiment in the United States. The North Vietnamese regime had mobilized its entire civilian population and military to quickly repair what the U.S. was damaging. It armed citizens with rifles and other light weapons to fire at low-flying planes. It increased its aid to the South and its resistance to us in the North. The North Vietnamese weren't becoming more compliant at all.

I knew I was stepping into a mess. There were few of us who believed that air power could work if truly sensitive targets were left unchallenged. My resolve was to achieve the mission but protect my guys, fight the Washington bureaucrats as hard as I could but still do everything possible within our imposed limitations to make us successful. During the three months prior to my taking over at Ubon, I knew the wing had lost a squadron's worth of airplanes, and more than twenty pilots were dead or missing. Things had to change, but I had already spent enough time thinking about the problems ahead. It was time for me to fly again!

At Davis-Monthan, I linked up with Chappie, Bill Kirk, and another instructor pilot, Tommy McNutt. We got down to work. I had my initial flight in the F-4 and knew that the normal fourteen steps in Bill's training syllabus would be compressed for my schedule.

On my second flight in the F-4 we were west of Tucson near Gila Bend and had just gone through the usual familiarization maneuvers. We had done high-g maneuvering, rolls, reversals, and routine acrobatics. I loved the Phantom. Everything about it felt right. It was light on the controls and quickly responsive to power changes, and it gave me a feeling of eagerness not normal in an object weighing more than 17 tons.

"Hey, Bill, how about showing me this adverse yaw everybody seems so worried about?" I knew what the principle was, but in this airplane it seemed to present some unusual problems. Basically the idea was that an airplane turns by moving one aileron up and the opposite aileron down, causing a roll. Adverse yaw was a slewing or skidding of the nose in the direction away from the turn. It was caused by the down aileron generating more drag than the one that moved upward. It was usually countered by a bit of rudder. I'd seen it all before.

Bill didn't sound too eager when he answered, "I dunno, Robin. Uh, well, OK. Let's get up some speed. Hit the burners, let the nose down, then pull up when you're close to mach to zoom and get some altitude under us. OK. Now pull up about 60 degrees."

Up we zoomed like a rocket.

"OK, we're through 40,000, bring it out of burner and back to idle. Let her slow down like a stall approach. Forty-five thousand, 50,000, don't touch the ailerons! OK, we're down to 200 knots, 175, hold it, hold it, 51,000, 150 knots. Now, touch the ailerons. Feel that buffeting? Watch out for the nose slice—"

"Whoops! Oh shit!"

The nose of the F-4 swerved left opposite my aileron input, sliced right, left again, then right, and tucked under violently. The ground spun around, stopped, and then spun the other way. The nose pitched up above the horizon, then slammed under again, the earth spun, and my shoulder harness bit me hard. A few years' worth of accumulated dust and dirt flew up over my head and lodged on the canopy. We seemed in an inverted tumble. I had seen spins in a lot of airplanes but this was something else. I worked furiously at the controls, but nothing seemed to have any effect. Then both engines flamed out.

We were gyrating like a falling leaf in a windstorm when Bill hollered, "Get out the RAT—the engines are gone!"

At least one of us knew what was going on. I found the handle on the console by my hip and extended the ram air turbine. I heard the small doors thump open as the fan device popped out into the airstream to run the hydraulics for flight controls. We continued tumbling crazily straight down, down, down; sky overhead, then under, the ground appeared, then disappeared, negative g-forces sucked at us, then a slam of positive, down we went. Thirty thousand, 20,000, 18,000, the altimeter unwinding. The bird tumbled, the earth spun, the horizon went crazy, and I kept feeling out all the controls, trying to break the violent stall.

"OK, Colonel," Bill yelled, "fourteen thousand, we better get out!"

"No, no, wait!" I called back. "I think I've got it. Just one more turn!" As the nose went straight down and paused in its gyrations I slammed the stick full forward, ailerons with the turn, and full opposite rudder. The aircraft hesitated, then kicked farther forward in a wings-level dive. I immediately relaxed forward pressure, and went neutral on the ailerons and rudder.

By God, that did it! I was back in control; the airspeed was building. I pulled gently out of our dive. We leveled out at about 8,000 feet above the deck, and with Bill's help, I restarted both engines. Whew! I could hear Bill gulping huge deep breaths in the backseat.

"Holy mackerel, Bill. That was fun! Let's go do that again!"

I laughed when Bill shouted, "Not on your life, sir!"

The g-meter was pegged in both directions, positive and negative. We flew gingerly back to base knowing the bird would have to undergo a thorough check for possible damage to the airframe and engines.

Well, I thought, that was an enlightening experience. I guess the tech order knew what it was talking about when it warned of deep stalls and aileron movement. I think I'll avoid it in the future. And I did. Bill, on the other hand, must have been out of his mind when he agreed later that week to join me in Thailand. Maybe it was because he knew we'd never have to be in the same aircraft together again.

After five training days it was time to get going, but there was a problem with clearing the base. Although there was a war going on on the other side of the world, peace prevailed at this SAC-controlled installation. Most of us in the F-4 training pipeline, officers and enlisted alike, were on full schedules as students. The only time we could work on out-processing was noon hour during the weekdays. That was the time when the base functions shut down for lunch. I tried twice to get my pay records from base finance, but the line outside the closed door stretched for 50 yards down the sidewalk and my next flight briefed at 1300 hours. Once that was over and debriefing was done, the finance office would be closed. Something was going to have to be done.

The next day at noon I barged past the line to the closed door, entered with a bang, and confronted a flustered sergeant. "Where's your boss?" I demanded.

"Still in his office," stammered the man.

"And where is that?" He pointed and I went. A captain sat behind a desk eating a sandwich.

"Come with me," I ordered.

I walked him outside to the end of the line, turned him around and pointed to the men standing there. As patiently as I could I explained to him that these men were going to Southeast Asia and this was the only time of day they could get their clearances from his office. I told him I was sure both his base commander and SAC headquarters would be fascinated with my report concerning his lack of concern for the needs of the troops and that both entities would recognize the basis of my complaint.

The captain sized up what was said and replied that I wouldn't have to go to all that trouble. All I had to do was go to the head of the line and his people would take care of my clearance. I glared at the man and told him that wasn't the purpose of my visit. It was about doing the job for all of the troops. That finally got him in gear and he asked what I expected him to do, since most of his staff were civil servants. I suggested he stagger their lunch hours and keep his air force people on hand during the time when they were needed. He did it. I found out later most of the base functions followed suit.

I still had to complete my training by firing two practice missiles, an AIM-7 Sparrow and AIM-9 Sidewinder, on the range at Point Mugu on the Ventura County coast. The airplane got loaded with the missiles and a travel pod for my gear. We briefed the mission, then flew out to the range, found the target being towed, fired our missiles (I never knew where they went), and landed at Travis AFB near Sacramento. Bill said his good-byes and headed back to D-M solo. I hung around Travis for a day, did more paperwork and prep, then was hustled into a chartered baby blue Braniff 707 loaded to the gills with an assortment of people: old, young, GIs in uniforms of all services, dependents, mothers with babies, you name it. It was business as usual, all on their way to various bases throughout the Pacific. I was just one of the passengers. God, what a contrast to going to war in 1944. I was on my way.

We stopped in Hawaii, Guam, and the Philippines. People got off and others got on in a constant, never-ending stream. The cabin began to stink of dirty diapers, vomit, and human sweat. It wasn't a crammed troopship on an ocean voyage, but it wasn't much better. We reached Tan Son Nhut, in South Vietnam. Some of the passengers deplaned for good and a harried-looking captain came on board. With an air of authority he ordered everyone to remain on board but announced that the colonel would be allowed to get off. I told him I would stay with my fellow passengers.

We sat there as the plane baked in the sun. The heat inside became nearly unbearable. The baby across the aisle fretted and screamed. His mother, who I learned was on her way to join her husband at the embassy in Bangkok, became frantic. I left the plane and found the captain in the terminal fussing around. He told me it would be another hour or so before departure. As he turned to go about his business I told him to come with me. He knew it was an order. We boarded the plane and I told him to sit next to me. I didn't say anything. We just sat. He began to sweat. The poor baby screamed louder. One of the women appeared about to pass out. The captain was a prolific sweater. He squirmed and tried to tell me he really had a lot to do. Too damn bad.

I responded, "That's fine. You can get off and so will all the passengers. Show me where they can get relief and a drink of water, and I assure you I'll have them ready when it's time to get back on board." That worked. Everyone had a break in the terminal. We reboarded after another hour and headed to Don Muang airport in Bangkok without further trouble. We deplaned there and were herded as a group to listen to a predictably boring "in-briefing." It was late in the day when a sergeant told us to report back the following morning for transportation to final destinations.

The next morning, September 30, I got on a cargo-laden C-130 with a number of enlisted troops. We spent the whole day flying from base to base around Thailand, unloading and loading people and supplies. Each stop let in another blast of hot, humid, fetid air. At last, five sergeants and I were dumped with our luggage out the back end of the "Klong" at Ubon RTAFB. I gazed about me with interest and no small amount of growing anger. We stood on a piece of hot concrete a mile away from base ops, the sun beating on us out of a brassy sky. No shelter and no base people to take care of deplaning passengers.

The C-130 did a 180 near us and took off in the other direction. We were left in the arming area at the end of the runway. In the distance I could see the familiar tails of a line of F-4s parked on what I presumed to be the main taxiway. Maybe that was why the 130 had to take off in the opposite direction. Mighty peculiar, I thought. It was quiet as the sergeants sat on their duffel bags and I sat on my footlocker. We waited. A fine greeting for their new commander. I had wanted to find out how replacements were received and I found out. This would be fixed!

A bored captain finally drove up in a pickup. I stared at him. He stared back. I identified myself and asked if this was a typical example of passenger service. He looked at me dully. I suggested perhaps he might give me a lift to wing HQ, since that was now my place of business. Even that didn't faze him. Without offering any directions on where to take our gear, how to sign in, or where the mess or quarters were, he delivered us to wing headquarters, where we were unceremoniously dumped out. The sergeants stayed with their gear out front, by this time looking a little nervous.

I stalked into the front door of the wing HQ, turned into the closest office, asked where the NCOs should go, and then reported back to the sergeants. They took off. I left my footlocker outside and walked back into the building. To tell the truth, I was having a hard time trying to look angry. There was sort of a "gotcha!" grin sneaking onto my face because I was just too damned happy to be there. Trying to look determined and offended and to show annoyance was just about impossible, even for a ham like me. My happiness at getting to what would be "my" base easily overpowered the lost "new guy" feeling. When I stalked down the long dark corridor from the entrance of wing headquarters I was more conscious of the smell of the ruddy teakwood walls than of maintaining my pose as an insulted new commander.

An air policeman stood at the end of the corridor outside a door marked COMBAT OPERATIONS. My scowl must have been sufficiently threatening because he didn't make the slightest attempt to prevent me from entering the nerve center of the wing. I slammed through the door and barely stopped myself from laughing at the look on the faces of the men working inside. There was annoyance at seeing a strange colonel burst into the sanctum, quizzically raised eyebrows at just who the hell I might be, dawning realization that they were looking at their new commander, then chagrin on realizing that no one was with me and that my arrival had been unannounced and unnoticed. They exchanged furtive glances, each man wondering who had dropped the ball, then bent their heads back down to work. It wasn't me. Don't look at me! One bright lad must have picked up the phone because 8th TFW vice commander Colonel Vermont Garrison suddenly appeared at my elbow. My old friend was not too happy with me. I couldn't blame him. It wasn't fair or very good form to arrive without warning.

Pappy was an old acquaintance. We had worked together in the Pentagon and I respected him as an extraordinary pilot. He was an ace in World War II, a double ace in Korea, a wise old sage, and a true Kentucky gentleman. He had a full head of silver hair and personified calm dignity, but today Pappy was mad clear through. He hustled me down the hall toward the front of the building and into a spacious office we would share with a male NCO secretary. Pappy's desk and mine were separated by a latticework partition sporting a thick growth of philodendrons. The checkerboard floor tile and spare, functional furnishings were not at all pretentious. I liked the place right away.

"Robin, why the hell didn't you let us know you were arriving? We could have met you down in Bangkok, brought you up in the Gooney Bird, given you some kind of welcome. Damn it, you've embarrassed us!"

"I truly apologize, Pappy. Embarrassing you was the last thing I wanted to do. I guess I wasn't thinking straight," I replied sheepishly. "It was the way I was sent over in that damned blue Braniff, with nothing said about procedure anywhere along the line. My only guidance was a vague order telling me to proceed to Ubon to assume command of the 8th TFW, and that's exactly what I did."

"You mean you didn't get your in-briefing at Hickam and Clark? What about in Saigon?"

"Nope, no place. I took the commuter route and those poor GIs and dependents on the plane were treated like cattle. Hell, we all were. Even the sergeants I arrived with this morning had no clear orders. Personnel handling is as big a mess as this war seems to be."

My friend sighed and shook his head. He obviously agreed. We both settled down and soon were chatting amiably. He brought me up to speed on all that had happened after the departure of my predecessor, Colonel Joe Wilson. The base had been set up well and things were pretty organized, but Wilson didn't fly much. In fact, he had flown only twelve missions in the thirteen months he had been there. His deputy for operations, Scotty Clark, had flown eighteen. Neither had the vaguest concept of tactics or the war itself. That wasn't good, not good at all, but it certainly set up the situation for my new command. Things were about to change drastically.

After that quick overview, Pappy told me where to take my stuff and where to sign in. I had inherited Joe Wilson's air-conditioned trailer so I dumped my stuff inside the door. Nice setup! Then I headed out to go through official check-in. At one point in the afternoon, I was standing in line for the military pay window with a bunch of other hot and tired new arrivals. There were only six or seven of us left to process when the airman on duty in the cashier window put up a CLOSED sign and told all of us to come back in the morning. I told everyone to stand fast and politely asked the cashier for a phone and the number for the base commander's office. The airman had no idea who I was, but my rank worked again. I got the base commander on the phone and asked, "Can you process a travel voucher?" He said he could not, to which I replied, "Well then, call the chief of military pay and the two of you come down here and keep this facility open around the clock. You're manned for it. If I can order a man into combat twenty-four hours a day, he should be able to get paid twenty-four hours a day." Since this guy's title was officially combat support group commander, he was my subordinate, and he knew an order when he heard one. It was a matter of minutes before he showed up with two other guys and we all got processed.

Afterward, I walked back to his office with him and got the lowdown on how things were going at Ubon from his perspective. I liked this setup of the base commander being under my command because it meant that I had the overall responsibility while he shouldered the day-to-day problems of running the base. If a toilet wouldn't flush, that was his baby. If he didn't have it fixed by the air base group people working for him, he caught hell from me. Operations, the flying mission of the wing, was similar. In that case the deputy commander for operations, a colonel, worked directly for the wing commander as a member of the wing staff. It was the same with the colonel in charge of running the maintenance and supply functions. USAF had made constant organizational rearrangements over the years and it always reminded me of an old dog turning in circles before settling down in front of the fireplace. No matter how many times he circled he always wound up in the same place, with the same grunt, and the same part of his body facing the fire.

The base commander gave me a good rundown on how things worked, who was who, what was what, and what his own immediate and most pressing problems were. All normal-normal, I thought. I told him I was surprised and delighted with the base setup. "I had no idea buildings and facilities would be permanent. I confess I expected Quonset huts and tents, but not this. There's even a swimming pool!"

He explained. "You have to understand, the entire facility really belongs to the Thai air force. We are just tenants, though we're five times the size of the Thai T-28 Squadron. You probably saw their aircraft out on the ramp. The Thai squadron commander is named Salukiat. He's a lieutenant colonel, and he normally leaves us alone. On the other hand, we must get his approval for anything we wish to build, and you can bet he becomes a pain in the butt if he doesn't like what Uncle Sam wants to do. The Thais will get everything when we leave."

I gathered there was no love lost between the two, and made a mental note to get to know my Thai counterpart as soon as possible. Then I made a request.

"I have a suggestion," I began, although my statement clearly meant it was an order. "I'd like you to assign one of your sergeants on temporary duty to Don Muang in Bangkok. I want him to be impressive, responsible, and gung ho. His duty will be to greet every batch of incoming replacements destined for this wing. He is to welcome them to the 8th, give them a short brief on the country and our mission, and present each of them with a wing patch. Meanwhile, when he calls, that C-47 Gooney Bird sitting out there on the ramp is to go down to Bangkok and bring our new troops directly here. I'll clear that with the detachment CO at Don Muang. He probably couldn't care less anyway. Got that? You can rotate your NCO as often as you see fit, but get cracking. I don't want another one of our new people, officers or airmen, to go through the same indifferent bullshit I experienced on my arrival. And another thing. I want you to reorganize the base in-processing procedure. Instead of each new arrival having to wander all over the place signing in, I want you to have a representative from each of the usual organizations at one table. I mean someone from finance, another from personnel, billeting, etc., you know who they must be. I hope you understand why I'm telling you to do these things." His expression told me he understood, but he wasn't particularly thrilled with the new tone of the place.

The round-the-clock mission schedule at Ubon meant the club was open twenty-four hours a day, both bar and dining room. My arrival hadn't been widely noticed yet, so I didn't feel conspicuous when I stopped at the O club at about 4:00 A.M. for breakfast. I wore a flying suit that I'd had for several years, both in the Pentagon and at Shaw for use when I'd been flying some of the support aircraft. I didn't think much of it. I was preoccupied with thoughts about the base, the morale, the troops, and the leadership that I'd seen so far.

I ate and headed to the cashier to pay my tab. I fell into line behind a couple of young lieutenants, both apparently backseat F-4 pilots who had been on the night schedule and stopped at the club for dinner and more than a few drinks. They glanced at the stranger standing behind them and then began in a stage whisper to discuss my attire.

"Must be a trash hauler. Probably on some Gooney Bird from the Philippines getting his monthly combat time."

"Yeah, sucking up the combat pay and tax exclusion. Patches say Air Defense Command, don't they?"

"Looks like an interceptor pilot maybe. Probably doesn't know that combat pilots don't wear patches. Check the leg! Is that his Gooney Bird survival kit? Even interceptor pukes don't pull enough g's chasing bombers to need speed jeans." He turned to me, "Excuse me, Colonel, are you a fighter pilot?"

"Let's make him one. . . ." The bigger one reached down for the knife pocket on the left leg of my flight suit and in one practiced motion grabbed the top flap, snapped it open, and smoothly tore it off my flight suit. Before I could react, the other one snuck behind me and grabbed me around the chest. "Now, let's get the patches."

Being manhandled by a pair of lieutenants on the day of my arrival seemed a bit out of place and I resisted. I turned and grabbed the one behind me. The second went at my waist and within seconds the three of us were rolling around on the floor of the dining room, wrestling, grunting, and grappling as my flight suit sleeves were ripped and both patches and chunks of cloth were removed. Other pilots gathered to watch the melee and the club manager frantically dialed the phone to call the air police.

By the time they had arrived it was over. The lieutenants were sitting with me, having another beer, and I was having a third cup of coffee. I told the cops it had been a brief misunderstanding and they left. The explanation the two, Kris Mineau and Lee Workman, gave me seemed reasonable. Combat pilots didn't wear patches, nor did they ever carry their issue survival knife in their flight suit pocket. It went in the pocket on the left thigh of the G suit. Anybody violating the rules got patches and pockets ripped off. Rank made no difference. I wondered why no one at Davis-Monthan had told me. But, I knew that there was a spark of morale at the flying squadron level that could be built into something bigger. These guys had spirit.

I headed out to spend the rest of the day exploring the base. I went roving through as many base facilities as I could to get familiar with the setup, locating work centers, unit orderly rooms, recreation facilities, mess halls, barbershop, PX, barracks, and hangars, asking questions and getting answers along the way. I knew the whole tour would take several days, but it was crucial to investigate every little thing at the start of an assignment. I planned to check out all the shops, check out equipment used by the men, look at their supplies, learn how things were put together and taken apart, even examine the gear designed for getting the pilots down from trees. The base functions were crucial to the success of the mission and the survival of the pilots. Even that first day I could sense lethargy among the troops. Morale seemed to be in the toilet. Getting up to speed quickly would be especially urgent for this command.

The base was small, tightly packed, and with an odd mixture of architecture. Tin-roofed hootches were open and screened, practical and reasonably comfortable. Flowers and grass were neatly done, everything fairly well kept. Most buildings were made of Thai teakwood weathering into a nice reddish brown color. Some goddamned fool had started to paint those attractive walls a terrible yellow or green. I raised hell and soon found out that someone up the chain of command said he "liked paint." I stopped the practice.

That night I headed to the officers' club, which wasn't far from my trailer. I met several of the guys and started talking to them over beer. It was easy to tell they didn't know what to make of me, and it was also pretty obvious they had little respect or time for wing commanders. Well, why should they?

None of the commanders flew much; therefore, they knew little about the missions. All the frag orders came down to lieutenants and captains. I got hold of Pappy Garrison before the evening was over and told him to gather all the pilots in the morning for a meeting and fit the meeting in between the flights. He told me this would be the first time a full wing pilots' meeting had been held. What the hell? Despite the staggered mission schedule, the pilots had never been briefed all at the same time? They were in for a surprise. It had been twenty-two years since I'd fought in a war, but it was obvious where my task lay.

The next morning, I let the pilots stew together over "this fucking new CO" for a little bit before I entered the briefing room, walked to the front, and turned to face them. They got quiet and their eyes glazed over. I glared at them silently for a moment and began, "My name is Olds and I'm your new boss. I've been around the air force a little while and I'm really glad to be here. You guys know a lot that I don't know and I'm here to learn from you. I'll be flying as your wingman for a couple of weeks. You are going to teach me, but you'd better teach me good and you'd better teach me fast because I'm going to fly Green Sixteen until I think I'm qualified to fly Green Three, and then I'm going to be Green Lead. When you get me ready, I'll be Mission Commander, and we'll get it done together. Now, you just stay ahead of me because as long as you know more than I do, we are going to get along just fine. I will listen to you and learn from you, but soon I'm gonna be better than all of you, and when I know more about your job than you do, look out."

From somewhere in the middle of the room came a quietly drawn out, "I see." The tone was a sarcastic "Yeah, right, Colonel," and I immediately sought out the offender. I could tell it had come out a little louder than he'd intended. My glance fell hard on a guy at the end of a row, Captain J. B. Stone, but slid quickly to the snickering major beside him, Cliff Dunnegan. I'd see about them both.

Over the next several days, I let the guys train me. Stone and Doc Broadway checked me out in the panhandle route packages, and soon I was scheduled with them to Route Pack 6. I wanted to see where the action was right away and I got what I wanted. Regularly I'd give the guys in the briefing room the same goading speech, "I'm gonna be better than you!" As soon as they stopped being pissed off, they got into the spirit of the challenge. When we weren't flying, I was stalking through the base looking over their shoulders, visiting the squadrons and hanging out with them at the O club. Pretty soon, I knew all of their names. They taught me well, both on the ground and in the air. I was out in front in less than two weeks.

This method of taking over a new command was deeply ingrained in me. My father had shown me how to be a leader by his own example. It was reinforced by other great commanders who had earned my respect, leaders like Hub Zemke, Tooey Spaatz, Jimmy Doolittle, and many more. They all connected with their troops on a personal level and learned everything they could about every part of their organization.

Here's what I'd learned over the years. Know the mission, what is expected of you and your people. Get to know those people, their attitudes and expectations. Visit all the shops and sections. Ask questions. Don't be shy. Learn what each does, how the parts fit into the whole. Find out what supplies and equipment are lacking, what the workers need. To whom does each shop chief report? Does that officer really know the people under him, is he aware of their needs, their training? Does that NCO supervise or just make out reports without checking facts? Remember, those reports eventually come to you. Don't try to bullshit the troops, but make sure they know the buck stops with you, that you'll shoulder the blame when things go wrong. Correct without revenge or anger. Recognize accomplishment. Reward accordingly. Foster spirit through self-pride, not slogans, and never at the expense of another unit. It won't take long, but only your genuine interest and concern, plus follow-up on your promises, will earn you respect. Out of that you gain loyalty and obedience. Your outfit will be a standout. But for God's sake, don't ever try to be popular! That weakens your position, makes you vulnerable. Don't have favorites. That breeds resentment. Respect the talents of your people. Have the courage to delegate responsibility and give the authority to go with it. Again, make clear to your troops you are the one who'll take the heat.

I worked my way around Ubon in the first few days, and after a week I could understand the malaise that permeated. Joe Wilson had run the base well but was completely disconnected and useless as a combat leader. His DO, Scotty Clark, was ignorant, dense, talkative, and lazy. He would have to go, and soon. The base commander was the same. The assistant DO, Bill Craig, tried his best but the squadrons ran the show. As far as I could tell, Pappy Garrison was the saving grace of the wing. He did things quietly, seemed to know what was going on, hadn't rocked the boat, and had actually made some progress while he waited for me.

It was clear that I needed a new deputy commander for operations and he had to be a personable guy that people would like and listen to, but he also had to be someone who would get along with me while carrying out my orders. I knew just the guy and quickly put the call in to Chappie James at Davis-Monthan. He said yes right away. We had always kidded each other a lot, and Chappie was only mildly offended when I told him that the base civil engineers would install additional foundation work under his trailer to keep it from sinking into the earth under his considerable bulk. At the same time, BCE would relevel the trailer so his beloved stereo hi-fi turntable could operate on an even keel. I warned him that morale building was active at the 8th, elevenses were encouraged, four o'clock tea was mandatory, social graces were observed, and we dressed for dinner. His orders were cut but he wouldn't be able to get to Ubon until sometime in December, not a moment too soon for me.

My favorite pastime had always been maps and history, so I headed to the intelligence section of the command center on the next day. It was a tiny storage room at the back of the briefing area, but the nerve center of the outfit, as far as I was concerned. That's where I'd really be able to put the scoop together for myself . . . read every report, study every photograph, absorb the wall maps, read intel from other bases. I spent many late hours learning everything I could, trying to get up to speed on what was going wrong and what we were doing right. A small bunch of guys were already there. I asked them, "Why are you here and what are you doing?" J. B. Stone, Doc Broadway, and Major J. D. Covington had been spending a lot of time in the classified area, studying photos and intel reports, trying to understand Vietnam People's Air Force (VPAF) tactics to figure out how to make the missions more successful. They were putting together a tactics manual for the 8th. Joe Wilson hadn't even known! I was impressed and told them, "Go for it, guys. I'm right with you!" J.B. had the well-earned reputation as the wing tactician after sixty or seventy missions north. He'd had an engine shot out from under him and several bullet holes in his bird. He was a steady, experienced cool customer. Doc and J.D. were also experienced guys and great pilots. Soon to be added to this cadre would be Lieutenant Ralph Wetterhahn. We were about to plan something spectacular.

Up to this point the results had been marginal for the level of effort the pilots were putting into missions. They were being sent in to targets in long sequences of four-ship flights. Going in at intervals, of course, gave the North Vietnamese gunners all the opportunity they needed to shoot at every flight as it came by. On top of that, maintenance had been severely hampered and compromised by a sortie generation test program called "Rapid Roger" that had started in August. The 8th Wing had lost twelve aircraft during August and September alone. We weren't suffering as badly as the F-105 crews out of Takhli and Korat, but, clearly the war was costing us dearly.

I looked at those losses as a new commander and believed I had justification to question them. Did they really have to happen? Was the environment really so tough here, or was the wing making mistakes? This is kind of presumptuous for a new guy because, hell, you haven't been shot at in their situation. If I could do better, I'd have to figure it out. There were some obvious places where improvements could be made. For one thing, they had been dropping napalm, using an awful lot of gun work in Route Pack 1, making multiple passes and really pressing in on low-value targets. I couldn't see any necessity for it. There were very few targets in Route Pack I that you could blunder across in broad daylight that were worth your ass and an airplane. You've got to kill a lot of beat-up old trucks to balance the books against one Phantom. So why not learn to deliver ordnance, with exceptions of course, in Route Pack 1 with the same techniques used in the harder packages? I became quite sure that 50 percent of the losses since January '66 in Route Pack 1 had been needless.

For the guys flying over the part of North Vietnam called Route Pack VI the situation was much worse. The Russians supplied the Communist North with all the matériel needed for fighting a protracted war: guns, ammo, food, clothing, trucks, gas, everything. There were more antiaircraft guns within a 60-mile radius of Hanoi than Germany had possessed in all of Europe. The guns ranged from automatic weapons like our .50 caliber machine guns up through batteries of larger radar-directed artillery spanning the gamut from 23 mm to more than 100 mm. Add the surface-to-air missiles and the MiGs supplied by China and Russia, and North Vietnam had a well-integrated and very effective air defense network. This was a very efficient and sophisticated adversary we faced.

In September we had introduced the surprisingly effective QRC–160 ECM pods carried by F-105 Thunderchiefs. Their initial results looked as though the pods significantly reduced the effect of the radar-guided guns and SAMs, but they also drastically changed the role of the MiGs. They had not been particularly aggressive or a nuisance before. The pods forced the North Vietnamese to increase the role of the MiG fighters for defense. As we entered the winter of 1966, the MiGs began increased efforts to harass U.S.

strike forces. The later-model MiG-21s had the capability to carry radar-guided or heat-seeking missiles. They and the highly maneuverable MiG-17s constituted a serious threat. It became imperative for U.S. forces to bring counteraction to bear on the MiG fighter threat.

The Rapid Roger program had also taken a toll on the 8th TFW in a short time. We knew RR was an order concocted by Robert McNamara and others with an obsession with statistics, who got LBJ to agree to it. The objective was ridiculous: "Produce a higher sortie rate with fewer aircraft." It meant airplanes that flew day missions had to turn around and fly at night, then be reconfigured again to fly the next day. That would be hell on the maintenance crews. During the day, bombers carried a 370-gallon fuel tank on each wing, plus bombs and missiles. For night flying, the birds had to be equipped with a flare dispenser in place of a wing tank and a centerline 600-gallon fuel tank. Added to the insanity of changing the aircraft configuration at dawn and dusk, the ground crews had to refuel, rearm, and repair. The maintenance crews did their absolute best, but how could they do their jobs when promised parts and personnel didn't show up, shifts were doubled, and there was little time for sleep?

If you fly one aircraft three times a day for three and a half hours each sortie, can you fly that same aircraft five times a day for the same sortie duration? Probably not. So what do you do to meet the requirement? Easy, fly it five times a day for one hour each trip—isn't that simple? You get five rides, five hours of combat, and fourteen hours in between to fix it and turn it around. What is the impact on your missions that took three and a half hours? What do you do, go faster to get to the same place? Move your base closer to the action? Or maybe encourage the enemy to come closer to you? Maybe you can load just one bomb between flights. That'll reduce turnaround time and increase rates. At the same time you might wonder how much effort you are putting up to produce what level of damage to the enemy. Am I being sarcastic? You bet.

When I got to Ubon, wing records showed that the "operationally ready" rate for aircraft had dropped from 74 percent to 55 percent between August 6 and September 22. Convinced of the failure, 7th AF HQ stopped the program for a while in an attempt to figure things out. The problem was evident to me. Promised personnel and parts never showed up. Lieutenants and captains were the ones fragged to go north, since the CO and senior officers seldom flew. The round-the-clock sortie schedule often had the guys going up without a wingman, and the loss of men and aircraft increased exponentially. It was bad news all around.

Washington had no clear idea that air power, particularly tactical air power, had to be flexible to be useful. Units were manned, equipped, and organized to produce a certain average output on a sustained basis. The entire support effort all the way back to programmed dollars was geared to that planned output. We bought gas, aircraft parts, food, munitions, aircraft ground equipment, blankets, vehicles, lox, oil, and even people on a preplanned basis. At the far end of this entire pipeline was the combat unit. That unit was flexible, up to a point. It could "surge" to a higher-than-normal sortie rate per assigned bird/aircrew, but you didn't get something for nothing. How long could you safely or efficiently compress or ignore maintenance phase cycles? How many delayed discrepancies, broken gadgets that you put off repairing, could you afford to accumulate fleetwide? How far down could you deplete spares and bench stocks? Could you ignore prudence and common sense in a turnaround cycle for very long? Were you willing to risk the degradation of weapon-system serviceability? Did you accept the high potential for a major catastrophe out on your ramp when you tried to repair a radar set, load bombs, and refuel the bird all at the same time?

For the first two weeks, as I flew tail-end Charlie, my eyes were opened to the mess the 8th was in on every level. Finally, after feeling that I knew enough to have a plan, I got a bunch of the guys together in a briefing and told them, "Captain so-and-so, who was here TDY from such-and-such place, is no longer here. He led me on a mission this morning, and we made a big turn over Route Pack I and then we bombed the doghouse down below Mu Gia Pass, and he briefed the flight when we landed to log a counter. Now, I went and changed that with the ops clerks. I told them, 'That was a non-counter. The mission wasn't into North Vietnam, but into Laos.' That captain is no longer with us. Now, I know a lot of you guys are old-timers here on your second or third tours and you're all kinda frustrated because you've had nothing to do but kill monkeys and snakes, but I'm going to offer a suggestion. If any of you guys want to be recce pilots and fly a quick turn over Route Pack I and then bomb in Laos claiming a counter, my good friend Brigadier General Vic Cabas up at Udorn is in real need of some recce jocks. I will be glad to transfer you right now. But, my friends, you log where you drop, and I don't want any mission faking or counter-sniveling going on around here, because I want you to leave this place tall and I want you to be proud of yourselves!"

The counter-faking bullshit had to be stopped. A lot of guys had gotten away with it, but I believed it would stop soon if they had a commander who led the flights. They would follow a commander into hell if he flew out front. Well, this wing commander wanted results, not statistics. One morning, I really got mad. A bunch of medal requests filled out by flight leaders for my signature showed up on my desk. I stormed into the briefing room with those papers crunched up in my fist and confronted the guys. "There sure is a shit-load of interesting reading in these forms, a lot about flak, SAMs, and MiGs, but not very much about targets being destroyed. Some of you want medals just for showing up. Well, here's what I think about that!" I dropped the whole stack into the trash can.

I also learned a big lesson on my first flight lead up to Route Pack VI. We had come off the tankers and I had been briefed to follow the last Thud flight into the target. It was soon obvious to me that the F-105 flight leader ahead hadn't a clue where he was or where he was going. He certainly wasn't any two minutes behind the flight in front of him, wherever they might be. We were snaking along at 540 knots, weaving this way and that, at about 3,500 feet above the ground. This was the tactic at the time: going in low, flights suppos-edly at two-minute intervals, stroking the afterburner at a pop-up point, then zooming to a predetermined roll-in altitude and pulling down on the target for bomb release in a 30- to 45-degree dive. I was almost at the point of break-ing off when bomb impacts off to our right gave the F-105 flight lead the loca-tion of the target his buddies were hitting. He broke violently in that direction. I followed him through his pop-up and thought this was perhaps the dumbest thing I had ever done in an airplane, especially when there were a whole bunch of bad guys down below throwing up a thick barrage of flak to the same piece of sky all the rest of the attackers had just passed through. I might be the new guy in town, but I knew that doing the same thing along the same route and from the same direction one after another wasn't a survivable tactic. It was the same old crunch: "We've been here, this is the way it is, and this is how we're going to do it." The mission stands out in my mind, not for where we went or what we bombed, but for how we went about it. On recovery that day I headed for intel again and dug out the records for the missions and tactics for the flights flown in the previous year to Pack VI. It wasn't a pretty picture.

I had never seen such a gaggle as a Pack VI strike package. I had the greatest and deepest respect for the F-105 guys, individually and collectively, but that business of going in at low altitude, jinking and weaving, pulling three negative and four positive g's at 4,500 feet, going like the hammers of hell in flights of four, in trail, was perhaps one of the dumbest things I had ever seen. You couldn't see to navigate, you were past points before you knew it, you weren't surprising the enemy, and you were taking incredible small-arms gunfire. If the pods were any good, they didn't need to do that anymore. We still didn't have our pods yet, so we had it all hung out, but we didn't lose very much by staying higher. I found out that there was some difference between the two F-105 wings, the Takhli bunch embracing the low-altitude, every-man-for-himself sort of rush into the target and the Korat flights doing it higher and with a bit more coordination between the flight members, but our Phantoms didn't work well that fast and we didn't have the radar for ground mapping that the Thud guys had. We did better with more altitude and a better chance with our air-to-air radar system. Our tactics were going to have to change, and we might benefit from talking between the wings to share what worked and what didn't.

I changed the tactics as efficiently and gradually as possible. In late October the MiGs were getting really brazen in reaction to the success of the QRC-160 ECM pods and they knocked down a couple of Thuds. The pods might muddy up the SAM radar picture, but they lit up the interceptor controller's radars as well. I hadn't been there long enough to know everything that was going on, but I was getting a pretty good idea. It was obvious that the three strike wings at Takhli, Korat, and Ubon were not really communicating with one another. There was an awful lot of bad-mouthing going on, particularly from Takhli about the other wings and specifically about F-4s. Maybe the F-4s had earned the reputation for themselves. I couldn't pretend to judge something that went on before I got there, but the bad rap seemed ill-deserved. We also had an increasing lack of radio discipline in the big strike packages. Chatter on the strike frequency as shoddy leads tried to herd their wingmen to the targets often blocked out essential communication needed to alert people to threats. In World War II, we went in and we never opened our mouths, even if someone was shot down. We would know it so there was no sense telling one another about it. We just kept our mouths shut. We had signals. We had wing rocks or rudder kicks, but we did not talk on the air unless it was absolutely necessary. It was a hard-and-fast rule. Communications were a mess among the three strike wings, both in the air and on the ground.

Contributing to the problems was a policy of the USAF not to share critical current intel with the combat units. We had facilities with information, but the aircrews were told they didn't have "a need to know." They were monitoring and translating everything the VPAF was doing, when it was doing it. Did they pass that info along to us guys in the line of fire? Of course not! We know what they are doing, we know it poses a threat, but if we tell you and you act upon it, the enemy will know they have been compromised, and we won't be able to know what they are doing in the future. Therefore we will know but we won't tell you. What logic!

The first fix had to start at home base: getting the guys talking openly to one another. I had learned it in World War II and it had worked over the years. You have to give your people an opportunity to think and express themselves. You can't knock them down if you don't agree with them. Think, talk things through, and keep minds open. Be flexible. I spent hours reading every combat report written by any outfit that went to Route VI. I read every damn one of them, where our guys were when they had MiGs sighted and where the rest of the force was. I would plot it all on a map kept in my desk drawer, so I knew what was happening up there. I made myself learn, and then I worked with J.B. and the guys in the intel room. Working like this, in short order you can see what is done wrong and recognize what needs to be done to fix it. It does not take great intellect to do this. Just study, learn, and listen. This is the situational awareness a guy has to have BEFORE he gets into the airplane.

After every mission in Pack VI, or a tough one in IV or V, we would gather for debrief. After all the debriefings, after all the reports were made out and all the maintenance forms were filled in, we would lock the doors in the wing's briefing room and I would say, "OK, guys, let me go over today's mission from my point of view. I want to point out a few things." I'd recap the parts I wanted to talk about by saying, "I screwed up today. I intended to do such and such at this point and I didn't do it for this reason," which I would then explain. Then I'd continue, "Looking back, now I realize I should have done what I first planned. That was a mistake. It didn't cost us anything, but I'm sorry I didn't do it. I goofed. Now you"—and I'd look at one of the guys—"you were one of the reasons I didn't, because you were out of position at that particular moment and I couldn't move without jeopardizing you."

Then the kid would stand up and say, "Yes, Colonel, but you just turned hard into me, or we just did thus and so, or I thought I saw thus and so, or you did not see the SAM that came up."

"Rog, sorry about that," I'd reply, and if I did wrong I would want them to tell me. They'd look around the room and someone would say to another guy, "Well, goddamn it, you were out of position," and the other guy would say, "Yes, but," and others would say, "You should have," and he'd say, "OK, OK." Then we'd go to the bar and that was all that was ever said about that. Every guy there would learn something. That's how it was done. We communicated, we learned, we improved. I decided at that point we should get pilots from other wings to come to Ubon for face-to-face meetings just like this. Our first tactics conference was a huge success, guys got to know each other, tactics were actually discussed, and the whole thing turned into a big party. This led to many future conferences at other bases.

Strike forces began to get on and off targets a lot faster. From studying the intel scoop, we decided to start staying away from the smaller guns by never releasing bombs below 6,500. The night owls got better at their night tactics. Through the latter part of October and into November things changed, and the 8th Wing's "operationally ready" rate rose while losses dropped dramatically. In a bad way, all the good news worked against us because General Momyer announced he was starting Rapid Roger again. I knew that McNamara's obsession with statistics was pulling the Pentagon puppet strings. Our sortie rates drifted back down. Those numbers didn't look good. I fumed and protested with the other wing bosses, to no avail. We had to reinstitute Rapid Roger.

This made it even more interesting for me with the guys in the intel room. The F-105 use of jamming pods screwed up the VPAF's ability to use SAMs and radar-directed AA artillery. The new tactic of keeping the Thuds above 6,500 kept our guys safer, which was good, but Hanoi started sending up MiGs to attack the force, which was bad. We were hampered by the U.S. policy of not attacking North Vietnamese airfields in the heavily populated areas right around Hanoi, so we couldn't get at the MiGs on the ground. A few tricks had been tried by flights of F-4s from other bases to get the MiGs, but nothing had really worked. By November, MiGs were coming up to attack U.S. flights aggressively and pursuing strike forces on egress beyond the Red River, often down to the Black River. Tactics were still not right. Since I was the new kid on the block and hadn't yet earned my spurs, it would have been fatal to come right out and speak my mind to HQ. Staff egos were easily bruised and a wing commander with any brains at all suggests changes only with consummate tact and deliberate subterfuge. Consequently, I had to bide my time, meanwhile watching the MiGs, reading daily mission reports, studying photographs, plotting the sightings and engagements on the map I kept in my desk drawer, and poring over intel reports trying to find clues about the operational habits of the North Vietnamese at that stage of the war.

J. B. Stone and I were sweating over intel one night when I said, "Damn it, we've got to lure those MiGs up where we can get at them." J.B.'s eyes lit up. "I think I've got a way we can do it." As soon as he started describing his idea, I knew we were in complete synch. We got excited and started throwing ideas back and forth. "Hell," I said, "let's do it!" Easier said than done—I had to convince General Momyer first.

The opportunity presented itself at the beginning of December when the big boss at PACAF, General Hunter Harris, invited/ordered a whole bunch of commanders to his going-away briefing/party at Baggio in the highlands of Luzon. His years as commander of PACAF were coming to an end, and this was, in a way, his swan song. The gathering was composed of three differing elements of the war in Southeast Asia. There were hordes of horse holders from Pacific Air Forces headquarters in Hawaii who thought they were running everything, the numbered air force staff people in the Philippines and in Saigon who knew they were running everything, and the operational types at wing level who really were doing everything. The interactions were fascinating. There were endless briefings on this and that all meant to educate us common folk. I thought the staff people from Hawaii and the Philippines were probably happy for a break from the arduous paper shuffling they endured each day, but those of us from the war zone resented being called away from our responsibilities. I knew my wing was in the capable hands of Pappy Garrison, so I wasn't worried about the mission or the troops during my absence; I was worried about the catching-up I'd have to do when I returned.

My immediate boss, Lieutenant General Momyer, the commander of the 7th Air Force in Saigon, was a man for whom I felt deep respect. He wasn't an outgoing personality. He seldom revealed his feelings, but we all knew he worked tirelessly to get the job done. We suspected that he often served as a buffer blocking the idiotic blandishments coming out of Washington. This gathering was not attended with any discernible enthusiasm by the people directly engaged in the war, specifically and particularly not by Spike Momyer, who had far more important things to do.

Those of us who worked for him sensed his mood at the party, and the wise ones kept a discreet distance. He barely tolerated all the blather going on around him, and I was apprehensive about approaching him at this social occasion with the idea I had in my mind, but when I saw him talking with an old friend of mine, Colonel "Dirty" Ernie White, I thought the time was as good as any. Ernie and I had played football together at the Point, and Ernie, bless him, interrupted his conversation with the general, turned to me, and said hello. General Momyer acknowledged my presence and asked how things were going at Ubon. That was my opening and I threw caution to the winds.

"Sir, the MiGs are getting frisky up north and beginning to go after the Thuds. I have an idea on how to counter their threat and teach them a lesson."

He looked at me hard and seemed to be thinking of what to say in response, but he only grunted, then turned away. I didn't take that personally, knowing his nature. In fact, I totally sympathized with him, but was deeply disappointed at having failed to make my point. I went back to the party wondering how to impress the man with what I thought was a crucially important matter.

17

★

Bolo

I shouldn't have worried. Back at Ubon a few days later, the phone rang. It was General Momyer's exec. He said the general wanted to talk to me about my idea concerning the MiGs. I was ordered to hustle my butt down to Saigon right away. I did that same night.

My session with the boss the next morning was brief and to the point. He asked what I had in mind. I told him I thought we in the 8th Wing could go north in the typical strike package employed by the F-105s, draw the MiGs up, and have a go at them in our F-4s in a good old-fashioned air battle. General Momyer thought a moment, then said, "OK, go talk to Don Smith about some of our ideas about going after the MiGs and then I want to talk to both of you together."

Brigadier General Don Smith was an old buddy of mine and I had great respect for him. It turned out we agreed on the general idea for the ruse to be employed. Don was so enthusiastic he told me we could use all of the 7th AF assets available, something I had not even hoped for. We went back to Momyer's office and told him. The boss said, "All right, draw up a plan and brief me as soon as you're ready. My staff here at 7th will help in any way needed. That's all. Get to work."

We were off and running! I put J.B. to work on the plan right away. He hauled in J. D. Covington, Ralph Wetterhahn, and Lieutenant Joe Hicks to work with us. We worked like mad for the next two weeks under the tightest security. I led them on the specific guidelines and major decision elements, and those young officers threw all of their NVM combat experience into developing the detailed plan.

The overall objective was to destroy any airborne forces encountered over North Vietnam. Intelligence gave us some highly probable MiG tactics. The MiGs were usually in the air anytime strike aircraft were in the area. Typically they were airborne approximately ten to fifteen minutes prior to the strike, about the time the Thuds crossed the Black River. Generally, two to four MiGs would orbit over Phuc Yen, the main MiG air base, to provide field cover. The rest of the MiG force was sent to two intercept points; one on the southwest side of the Red River, in the vicinity of Phu Tho and the other to the northeast of "Thud" Ridge, near Thai Nguyen. The MiGs attacked the F-105 strike forces at varying points along their routes. Additional intelligence showed that the MiGs exhibited a tendency to avoid the F-4s.

Our ruse was simple. Our F-4s would mount a typical large strike using the F-105 call signs, routes, and timings, the routine stuff that the North Vietnamese were used to seeing in the predictable bombing raids by the Thuds; but we would be armed for air-to-air combat with four AIM-7E Sparrows and four AIM-9B Sidewinders each instead of for bombing. Since we were not allowed to attack the North Vietnamese airfields, and they knew it, the MiGs would come up after us and get a deadly reception. Flights of Phantoms would come in from different directions and orbit the VPAF airfields, preventing any MiGs from landing and, we hoped, running the bastards out of fuel. Finally, if they chose to escape to Nanning in China, there would be other flights of F-4s airborne waiting to block their escape and counter any possible support from Nanning into the battle area.

First things first: Emulating F-105s depended on making the North Vietnamese think the approaching force was a typical strike package. This they usually did by reports from ground observers and by radar interpretation. To fool the radar system we planned to fly the same formation and at the same speed as the F-105s, using Thud call signs. It was simple. But could we fool the ground observers? That depended on luck and the cloud cover. Knowing that the MiGs were scrambled each day when the incoming strike force crossed the Black River, and assuming they were sent to orbit points out of the anticipated path of the incoming fighters, planning to intercept the enemy was an interesting challenge.

It was crucial to accurately predict the capabilities and possible reaction of the MiGs. How long could the MiGs stay airborne with five minutes of air-to-air combat? How would they react to the aggressive F-4Cs and how many suitable fields were available in the area for their recovery? Next, our F-4 capabilities: How long could the F-4 engage in battle and return home safely? How long could the F-4 stay over the airfields if not engaged? How many airfields did the F-4 have to cover? For how long? Also of prime concern were the concentration and effectiveness of the defenses in the battle area and the exposure time of our forces. Each of these matters bore significantly upon the final decisions of our force structure. It was determined that the MiG-17s and 21s could remain airborne for approximately fifty minutes with five minutes of engagement time and could recover at any of five airfields in the battle area.

In this phase of planning, Captain Stone, Lieutenant Wetterhahn, and I plotted possible inbound routes, then took turns playing as if we were sitting at a scope in the enemy radar network. Using technical data available, we calculated how far our strike force would move between each rotation of their main antennas. Then we guessed how many antenna sweeps it might take for an operator to detect a change in the blips denoting our approaching path. After two, hopefully three, sweeps, the operator would notice something different and then advise his supervisor, who in turn would have to call his boss up the line, which would take time. Assuming that the VPAF air defense director was an experienced battle commander, he would still need time to interpret the information and issue orders to his own aircraft to counter our movements. These estimates seemed critical to me, considering we would be moving at an indicated 540 knots covering 9 miles each minute. Any delay on the part of the defenses gave us just that much more time before they caught on to our ruse.

The more we played this game, the clearer the picture became. Each of us really got into the scene. I felt like I was actually the air defense commander in Hanoi interpreting and countering the moves reported to me. We hoped our attacking moves would appear to be normal until the last possible moment, at which time we would spread out into a sweep formation, turning down Thud Ridge with our first three flights line abreast and scanning the sky ahead with our own radars. I hoped this would detect any MiGs airborne in front of us. Also crucial to success was allowing the first three flights entering the combat area to have "missile-free" firing options. For a few short minutes, these F-4s would know exactly where all friendly aircraft were. Any other aircraft could be assumed to be enemy and could be fired upon without need for close-up visual identification. Within this specific time, we would have the element of surprise, be safe from counterfire, and be able to launch missiles in ideal conditions, i.e., without battling excessive g-forces.

It would be my responsibility to lead the first flight into the area, and we had to simulate a Thud feint all the way in. We planned to use the same tanker track, refueling altitude, ingress route, altitude, airspeed, and radio communications as were used daily by the Thud strike forces. Once the MiGs were lured up, they'd realize the trap, and there would no longer be a need for the rest of the force to continue with any F-105 tactics.

We had to devise code names for the flights, and J.B. thought it would be funny to name us after cars. Naturally my flight would be "Olds." Chappie's would be "Ford" because J.B. thought of Fords as big, black, and fun. J.B. would be "Rambler." Other flights were named "Lincoln," "Tempest," "Plymouth," and "Vespa." Olds Flight would be followed in five-minute intervals by Ford and then Rambler, and the remaining four Ubon flights were timed to cover the enemy recovery bases: Phuc Yen, Gia Lam, Yen Bai, and Hoa Lac. One of my flights would be approaching or over each of these bases for a bit over an hour. I knew any MiGs still airborne would be running out of fuel and desperate to land, but their ground controllers would see Phantoms waiting for them at each place. With luck, we could run one or two of them out of fuel.

Phuc Yen was used as the primary target at H+00, with the remainder of the force timed into the battle area after that. Based on airfield locations and tanker requirements, we decided that the force would be composed of an east and a west element. The west force, composed of seven flights of F-4Cs from the 8th TFW, would be responsible for getting the MiGs airborne, sweeping the suspected orbit areas, and covering Phuc Yen and Gia Lam airfields. The east force, composed of five flights from the 366th at Da Nang, would be responsible for airfield coverage of Kep and Cat Bi and for blocking egress and/or ingress to the ChiCom field at Nanning. The whole plan would be supported by EB-66s for jamming, with Iron Hand aircraft (F-105Fs) positioned for SAM and flak suppression and some F-104s used as a barrier cap to protect the main attack forces on egress.

The east element from Da Nang was to come up the coast, top off from tankers over the Gulf of Tonkin, then proceed inland as though they were on a strike to the bridges on the northeast railroad. Their first flight would turn suddenly for a spot just northwest of the airbase at Kep. There they would surely find the MiG-17s in orbit, awaiting orders from their ground controller. The second Da Nang flight would back up the first, and the third was to go to a point blocking escape of any MiGs north into China. The rest of the Da Nang force would spread out and cover the known MiG bases east of Hanoi and the port of Haiphong.

The next step in the planning was to establish a missile-free environment for as many of the counter air forces as possible, to take advantage of the surprise element and to optimize the AIM-7E Sparrow launch environment. Our plan allowed the first three flights, Olds, Ford, and Rambler, a full or partial missile-free environment as we passed through the suspected orbit areas. My flight, being first in, was provided a full missile-free option as we crossed the Red River. Our main purpose was to pick off the top cover orbit, then proceed directly to Phuc Yen to provide airfield coverage in spite of MiGs or other obstacles. Ford Flight, second in, was to fly through the orbit area to the west of Thud Ridge, and Rambler was to sweep the area east of the ridge. All twelve F-4Cs would remain missile-free until I ordered them otherwise. At that point the battle area would be saturated with Phantoms and visual identification procedures would prevail. Any MiG sighted by any flight would be aggressively engaged and pursued with every attempt made to destroy.

The details we had on MiG capability told us that the ideal counter air force would be composed of sixteen to eighteen flights of F-4C aircraft. This required twenty-five tankers to supply pre- and poststrike refueling. The predicted battle area was within the most heavily defended airspace ever faced by U.S. forces. These defenses of SAMs and radar-controlled AA batteries meant our F-4s would be at great risk without the QRC-160 ECM jammers. We had watched them effectively employed by the F-105s for the last several months and knew they felt confidence in them. Exposure was a problem for us but solutions were in the works.

Most critical to the success of Bolo, we had to have clear, real-time intelligence from USAF monitoring stations listening in to VPAF transmissions—no more of the bullshit of keeping essential knowledge secret from the strike force. VPAF transmissions had been monitored and translated but never shared down the line. It was sensitive, but it was imperative to have this intel for Bolo. We knew the VPAF would be monitoring our transmissions, so we gave code names to ground locations corresponding geographically to well-known cities in the United States so that the monitoring sites could tell us what the enemy was doing and where. Phuc Yen, northwest of Hanoi, would be called "Frisco," and Gia Lam, in Hanoi, was "Los Angeles." Getting the requirement for the real-time communication info across to 7th AF HQ became my urgent goal.

Finally satisfied that the plan was the best we could produce, I went to Saigon on December 22 to brief General Momyer and his staff. Momyer said "Go!" right away and accepted the plan without a change. Execution was set for January 1. To my relief and satisfaction, he willingly authorized the release of the monitoring data in real time. This concession would finally break the intel logjam. It had significant impact on the success and safety of forces for months and years to come.

Operation Bolo was under way. It would be the first offensive fighter sweep of the Vietnamese conflict. We had nine days left to get ready. Once HQ approved, a lot of the air force participated in both preparation and execution. The 8th and 366th wings were the strike force. The 355th and 388th would provide SAM suppression. 7th AF planned the support of the EB-66 ECM forces, KC-135 tankers, Big Eye EC-121 battle monitor, SAR (search and rescue) elements, C-130 airborne command post, and in-country radar ground-controlled intercept (GCI) sites.

From Saigon I went directly to the 366th TFW in Da Nang and briefed them on their part of the plan. As it turned out, I gave two briefings at Da Nang. For some reason I wasn't sure the pilots and their leaders in the 366th Wing were taking me seriously. I couldn't blame them. With General Momyer's support behind me, they listened.

General Donovan Smith called from Saigon. "Robin, we want you to carry ECM pods. I know the F-4s have never done that, but the Thuds have. We're scarfing up all we can find and I'll have them sent to you and the 366th. I think carrying the ECM gadgets for radar jamming will convince the guys up north you're really Thuds." We'd cram a quick course in handling the pods into the time remaining for our aircrews and maintainers. The F-4C had never used the QRC-160 pods operationally. There were no provisions at either Ubon or Da Nang for adapting the pods to the F-4C, no technical orders for loading or checkout, and no test equipment.

Every aircraft in the fighter sweep would need a QRC-160 ECM aboard to minimize possible U.S. losses. This became the limiting factor in the size of the force because of the small number of pods available in theater at the time. A quick inventory showed fifty-seven pods available, thirty-two at Korat and twenty-five at Takhli. This number became the basic planning factor for force structure. We would need to adapt the Phantoms to carry the pods, but to maintain secrecy, the Thuds would have to continue to use the pods on normal missions until two days before Bolo. Then F-105 ground crews would have to remove the pods at night and get them shipped up to us for immediate installation. The pods would then have to be removed after Bolo and sent back for immediate reinstallation on the Thuds.

8th Wing guys got to work right away on the problem. The sway braces on the F-4 bomb racks didn't hit the pods in the proper place. "No sweat," said one of my young NCOs in the fabrication shop. He worked thirty-six hours straight to fabricate a replacement top panel for the pods so our birds could carry them. Then another glitch cropped up. Long ago, some engineer had designed the F-4 wiring so that we had to carry the little pod on the right outboard pylon. No other weapon station had the proper wiring. In our case, the F-4 carried 370-gallon fuel tanks on the outboard stations. These could be jettisoned if necessary and usually were if a hassle with MiGs was imminent. The inboard pylons could accommodate a wide variety of weapons. With a TER, or triple ejection rack, that station normally carried three 750-pound bombs. Heat-seeking air-to-air missiles were also carried on those pylons. The fuselage centerline station was the granddaddy. It could carry a 600-gallon tank or six 750-pound bombs on a MER, or multiple ejection rack. Half buried in the fuselage were four long-range radar-guided missiles that could reach out some 20 miles depending on the target aspect, relative closure speeds, and altitude. We had to carry a 600-gallon tank on the centerline to get to our targets. The tank was not stressed for heavy maneuvering and was almost always jettisoned on combat missions.

With three tanks and a full load of missiles we normally grossed out over 50,000 pounds at takeoff. Now, with only 190 pounds under the right wing and 2,200 pounds under the left wing, the unbalanced load might make takeoffs interesting. Nobody had done it in an F-4 before but we would have to start now. For the future we had to figure out how to move the tiny ECM pod from the outboard to the inboard pylon and be able to keep the right wing tank. But for now, the asymmetric load was going to be a fact.

The pod itself got power from a generator powered by a small propeller-driven turbine in the pod nose. It didn't need to draw on aircraft power except for controlling it on and off. We still needed to get it connected electrically. My lead avionics NCO, Ernie, checked the diagrams and schematics, then looked at what kind of umbilical and cannon plug were required. We had suitable power to the outboard pylon but still no connectors. We sent messages to the Air Material Command headquarters in Utah, only to discover that the power was dedicated exclusively for nuclear weapons. We weren't supposed to have access.

"So? Let's get it done," I said.

Ernie explained, "Boss, I'm with you, but we need and don't have a certain cannon plug that is controlled by the Atomic Energy Commission back at Sandia. We could jury-rig something if we had that plug, but not without it."

"Well, who do we know at Sandia?" I asked.

I got on the phone and finally talked to someone and explained our need, giving him the part number of the cannon plug in question.

"How many do you want?" was his only reaction.

On Christmas Day, a C-141 departed the States with forty-eight adapter kits and an engineer from OAMA (Ogden Air Material Area). The aircraft arrived at Ubon on December 27 and brought us a crate full of the needed items. Not one piece of paper was exchanged in the transaction and my maintenance guys soon had every jet wired ready for the pods to be hung on the right outboard. It wasn't a permanent fix, but it worked! Eventually correct parts would have to be engineered and manufactured if we were to carry the pods for missions after Bolo. That guy at Sandia was a shining example of what good people did when the chips were down.

As part of the mission secrecy, the frag order to "borrow" the pods from the F-105 wings was hand-carried from Ubon to the other wings. Thanks to the effort of all the ground crews and many people all the way back to depots in the States, a C-47 arrived on December 30 with all the jammers we needed.

Maintenance worked around the clock. So did supply, mess, fuels, munitions, electronics, everyone. We had to maintain our regular flying schedule in addition to preparing for Bolo. Our normal daily ops plan, fouled up by Rapid Roger, meant sixty-four missions every twenty-four hours required an overall maintenance effort geared at producing armed and loaded aircraft as needed. Now all of a sudden the maintenance and armament troops had to generate more than thirty in-commission F-4s all at the same time.

We still had to maintain secrecy about any kind of plan and/or execution date. The last few days of December, I canceled all leaves and postponed the New Year's Eve party. The rumor mill got into full swing. I went out on the flight line in the wee hours to see how the troops were doing. The place was a beehive of activity, men working far beyond their normal shifts. I saw one young airman hobbling about on crutches and asked his line chief about him. "Fell off his bike the other day and busted his leg. But he's all right. I'm watching him. None of us know what's really up, but he said his bird is going to go, whatever!"

God, how I loved those men! The sarge made me realize it was high time to cut the men in on our plan, at least as much as I dared tell them. Briefings for the pilots weren't given until absolutely necessary—that was December 30, when the flight crews were chosen. Since the normal twenty-four-hour-a-day flying schedule was still in progress, we had to conduct two aircrew briefings per day to cover the entire spectrum. There were seven briefings conducted between December 30 and January 1. It was ridiculous to think we could pull this off in absolute secrecy, but I was sure the rumor mill was responsible for the extra energy and dedication seen everywhere.

The planned day arrived and we stood by for the execute order from the 7th. It didn't come on January 1. We were put on hold because of bad weather in the Pack VI area. That night, every man felt tense. We briefed again the next morning and then sat and waited. Stormy wasn't helpful when he informed us that the weather up north was the same as the day before, solid cloud coverage with tops at 7,000. That wasn't good. We couldn't see any SAMs launched our way until too late to dodge the damned things. But what the hell, we'd worry about that when the time came.

There was little talk as we waited for the word on January 2. Come on, come on, we were all thinking, when one of the men from the combat operations center stuck his head in the door and shouted, "You're on! EXECUTE!"

"OK, Wolfpack, go get 'em!" I yelled as a recollection of Hub Zemke's famous send-off to his guys suddenly blazed into memory. The Wolfpack was reborn.

We rushed to the squadron personal equipment rooms for our gear, donned harnesses and G suits, grabbed our helmets, and headed out to the jets. This last walk across the ramp was solemn for everyone. I smoked a final cigarette on the way. Would this be the last time we saw one another, saw Ubon, saw home? I felt a searing pain in the pit of my stomach and was already drenched in sweat by the time I reached my bird. When I stamped out the cigarette, my jaw was so tightly clenched that my teeth hurt. The pain blended well with my grim mood. Dear God, please let me lead these wonderful men into a successful battle and safely back home.

As I taxied out of my parking place I saw the young airman with the broken leg stretched out on the concrete with his head on a wheel chock. He was dead to the world, exhausted. I wondered how many hours he had spent out there getting his bird ready. I'd make sure to find out when I got back, if I got back.

Our Ubon package refueled on Red track and topped off, and on my call the tankers headed out of orbit northbound to lead us all the way to 20 degrees north, well into Laos. Six tankers stacked in trail, each dragging a flight of four Phantoms refueling all the way to get us as far north as possible with a full load of fuel. I waved at the boom operator of my tanker and dropped my flight away, then pushed up the throttles to 480 knots, starting to do my best F-105 impersonation. We switched over to the mission strike frequency along with Ford and Rambler flights. The rest would follow in about fifteen minutes.

Solid undercast greeted us as we crossed the Black River and I checked slightly right to head to the Dog Pecker, a conspicuous bend in a Red River tributary a bit east of the riverside town of Yen Bai. I kicked the rudder back and forth to signal Olds Flight out into combat spread, not our usual wide fluid four, but the more compact 1,500-foot spacing of a Thud flight in pod formation. "Olds flight, clean 'em up, green 'em up, start your music" was the unfamiliar combat preparation call of the F-105s. We were in character.

Past the Dog Pecker and then onward to Thud Ridge, right turn and down the east side of the ridgeline, which is a gigantic finger pointing directly at Phuc Yen airfield. According to plan we are missile-free and anything ahead of me will be hostile. My GIB or guy-in-back, Charlie Clifton, is sweeping the area with his radar, searching for the MiG orbit we had predicted would be over the airfield. Solid undercast at about 7,000 feet beneath us and no MiGs! Chappie is coming behind me and then J.B. I'm over Phuc

Yen and nothing yet. A few miles past and I'm forced into a reversal, back toward Ford and Rambler flights. I cancel the missile-free condition and we revert to mandatory visual identification before firing anything.

Ford flight arrives on time. Chappie calls a MiG-21 on my flight that has popped up out of the undercast beneath us. I break hard right just in time to see another MiG at my eleven o'clock. We're set up for radar missiles and he's right at min range. Clifton hears my call and aims the radar that way and is locked on almost immediately. I squeeze the trigger and launch one, then another Sparrow. They zoom away but apparently aren't guiding. I slap down at the missile switch on the panel ahead of my left knee and hear the growl of my first Sidewinder. I shoot again. Nothing! It heads abruptly toward the undercast.

MiGs are popping out of the cloud deck everywhere. Chappie's flight is engaged and his wingman, Ev Raspberry, gets the first one. Meanwhile, I've got another 21 engaged. I get a growl and fire. As the missile leaves the rail, the next Sidewinder is already howling, I shoot again. Splash! The MiG's right wing comes off and he snaps right and down. My wingman, Ralph Wetterhahn, has slid behind a second MiG that had been attacking us, and he snaps off two Sparrows, which hit. Three down now! Olds Four, Walt Radeker and Jim Murray, have got a MiG-21 in front of them attacking Olds Three. They shoot. We've got four now!

Rambler Flight gets on the scene. The battle has now been swirling for almost ten minutes. J. B. Stone and Cliff Dunnegan are engaged almost immediately. J.B. fires first in Rambler Flight and takes one. Rambler Two, the two Larrys, Glynn and Cary, get yet another. Major Phil Combies in Rambler Four chalks up the seventh MiG. His claim is a "probable" but later confirmed. The MiGs have had enough and suddenly the air is still. Olds, Ford, and Rambler flights head outbound exuberantly. The second wave from Ubon of Lincoln, Tempest, Plymouth, and Vespa flights find nothing. The Da Nang force is destined for Haiphong and hopefully the MiGs of Kep airfield abort their mission because of even worse weather on the coast.

The mission took a huge toll on the small fleet of new MiG-21s. It also proved the ability of the F-4 and its missile armament to effectively engage the enemy aircraft. A gun would still be a priority for future models, but we could accomplish the mission with what we had. The pods had worked well for us with only five SAMs seen during the entire mission and virtually no 85 mm radar-directed flak from beneath the clouds. Our tactics, our team-work, our planning, and our training could always be improved, but we could prevail if given the opportunity. We returned home triumphant.

18

★

Rolling Thunder

Activity on base was hectic through the rest of January. Everyone was energized by Bolo. I was proud, happy, and busy just going through my daily command activities over the weeks that ensued, but totally unprepared for the public-relations firestorm the mission had created. Good God, why couldn't they just let us get on with our business? It's not the war that wore me down, although by then I'd had four months without any time off; it was the people who ran the blasted thing from their perches on the various dead tree boughs between SEA and the hallowed halls of that empty "headquarters." My diary for January recorded over three hundred visitors to Ubon, a daily stream of "do-gooders" and "fixers" one by one or in various-sized groups. It was difficult to avoid the feeling that over half of these people were just hangers-on, longing to be near the thrill of action in the hopes that it rubbed off on them. Not a good attitude, I know, but hardly anyone in that constant stream of "VIPs" seemed to have a real purpose for being there. By purpose, I mean to contribute and help, not to take or to suck some of the 8th Wing's high energy for themselves. Protocol demanded I temper my growing reputation as a maverick; I had to give each visitor the proper time. Reporters and so-called journalists showed up from all over. I lost track of the interviews. How many damn times did people need to hear the same story? I knew their reports would have inaccuracies, exaggerations, and omissions, all impossible to control after the fact. It drove me nuts. Often I'd hear Chappie chuckling and snorting on the other side of the vine-covered trellis between our desks. If his amusement became too great, he'd suddenly pretend he was on the phone. That drove me nuts, too. He was also doing quite a bit of grandstanding with the VIPs when he thought I wasn't watching. There was little I could do about it. We were too busy. On the positive side, letters and calls flooded in from folks I knew and respected around the world offering their support. A telegram came from Bill Kirk, still at Davis-Monthan: "OK, you've got yours, now save one for me!"

Evenings at the O club were great fun. The "Wolfpack" had taken on a life of its own. A new spirit and camaraderie evolved. One evening I sat at the bar talking to a young guy named John Harris, who sported a nice, neatly trimmed, regulation mustache. I asked him if he thought I'd look good in one. What did I expect him to respond, "No, Colonel"? Starting that day, I grew my mustache. When it had respectable growth to the edges of my mouth (still correctly trimmed) I decided the David Niven look wasn't for me. What the hell, I'd look a whole lot better with a full Tommy Burne–type World War II mustache, so it grew well beyond the regulations. What was anybody going to do—send the secretary of the air force over to knock me out, sit on me, and shave it off? It became the middle finger I couldn't raise in PR photographs. The mustache became my silent last word in the verbal battles I was losing with higher headquarters on rules, targets, and fighting the war.

High morale and focus were needed, but occasionally the activities became excessive. Phil Combies was irrepressible. A knock came on my trailer door one night. Glancing sleepily at my watch I saw it was about 0245. Thank God I wasn't scheduled on the first go in the morning. A captain dressed in typical off-duty civvies stood there, looking a bit nervous.

"What's up?" I muttered, rubbing the sleep out of my eyes.

"Colonel sir, you'd better come down to the club. Your wingman is raising hell and we can't get him under control."

Oh shit, I thought, it's Phil. "What the hell is he doing now?"

"Sir, he's tearing the place apart and—"

I cut him off. "Go back and tell 'em I'm coming. And for Christ's sake, all of you back off till I get there."

I put on a flight suit, pulled on a pair of flight boots, headed the two blocks to the club, and walked into the bar. The place was a shambles. There were two or three guys facing Phil, who had fortified himself behind the bar. Broken glass littered the floor. One window was broken out and a barstool was destined for the junk pile. Phil was raging, cussing at the top of his voice and daring any bastard to come closer. I assumed that included me, so I went over, walked around the end of the bar, and approached him. Now there was one drunken, angry Irishman! God, he was a mess and smelled like a busted beer keg. He started to raise a fist, but I could tell his heart wasn't really in it, so I grabbed him, whirled him around, got him by the scruff of the neck and the seat of his pants, and propelled him out onto the sidewalk.

Phil ranted something about a damned nonrated SOB who tried to keep him from pouring himself a drink. He'd show that SOB. He was going to wipe up the whole base with his nonrated ass. I told Phil that would have to wait; now he'd go to bed. No such thing. He raved and struggled to get back into the bar, where he was going to kill someone. I shook him and said, "Get your ass to bed, Combies, NOW!" It took a while for that to have an effect, but finally he stumbled away with my parting order for him to report to my office in uniform at 0800.

Since the day had already started for me, I went to my trailer, shaved, re-dressed, and headed back out. There were plenty of troops on shift and I spent some happy predawn time drifting around the shops along the flight line. After breakfast at the club I went to my office, arriving at about 0840.

There sat Phil in the outer office in fresh 1505s looking like death warmed over. I ignored him, pretended to busy myself with the morning's in-basket, and exchanged a few pleasantries with Chappie. Finally I had Phil ushered in.

He marched the length of my office up to my desk and saluted. "Major Combies, reporting as—" He stopped as I stood up and lit into him.

I roared, "Shut up, Major! You are a disgrace. Your behavior last night was inexcusable. What do you have to say for yourself?"

Combies seemed to be struggling to get out the usual "No excuse, sir," but what came out of his mouth was a defiant "Sir, you're forty minutes late!"

It was all I could do to keep a straight face, especially when I saw and heard Chappie choking behind the ivy. Trying to be the stern disciplinarian,

I glared at Phil and issued the worst possible punishment I could have devised for him. I told him, "You are grounded. Furthermore, you will report to the club each evening and stand duty in the bar. Your instructions are simple. You are to maintain order and discipline. You will not drink, and if one, just ONE, glass is broken during your watch, I will send you back to ADC forthwith. UNDERSTAND?"

"Yes, sir!" He saluted, about-faced, and marched off, not quite steadily.

He took his punishment like a man, did as he was told, and took an unmerciful ribbing from the rest of the pilots without as much as a murmur.

I don't remember how long I let the situation stand, but it wasn't too long. I needed him in his invaluable role as a combat leader, and often as number Three in my flight. He was one hell of a pilot and a good man. The North Vietnamese soon put a $5,000 reward out for his pink body. I had to remind him not to get too big a head, because the bounty on me was $25,000.

The MiGs seemed to be hiding after Bolo. Guess we really got to them. We wouldn't see any again until the middle of March. It was OK; there was plenty to do. Properly configured parts arrived from Ogden to replace the jury-rigged wiring from the cockpit to the QRC pod from Bolo. Our ECM pods arrived and we flew missions into Route Pack VI with pods thereafter.

My main focus at that point was the continuing problem of communication among the wings. Why all the bad-mouthing? The wings didn't look any bigger and their targets didn't look any smaller. It was simply counterproductive. I had to figure out how to get them really talking to one another so I went to Saigon and asked General Momyer if I could host a tactics conference at Ubon. He thought it was a great idea. Reluctantly the other wings agreed to participate. Korat and Takhli came, plus the tanker guys, Weasels, and ELINT group. We made a big party out of it. There was a dinner downtown and a lot of whiskey drinking, fun and games, songs, skits, and stuff, but the serious business of talking to one another went on, too. It was good for the guys just to see what the other fella looked like and how he thought. I can't say we accomplished a hell of a lot tactically, hard to call it a "symposium," but it was the beginning of a dialogue among the wings; the foundation was laid. We agreed we would meet again. An agreement! Good God. A few more casual tactics get-togethers/parties were planned over the following months and the communication among the wings started to improve, although Takhli remained a bit rebellious.

Toward the end of January, Rapid Roger was finally terminated, great news for all of us. The final demise was an event we celebrated with an official burial and wake on Groundhog Day, February 2, complete with black casket and a grave dug outside the ops building. We took turns urinating on it. An official death certificate was drawn up. I signed it above the title "Mortician Preparing Remains." Chappie James signed as "Funeral Director." Others signed as "Medical Officer" and "Flight Surgeon." The document read:

Name of Deceased: ROGER, Rapid (NMN). Branch of Service: Decaying. Service No: 69696969. State: Decomposed. Organization: Excellent in spite of severe handicaps. Date of Birth: August 1966. Sex: ?? Color or Race: Non-specific. Marital Status: Castrated. Religion: Agnostic. Medical Statement, Cause of Death: Rejection by those who really count. Doomed to nonaccept-ability from birth obstruction (intestinal) to USAF mission. Other Signifi-cant Conditions: Gonorrhea. Major Findings of Autopsy: Very little muscle tissue to fulfill requirements of inadequate cerebral functions. Mode of Death: Homicide. Circumstances of Death: 8th TFW simply had enough. Burial Grounds: TOC Memorial Gardens APO SF Gates of Hell, Ubon.

Noises were coming from the Pentagon about my reputation. The chief of colonel assignments, Brigadier General Jimmy Jumper, wrote about moving me "up" into some sort of high-level staff job. I responded, "I'm going to slit my throat if you assign me to ADC. Leave me right here." Jumper wrote back acknowledging my refusal but announced that Colonel J. J. Burns would be coming in May to replace Colonel Daniel James as DO. I took perverse delight in reading the letter out loud to Chappie.

He went through the ceiling, "May? I just got here! I'm not due till December. They can't make me leave!"

It was too much fun so I let him stew for a while, then said, "Calm down, Chappie. You're moving, all right, but only about thirty feet forward into the vice slot."

He grinned. "Shoot, boss, you almost had me turnin' white!"

Things up north had changed drastically. Missions got tougher than ever. Uncle Ho had lost a lot of his MiGs but he rewarded us with barrages of SAMs plus dense and accurate 37/57 and 85mm fire. Our birds were often taking hits. We needed guns on the airplanes. We needed better targets. The bullshit from Washington was maddening. On the ground, I fought daily battles with the chain of command, endured interruptions by visitors, pushed paper back and forth across my desk, and spent way too much time on the phone, usually slamming it down.

Cares of the workday faded only when I existed in the suspended time capsule of a mission. My mind could easily turn to the grim business at hand, thoughts quickly disciplined away from the extreme discomfort of ticklish sweat trickling down back and face, hands already slippery and wet, groin area clammy and chafed, the morning's shower and application of Old Spice deodorant already transformed into Robin's unique Eau de Jungle Rot.

We sat in the bird, my GIB and I. We waited, along with many other crews, for the tick of the second hand to mark start-engine time. Far away, tankers were already climbing to their orbit points to await our arrival. We sweated; the howl, blast, and fumes of the Dash-60 carts plugged into each of our aircraft added to the discomfort. We listened to our crew chiefs talking to us from their ground stations: "Intakes and exhaust clear, external power checked, steps up, fire bottle manned, air ready on number Two, pressure reading in the green, you're clear to start number Two, sir." I'd push the START button, watch rpm build, oil pressure rise, generators check out OK. I'd throw the throttle out of idle—fuel pressure responding, mighty engine reacting with a growl that rose to an ear-shattering scream. System checks were completed quickly, the other engine started in similar fashion. Inertial nav system ready, flight controls checked, chocks pulled, ready to go.

The idling howl of forty-eight engines along the flight line dominated. Our jets were unbelievably heavy with bombs, missiles, and extra fuel, grossing over 56,000 pounds. Taxiing wasn't routine, but slow and cautious. A blown tire could spell disaster. An overheated brake might mean death. Arming and a last-chance inspection for leaks, loose panels, cut tires, or loose weapons, then onto the runway. Screaming engines checked for power; then one by one we released brakes and accelerated to liftoff. Watching the jet ahead, turning to cut off his circle and close to formation for departure, we'd assemble into flights of four and head to our tankers.

The course was north, always north. Underneath us, the dry-season plains of Thailand gave way to the green jungle hell of Laos. Mountains rose, clad unbelievably in solid green. Silver gouges laced facades of limestone cliffs, the landscape eerie, exotic, strange, compellingly beautiful, but also hostile, menacing, and uninviting. Soon we'd cross the Black River, gateway to purgatory, then descend from our cruise altitude to turn toward a landmark across the Red. It didn't take long for the challenged beast to respond to the intrusion. His missiles came in salvo. "Wait—wait—not now—wait, let them track—watch—watch, hold it. OK, they're tracking! Hard down. Harder! Now pull, pull up! OK, they're past." An explosion 500 feet to the rear, a first hurdle passed in our race to the target. The blue sky turned dark with the fury of shrapnel and black explosions. Unconsciously our throttles seemed to edge themselves forward seeking more power, more speed, harder turns. Twisting, weaving, turning, we dodged and fought our way to the target.

Nothing I had experienced in World War II matched it. Missiles streaked past, flak blackened the sky, tracers laced patterns across my canopy, and then, capping the day, MiGs would suddenly appear—small, sleek sharks, cutting and slashing, braving their own flak, firing missiles, guns, harassing, pecking. God, if only we had guns! A flight member disappeared in a blinding explosion, caught by a SAM, only small pieces of flaming debris marking the end of two young lives, but on we'd go, 20 miles yet to the target. There it was, just ahead: an insignificant damned fuel depot with untouchable belching factories surrounding it, crying for destruction, forbidden to be touched by our commander in chief, so up we'd go, pop up to the roll-in point, then down into a screeching dive, sighting on target, allowing for wind, speed, dive angle, altitude, concentrating, ignoring the threat of guns stitching patterns around us. If we didn't hit the target, we'd be back tomorrow. Down we'd press at 500 knots. The aircraft shuddered with the release of 3 tons of bombs, responding to demands for escape. With gut-wrenching, searing, nearly blinding turns, and speed now pushing over 600 knots, we'd claw our way outbound, fighting through streaking missiles, flak, SAMs, all conspiring against our escape. The Red beneath again, then the Black, and the frantic cauldron of the battle became the slow, quiet hell of the green jungle until we met our tankers again. We'd coast home, gingerly feeling out our aircraft, checking everything slowly, making sure that no unsuspected damage impaired our ability to land. My wingman would swing close underneath my jet, looking for damage, giving me the OK, no visible leaks, just some loose fasteners. I'd reciprocate and check out his bird. All OK. Then gratefully back to home base, down safely, taxi in, untangle from harnesses, climb out of the cockpit, sweat-soaked, stinking, get through maintenance and intel debriefs, wanting a beer, getting it, maybe too much of it, too tired for dinner, still paperwork to do, reports to answer, reports to write, "commander" problems to solve, new facilities to build, policies and procedures to implement, supply problems to meet, people to encourage, chastise, discipline, praise, then fall into bed at midnight, the whole cycle to repeat the following morning at 0600 or possibly the day after if a visiting delegation didn't tie me up with meandering banalities.

That was the war: an ugly, brutal, demanding, and soul-crushing beast. Why in the name of God couldn't the people of the U.S. understand what they had a hold of? We couldn't turn it loose. Once committed, it had to be finished. The only way to win a war is to win it. It seemed so obvious. Those of us in SEA could not understand the antiwar protests we were hearing about. Nobody seemed to understand that it was our president and the administration drawing it out. The boys safe at their desks and going home to Georgetown cocktail parties thought that Uncle Ho would roll over and come to his senses simply from dropping bombs on the same old targets and doing away with some of his airplanes. Ho knew we weren't allowed to bomb airfields or hit targets that would really hurt. Why should he stop under the pressure of our good manners?

In the middle of all this, I barely had a sense of home or family. My daughters sent me wonderful, chatty letters, nonsensical teenage-girl talk about friends, school, the cats and dogs, snow, the latest TV show, but always, "I love you, Daddy, please be safe." I read and reread these precious notes, my emotions sometimes spilling into private tears when alone in my trailer late at night. In stark contrast were the letters from Ella. I longed for a few kind words, for any words of love. None came. She was angry at me for being at war, for abandoning the family. There was always something wrong. Couldn't I understand how hard it was on her? She demanded I take leave and at least meet her in Hawaii. Leave my men for a week to face that kind of hell? No! I couldn't bear leaving Ubon even to fly to Saigon for meetings at 7th HQ. Why would I go knowingly into the maw of a disintegrating marriage when I knew nothing would change? Ella had no idea that her unending criticisms and admonishments wore me down. I tried to tell her both in letters and phone calls. Nothing worked. Toward the last week in February, I received a telegram: ARRIVING BANGKOK MARCH 8TH. MEET OR DIVORCE. I knew I'd have to go. The daily grind of work went on. It was nonstop, my only downtime at night in the O club with the guys, then back to my trailer to crash. I had no time to think about Ella.

Replacement crews flowed in and I always met them with a little pep talk. My greeting was enthusiastic but harbored lingering skepticism. Were they qualified? What was their experience? Did they have the chops needed to fly

F-4s in combat? Everyone came in as a pilot, no doubt about that. Every single man loved airplanes. That was plain to see. When I met the various groups, the faces of the young guys were burning with eagerness and impatience, tight with nervous energy, smug with bravado for their new challenge.

Fighter pilot is not just a description, it's an attitude; it's cockiness, it's aggressiveness, it's self-confidence. It is a streak of rebelliousness and competitiveness. But there's something else; there's a spark. There's a desire to be good, to do well in the eyes of your peers and your commander, and in your own mind, to be second to no one. The sky is your playground and competitiveness is your life. You don't understand it if you fly from A to B straight and level, or merely climb and descend. That's moving only through the basement of that blue playground. A fighter pilot is a man in love with flying. A fighter pilot sees not a cloud but beauty, not the ground but something remote from him, something that he doesn't belong to as long as he is airborne. There's something in the eyes. That's what I looked for in replacement crews, but sometimes it was a crapshoot.

One particular group of seven at least looked mature, not like brand-new lieutenants. There was nothing wrong with being a lieutenant, but I had learned to doubt the thoroughness of the combat training given to pilots being sent to SEA. Those of us there knew it was one hell of a war. Practically no one sent over had ever dropped real bombs, had made a max weight takeoff, or had fired his guns on an air target. The first time most of the replacement pilots ever saw a fighter loaded with live ordnance was when they arrived in Thailand. They hadn't a clue what they were looking at. Any fighter experience among them was a welcome asset. The others would have to learn quickly.

The bunch sitting in front of me looked only slightly promising. I did my usual welcoming speech, "Glad to have you, looking forward to serving with you, etc, etc." Then I said, "How about standing up right to left and hollering out your name, tell me where you're from, what your background is. I'll remember you and I will remember your name."

Names were given, followed by, "Training Command, Air Defense Command, Logistics Command, Systems Command, Training Command, Air Defense Command, Headquarters." Logistics Command? Systems, for Christ's sake? Not one of them was from TAC, from USAFE or PACAF. Not one of them had a fighter background. So I looked at them and said, "Dear God, don't tell me there isn't a fighter pilot among you! What we need over here are raggedy-ass fighter pilots and they send me you guys. What am I going to do with you?" I was deliberately trying to get them mad. And I did. They seethed. They were boiling. I read them the riot act. "I am going to use you but I do not want you. This is tough business. This is big league and you guys are not qualified. Goddamn it, why don't they send me some fighter pilots!"

I looked at them hard and taunted, "Hell, I bet you can't drink, either. I'll meet you in the O club in five minutes. I'm buying." We proceeded to the bar and bellied up for several rounds. They soon relaxed and realized their legs had been pulled more than just a little bit.

I knew they'd be a great bunch when one named Danny Fulgram came up to me with a slight blur, looked me in the eye, and said, "Colonel, you know you made me damn angry, but I didn't tell you the whole truth. Yep, I was in Systems Command all right, but I was a balloon pilot!"

That stopped me cold until I got out of him he'd been testing pressure suits for the space program. He and other guys like Red Kittinger would suit up, ascend in a balloon to 90,000 feet, and then bail out, for God's sake. What Danny did was unimaginable. He had pulled my chain but good and I loved him for it. He turned out to be one hell of a fighter pilot. All in that group turned out to be great pilots and good friends.

That was my "new guy" routine, and 95 percent of the time I'd end up with great kids. There was just no way I could take a guy at face value. I didn't care if he had four thousand hours in Huns, F-104s, 86s, 105s, or F-4s—I wouldn't send him off to fly combat right away. I'd stick an experienced backseater in with the new guy to get twelve or fifteen missions on targets in Laos and Route Pack 1 before I'd think of sending him up on the harder missions. It made sense, and this applied to anybody. It was how I ascertained whether the new kids had any mettle, what they were made of, if they were eager, how much they loved to fly. They had to prove themselves.

For pilots, no matter the background, flying is not just a job, it's a love affair. No pilot calls his plane an aircraft, any more than a sailor calls his ship a boat. The names he uses are many, some even profane, but to him and to him alone, they are terms of endearment. He may call it a bird, a beast, a jug, or a gooney. He may call it a bucket of bolts or "Old Shaky." It can be a dog whistle or a tweet, a bamboo bomber or a boxcar, a trash hauler or a crowd killer, an aluminum overcast or a peashooter. It can be any of these, but only he can call it that. The use of most of these names by any outside the brotherhood can easily earn a bloody nose. Pilots and mechanics are like that. Even within the fraternity there are certain taboos. Before the Vietnam conflict it was downright dangerous to call a Thunderchief a Thud in the bar at Seymour Johnson. Since then, F-105 pilots have wrought such deeds of valor and sacrifice that the name Thud denotes a proud history.

A pilot is a man in love, a man whose emotional ties with a piece of machinery run deep. His bluff expressions are protective devices meant to hide the tenderness in his heart when talk turns to flying. Man merges with machine; he doesn't simply use it. You don't climb into an aircraft and sit down. You strap the machine to your butt, become one with it. Hydraulic fluid is your blood; titanium, steel, and aluminum, your bones; electrical currents, your nerves; the instruments, an extension of your senses; fuel, the food; engine, the power; the control surfaces, the muscle. You are the heart, yours is the will, yours the reasoning power. You are something more than earthbound man. You are augmented and expanded by the miracle of the machine. You are tied to it physically and you are part of it emotionally. Together you conquer the bonds of earth and, in the words of Flight Officer John Gillespie Magee, "join the tumbled mirth of sun-split clouds . . . wheeled and soared and swung high in the sunlit silence . . . chase the shouting winds along . . . and, while with silent lifting mind, you tread the high untresspassed sanctity of space, put out your hand, and touch the face of God."

To some, these feelings seem utterly inappropriate in relation to military flying and the grim purposes of war, but for combat pilots there is no such ambivalence. The realities of danger and the tensions of conflict serve only to heighten the bond between man and machine. The pilots new to the 8th TFW soon transformed themselves. When you've rushed headlong at treetop level into a storm of flak, when the tracers from an enemy's guns flick past your canopy and your bird shudders as others strike home; when you twist and turn in mortal combat, outnumbered and far from help; when you strike with savage, thunderous power and wheel in white-hot anger toward another foe; when your bird responds to your impossible demands, slamming you into near unconsciousness with crushing g-force, leaping like a cat when you unleash the full energy of 40,000 pounds of thrust, beating the earth below with one rolling thunderclap as you exceed the speed of sound, hurling iron bolts of destruction with deadly accuracy, and then quietly, serenely lifts you home, physically battered, emotionally spent, and numb with weariness, then that bond is as solid and as personal as any relationship you will ever experience. You and your bird have survived another day and for the moment tomorrow is a long way off. As you shut down, each switch stills a part of the pulsing energy that has been an extension of you. The radio fades to stillness, gyros unwind, hydraulic pressures fall, radar images fade; lights flicker, dim, and are gone to blackness. As the engine clicks down to silence, air pressure from the fuel tank hisses free, like a long sigh before sleep. You love deeply the crewmen who swarm around to care for what has now become "their" bird, and you unfasten yourself from your metal body and climb out. It's a rare pilot who doesn't feel these things as an act of gentle severance, and his final, gloved touch at the bottom of the ladder is a secret gesture of parting.

These thoughts obsessed me as I flew to Bangkok and steeled myself for the meeting with my wife. I remembered being in love with Ella with the same undeniable force twenty years earlier. Our passion for each other brought us great joy. With laughter she had accepted my warning that I'd always be a fighter pilot, her beautiful face and light green eyes full of love. We adored each other, but the years and our differences wore us down. Little was left that was familiar, loving, or even comfortable. I was unhappy to leave Ubon for the mandated meeting in Bangkok but I tried to turn my dread to optimism. It was truly good to see her—at first. The fun lasted less than two days, then retreated under her sharp demands to return home, to leave the foolishness of war, to accept an assignment in Washington, D.C., to keep my family anchored, to do something SHE wanted and to turn away from what she saw as my complete selfishness and betrayal. In my heart, our marriage ended at that moment. Her unyielding negativity bored into me like a knife. We were from different worlds. I departed two days before the end of the planned six-day leave to return to my men. Ella stayed in Bangkok to visit tailors, order custom-made silk and suede suits, and buy a leopard skin coat before flying home. I wondered if I would ever see my children again.

A problem had come to Ubon in my absence. Captain Bob Pardo had pulled a heroic stunt on March 10 that HQ deemed unseemly and unnecessary because it was against regulations. His feat became known as "Pardo's Push." I returned to my office to find Chappie in a lather, commencing court-martial proceedings against Bob. I plunged into damage control. After learning the facts, I went to Saigon to meet with Momyer.

Pardo's escapade was another in a string of incidents from our futile attacks on Thai Nguyen. Before the 8th Wing strike flight reached the target on the tenth, ground fire hit and damaged Captain Bob Aman's F-4, but with his backseater, Lieutenant Bob Houghton, Aman stayed with the formation. Over the target, they were hit again and began to leak fuel badly. Bob Pardo, with Lieutenant Steve Wayne in the backseat, was hit and damaged as well. Pardo might have been able to reach a tanker and ultimately save his own aircraft, but Aman was going to run out of fuel before he could get to Laos, where he and Houghton could bail out with a reasonable chance of rescue. He was still over North Vietnam when he flamed out. Pardo decided to push Aman to safer territory. He brought the nose of his F-4 into contact with Aman's aircraft, but turbulence off the other aircraft made it impossible to hold his position. He told Aman to drop his tailhook, then positioned the tailhook against his windscreen and pushed. Although the hook slipped frequently and had to be repositioned, the push succeeded. Aman's rate of descent slowed. Pardo's left engine caught fire. He was almost out of fuel himself. Both crews bailed out near the Laotian border and were rescued. Two F-4s were lost.

AF regulations forbade pilots from attempting to push one airplane with another, so Pardo was in trouble for that plus the loss of his own F-4 in the effort. After learning the facts, and heated arguments with Chappie, I went to Saigon to intercede with Momyer. My position was that Bob had done something heroic, and while he'd lost the aircraft, four valuable crew members were alive at Ubon. It was a worthwhile trade. Bob eventually was awarded the Silver Star instead.

The incident marked a turning point in my relationship with Chappie. There had been numerous instances when he was "talking the talk but not walking the walk," often finding ways to hang back from the action in combat, yet glorifying himself after the mission. It disturbed me, but we had a wing to run and he was still the man to do it. Everybody loved Chappie for his great personality, his glib talk, and the sheer ease with which he connected with the men. I loved Chappie, but I knew that combat, specifically leadership in combat, proved the real mettle of a man. We had a deep friendship but I needed him to reach past his obsession with appearances and just think and act like a fighter pilot. Our greatest challenges at Ubon still lay ahead.

In March the targeting opened up. The weather patterns shifted and we were going back to the hard ones in Route Packs V and VI. For the first time we could hit things that we thought were worthwhile like the steel mill at Thai Nguyen and thermal power plants. The navy hit a thermal plant at Haiphong and then one right in the middle of Hanoi. It was about time! Our own action was hot and heavy. On Easter Sunday, Phil Combies and I went round and round with seven MiGs. Fred Crow took a SAM and went down.

The air force, navy, and marines were all working together for once. J. B. Stone finished his tour and went back to the States in the middle of the month. He would be missed.

The word coming from Washington was about reassigning me to the Pentagon: Directorate of Operational Requirements and Development Plans in USAF HQ, report NLT 10 Oct 1967. Hell no! I fought back with a letter to Jim Jumper at personnel, and he responded with a request that I suggest something more specific than "no preference except TAC," since there were no good TAC assignments, only ADC commander jobs at different bases, or maybe overseas with PACAF or USAFE. General Jumper told me the best idea was to come home for air staff or Joint Staff. Ella had called him personally and wanted me in D.C. Her influence in Washington was causing me problems.

Then came a low-altitude strike at Thai Nguyen Steel Works on March 30. I had returned from 13th AF headquarters in the Philippines the afternoon of the twenty-ninth and was still fuming from a round of so-called Star Talks, a procedure invented by some headquarters fiend as a way to harass and intimidate wing commanders who had the misfortune of suffering an aircraft accident in their wing. The CO was supposed to divine the cause immediately, then proceed up the chain of command explaining the situation to the generals and their staffs. Such procedures sometimes precluded recurrences, but in combat they often simply detracted from the ability to focus on the mission.

Before retiring that night, I posted myself on the next morning's schedule to lead Plymouth Flight, escorting an F-105 strike force into North Vietnam. If the weather precluded the Thuds from getting to their primary target, they would proceed to their secondary target, and we'd drop off and sweep the airspace around Thai Nguyen. Briefing would be at 0600 with takeoff at 0800.

A knock came on my trailer door close to midnight. That always meant trouble and this was no exception. One of the officers who worked in the command post stood there with a worried look on his face.

"What's up?" I asked.

"Sir, tomorrow's strike package has been canceled and—"

"Thanks for telling me," I cut him off. "But why come all the way over here? Why not just call?"

"Uh, sir, Plymouth Flight has been rescheduled to make a low-level run on the blast furnaces at Thai Nguyen and—"

"Holy shit, you gotta be kidding me!" I couldn't believe it.

"No sir. Do you want me to schedule someone else?"

He shouldn't have said that and he knew it. "Hell no. Get hold of Bill Kirk, Combies, Greaves, and some of the other old-timers and have them meet me in ops plans, right now."

"Yes sir!" He hustled off.

As I pulled on my flight suit I tried to imagine what idiot had ordered this strike. The blast furnaces; my God! Thai Nguyen! That damned steel mill had been under severe attack for a month. The enemy defenses were murderous. Both the Thuds and my outfit had lost a number of aircraft, making the ground around the complex look worse than the craters of the moon. Who was worried about the damned blast furnaces? What did those ops analysts in Washington think those furnaces were going to blast? This was going to be a bitch!

An hour later, I finished up my briefing at ops and said, "OK, guys, that's it. Six 500-pound high drags, three each on the inboard pylons, all with eight-second delay fuses. ECM pods on the right outboard, a 370-gallon drop tank on the left, 600-gallon centerlines, and only three of us. I don't want a number Four flailing away and trying to cross the target before my bombs go off. We'll hit the tanker, then drop down to the mountaintops, go low level the rest of the way in. And when I say low, I mean LOW. The weather stinks, so I'll have to play that one by ear. Thanks, guys. Let's try to get some sleep. See you at 0600."

Sleep, hah! Everyone, including those not going, had butterflies.

My backseater was Captain Dan Lafferty, Major George Greaves was number Two with Captain Gerald Finton, and Phil Combies was Three with Captain Lee Dutton. We hit the tanker right on time, headed north, topped off, and started down. We were over a mountainous section of Laos where our maps declared "Relief Data Inaccurate." Bloody hell, that sure was comforting. We descended into the typical humid mist with about half a mile visibility. Dan called off our altitude as I peered ahead, watching for terrain to appear in the murk. Suddenly, there! A mountain ridge right in front of us! I pulled up to miss it and the three of us started ridge hopping our way north. I kept the airspeed at a comfortable 480 knots, and held our predetermined compass heading while Dan counted off the minutes as we ate up 8 miles for each of them. Just after we crossed the Black River the mist thickened into cloud. I called Phil and George to close in and climbed up to 4,500 feet. We were totally engulfed in cloud and on the gauges.

"Dan. Alpha."

"Two forty-two," he quickly responded, meaning we had two minutes and forty-two seconds to go to reach our checkpoint on the Red River.

This was getting tense, particularly when my RHAW gear flashed a warning that we were being tracked by enemy radar, might be early warning, could be guns or SAMs. If they launched there wasn't a damned thing we could do about it but hope the missile missed.

At two minutes forty I called, "OK, boys, here's the river. Let's go down."

God, please let this be right. We descended and didn't break out. When we passed through 500 feet on the radar altimeter and hadn't hit anything, I knew we were at least over the Thai Nguyen Valley. At about 300 feet we broke out, and sure enough, there was our checkpoint: a loop in the river not a quarter mile off my right wing. I didn't want to think about the 3,000-foot mountain we had passed over during our letdown a mile back.

"Good job, Dan," I said quickly.

I didn't have to tell Phil and George to spread out. They already had. So down I went to about 25 feet off the deck. Later, Phil told me he thought he had flown low many times before but when he looked over at me he was looking down at the top of my aircraft. We skimmed treetops and flattened grass as we went. A small herd of water buffalo leaped straight up as we passed over and our shock wave hit them. We hurtled across the valley toward a gap near the north end of Thud Ridge. I pushed the airspeed up to 540 knots, flew through the gap, then pulled a hard right turn to proceed down the valley on the northeast side of the ridge. The weather was better here, if you want to call a 400-foot ceiling better; at least the visibility was good. Suddenly, there was a tremendous amount of "twinkling" on the ridge. All our low-level maneuvering hadn't fooled Charlie one bit, and he let loose the damnedest barrage I'd ever seen. Flak mostly came in streams, often intense and heavy, but here, in this humidity, the stuff was coming into our faces like an orange-red blanket. They threw everything at us: 85s, 57s, 23 mms, God knows what else! The rice paddies around us boiled from the falling shrapnel. I felt my bird taking hits, but we were still on course. To hell with it, one of us might make it to the target, so nothing to do but press on.

I glanced over at George, then at Phil. Yep, they were hanging in and still flying. I could see only the front third of their F-4s. The rest was hidden in vapor condensation, a pretty spectacular sight. If we weren't under such heavy fire it might have been fun to watch.

The target, those damned blast furnaces, stuck up like apartment buildings off our nose to the left. I waited until the proper moment, then made a hard left turn to line them up. George slid over to make his run behind Phil. We were flying so low that gunners on rooftops were firing down on us! The first two bullets hit my wing from above. As I pulled up to 200 feet I took a hard hit on my right wing. Oh shit.

Phil called, "Plymouth Lead, you're on fire!" Hey, that wasn't good news at a time like this. What the hell, I determined if I took more bad damage on the run in to the target, I'd just fly directly into the blast furnaces and blow the whole place up to spare other pilots from having to attack it later. I poured on a little more speed to blow my wing fire out and descended toward the target. As we closed in we had to climb to clear an 80-foot chimney dead ahead. The furnaces came up, the sight picture was right; I pickled my bombs. Phil and George followed. As I made a hard left turn to get the hell out of there I looked over and saw our bombs going off all around the three furnaces. There were no more transmissions from Phil or George, both of whom I could see under the cloud, so I figured Lady Luck was with us and continued on toward the gap and the Red River beyond it. Once there, we sped across the flat plain, then the river, and entered a promising-looking valley that could hide us from SAM sites. Suddenly, we were in a cloud deck again and I couldn't see anything but blackness beneath it.

Holy crap! "Pull! Burners! PULL!" I yelled.

We shot straight up in a 60-degree climb and broke out of the cloud like rockets, only 50 feet off the sheer face of North Vietnam's highest mountain, each of us practically grazing the trees. *My God*, I had nearly run us straight into the side of that mountain! To hell with the SAMs, I thought, and continued on up to 20,000 feet. That was the worst moment of the whole mission, the absolute stuff of nightmares.

Once at altitude I called for the tanker. At first he refused to leave his assigned track, but once I identified myself, he said, "Yes, sir!" and cruised to meet us. I had only 1,200 pounds of fuel remaining. We rendezvoused and took our normal off-load for the trip to Ubon. I had a big problem because fuel was streaming out of the right wing. Since I didn't know the extent of the damage or if I could make it home, I asked the tanker pilot to stick with us all the way to home plate. Bless his heart, he did. I loved those tanker guys.

When we landed, the whole base was out to greet us. Word had spread that the Old Man had been hit. During debriefing I asked Phil what he expected me to do when he told me I was on fire, get out and piss on it? He laughed, and showed me the piece of flak that had hit his right quarter panel and bounced around his cockpit. The blast of air through broken plexiglass rendered his radio useless, so he couldn't transmit during the rest of the mission. By some miracle George's bird didn't even get scratched.

It turned out I had taken five hits on our way to the target and then took that last one right through the main wing spar into the fuel tank. The hole was the size of basketball. Later it was found that the reverse flow check valve in that tank was inoperative. Fuselage fuel could flow backward to the wing tank, so it was a lucky thing I even reached the tanker, let alone made it home. My poor old F-4 was dismantled and shipped back to the depot in Utah. I don't know if it ever flew again, but in my book, the old lady had done her work and had let us live to fly another day.

The MiGs had been pretty quiet since we knocked the shit out of them in January, but they came up hard again in late April. They started hammering away at the Thuds, who had to jettison bombs to avoid being shot down. Thuds were lost, three in one day. It finally dawned on the 7th AF that we'd better have MiG combat air patrol (CAP) again. I convinced HQ that we could both escort and bomb. Escort only was an awful waste.

F-4Ds loaded with pods started arriving at Ubon on May 8 and that changed things more than anything. Getting the Thuds up to about 12,000 to 14,000 feet in pod formation, going in like the hammers of hell, everybody was together; everybody knew who everybody else was, where they were, where they were going, and exactly what they had to do when they got there. If there were any other airplanes around, they were enemy—who else could they be? The Thuds weren't to worry about that. I would worry about those. Thud guys go on! I'd be right back behind and wouldn't let anybody get hurt. Ubon and Da Nang were put on the job of MiG CAP, and we got tied in with Takhli. For three or four weeks, and through May, it was escort. From the time of our first MiG CAP mission until the thing finished in June, not one Thud was lost to MiGs, but we lost Herm Knapp and his GIB, Chuck Austin, on egress April 24, best of officers and a damn shame.

Late in April I was leading what was supposed to be a normal mission up north when I got all of us in big trouble. It started as I led Buick and Plymouth flights toward our prestrike tanker.

"Orange 56, Buick Lead here, we have you at 1130. Closing for prestrike."

"Roger, Buick Lead. Take the perch."

Take the perch? What the hell was that? That was a Stateside procedure.

We didn't do that over here. This must be a new guy fresh from SAC and he was trying to pull the procedures he'd used over Nebraska. Well, to hell with that "perch" crap.

"Orange 56. You just hold nice and still and we'll work the prestrike refueling. That's a good boy."

Orange 56 got the word because he held still as he was told. We bored straight in, each of the four of us taking our prestrike load and moving out to let the next man come in. The boomer was good and my guys were pros. The operation went smoothly as we flew north on Orange tanker track to our final top-off point over central Laos.

I bid Orange 56 a fond "See ya" and headed my two flights of F-4s over for a rendezvous with our Thuds. The strike mission went smoothly, if you call dodging flak and SAMs smooth. Then we were hit by MiGs. As usual, all hell broke loose. During the ensuing tussle, Plymouth Flight became separated and wisely headed for home, as they were supposed to.

Meanwhile, I kept Buick at it much too long and fuel became critical. I took a horrified look at my fuel gauge and shouted, "OK, guys, break it off. Break it off! Disengage heading 240 degrees! Bingo minus two. Egress!" and we streamed back over Thud Ridge at high speed. We were close to our "no-shit bingo" and I began to worry about reaching the tanker, let alone the nearest recovery base.

In order to save fuel, I started climbing before we reached the Red. Considering the missile threat, that was not the safest thing to do, but it was certainly the lesser of two evils. I knew the tanker was waiting for us at the south end of his track and I wanted to get him headed north as soon as possible. Then I began to fret about the responsiveness of a new tanker crew, probably on their first refueling mission over here.

I switched to the refueling frequency and called, "Orange 56, this is Buick. Head north, now!"

He answered, "Roger, Buick Lead, as soon as I check in with Brigham."

"For Christ's sake, Orange, Brigham is busy! Head north as fast as you can. I'll work the intercept."

"But I—"

"No damned buts, head north! NOW!"

He must have sensed my urgency, as he let me know he was heading our way. I soon picked him up and told him I had him on radar. He knew he was already north of his normal track limit but, like a good fellow, kept right on coming.

When he was 27 miles off my nose I told him to make the tightest 180 he had ever done. He was in an almost vertical bank when I got a visual of him. What a beautiful sight it was! He rolled out and headed south just as we came up under him. I moved into position first, and as the boom plugged in I saw I had about 400 pounds remaining. That's less than four minutes' flying time in the F-4, assuming the gauge is accurate and you're at cruise power at altitude. As Lead I'd been tapping my burners during our engagement with the MiGs, and I knew the other guys had a lot more fuel than I did. I told the boomer to give me only 2,000 pounds and then I backed off so my wingmen could take on their full poststrike load of 4,500 pounds each. By the time number Four was finished refueling, I was back down to 300 pounds. I went under the tanker for my full share and gave a huge sigh of relief when the boom thudded home.

Then it was suddenly disengaged and stowed under the KC-135 in the trail position.

I hollered, "Hey, wait a minute, give me my fuel!"

The tanker pilot responded, "We're bingo. Returning to base."

"Bingo, hell! You don't know what bingo is! Give me some fuel!"

"No, we're bingo, headed home."

I knew his bingo meant he could go from our position over Laos clear down to U-Tapao in southern Thailand, turn left, and proceed all the way to the Philippines. Even then, he'd have some fuel left over.

"Look, buddy, I'm about to flame out. Give me some damned fuel."

"Sorry, I'm at my bingo and headed home."

"For God's sake, those people down there in the jungle don't like us at all. Give me fuel!" I even tried to pull rank on him, but in spite of my pleading and cussing, the tanker guy was adamant.

Finally I said, "OK, I have a couple of Sidewinders left. I'm going to drop back behind you, and before I punch out, I'm going to pull the trigger. Put your parachutes on!"

There was a moment's hesitation before the boom came down with a twang. The boomer thudded it home and began pumping just as my left engine flamed out. I hung on desperately, hoping the incoming fuel would keep the right one going before it, too, quit. In what seemed like minutes but could have been only seconds, I got the left restarted and things settled down to normal.

In a shaken voice, the tanker asked how much fuel I wanted, and I told him, "Fill 'er up!" I didn't need or want that much, but I wanted the tanker guy to get the message. I said, "Look, 56, old buddy, we're all in this together. You scratch my back and I'll scratch yours. Over here we help each other out. If you're really low on gas you can stop short at Ubon and we'll fill your damned tanker with bourbon."

That evening I called his boss and explained what had happened. He wasn't all that happy, but he assured me he'd have a talk with Orange 56.

The fighter guys knew we couldn't operate without the tankers. We never forgot the many times they broke their own rules to save our butts. They were our safe ticket home, and our admiration for them ran deep. For all the old heads in SEA, the feeling was mutual. I'd goofed that day in more ways than one and I knew it, but I couldn't help smiling at the thought of all that bourbon sloshing inside a tanker. Hell, there probably wasn't that much booze west of Hawaii.

Around the end of April, my notoriety was such that General Momyer, convinced by his staff officers (and probably Pentagon brass), told me I shouldn't fly into North Vietnam anymore. The thought of me shot down, captured, and exploited by the People's Republic PR machine was more than anyone could bear, so an order came down from 7th HQ directing that "Colonel Olds can no longer lead missions over North Vietnam." Christ, they couldn't even get that right! I called Phil Combies into my office, showed him the TWX, and said, "OK, Phil, YOU lead the missions. I'll follow you and if the silly bastards figure that out, then I'll change my name!"

Also at this time I was keenly aware that the magical one hundredth mission would send me home sooner than end of tour, so I started covertly erasing my missions off the board. Nobody could figure out what number I had or hadn't flown from that time forward. I kept the number hovering in the high eighties and low nineties. Damned if I was going to record one hundred before I was ORDERED home. We were busier than hell. No way was I going to leave.

May started off with a bang. On the fourth we provided two flights of four F-4Cs each as MiG CAP for the strike forces of the 355th TFW. Chicago Lead was flight commander. I led Flamingo Flight. Dick Pascoe, Kirk, and Allen were my three wingmen.

We were one mile in-trail of the last two Thuds in the strike force when four MiG-21s were sighted coming in from seven o'clock. Two of them sliced right up between my flight and the Thuds. I told the next-to-last F-105 flight to break and turned to take on the two 21s. The first one broke right and headed down and out. The other tried but was blocked, so he crossed and tried the other way. I pulled up high, staying inside the MiG's turn, and hovered for a second to let him move forward on me. I dropped the nose and flipped the missile toggle down from Sparrow to Sidewinders, then waited for a growl. I finally got a Sidewinder off under marginal parameters. It tracked and exploded right beneath the MiG. Damage was not immediately apparent so I stuck with him. The MiG began turning madly, alternately losing control then recovering, some turns so violent that the aircraft snap-rolled in the opposite direction. He finally straightened out in a steep, steady dive heading directly for Phuc Yen. I closed to about 2,500 feet and saw he had brilliant magnesium flames erupting from the left side of his fuselage. He continued straight for the runway. Flak became dangerously thick. Then Bill Kirk saw MiGs on my tail and called, "Flamingo, break right! Break!" Just as I did, Bill saw the MiG crash about 100 yards south of the runway, right in the middle of an active flak site. I was pissed I'd missed watching him go down. I inserted myself back between Bill and the MiGs. He moved off a bit to gain separation but kept asking, "Hey, Colonel, can I come in now?" which meant "Get out of my way!" On his third repeat, I growled at him, "Do you need an invitation?"

When that donnybrook ended I took Flamingo Flight over Hanoi to cover the last of the Thuds coming off target, then turned right and headed for Hoa Lac. We dodged a pair of SAMs, then spotted four or five MiG-17s in the landing pattern. We tore into them like foxes in a henhouse at 1,500 to 6,000 feet, right over the center of the airdrome. The mix of F-4s and MiG-17s was thick enough to prevent the flak gunners from shooting. It was a dogfight reminiscent of World War II. Those MiG pilots were damned good. Round and round we went, me with no missiles left at all but enjoying myself immensely, making dry passes on the various MiGs. If only I'd had a gun! Would have had some lovely shots. We separated at bingo fuel. Number Four tapped the tanker with only 800 pounds remaining. Kirk confirmed my MiG. That made two for me.

Back at home, it was business as usual for two weeks, nonstop in the air and on the ground; new F-4Ds started coming in with replacement crews, the F-104 pilots of the 435th at Udorn were transitioning out, and the 435th name and number were reassigned to Ubon as an F-4D squadron. When I wasn't on missions, my days were filled by arguments with HQ, piles of reports to review, nonstop paperwork, and endless visitors. Days started early and nights ended late, either at the O club or back at my trailer doing home-work. My office was rarely a sanctuary, but my administrative duties were held together by a ray of sunshine named Ruby Gilmore. Ruby had arrived in late March from Randolph as a replacement secretary. She thought she was headed for a civilian job in Bangkok when they suddenly shipped her to the 8th. The poor girl got to Ubon knowing nothing about the wing, but within a week she had whipped the whole office into shape. Her efficiency and pleasant personality had a calming effect on me. After grueling missions, I'd flop down on the sofa near my desk, falling asleep to the rhythmic sounds of typing and her voice on the phone.

We all loved the C model of the F-4, but with the advent of this new bunch of upgraded jets, we old heads would be flying the new birds. We had to at-tend ground school to learn the main differences with the new Phantoms. The courses were taught mostly by tech reps, civilian experts from the various systems manufacturers and aircraft plants. The differences were minor, ex-cept for the new missile, the AIM-4 Falcon carried on the F-4D. Like our Sidewinder, it was a heat seeker. The tech rep extolled the virtues of the weapon, but to my way of thinking it didn't have any, certainly not in the en-vironment we faced each day.

"Go over that again," I asked the instructor.

He did.

"Once more," I said.

He did, this time with a bit of exasperation.

I must have growled when I said, "Your damned missile might be OK for an Air Defense mission, but it won't work here."

"How do you know, Colonel? You don't know anything about it. It has been thoroughly tested by Systems Command and the Air Defense Com-mand. It's been fired at airborne targets at Eglin and out over the ranges at Point Mugu. It's been adopted by ADC and installed on a good portion of the alert birds. It—"

I interrupted. "I don't give a rat's ass where or by whom it's been tested and accepted. I'm telling you the switchology you describe doesn't fit our situ-ation. Whoever thought up that gadget didn't know a damned thing about air-to-air fighting, and didn't ask anyone who ever had." I left the briefing room in anger, not at the tech rep, who was only doing his job, but at whatever bunch of designers, developers, and procurers had put that creation on an air force fighter. I wondered what command wanted the damned thing in the first place. The Falcon required a complex set of steps to cool the seeker before the missile could be fired, sometimes taking up to a minute. Once cooled it was good for a limited period of time and couldn't be cooled again. This was intolerable in dogfights. Who in hell thought we had the luxury of checking our watches? Unlike the Sidewinder, which had a proximity fuse and a sophisticated warhead, the AIM-4 had a contact fuse, which required a direct hit to explode. Assuming it locked on, launched, and guided, it had to hit the target with its little 3-pound warhead in order to do its job. What a classic fuck-up.

It occurred to me that we were the warrior victims of an ongoing battle between the air force and navy. Our Sidewinder was a navy missile that had been thoroughly tested and proven in actual combat. That meant the air force procurement people had to go hat in hand to obtain a share of the production, and it also meant the operators had little or no control over any future changes and improvements. Bureaucracy! What the hell did I know about such things? All I had to do was determine if my reservations were valid and then find a way to do something about it. All of it could wait until the new squadron arrived. That would be soon.

The F-4Ds would replace the F-104s in the 435th Tac Fighter Squadron. The pilots and crews of the 104s would return to the States, and the squadron designation would go to the F-4 crews and maintainers. The construction of the new 435th Squadron operations building proceeded on schedule and was just about complete before the first F-4Ds arrived. Telephones were installed; lockers were moved in; the squadron briefing room and the pilots' lounge were the best on the base, with only a few bits of furniture still needed. The ground cadre arrived ahead of the pilots and settled into their hooches. The Combat Support Group's construction people did a first-rate job all around. We hoped the new guys would appreciate what had been done for them.

I admit all of us were impressed by the formation fly-past put on by the new squadron on arrival. After a near perfect transpacific crossing, they came over in squadron formation from their last stop in the Philippines. I met the squadron commander as he climbed down from his cockpit and offered my heartiest congratulations on the impressive show he and his troops had put on. As we stood in front of his aircraft we had to give way to one of my armament men driving a small tug. He pulled to a stop just past the bird. The squadron CO turned to see what was going on. The young airman was bare to the waist, tanned bronze, and wore one of those popular copies of an Aussie hat with the right brim pulled up tight against the crown. On top of that, he sported a truly impressive blond mustache sweeping jauntily out past his ears. Behind him were three small bomb dollies loaded with a total of nine 750-pound bombs. Farther back, another armament troop waited with four of the new AIM-4 Falcon missiles we were supposed to start using. Behind him were two men with a QRC 160 ECM pod.

The lieutenant colonel's reaction was amusing. I wondered what shocked him the most, the getup and mustache of the young bomb loader or the immediate appearance of all those bombs. Perhaps it was both because he turned to me with an air of bravado and asked, "Oh, going out tomorrow, are we?"

"No, Colonel, you're not, but the aircraft is."

"But that's my aircraft!"

I tried to control a growing exasperation. "Not anymore, Colonel. The minute that plane touched ground here at Ubon, it became part of the 8th TFW. I'll use it as I see fit, for whatever purpose and whenever it fits the schedule. I assure you it will always be a part of your squadron. Your men will maintain it and you and your pilots will fly it when it's available to you in the daily cycle. That's the way we operate around here, and it would be wise if you understood and accepted what I'm telling you."

"But it's a brand-new D," he almost whispered.

"I don't give a damn if it's a P!" I shot back. "It goes into the daily overall schedule, and that's that." I didn't tell him we had all already gone to school on his precious D. He'd find out for himself in due course.

Now it was his turn, and he replied with more anger than was prudent, "And what do you intend doing with me and my pilots?"

"You are all going to ground school," I replied.

"Ground school? The hell we are! Every pilot in my squadron is combat ready!"

"Combat ready by whose standards?" I snorted. "You don't know your ass from a hole in the ground about combat ready. If it makes you feel any better, neither did I, or anyone else around here, when we arrived. I'll let you know when I think you're ready to be called combat ready and then you'll fly with someone who'll keep your sorry asses alive. Furthermore, I'm splitting your pilots into three groups. One you'll keep and the other two will fly with the 433rd and the Triple Nickel. I'm going to fill your outfit with an equal number of my old heads, each of whom has less than ten missions to go. You will listen to them, they will lead in the air, and they'll teach you as they complete their hundred. In due time, you'll get some of your guys back, but not until I'm satisfied all of you have learned how to survive this damned war."

To mollify my tirade, I added, "OK, I know you have a fine bunch of troops and I look forward to flying with you and getting to know you personally. Meanwhile, you'll do exactly as I say." I walked off. I hadn't meant to get so pissed. I knew I hadn't made a friend, but getting this job done properly had become an obsession, and I didn't intend to take a bunch of losses by not doing what I knew had to be done.

One day ground into the next, punctuated by a few highlights. Bill Kirk got his MiG on May 13. We rocked the O club that night. Colonel J. J. Burns assumed position as deputy for operations, and Chappie moved into the vice wing commander slot when Pappy Garrison headed for home. He was a great fighter pilot and ace in two wars. My God, how that Kentucky gentleman schoolteacher could handle an airplane! By Ubon he was so nearsighted he carried about four different pairs of glasses with him. He sneaked his way over to the 8th and never did get checked out properly in the F-4. He didn't know the emergency procedures from sour owl manure. I always put an IP with him instead of just a GIB, but by God, if you wanted a target bombed, he would hit it. He would hit it when everybody else missed. That old-timer flew his fifty-second mission on his fifty-second birthday. He got furious with me because I wouldn't let him get up there among the MiGs. I told him, "Pappy, every fighter pilot in the air force knows and loves you, and I am not going to be the guy that sends you up there to get your butt scragged." He just could not see anymore. He would swear that he could, but I knew damn well that without his bifocals he could not see a thing. Those weren't going to help him at six g's. God, I would miss him.

May 20 started out like many days. The morning mission went out as scheduled. The afternoon frag was a MiG CAP escorting a large force of Takhli F-105s to the Bac Giang railroad yards in northeast North Vietnam. The route in was from the Gulf of Tonkin, straight west along MiG Ridge. Usually two flights of F-4 Phantoms were inserted into the strike force, but this day was strictly CAP. We had two flights of four F-4s each, loaded with four AIM-7s and four AIM-9s. Lead of Ballot flight was Major Phil Combies with Dan Lafferty. Ballot flight flew up front near the lead Wild Weasel flight, offset about a mile to the left. I led the second flight, Tampa, with Lieutenant Steve Croker in my backseat. We were offset to the right two miles and behind the strike force about three miles. Jack Van Loan was my wingman; his GIB was Joe Milligan. Bob Pardo and Steve Wayne were Three, and Ron Catton with Ron Ayers, number Four.

The current MiG CAP tactics had been very successful. A lot of mutual respect had developed between the 8th and the 355th. Takhli's formations were 100 percent improved over two months before. They got their gang of brass-balled Thud drivers in and out in one hell of a hurry while still making the MiGs commit themselves to come up after them. This certainly made our job easier. Plus, the new system of MiG calls was working pretty well. Ever since Bolo we'd greatly improved communication among all of the players. Whoever was doing the calling certainly knew what they were talking about. We thanked our unknown benefactor every day. We had no idea how much they were still holding back.

Fifteen miles short of target, all hell broke loose.

"Tampa, Break left!"

That scream from Pardo meant only one thing: MiGs! And they had to be behind us and close. I rolled left and hauled the stick back into my gut. Head over my shoulder, eyes straining, looking, searching . . . there they came, up from our deep six o'clock, looked like twelve to sixteen of them, God knew how many—some were already through us. The sky was full of whirling, shooting aircraft. One MiG went down. Pardo's. My wingman was hit hard. I looked back over my shoulder and saw his F-4 nose straight up, a ball of fire, out of control, two bodies ejecting; two good chutes. Van Loan and Milligan had gotten out. No time to worry. One of the bastards was off to my eleven. I continued my turn, switched to Sparrow missiles, got a bead on him, went interlocks out, mashed the button, and squeezed the trigger. The two-second delay was a lifetime. I willed it away, "Go, damn it, go!" With a whoosh, the Sparrow blasted out in front of me, arced toward the MiG, and exploded in a burst of fire. The MiG tumbled down to the left. Damn! Too close to get radar lock-ons for Sparrows. I switched to Sidewinders. There was another one, closing on one of my guys. I pulled up in a rolling turn, breaking down and behind that MiG, close enough, but too close for the AIM-9. He saw me, broke hard left, and disappeared. More MiGs were all around us, and one was down on the deck slowly circling. He was doing a figure eight, the shadow close beneath him giving him away. MiGs everywhere—one took a head-on at me, but no way for me to fire back with a Sidewinder. Christ, I wish I had a gun!

A damned SAM came right through the middle of the melee. The bastards didn't care if they hit their own people! Then, "Look out! Thuds at nine!" Right through the battle they came. They'd hit their target and were headed home like a herd of stripe-assed apes, moving at warp 2, it seemed. As fast as they came they left, scarcely interrupting our private fight.

It was quiet for a few seconds before calls came from my guys, warning one another in excited voices, too much noise. This was no time for me to lecture about radio discipline. The MiGs had formed a huge circle, were following one another, protecting the rear of the guy in front; pretty good tactics. All of us were trying to get a crack at them. Each time one of us tried to line up for a shot we'd have to break off as a pair of MiGs from the opposite side of their circle came at us. Damned good discipline, I thought, giving the devils their due. Without a wingman, I was particularly vulnerable and had to watch my back constantly. It occurred to me they were being directed by that loner down on the deck. He was probably watching our telltale smoke trails and giving warnings and orders to his people, but there was no time for him—my fuel gauge told me the fight was over. This was the longest aerial battle I'd ever experienced, fourteen minutes of pure dogfight. It was high time for us to get the hell out of there.

"OK, guys, this is Tampa Lead, we're bingo, RTB, all of you, haul ass!"

As I completed one last circle of the area checking for any of my stray guys, I saw the main body of MiGs turning for Kep just over a small range of hills. That loner was still down there, still circling, probably doing his own check-ing for any of his troops. I turned for the coast, certain I was the last out. Then it struck me: I've got enough fuel (I hope). Why not go for that MiG leader? At least I could scare him a little.

Calling ahead I said, "You guys go on. I'm going back to find the loner I spotted."

I went out about five miles, pulled a hard 180, went back to the scene of action, and there he was, just turning for the small range of hills between him and his base. I pulled the throttles back to idle to avoid an overshoot. He saw me or was warned by a ground observer because he frantically jinked right and left, hugging the ground for all he was worth. I stayed below him at 30 to 50 feet as we tore across the deck. I knew I was too low to fire a Side-winder. There was too much reflected heat from the rice fields below us. I could only watch his frantic maneuvering as he approached the hills through a small valley.

"Look at him, Steve," I called over my left shoulder. "Watch, he's in a real bind. He's going to hit that ridge in front of him, bail out, or pull up and give us some blue sky. No good choices. Oops, there he goes, up over the ridge! There goes our Sidewinder. It's tracking—come on, baby, do your stuff, come on!"

Just as the MiG cleared the hill, nose starting down, the Sidewinder struck near his tail in a great blast, blowing off a cloud of debris. He pitched violently left just as I cleared him by about 75 feet. I couldn't see if he crashed and couldn't go behind the ridge to check because it was way past time for us to head out.

Fuel was really a problem now and I began to wonder how I could explain to General Momyer why we'd had to bail out over the gulf. We reached the coast but were still a long way from help. To my relief, a frantic call to our poststrike tanker brought an immediate response, and he headed north to meet us. By the time I got there, Pardo and Catton had taken on fuel and were cycling through again. The tanker pilot asked why there were only three of us, but I was in no mood to talk. I said little, but hooked up quickly with only 300 pounds of fuel remaining.

I don't think Steve and I talked all the way back to Thailand. There was too much to think about, too much adrenaline, too many dark thoughts about Jack and Joe interspersed with our own thought that we had lived through another one. There were no victory rolls over the airfield. We landed without fanfare and went to debriefing. Combies and Pardo got a MiG each. As it turned out, I was given credit for that last MiG, too; our intelligence people had their own way of knowing those things. That made numbers three and four for me, but this was the first time I had ever lost a wingman in battle and it felt like shit. I found out later that Van Loan chased two MiGs off my tail just before he was hit and bailed out. No beepers were heard. I hoped like hell they were alive. We learned later that both survived the bailout but Jack was engulfed in fire around his head and neck. They were captured and hauled off to a POW camp. Jack learned to use maggots to treat his burns; they ate the dead flesh, leaving the good. He recovered well, with few scars to show for it. Both of them were Uncle Ho's guests for five and a half years.

Two days after that battle, I headed off with Chappie, Dee Simmonds, and several other Ubon pilots to the 388th Wing at Korat for another tactics meeting. This was held on Buddha's birthday because we were all standing down for the holiday. Scrappy Johnson determined this one would be the First Practice Reunion of the Red River Valley Pilots Association. We wouldn't have a "real" reunion until the war ended and all POWs came home. The

388th really did it up. We landed at Korat and were met by six elephants, lovely Thai hostesses in traditional dress, and a band from the 13th AF! I was ordered onto the first elephant and led a parade from the flight line to the O club, where we were greeted by a forty-foot banner proclaiming, WELCOME, RED RIVER VALLEY FIGHTER PILOTS ASSOCIATION. We had one hell of a party. Chappie, in his most natural state as grand orator, was master of ceremonies. I instigated the first River Rat MiG Sweep. The club and all pilots survived. The tactics conference was also worthwhile, with much agreed upon by the various wings. It remained to be seen what decisions would be enacted.

19

★

The Ending Battle

May and June brought a resurgence of MiGs. We took a heavy toll on MiGs in May battles and they disappeared completely for over three weeks. I believed they retreated into one corner of their hangar, sulked a bit, then tried to revise their tactics. Many of my guys were strutting and celebrating, "We mauled 'em all!" Chappie was all puffed up about it, which tweaked me no end, due to his basic noninvolvement in actual battles. We had several words in private about it, to no avail. His new title of vice wing commander appeared elevation enough to justify the grandstanding. What was I going to do with my good friend?

While the 8th and the other wings on regular strike missions were appreciating the breather from MiGs, I was fretting about what was really going on behind the scenes. There were few stories in the press or coming out of Saigon about the MiG-17, only disparaging remarks belittling the North Vietnamese combat capability. Pretty strong stuff, coming from armchair strategists and performance data analysts, but I knew the MiG-17 to be a vicious, nasty little beast. As marvelous as our Phantoms were in air-to-air combat, they were no match for the MiGs. We were heavily loaded with bombs, external tanks, missiles, and pods, just pressing in with one objective: the ground target. It was fine to advertise that the F-4 could do Mach 2 plus, or that the F-105 was the fastest thing down low that was ever built, but we weren't going fast with all those bombs, nowhere near as fast as our capability. Our first hard turn put us at the speed where the MiG-17, as old as it was, was at its best. He could intercept and close with us. Once he did that, his wing loading was so light that his turn capability was fantastic. There was no way to turn an F-4 with a MiG-17 and no way to battle with it in a classic World War II dogfight. I liked to think that if I'd been a North Vietnamese pilot, I would have been an ace ten times over. Give me a little plane with a great big gun; Snoopy flying alone on his doghouse shaking his fisted paw at the sky, shouting, "Curse you, Red Baron!" I was Snoopy in my dreams, but only in my dreams. The real world SEA conflict was a much bigger dog.

Statistics showed we had a four-to-one advantage over MiGs in air combat kills. We had that advantage only because we had the combination of damn fine aircraft, training, skill, discipline, and leadership across the board. The MiGs found our strike forces a tough nut to crack, but they cracked it increasingly often. Despite our advantages, we often fought them to a draw. Sometimes our flight of four would be hit by twelve MiGs. The eight of us flying the MiG CAP on May 20 were hit by a force of sixteen MiGs—hardly a superiority of numbers. We got lucky that day. I got two, Pardo and Combies each got one. The U.S. got five total.

By the beginning of June, we all hated the new AIM-4 Falcon missiles. I loathed the damned useless things! I wanted my Sidewinders back. In two missions I had fired seven or eight of the bloody things and not one guided. They were worse than I had anticipated. Sometimes they refused to launch; sometimes they just cruised off into the blue without guiding. And then, in the thick of an engagement with my head twisting and turning, trying to keep track of friend and foe, I'd forget which one of the four I had selected and couldn't tell which of the remaining was perking and which was already expired on its launch rail. Twice upon returning to base I had the tech rep go over the switchology and firing sequences. We never discovered I was doing anything wrong.

The June 5 mission became the last straw. It started with a ray of hope when I locked onto a MiG-17 and completed the firing. Away went the Falcon. Oh shit! The bloody missile was guiding! Now what? After all my bitching and complaining about the AIM-4, one was about to work. It was tracking straight and true at the tailpipe of the MiG-17 in front of me. Then, suddenly, it went almost straight up, nosed over violently, and disappeared, going straight down. Damn it.

The MiG headed for the deck and home. The fight was over. I called out to my troops, "OK, guys, time to RTB. Head out 310 to the Dog Pecker, then the tanker."

I turned to that heading and glanced around for any other Phantoms that might be around.

Sure enough there was my wingman, Dick Pascoe, right in position. Dick was a wonderfully aggressive bastard. He and his backseater, Norm Wells, were among the very best: Dick flying the jet, and that crazy Norm with his Leica slung around his neck, taking pictures during the roughest moments of a mission. Unbelievable!

Suddenly, there! I saw one lone MiG down low behind us in a turn headed back toward his base. I called to Dick, "Two, slice back left. MiG will be low and just about on your nose. I'll cover you. Got him?"

"I got him!"

"Go, man, you're covered!"

Down he dove with me out on his right wing, down, down. And I was thinking, Shoot, for Christ's sake, shoot!

Not Mr. Cool. He went down till he was below and in perfect range, then fired one Sidewinder. It tracked true, exploding just below the MiG. Over went the MiG, smoke and parts streaming, and the pilot punched out low, too low. The MiG crashed in a quick explosion.

"Good work, Dick. Now let's get the hell out of here."

That was Dick and Norm's second MiG. He wasn't excited, oh no, not at all, just did victory rolls all the way to the tanker and home. I shared his elation but was also seething at the worthlessness of that blasted AIM-4, foisted upon the air force by a group of idiots who didn't have a clue.

As we neared home plate I called ahead and told command post to have Ernie Timm, the maintenance honcho, meet me out on the flight line when we landed. After dearming I taxied to my parking slot and shut down. Ernie had a quizzical expression on this face. I didn't keep him waiting long.

"Ernie, I want you to take those goddamn AIM-4s off all the D models and replace 'em with Sidewinders. I don't give a rat's ass what you do with those pieces of junk, but I don't want to see another one on this ramp, ever!"

"Boss, for God's sake, we can't do that! It's not—"

"Ernie, I know what you're thinking, and I'm not going to quarrel with you. Do the D models have proper circuitry to fire Sidewinders?"

"I don't know right offhand but I can sure find out in a hurry. But, boss, it's against regulations!"

"No buts, Ernie. Let me know ASAP!"

He was back within the hour. "Boss, there's proper power and we can mount the LAU-12 launch rails and missiles on the D model inboard pylons. They'll fire off the stick trigger just like the C models, but you won't get steering information."

"Christ's sake, Ernie, do you think we're interceptor pilots? We don't use steering information in our kind of fighting! Look, while you're at it, I want you to have the maintenance shop fabricate shims just about the size of my fist to move the launch rails out from the pylon."

"Why, boss?"

"Because I want the lower inboard fin on the Sidewinders to clear the sway braces on the TER if we load it on the same pylon."

"My God, boss, we can't do that!"

"Why not, Ernie?"

"Because, because, uh, the tech orders for our birds don't cover both bombs and missiles on the inboards, and no one has flown or tested the F-4 with that configuration, and—"

"OK, my friend, I know you're right and I appreciate that's your job, but do as I say. And I want that shim on all the older C models, too. Understand? When you've got one ready with bombs and missiles, let me know and I'll take it out over Laos for testing. I'll fire the AIM-9s at the sun first. When I come back you'll know the change has worked and you can write an addendum to the tech orders if you like. Oh, by the way, I don't think it's necessary to bother higher headquarters with our little change. They have far more important things on their minds. Also, Ernie, I really appreciate your concern about these changes. If any flak comes down from above it won't reach you. I'll just let it bounce off my head. But think what we're doing. Instead of either/or, we'll now go up north with bombs and missiles, giving the Thuds MiG coverage as well as delivering ordnance ourselves. I expect it'll change the whole damn way the strike force does business: Double our pleasure, double our fun!"

I figured I'd be in a lot of trouble when headquarters found out what I was doing, but by then it would be too late.

A couple of weeks later Al Shintz, an old friend, was at Ubon checking up on the performance of the D model in combat. He was in the system at Eglin at the time. Responsibility for upgrading to the D model was his baby. We were standing out on the ramp in front of one of the jets and Al was asking questions.

"Well, Robin, how do you like the D?"

"Al, it was great getting some new birds in the maintenance flow. These low-time Ds really helped."

"That's not what I mean, Robin. How do you like that new lead–computing gun sight?"

"I suppose it's fine, Al, but we don't carry a gun."

"You what?!"

"I said we don't carry a gun, Al."

"Why not, for God's sake!"

"Al, out of all my fighter guys, only a precious few have ever fired a gun at an aerial target, let alone learned how to dogfight with guns. Hell, they'd pile into a bunch of MiGs with their hair on fire and be eaten alive. Besides, a gun pod hanging on the belly eliminates five or six bombs and induces tremendous drag. On future models get an internal gun where it belongs and teach the new pilots how to fight with it." I really had to argue with myself about my own desire to carry a gun. I knew I could hit anything I shot at but was damned sure I didn't want to tempt my men to engage a MiG-17 in an old-fashioned dogfight or give them the urge to go down in the mountain passes in Laos to strafe a stupid truck. In either case, I would have lost bunches of them. We needed guns, no doubt about it, but we needed pilots trained to use them even more.

"OK, Robin," Al responded, "I see your point, but how about that new RHAW [Radar Homing and Warning] gear? That's supposed to be a great improvement over the stuff we jury-rigged for the Cs."

"Yes it is, Al. But a lot of us turn it off when we cross the Black: too many false alerts when your life depends on your eyeballs. All that zit–zit noise and flashing colored lights in the cockpit is a bother. We know the enemy radar is searching, tracking, and locking on. He's paid to do that, and he does it every time we're up there. We don't need some fancy electronic gear to tell us he's doing his job. We know he'll launch when he can provide guidance to his SAMs. It's our job to see the missile launch if possible, then determine if we are the target. If the SAM doesn't move on the canopy, we know we're it, and if we take the evasive action we've learned, it will make the damned thing miss, we hope."

"Damn. Well what about that new bomb-delivery sight system?"

"It's good, Al, but we are learning to use it in the easier target areas. We don't like anything that makes us do a lot of straight tracking during the bomb run when we're in Route Pack 6."

"How do you bomb then?"

"Now we're flying a 'pod' formation. We're spread out about 1,000 feet and stack 200 or 300 up or down. A little rough at first but the guys are used to it now, and it gives our pods optimum effectiveness against the radars. When we get to the target, each flight lead calls the roll in and everyone in his flight of four rolls-in at once. That means all of us are going down the chute at the same time, each at his predetermined dive angle and converging on the target. We pickle at 7,500 feet and break hard to a predetermined departure heading. That gives us the least amount of exposure to his ground fire and puts us right back in formation for getting the hell out of there. It works, Al. Believe me, it works. Our bombing is better and our losses over the target are practically nil."

"OK, my friend, but what about the AIM-4 Falcon missile? Take this old C model here, it—"

Uh-oh. I knew the shit was about to hit the fan. "That's actually a D, Al."

"No, it's a C. It's got Sidewinders on it."

"I assure you that F-4 is a D, Al. I had to put Sidewinders on the whole fleet of Ds. The AIM-4 isn't worth a damn."

"Robin, what in hell have you done? You can't do that!"

My ensuing explanation was rather long and drawn out, but apparently Al got the message and didn't blow his stack. He merely said that he'd look into the matter when he returned to Eglin. The rewiring of F-4Ds for reliable Sidewinders was eventually done fleetwide. Later, I was told the air force kept working on the Falcon for years and finally gave up.

In mid-June, Jimmy Jumper, colonels assignments at the Pentagon, let me know there was a bunch of hoopla about my fourth MiG. Everyone was lathered up that I would get number five, become the first ace of the war, and summarily be sent home. The SAFOI (secretary of the Air Force Office of Information) had the urge to popularize the air war by producing an "ace," which the public could identify with. The situation angered me deeply. The PR machines were really cranking up with rumors of a big homecoming parade in D.C., a promotion to brigadier general, and a highly visible assignment at Systems Command to head up the Limited Warfare Deputate at Wright-Patterson. I called the information office at the 7th to confirm this. He explained it was Secretary of the Air Force Harold Brown and SecDef McNamara ordering it.

"Tell them both to go screw themselves! They can court-martial me. I just won't get number five! It means more to me to command my wing than to satisfy their childish exploitation of me for PR purposes!" I understood that getting the fifth MiG and retaining my command would make me a particular target and endanger my guys as well. My propaganda value to the North Vietnamese as a POW would be staggering. Damn! We've got a war raging over North Vietnam, and some little prick behind a desk in the Pentagon has me by the balls! Why was the number five so important?

It came on the back of those months after Thai Nguyen when Momyer had forbidden me to lead missions. So I didn't fly lead; I pushed from the rear. How was I going to stop myself from shooting at MiGs? This was the ultimate Catch-22. How could I be in the cockpit facing a MiG yet hold back? It was hard for this old warrior to simply not fight, when I knew with all my heart that I was the best fighter pilot out there. It wasn't ego; it was experience, desire to win the battle, and honest love for my men. How could I passively watch the battle because of a number? It had happened to Gabby Gabreski in World War II. He let his wingman get the kills. I'd have to do the same.

I wasn't worried about after my tour in September. If it was TAC it was OK, but the current plan had me going back to the Pentagon. That's what Ella expected and wanted. Brigadier General Jumper let me know that she was very vocal about it, so we would keep any talk of any assignment away from D.C. on the q.t. Jimmy was a tremendous ally on that subject, but he had no recourse on the "ace" mandate. Ella was also hoping I'd get my fifth MiG and be sent home early, and in glory. Well, I had big news for both of them. I told Jimmy I would slit my throat if they put me back in Air Defense. I also wasn't going to come home anytime soon. There would be no fifth MiG. There was no way in hell I'd leave my men.

From that point forward in the many missions of June, July, and August, I deliberately chose not to shoot down number five, wanting instead to finish my tour and lead my wing. My neck was stuck way out. I wouldn't stop flying, but it meant I couldn't fight, even when in a fight. There would be nine or ten more opportunities to get a MiG, sometimes so easy I could have closed my eyes and hosed off a Sidewinder, but I just sat there and looked at him. I let my wingman take him. It was hard.

About that time, I became embroiled in an incident that took on international proportions. I saw it as fallout from the continuing bad-mouthing going on between wings, especially from a few guys at Takhli toward everybody else. The wings showed personalities, both good and bad. Despite the fun parties and serious talking enjoyed at various tactics conferences, despite how much we were all visiting one another at different bases, despite gaining more respect and confidence in one another and working well together, the trash talk was still going on. Korat and Ubon were behaving, but Takhli had a real problem.

We were all frustrated about the target limitations imposed on us by Washington. Haiphong Harbor near Hanoi was the worst insult of all. We should have closed it down, blockaded, done whatever necessary to keep it from operating, but we couldn't touch it. Ships came in and went, bringing in supplies: MiGs, trucks, ammunition, food, cement to fix the blown bridges, you name it. The Vietcong troops received their stuff within days—and we were letting it happen!

There's a fine line between constructive competition and downright destructive bad-mouthing. That's what was happening with Takhli. They said nobody died as nobly as the boys from Takhli. Even between the F-105 wings, Takhli called themselves "Hertz" and insulted Korat as the "Avis" wing. Their tactics were right and everybody else was wrong. Everyone else stank and they were the only ones that were good. It was like standing in the middle of a grassy field with a circus mallet and pounding the earth around you for five or six hours until you are standing on a little tuft of grass surrounded by a sea of mud. You're not any higher than you were when you started pounding. In telling yourself, "Look how high I am, standing above all this!" you've just made yourself look silly. Worst of all, that field mouse pounded down into the mud will eventually recover and come back to bite. That is what happened with this incident.

We were coming off target on the northeast railroad. It was a tough mission in and out because of thunderstorms. Crossing out over the gulf I looked south and saw somebody in the process of attacking the dock at Hong Gai near Cam Pha. A couple of bombs went off near the dock. There had been a Russian ship tied up there for several days, an easy target for sure, but prohibited. I thought, Who in the hell is doing that? They weren't smokers and I knew where all of my guys were, so we pressed home.

About three days later, wires started coming in: "Who strafed the ship?" I thought, This is funny. Why are they asking me? I don't even have guns, for Christ's sake. About two weeks later, another message came in demanding the name, rank, serial number, and position of the flight and flight path in and out for each guy in my flight on that mission. I thought, Uh-oh.

Finally, the commander of PACAF, General Jack Ryan, showed up at Ubon and based himself there. He was conducting the investigation himself. I will never forget the night he told me how the investigation was going. He sat down in front of my desk and told me what he and his staff were finding. Somebody had strafed the ship and killed a Russian sailor, and it got all the way to the Kremlin. The Kremlin called the White House, and the White House told them to go to hell, the U.S. didn't do it. President Johnson's staff had asked the troops and they said they didn't do it. Everybody denied being anywhere near it. Brezhnev said, "Well, I am coming to the United States for a UN meeting and I'm bringing the evidence with me: photographs, shell fragments, damage reports, plus maybe the autopsy on the dead sailor." Still, there were utter denials.

General Ryan got a phone call toward the end of his meeting with me. He jumped in a T-39 to Takhli. He was back about three or four hours later, came into my trailer, sat down, shook his head sadly, and said, "I can't believe it. I have personally interviewed those people before. I've talked to everyone there and they had nothing but absolute flat-out, right-in-the-eye denials." Ryan told me that a sergeant finally broke. It was getting way over his head and he told one of Ryan's people that they ought to look into something that had to do with a film pack being deliberately destroyed. This sergeant was accountable for those film packs and he thought the trail was going to lead to him so he blew the whistle. Ryan's staff got the records and proved that a particular flight had shot their guns that day. There was denial that they had. It was found that the guns had been recharged but the film packs couldn't be accounted for. The packs were serially numbered and were assigned to each airplane by that number.

What happened was the guys who strafed the ship came back to Takhli when the wing commander, Bob Scott, was away. They took the film packs out of their bird to take to him. The NCO responsible told them he couldn't let the film out of his sight, so he accompanied them to the O club, where a party was going on. Colonel Jack Broughton, 355th Wing DO, who was a hell of a fighter pilot, came outside to meet with them. When they told him what had happened, he opened the film pack in front of the headlights of a jeep and exposed the film. The film went blank, and when asked by the investigation team, he said, "Sir, I have no evidence." The statement he made was not an outright lie, since the evidence of the strafing no longer existed, but he was brought up for court-martial along with the two pilots for destruction of government property instead of for violating the explicit rules of engagement. I know that he didn't want his guys nailed for strafing the ship, because everyone hated that damned off-limits harbor. His action was understandable, but clearly dishonest. A couple of fine young pilots got screwed over by a cover-up intended to preserve the wing's image. The real tragedy of the whole subterfuge was that the president of the United States got caught in a lie. Jack Broughton's career was ended.

After General Ryan left, I held an aircrew meeting and said, "Don't you guys ever do that to me, because I will never, ever do that to you! My loyalty is first to the oath that I swore as an officer to the Constitution of the United States. My loyalty is upward. My loyalty to you is as your commander. I will fight for you, I will protect you, and I will do everything I can, but I will not lie for you. I will not steal for you and I will not cheat for you. Don't you ever try to do it for me. If you screw up like that, come and tell me. You are in my outfit. It is my responsibility and I will make the decision and take the brunt of the reaction. That is my job and don't you ever try to deny me the fulfillment of the responsibilities of my job. Take this as a lesson, guys."

The 13th AF staff judge advocate soon called and said, "You have to report to Clark. You've been assigned to serve on a general court." I said, "Morey, I can't do that." He said, "Why not? It's an order from General Wilson [commander, 13th AF]. You have to." I said, "No, Morey, I can't do that. You will just make yourselves look silly." He repeated the order, and I knew I could not divulge what Ryan had told me. Ryan had spoken to me in confidence and I treated it in confidence. So I had to jump in an F-4, fly all the way to Clark, and sit down to wait for half a day while they went through the bullshit. When the staff judge advocate finally asked, "Does anyone on the court, or on the board, know of any reason why he should not serve?" I stood up and said, "Yes, I do." The judge asked me why. "Because I have material knowledge of the evidence in this case." Then I marched out of the courtroom and flew back home.

Throughout June and July MiG CAP missions worked well, the result of good tactics developed with the F-105s. Targets were nearly all railroad yards, where we encountered heavy flak yet few SAMs and even fewer MiGs. I questioned the effectiveness of railroad strikes day after day and had several go-rounds with HQ on it. We needed to broaden our target base. Good military targets still existed—supply dumps, warehouses, barracks, training areas, lines of communication, bridges—but we were hampered by Washington's policy of politeness. It was a daily frustration.

The battles went on. We were fighting for all we were worth. God, I loved my guys. They all understood why the Old Man wasn't firing at MiGs and they became even better pilots in the deal. The old wolf taunted the enemy, snarled face-to-face, wore them down, then danced aside for the pack to come in for the kill. My own tactics under my self-imposed no-kill zone became sharpened by the new challenge. Briefings intensified and debriefings shortened and sharpened; nights at the O club were ribald, loose, off-the-charts fun.

Daytime desk duties droned by, almost with a sense of normalcy. Ruby was the most professional secretary I'd ever known and she ran a tight ship. It freed me to do all the running around necessary to my job, but there were also light moments around the office. There was the day Chappie casually mentioned that I ought to review the end-of-tour report prepared by our Catholic chaplain.

"Who?" I asked.

"Our Catholic chaplain," he responded.

"Damn, Chappie, I didn't know we had one."

"Come on, boss, stop kidding. He's been picked for an out-briefing and I think you should review his report."

"What's the matter?" I asked. "Why don't you take care of it?"

"Now, boss, you're getting upset. We'll drop it for now."

His concern told me there was something I should see, but when he sensed my reaction, he clammed up. In those days an out-briefing meant the selected individual gave a written and oral report at each echelon of command all the way back to the Pentagon. I'm not sure what was done with the information, but it seemed to be a prying effort on the part of staff officers involved. Several days later I reminded Chappie of his concern and asked to see the report he was so worried about.

"Now, boss, don't get mad."

"OK, Chappie, I won't. Just give me that report." I took one look at the first paragraph, and shouted, "Damn it, Chappie, get that son of a bitch in here!"

"My God, boss, you can't call a chaplain that! See, I knew you'd get mad."

"OK, OK, I'll try to be good. Just get him in here."

The chaplain showed up and sauntered up to my desk. He was in uniform with his captain's bars on one collar and his chaplain's insignia on the other. He was sort of roly-poly and just stood there.

I looked at him and asked quietly if he considered himself an officer in the United States Air Force. He acknowledged that he was.

"Then salute!" I said, which he did with some difficulty.

"Now, Chaplain, about this report of yours. In the very first paragraph you clearly state that the wing commander openly tolerated and even encouraged his senior enlisted personnel to live off base and to cohabitate with the native women. You go on to condemn my actions, inferring I approved of the men hiring cleaning ladies and domestic help for sexual reasons. I'm not at all sure how you know this, but let me tell you something. There are over eight thousand men on this base, more than we have barracks for. So the senior NCOs have to live somewhere. Now, I am responsible for their food, their work, their clothing, their on-base recreation, and their total response to our mission. All that and more are the things that fall under my responsibilities as the wing commander. Their morals are YOUR responsibility, and it appears to me you are trying to shift the blame for your failure onto my shoulders. You may be sure I shall make note of that in my evaluation of your performance. Now, please remove yourself and think about what I've said."

I could see Chappie watching the proceedings through the philodendron screen between our desks. When the chaplain departed, he came around to my desk and wanted to know what I was going to do about that report.

"Why, nothing about the report, Chappie, but get the transportation officer over here and find a copy of the chaplain's orders. Meanwhile I'll call the Chief of Chaplain's Office in Washington and explain what happened and what I'm going to do about it."

With some changes to the wording of his orders, our chaplain found himself returning home the other way around the world. The last I heard he was having quite a problem finding transportation out of Saudi Arabia. I presume he ultimately arrived back in the States because, surely, God was on his side.

Days later, my vice wing commander committed a breach of etiquette I just couldn't forgive. I had a pair of flying socks in my desk drawer—mind you, they were my lucky socks, left over from World War II. I wore them on every mission and washed them from time to time, but obviously not enough for Chappie. He opened that drawer one day when I was gone and threw my socks away. The next morning before a mission: no socks. Ruby looked puzzled and was honest in her denial of any knowledge, so I immediately confronted Chappie. I was pissed. He relented under my anger and confessed to throwing them away. I ordered him outside into the trash container to retrieve them. When he came back into the office some time later, it was obvious that the previous night's garbage from the mess had been thrown on top of the socks. Chappie was a mess and stank to high heaven. I let him know in no uncertain terms that he smelled far worse than my socks ever could. Then I put on my socks, pulled on my boots, and went out to fly another successful mission.

In late July a tech came over with a helmet camera that Hughes Aircraft wanted me to wear in the cockpit. It looked like the head of Medusa, with tubes and wires coming out all over the place, connecting to God knows where. I was supposed to capture live-action combat film as I turned my head in flight. My F-4, now *SCAT XXVII*, was out of commission for days as the tech worked with the ground crew to get the support equipment for the headset installed. I argued that the gadget was useless but finally agreed to test it. The first flight proved it all. While pulling g's in a hard turn around some MiGs, I tried to check six. No dice. Couldn't even turn my head back over my shoulder. I pulled up and out of the fight and came home raging mad. That helmet disappeared overnight. It probably ended up on a shelf behind some guy's basement bar in Utah.

Pilots from other wings often dropped over for social times at the O club, as we did at their bases. One of my favorites was a kid named Lieutenant Karl Richter, a 1964 Air Force Academy grad. We liked each other enormously. He was an F-105 pilot from Korat with a great career in front of him. At the age of twenty-three, he was the youngest pilot to shoot down a MiG. Tragically, he was killed on July 28. At the time he had 198 missions over North Vietnam, more than any other guy in the theater. I was really broken up when I heard. Richter had been flying with a new pilot on his wing when he spotted a bridge. He instructed the trainee to stay above to watch as he rolled his F-105 toward the target. Enemy antiaircraft artillery opened up, hit his Thud, and forced him to eject. His trainee watched Karl's parachute disappear into cloud cover. Rescue forces reached him but he died en route to the hospital from injuries received during his ejection. It was a hell of a loss for all of us.

Richter's buddies at Korat knew that Karl and I were great pals. They decided to give me a remembrance, something of Karl's I admired: his pet monkey. Just a day or two after Karl went down, I opened the door of my trailer to utter disaster: all cupboard doors and drawers stood open, toilet paper lay in ribbons from one end to the other, a potted plant was dumped over, and dirt was everywhere. My pillow had been dismantled, dishes and glasses were broken, files were hurled, work papers and maps were shredded beyond recognition. That damn monkey sat screeching and laughing on the top of a cupboard with his next missile clenched in a tiny fist. I roared and lunged at him. The comedic chase scene that followed ended only because the Korat guys had kindly left the harness and leash on the critter. I threw the little beast into the head and slammed the door. But there might be the potential for some fun.

The next morning, I showed up at the office with the monkey perched docilely on my shoulder. Ruby just laughed at my story. Chappie was horrified. "Boss, you're not going to keep that thing, are you?" Yup, I sure was. Then I announced the monkey's name would be "Stokely Carmichael." Chappie's face was a sight to see at that news. It tickled me no end. Well, Stokely didn't last more than half an hour in the office. His mischief and chattering were impossible. I ordered a cage built and installed outside my trailer. That became his home. He became the wing mascot. Nights at the O club were especially entertaining. The guys would bail out and dive for cover when I walked in. The Thais on the O club staff were scared to death of the monkey but knew they couldn't do anything. I'd put Stokely down on the bar and that damned monkey would make one pass down the length, knocking over every glass in his path. Sometimes he'd stop to jam nuts into his mouth or stick his fist way down into a glass and fling beer in all directions. Then he'd jump onto the back shelves and make one pass down behind the bottles, screeching the whole way. It was chaos: bottles breaking, guys yelling while protecting their drinks, Thai waitresses screaming, the bar manager shouting a stream of Thai curses, and me laughing. What was their problem?

I was not immune to return favors. Bill Kirk and Joe Moore plus three or four other guys decided to haul an F-4 drag chute behind a jeep at a great rate of speed to see if it would blossom and slow the jeep down. They dragged it all over the ramp and never did get the damn thing to open. With that failure they thought it would be fun to drape the chute all over the inside of my trailer. Maybe they didn't realize how dirty it was, or then again maybe they did. When I returned to base the next day and opened the door to my trailer, there was grime and gravel and oil all over the couch, chairs, table, and bed underneath the chute. I knew instantly who had done it.

The guys were in the tactics room when a note was handed to Kirk. It read, "An unauthorized piece of Air Force property was stolen, damaged, and improperly displayed. The perpetrators of this offense are put on notice. A report will be placed in the appropriate personnel files." Best of all, when Bill and Joe returned to their room, Stokely was there to greet them. Their bedroom and bathroom were totally destroyed, every surface was covered with shaving cream, and monkey shit adorned the walls. Those guys avoided me for weeks.

New tasking came in August. Target: the mile-long Paul Doumer Bridge spanning the Red River at Hanoi. The bridge was a principal link for both road and rail traffic from China and the industrial area north of the Red to the capital, Hanoi. It had been on the list of restricted targets. On August 11, it was released. We'd seen the bridge and knew it was a significant target. We knew the enemy would fight like hell to defend it. We'd have to fight like hell to destroy it. If this first effort was unsuccessful, the defenses would only get bigger. The bridge had to be dropped on the first strike. Accuracy was imperative. No civilian areas near the bridge were to be hit. We were told to expect the heaviest defenses yet encountered in the war. We believed it.

Colonel Bob White led the 355th strike force out of Takhli. He would also coordinate the entire package planning and serve as the mission commander. The F-105s from the Korat wing would be led by the 469th Squadron commander, Lieutenant Colonel Harry Schurr. I would lead the 8th. We would have the usual package of MiG CAP, Wild Weasels, EB-66 jamming, and two four-ship flights of F-105s with cluster bombs dedicated to flak suppression.

The frag caught us by surprise. Takhli had already loaded 750-pound bombs and wing tanks for a second mission of the day. Crews scrambled to download everything. They reloaded the Thuds with 3,000-pound bombs and centerline tanks. Crews were quickly briefed in all the wings, and by early afternoon the force crossed the Red River and was moving down Thud Ridge toward Hanoi.

Heavy flak and missiles showed up before we reached the target area. The strike force, moving en masse, sailed right into it. Damn I was proud of those Thud drivers for not dropping their ordnance early and hightailing it out of there. The flak-suppression flights dropped their CBUs on the active flak sites on the approaches to the bridge and blew several of them to hell. My gut was clenched when I saw the first of their flights disappear ahead into the ugly black smoke, followed by the first force of bridge-bombing Thuds. MiGs suddenly came out of Phuc Yen about 20 miles out but passed right under the formation, making no attempt to engage. What the hell? More showed up to harass the force and we engaged them. MiGs made several unsuccessful attempts, but couldn't outbattle us. As we rolled and feinted with the MiGs, I watched the flights of Thuds roll in one after the other, releasing their bombs through the flak. The impacts of 3,000-pounders enveloped the bridge!

Following them, I roared the Wolfpack over the target, the wail of the Phantom J-79s adding a new tone to the cacophony over Hanoi. If it was possible, the flak seemed intensified. They threw everything they had at us. We dove into the chaos and dropped our 750-pound Mk-82s on target, then pulled up to resume defending the departing force from MiGs. Another wave of F-105s screamed in to ensure the strike. More M-118 3,000-pounders. Huge orange balls of fire exploded. With each detonation, the humid air flashed clouds looking for all the world like miniature A-bombs. As I led my flight up and out, two unarmed RF-4Cs drew a tremendous barrage of antiaircraft fire as they flew low over the bridge to film the results of the strike mission. Two spans of the bridge were dropped and not a single bomb fell on civilian areas. Best of all, we all made it safely home: a perfect mission made perfect by outstanding coordination among the wings and the extreme bravery of many pilots against the heaviest odds seen to date in North Vietnam. I was extremely proud of the Wolfpack.

On the thirteenth, the 8th Wing's morning mission was a MiG CAP to cover F-105s inbound on the Canal des Rapides Bridge just upriver from Doumer. My force would bomb the marshaling yard northeast of Hanoi on egress. I named Ron Catton, call sign "Cadillac," mission leader. I took up the flank, leading the fourth flight as "Chevy." The MiGs were stirred up by our recent bridge strikes, so we expected some action. My flight would be first to engage any MiG attack, and sure enough, just before we left the Thuds and turned toward our target area, a single MiG-21 came screaming through our formation from five o'clock going to eleven o'clock, heading toward Thud Ridge. I gave chase and told my flight to hang in with the others. This might be fun! I zoomed after that little fucker, knowing I could scare the shit out of him. Just as he crossed over Phuc Yen, two SAMs came up at me and I dove to evade. I lost sight of one SAM, but the other curved right around and hit the MiG! It was beautiful! I laughed cynically as the MiG crashed just off the Phuc Yen runway. I knew they were listening on the radio so I said, "Congratulations, you dumb bastards!"

I turned hard back toward the battle and joined up with my flight. One of my guys—it turned out to be Catton—was in a vertical climb, pouring smoke from a direct hit on one engine, with three MiG-17s hot on his trail. He called to me, "Hey, Chevy, I've got three MiGs cornered at six o'clock!" That wise-ass, I'd have to chew his butt later for that remark. Just as Catton reversed, head-on, straight down through the MiG formation I ordered him, "Come out on the grass toward Thud Ridge and shut up!"

He went down low over the rice paddies and into the small-arms fire of farmers whacking at him with their rifles, the MiG-17s right behind and closing. An F-4 on one engine even in afterburner was easy prey for a MiG-17. He was a sitting duck. I called my flight. "OK, Chevy. Let's go!" We screamed in off the ridge just as the MiGs got into gun range behind Catton. We fired Sparrow missiles head-on at them over his canopy. So much for my decision not to get number five. Oh well, only a month left anyway. Damned if I was going to let the enemy get one of my guys! The MiGs wisely broke northeast for home. We chased for a minute until I called, "Egress!" My flight turned southwest, toward our tanker.

I called Catton, who was alone and headed outbound. "Cadillac, Chevy Lead here. What's your status?"

"Smoke in the cockpit, fire light on, losing fuel rapidly, will bail out over Laos. Call rescue."

"OK, Cadillac, you hang in there!" I knew he was in deep shit, losing fuel big-time and still over enemy territory.

A KC-135 tanker pilot listening in immediately got on the horn. "Negative, Cadillac Lead, Red Anchor 31 here. I'll come up to get you. Give me your coordinates." The tanker pressed far north of his limit and met Catton's F-4 just south of the Black River. They joined up and headed out back toward

Udorn. Catton described his battle damage and fire-warning light to the pilot, concerned for the tanker's safety.

"Cadillac Lead, get your sorry ass in position for hookup before I change my mind!"

What a warrior! There aren't many tanker guys who can buy a drink in a fighter bar. Turned out that KC-135 dragged Catton all the way to Udorn, where he dropped off for a flameout pattern. After landing, his left engine quit, damaged when the right was destroyed. Quite a day at the office!

A week later, Catton appeared at my office with a rumor coming out of HQ that Red Anchor 31 was to be court-martialed for coming after him over North Vietnam. After thinking about it for a moment I said, "Hell, no sweat. Put him in for the Silver Star!" We did just that and the court-martial was canceled.

The day after the battle, I went to the 7th for a meeting and laughed with some guys from intelligence and ops about the SAM hitting that MiG. We chuckled over how beautiful it was. I said, "You know, I still can't figure out how they goofed. The only thing different I noticed was the MiG was up pretty high. Usually, they aren't."

The intel guy said, "Oh yes, he was above his missile-tight altitude."

I asked, "What is that?"

"He blundered up above 3,500 feet, and they have missile-tight below 3,500 feet. That keeps their MiGs from being engaged."

"No shit. How long have you known that?"

He said, "Oh, that has been the rule for a couple of weeks now."

"You dumb fucking asshole, why didn't you tell us?"

"Colonel, it's up to ops to tell you."

The ops guy said, "Hell, we didn't know it!"

I was furious. "Why didn't you bastards tell me? Just three days ago I came off a target, went whistling across the Delta just north of Hanoi, and had twenty-eight SAMs shot at me in about two minutes. All I had to do was go down to 500 feet? Why didn't you tell me?!"

"Well, it's highly classified."

Classified, my ass! Keeping a secret from whom? The enemy knew their policy already! Intelligence and operations weren't working together. Un-fucking-believable. The real tragedy of this screwup would hit us hard in the last week of August.

The edge was taken off my anger for a couple of days, August 18–19, when Ubon hosted the second practice reunion for the Red River valley pilots. Guys came in from Takhli, Korat, Da Nang, and Udorn for a great tactics session. The first night's party was at our O club. Stokely nearly got shot during one of his sweeps down the bar, so he stayed in his cage for the rest of the gathering. The next day's meeting accomplished more good tactics discussions and selected an emblem for the group. The RRVFPA came into being. All wings had finally developed some friendship and mutual respect on the ground and in the air. We had progressed and improved on missions together. The reunion finale was a monumental blowout in downtown Ubon. Everyone survived, I think.

Eighth Wing's tactics continued evolving over my last two months. We learned a ton as we flew supporting the F-105 wings on strike missions, slipping in sequence with them, enjoying the protection of all the pods, and completing some damned fine strikes. But tactics had to be flexible to meet changing conditions and situations up north. MiGs were up in August, snapping at our heels, hitting hard and flying smart. In intel at Ubon we were going crazy trying to figure out what was happening that was different. I studied photos, drew different coordinates on my desk map, then erased and plotted again, trying to find a pattern, working like hell to change our tactics to beat the enemy's.

On August 23, I led a MiG CAP from Ubon as part of the overall force hitting the Yen Vien railroad and Doumer Bridge in Hanoi again. Those industrious little bastards had put every available citizen immediately to work repairing the bridge. It was functional again. We kept bombing. They kept rebuilding. It was a hellish game of tag.

About 60 miles northwest of our target, Big Eye called, "Bandits! Bandits!" If the MiGs were up, there would be no SAMs. I couldn't split off with my flight and go hunt them down, so we had to follow protocol, sticking close to the Thuds to protect them when MiGs appeared.

Suddenly, Jesus Christ! Two MiG-21s came screaming in supersonic at six o'clock and knocked two of my guys down with Atoll air-to-air missles before we knew where they were coming from. That broke up the package as we turned after them to fight. Everyone was turning, calling wingmen, pulling g's, firing missiles, diving and climbing. Our sequencing and bombing plan was shot to hell as we reformed approaching the target. Another F-4 was lost just as we got there. It was becoming a disaster. I turned to engage a number of MiG-17s just north of Phuc Yen. In the course of this fight, the F-105 force egressed through the area, going like bats out of hell. As I turned right from an unsuccessful pass on two 17s, I saw an F-105 in afterburner in a steep inverted dive closing on the tail of a 17, which was on the tail of an outbound F-105 barely 200 feet away from me at 2,000 feet. That Thud had to be going at least 1.25 Mach! He looked like a shark after a minnow. I could see his tracers and the muzzle flare back from his 20 mm Vulcan. He was firing like mad, scoring numerous hits on the MiG. I breached radio discipline and shouted at the unknown pilot, "Go get 'em, Thud!" The MiG caught fire, rolled inverted, and went into a nearly vertical dive. God, it was a thrilling sight. The next instant I was worried that the Thud's closure rate was so fast he wouldn't be able to pull out in time. I rolled left to watch him and saw the MiG strike the ground in a fireball as the Thud pulled up just above the ground and tore off after his outbound flight.

When I got home I jumped on the phone after debriefing and called Colonel Flynn at Korat. "I want to confirm some great goddamn son of a bitch's kill today!" Flynn walked back into the 388th debriefing and told Lieutenant Dave Waldrop that Colonel Robin Olds had just confirmed his kill.

The sight of Waldrop saving the ass of a fellow F-105 and knocking down a MiG in the process was the only good thing about that black day. Six of my guys were gone. I learned that three had bailed out, one was dead, and the fate of the other two remained unknown until the POWs were released in 1973.

How the hell had it happened? I charged down to the 7th two days later to find out what they knew. The same intelligence fellow told me, "Well, yes, the MiGs have been practicing for two weeks to get into a position to do that. They've been taking off when the strike force is coming in, circling at high altitude, and practicing dives in pairs to come in behind you."

I thundered at him, "Why in hell didn't you tell me?"

"Well, it's too . . . it's sensitive. It's classified."

"Goddamn you, there are six young fighter pilots up in Hanoi right now because you did not tell me, because you did not let me know. Something like that would have been easy to counter, but you chose to withhold vital information. You are the direct cause of our loss of six men and three airplanes. Goddamn you to hell!" We almost came to blows.

With the end of my tour coming up in late September, I dreaded the assignment coming my way. My requests to stay at Ubon for another tour, or at least stay in a combat command someplace, anyplace, were getting nowhere. Please, God, not a staff job; not the Pentagon again. I was doomed and I knew it. When the news came in early August, it was a complete surprise. Chief of Staff John P. McConnell sent a letter informing me that Lieutenant General Thomas Samuel Moorman, superintendent at the U.S. Air Force Academy, had personally requested my assignment there as commandant. What? Were they nuts? What would the Air Force Academy do with a grizzled old disgruntled fighter pilot in charge of the cadets? I was stunned and questioned the news immediately. Word was they wanted something completely different from the norm. A combat veteran could energize the corps. Cadets were looking for a hero. McConnell thought it was a great idea. He told me General Gabe Disosway had a son there and Brigadier General Herbert Bench had two. Those boys reported that my picture was up in 50 percent of the rooms. The academy was short on spirit, enthusiasm, and dedication. They needed my guts and fire.

My reporting date was October. Oh God, what on earth could I do with a bunch of eighteen- to twenty-two-year-old kids? I called my old friend Ben Cassiday, now a brigadier general, for his opinion. Ben was a World War II combat pilot, recently flying F-4s as commander of the 36th TFW at Bitburg, and he had been on the startup of the academy in the late 1950s. He had been deputy commandant and commander of the Cadet Wing through the graduation of the first class in 1959. He would give me the straight word. He did; he laughed. Ben's amusement was about my confusion, but he assured me it would be a great assignment, a new challenge, not to worry. I thought about Karl Richter and the many other academy grads I had in the 8th. Maybe it was OK. There were far bigger problems than moving to Colorado to a job I thought unsuited to my abilities; there was telling Ella we were leaving D.C.

With the end of my tour in sight and all hell breaking loose with the MiGs using their new tactics, I ramped up training and tactics meetings in the first three weeks of September, flying lead on as many missions as I could. I made another pitch to the Pentagon to stay for another tour. No deal. Office hours were spent preparing a report to be delivered in a speech to the guys on my last day: a recap of the past year plus vital information I wanted to cram into their heads. I was exhausted. I felt frantic, cornered, trapped by my ordered September 27 departure. My replacement, Colonel Bob Spencer, arrived two days before my final mission, and my time was filled with showing him the ropes. I could tell he'd be a different kind of commander. I scheduled my last mission on September 23 because we were fragged up north. This would be my one hundredth "official" mission, fifty-two short of the actual number I'd flown.

To my disappointment, the twenty-third dawned with weather preventing missions to Hanoi. The alternative was Route Pack I so I decided to do something a little special. Three men, Bill Kirk, W. T. "Mac" McAdoo, and Joe Moore, had been flying with me since Bentwaters. We knew one another well. I trusted them implicitly in flight, knew they would follow my lead, and tapped them as my wingmen for that final mission.

We took off as scheduled. We roamed around Route Pack I looking for targets, found a few minor things, dropped bombs, then formed up at altitude. I'd briefed them before the mission on my intentions. "OK, guys, let's put on a little air show for the gang at home, tight diamond formation, Thunderbird style. We're gonna practice for a few minutes." We practiced a series of maneuvers for less than ten minutes before heading home. I called ahead and got traffic cleared. We came screaming in low over the runway in tight diamond for the first pass, then up into a loop, followed by a barrel roll. Each pass was tight and low over the runway. When we landed, drenched with sweat, we could hear the shouts and whistles from the crowd over the whine of our engines while we taxied in. Debriefing was a nonevent. Colonel Spencer had watched the show and predictably wasn't happy. He later told the guys they could never do that again. Beyond that, even traditional victory rolls over the runway were prohibited.

I climbed out of my gear in the equipment room and, still in my sweaty flight suit, headed toward the O club; the guys surprised me by hoisting me on their shoulders and carrying me to the club and up the front steps. It's a good thing there was a lot of shouting going on, because I couldn't stop the tears running down my face. It was, without question, the proudest moment of my career.

The club was jammed with the crews. Our three American girls, Ruby, Kathy, and Marge, were there, along with the Thai staff and people from across the base. It took a while to settle everyone down to listen to my prepared speech. I choked down a ton of emotion when I faced my Wolfpack for the last time.

"Hello, gang. I'd like to take the opportunity at this last pilots' meeting not to really say good-bye to you, but to at least talk to you while I'm sober! This afternoon I'd like to recap this last year for you. I'll try to be as brief as possible, go over some of the things that influenced the changes around here, point out the current problems, perhaps even anticipate some of your future problems, and certainly during the course of the monologue, to express my deep affection for you all. Anyhow, where's my board? Damn it! Somebody go get that working board." There was laughter as the large map of North Vietnam and Laos was dragged from the back of the room.

I spent the next half hour describing the events, battles, tactics, HQ orders, enemy maneuvers, missile snafus, characteristics of MiG-17s and MiG-21s, SAMs, strike logistics, communication glitches, mission successes and failures, base problems and solutions, and wins and losses the wing had experienced under my command. From October 1, 1966, through August 31, 1967, the 8th TFW flew 13,249 combat sorties over North Vietnam and Laos and 1,983 combat support sorties over Laos, for a total of 15,232 sorties and 27,880 hours. The wing experienced 37 aircraft losses, 29 in combat, 18 in RP 6A, 2 in RP 5, 5 in RP 1, and 4 in Laos. Seven were operational losses, and 1 was lost while on loan to the 366th at Da Nang. A total of seventy-two 8th TFW crew members were involved. Six were killed, thirty-two were missing in action, and thirty-four were rescued, a 47 percent recovery rate of lost aircrews. I went on to name every man down, the date he went down, and his current status. It was hard to get through that list.

I drilled down with advice: Stay alert, listen to the Wild Weasel calls, maintain radio discipline, don't screw around with fuel, don't go in alone, be flexible for changing tactics, use the intel library, don't go dead between the ears. "Don't be complacent! Don't be pigheaded! You guys in the front seat think you know it all, that you don't need the checklist. Have the guy in the back read the bloody checklist to you. Your bomb switches, your pretakeoff, postlanding, the emergency procedures, the whole nine yards. Even the little bit about the pretanker check. For Christ's sake, be a team!

"All of you guys are the greatest. The squadron's the best. You Night Owls are something else. I tried flying with you a couple of times and was terrified. I can't do what you do. I chickened out! All of you—remember, when you go home you're not going to be the same young guy that swaggered in here. You've had the experience of a lifetime and it'll be tough when you get home. That sweet wife who waved good-bye is not going to recognize you when you walk back in that front door. She'll sense immediately that you've changed. She's going to want to know why and how you've changed because she'll want to know where she stands with this stranger she's married to. I guarantee you, within the first ten days home you're going to have a fight. You'll probably go to a party or two in your hometown, where they'll sort of half-ass welcome you back. Your best friend from high school or college will walk up to you and tell you what a dumb shit you are for having been fighting this stupid war. Then you'll fly off the handle at him, or you'll want to tell someone what it was all about, and you'll realize that nobody gives a damn. Remember I told you this; it might make it easier.

"You still have a helluva war ahead of you, gang! There are an awful lot of MiGs up there, and they're getting more aggressive every day. You're sure going to have some fun, and I'm certainly going to envy you. I know the 8th Wing is going to go at it with great spirit, high morale, superb skill, and the application of absolutely the best tactics. I know the Wolfpack will keep right on improving! I hope those MiGs show soon because it's been a long dry spell since June. You've got some hard work in front of you. In closing I'd like to remind you of something: The period of time you spend here with the 8th Tac Fighter Wing is going to be one of the finest experiences in your lives and it will influence you for the rest of your days! You're going to look back on this as the highlight in your career. So I ask you, give it everything you've got; enjoy it to the hilt! Be soldiers, be warriors, be men, not babies but men! Take every scrap of pleasure in your comradeship with one another and your growing knowledge of yourselves. You know what's in your heart and how hard that old heart beats sometimes when you're lying in bed at night facing a hard one in the morning. Go anyway! You're learning a lot about yourself. It's true for everybody else in the damn hooch lying around you. You're not alone. That's the greatest thing, troops—it's teamwork that does it. It's friendship that cements it together. It is dedication that accomplishes the mission. You've got those attributes and more! Godamn it, I am so proud of you I could cry. God bless you shit hot fighter pilots. I love you all. I wish you all the best from the bottom of my heart. Carry on."

With emotion I couldn't contain, I had to turn away to go behind a curtain as bedlam broke out. The kids had never seen this side of the Old Man. It was the most deeply felt moment of my life, I wanted to bawl like a baby, but the party was on! Someone thrust a shining silver tankard of beer into my hand, and the cheering crowd propelled me over to a cake, which I cut with a great, dramatic flourish. We nearly blew the roof off the club for the rest of the day.

As the afternoon wore into evening, I found myself seeking a quiet corner with Ruby to thank her for her fine work and dedication. We had developed a strong friendship and mutual respect over the months since her arrival but had kept the relationship strictly professional. I trusted her and enjoyed her easy banter. She had made my office a sanctuary. As we talked and spent time together at the party, other feelings emerged. There was something more, something deeper between us. I had less than a week left on base, with no flying and no official duties. It was obvious where I'd spend most of my time. Ruby and I left the club together that night and I melted into the arms of a woman who welcomed this weary old warrior with sweet tenderness and grace.

The following few days became a blur. I dropped into the background of life on base. Most people thought I had already left. I spent some time visiting each of the shops, said my good-byes to the Thais, sorted through papers, packed up belongings, and shipped my footlocker. Stokely found a home safely behind bars in the local zoo. Mostly, I spent time with Ruby. I knew she'd be a friend for life.

On September 27 I headed home with a heavy heart. I didn't want to go back to Ella. Affection, friendship, and passion had come my way again. It bore no resemblance to my bleak marriage. From Clark AFB, I flew in another baby blue Braniff to Honolulu. The plane was met by a crowd of reporters. Oh Jesus Christ! In answer to their questions I told them, "Look, I haven't had a wink of sleep in twenty-four hours. I want breakfast, a hot shower, and to go hide somewhere for four days. I'm honored to have had this tour and feel a great deal of humility when I think of all the fine young men still fighting. Right now, all I want to do is get used to the fact that for me, from here on out, there will be a tomorrow. I consider my new job at USAFA a tremendous challenge and I'm quite flattered with the assignment."

I checked into the BOQ at Hickam. I needed time to think, to be alone, to hold still, to decide. The mirror in my room reflected a man hollowed out by a year of war. Thirty-five pounds were gone, my face was gaunt, my jaw was clenched, my hair was thin and graying, and there were deep circles under my eyes. Only my mustache was alive and well. I noticed my hands shaking when lifting a glass later at the Hickam O club. Being around the guys felt familiar and right. Many of them looked like hell, too. It didn't matter. We were family. After several drinks at the club I went out to the beach, swam out into the ocean, and just floated on my back. Despite the Honolulu lights, the stars were bright. Looking up at them, feeling totally alone, I cried. The tears finally came in the privacy of that warm, safe water. The decision was made. I was not going home. There wasn't enough left of me to go from one war to another. I could stay in Hawaii for a while, go over to my maternal aunt Steve's house on the Big Island, eat avocados, pineapples, and bananas from her trees, sleep, get fat, carve wood. I didn't care. It didn't matter.

Two days later, an hour before the scheduled late-afternoon flight, I picked up the phone to call Ella with the news. The long-distance line crackled and hissed; the phone rang once, twice, three times. "Hello?" It was my daughter Chris.

"Hi, Chrissie. It's your old man." God, I hadn't heard her voice in a year.

"Daddy! Oh, Daddy, when are you coming home? I've missed you so much."

"Baby, can you put your mother on the phone?"

"Uh, no, Daddy, she's out somewhere." At 8:00 P.M. Washington time, I knew that meant Ella was deep in her cups. Chris lowered her voice and said tearfully, "Daddy, please, please come home. Susie and I really need you."

And that was that. "OK, Chrissie, I'll be home tomorrow. Don't worry."

All the way across the Pacific and the mainland I thought hard about my year at Ubon Ratchathani. My command was the culmination of many years of preparation. It was a highlight of this man's career, not, as many outsiders supposed, because of the physical action of the mission, but because of the total experience: serving with dedicated men, sharing deep respect and comradeship forged on an anvil of challenge and danger. It was a time of maximum effort where every single man contributed his best for the good of the whole. Each man was as important as the next in getting the job done. It was a time of courage and self-discipline, of deadly seriousness and riotous fun. Each man was measured and stood revealed in the esteem accorded him by his comrades. The unit became larger than the sum of its parts and buoyed each man in his performance. It was a deep human experience for all of us; each was made a better man for it, each a better member of our air force, and a more dedicated member of our American society. All that we stood for, everything that we meant to one another, would last all of our days. We needed to remember our days with the Wolfpack, and in remembering, keep the faith in each other and in our nation. Battles would surely continue on a different scale in different arenas. We would carry on that battle wherever the enemy appeared, be it national, neighborhood, or personal. I prayed we'd never shirk our fight for truth, decency, law, integrity, and justice, and for our home, America. We fought for her; many of us died for her. We believed in her, and under God, we would preserve her.

On the long flight toward D.C., I remembered the people, the pilots of the 8th TFW, all the ground crews, what they did and how they felt. I remembered the supreme effort made by all: laboring under the scorching sun or a tropical downpour, working to meet the frag, supporting our daily lives, feeding us, housing us, supplying us. I remembered lines of bomb-laden trucks outside the gates of the ammo storage area, the surgical delicacy of a young airman working in a precision-measurement equipment lab or in the electronics shop, the curses of load crews faced with almost impossible weapon changes, the old sergeant major proudly escorting a crowd of VIPs through an immaculate shop, the hustle of crews on the arming ramp, a crew chief or dock crew working long past the shift change, the guys in the lox plant or over at the avionics shop, the firemen and rescue troops, the medics and communicators, the stock chaser, every man in every job doing his best, making the Wolfpack an efficient and proud combat unit. I also remembered the wonderful Thai women who took care of us in the O club and base services, how proud the waitresses were when I insisted they wear their traditional Thai dresses instead of the ridiculous and demeaning club waitress outfits. I will never forget the gentle humor and sweetness of the Thai people, always a smile, always a teasing remark, always such peacefulness in their attitudes and thankfulness for everything in their lives. They are a people full of grace, and I thanked them.

I thought back to the night we buried Rapid Roger, our return from Bolo, Thai Nguyen, Kep, Hoa Lac, Bac Giang, Gia Lam, SAMs, MiGs, endless flak. I remembered Mu Gia and Dong Hoi, Banana Valley and the Y, Thud Ridge and the Elbow, the Loop and Yen Bai, Cricket and Brigham, Panama and Lion, Orange Anchor and Channel 97, Ban Ban and San Nuea, 2:00 A.M. mission planning, Doug Cairn's face after the Valentine's Day mission, and Phil Combies's remarks on Easter Sunday. There was the BRIDGE, Aussie snow on Christmas Day, the navy commander who tried to close the stag bar, my birthday party on July 14, Bill Kirk's request on May 2 over Hoa Lac. How could I ever forget Dick Pascoe and Tom Hirsch playing Recce Jock on January 6, Mother Baader and the Night Owls over Hoa Loc and Kep, J. B. Stone, Bob Pardo, Bill Kirk, McAdoo, Moore—some of the finest men on earth—Doc Broadway, J. D. Covington, and great guys like Clifton, Wetterhahn, Raspberry, Dunnegan, Croker, Wayne, Wells, and all the great backseaters. I remembered Chappie James, who was a friend for life and destined

for greater renown, both good and bad. I'd never forget the first tactics conference, then practice reunions, Scrappy Johnson, elephants, and the welcoming
parades for the new squadrons from Eglin. I'd never forget any of it.

As the airplane touched down at Andrews AFB on October 2, I knew I
was leaving a big chunk of my heart behind in Thailand. I would need a good
chunk of my courage for what lay ahead.

20

★

The Painful Way Home

I stepped off the plane in D.C. into glaring midday sunshine. Ella, Chris, and Susie ran into my arms at the bottom of the ramp. A group of photographers started a feeding frenzy. Chris said, "Daddy, you're so skinny!" Susie curled her long hair from each side across her upper lip in imitation of a mustache, and a photo was taken that would be widely published in newspapers. It was very emotional to hold my children again. Now fully teenagers at fifteen and fourteen, they had changed greatly over the year.

An aide to the chief of staff led us to an air force car parked on the ramp, and we piled into the back, the aide into the front. He swiveled back to tell me that I had to meet right away with McConnell at the Pentagon before going home. Ella's plans had been for a private but elegant dinner at home with just the family. She started to protest this interruption but stopped when I put my hand on her knee and squeezed. Hard. The driver dropped me with the general's aide at the Pentagon and took the girls to our house in Spring Valley.

On the hallowed D Ring floor, the aide placed an eye against a small peephole, opened the door, then turned and said, "OK, you can go in now."

I stepped through, came to attention, and saluted. There sat General John P. McConnell, chief of staff of the United States Air Force. His huge desk fronted a window giving a panoramic view of the Mall, complete with the Washington Monument and the Capitol in the distance—just like a movie set. The office was huge, with a seating area and coffee table to my right. Paintings hung on the walls, and drapes were air force blue. The American flag, the air force flag, and the chief's four-star flag stood in the corner. All of this was assimilated in a second, but there was one thing slightly wrong: The chief sat in his shirtsleeves, had a piece of Kleenex stuffed up one nostril, and was trying to light a cigarette with a flaming Zippo. I watched with horror, wondering what I would do if he set himself on fire. Luckily, there was a pitcher of water nearby on the coffee table.

I dropped my salute as the boss walked toward me. He gave up on lighting the cigarette. With it dangling from the side of his mouth and Kleenex billowing from his nose, the general pointed a forefinger under my nose and said, "Take it off!" Just like that. He obviously meant my rather flamboyant mustache, which I knew somehow had outgrown all semblance of air force propriety. To tell the truth, I wasn't all that fond of the damned thing by then, but it had become a symbol for the men in the 8th Wing. I knew McConnell understood. During his visits to Ubon over the past year he had never referred to my breach of military standards, just seemed rather amused at the variety of 'staches sported by many of the troops. His "Take if off!" was the most direct order I had received in twenty-four years of service.

"Yes, sir!"

We sat on the sofa and the boss chatted amiably, welcomed me home, and flattered me with some Well-dones." Then came the bombshell: "You're going over to the White House this morning. The president wants to see you." McConnell continued, giving me advice on how to handle myself in the Oval Office, but I scarcely heard him. I was in a state of shock.

He continued, "After that there are some people over on the Hill who want to say hello. My aide will go with you to help you find your way around. Any questions?"

Any questions? Hell yes I had questions, but I could only manage to say "Yes, sir" again, wondering, Lord, why me?

During the ride to the White House the aide chattered away, trying to put me at ease. I'm afraid I didn't pay much attention. My thoughts were someplace else. I was supposed to be on leave for most of October. I hadn't seen my daughters for over a year, and the short visit with Ella in Bangkok back in March had been a disaster. I had a lot of personal catching up to do, to say nothing of the need for mental readjustment, time to try to get back on a civilized track. There were a lot raw nerves and tender edges to heal after twelve months of combat and putting my heart and soul into doing my best to be a good commander. Meanwhile, outside the car, D.C. and its inhabitants appeared completely foreign. The scruffily dressed hippies with long, dirty hair carrying peace signs, exchanging joints of marijuana as they walked down the street or lounged in groups in front of buildings near the Mall, thoroughly shocked and disgusted me. I finally tuned into what the aide was saying: ". . . and there's going to be a peace march on the Pentagon over the October 21 weekend. Thousands of these kids have already descended on D.C." This day was already too much. What had happened to my America? Now, I had to face the president?

After passing through the White House gate, we parked under the West Portico. The president's air force aide, Colonel James Cross, met us in an outer office. I didn't have time to ask whether or not it was proper to salute the commander in chief, so taking no chances, I saluted as we entered the Oval Office. President Johnson stood ready to greet me and stepped forward to shake my hand. He was an imposing figure. Even slightly stooped, he was every bit as tall as I. His grip was firm and he was all smiles as he led me to a couch near the fireplace. He sat in an overstuffed chair on my left and Colonel Cross sat on the sofa to my right. Johnson made some very pleasant small talk, welcomed me home, asked about my family, and wished me well in my new assignment at the Air Force Academy. Then he asked my impressions of returning to Washington. I told him I had heard about but had never seen a so-called hippie before. It was something of a culture shock to encounter thousands of them on the drive over. The president frowned a bit as he said, "They jus' don't unnerstand what's goin' on and they raise hell about it. I got two hunnert and forty thousand boys over there in Vietnam and they'll surely tell the American people what's goin' on when they get home."

This stunned me. I couldn't believe what I was hearing. A thought struck me hard: That's your job, sir, yours and the Congress's. I'm afraid my next remark lacked any tact and diplomacy. I blurted out, "Sir, I've been home for only about two hours but all my friends who've been back for a while tell me civilians aren't even slightly interested in what we've been doing this past year. In case I do run into someone who's curious, what do you suggest I tell them?" With that, Colonel Cross damned near jerked my right sleeve off, but I had the bit in my teeth and paid no attention to his warning.

The president looked at me sternly, then relaxed and said, "Why, Colonel, you just tell 'em we're preventin' the North Vietnamese from interferin' with the South Vietnamese so those good people can exercise their own democracy."

I guess I lost it, for I replied, "Sir, I can't say that."

LBJ looked at me hard and asked, "Why not, Colonel?"

The tugs on my sleeve grew more intense as I responded, "Sir, if that's the reason we're over there I don't want to be the one to spread the word." There went my future in the air force! Robin, you dumb shit. Why can't you keep your big mouth shut? The president's words on top of a year of intense combat and frustration undid me.

To my surprise, the president didn't seem ruffled. He leaned forward, put his elbows on his knees, bridged his hands under his chin, and asked, "Well, what do you think we should be doin'?"

OK, here it was. Colonel Cross had stopped yanking at my sleeve. I guess he was fascinated at the turn of events and was waiting to see how this would play out, sort of like the thrill of watching a guy at the circus put his head in a lion's mouth.

"Sir, it takes three things for a country like North Vietnam to wage war: manpower, willpower, and industrial power. They possess the first two requirements in abundance, but they have little if any industrial capacity and must rely totally on others for their matériel needs. The bulk of those needs arrive in ships at Haiphong and several minor ports. Our bombing pressure keeps very little coming by rail out of China. Let us attack those ports, stifle their will, bottle up their manpower, and the job will be done." The president was looking at me hard this whole time but didn't interrupt. I plunged on. "In other words, mine the harbors, drop the road and rail bridges on the Chinese border, get the supply dumps in Cambodia, and most important, totally destroy the seat of government in Hanoi. It's simple, sir, and with all due respect, the way to end this war is just to win the damned thing!"

Johnson was startled and frowned, but he didn't kick me out of his office or even suggest my future in the air force was limited. He was pensive for a few moments, then said, "Tell you what, Colonel, tomorrow morning you come over and see old Walt, tell him what you told me. Thanks for coming by. It was a real pleasure." He stood up.

A real pleasure? This was a real lesson in top-level political diplomacy. The Man shook my hand and stepped back to his desk. What was supposed to have been a ten-minute "Welcome home, boy. You done well!" had turned into an intense thirty-minute outburst on my part.

Colonel Cross led me out, closed the door to the inner sanctum, shook his head in disbelief, and said, "Robin, that was the dumbest session I've ever sat through. I can't figure either one of you—you blurting out like that, or the president just sitting there listening. I've seen him bite heads off for a lot less. My God! Well anyway, I'll set up the meeting with Walt Rostow for tomorrow morning. How does nine o'clock sound?"

Did I have a choice? "Uh, sure, that's great. What do I do, where do I go? And who is Walt Rostow?"

The way Cross looked at me said volumes: Where have you been? How naive can you get? Don't you guys at wing level know anything? He said none of that but explained, "Mr. Rostow is the president's national security adviser," as though that was supposed to mean everything to me. It helped, but I wondered if my impression was correct. National security adviser? Advice about what? Cross detailed the morning activity. "I'll send a car for you. Your meeting will be down on the lower floor here in the White House. I'll meet you at the West Entrance and see that you find your way to Mr. Rostow's office. Now it's time for you to go home and enjoy your family. I'm sure they're anxious for private time with you."

I thanked him and wondered how I was supposed to find my way past all the White House security and back to General McConnell's aide. There were more surprises in store. Colonel Cross found the aide in an outer office and led the two of us down to a room full of people. "These gentlemen want to ask a few questions. They are the White House press corps."

Holy mackerel, I wasn't prepared for a press conference!

The session went along easily for the first few minutes. Questions were mere banalities and fairly easily covered, or so I thought. I was asked about my trademark mustache and told the assembly that Johnson had no opinion but that General McConnell commanded, "Take it off." I would, but not right away. Then one reporter asked what I thought of the aerial campaign in South Vietnam. The question vexed me and I responded somewhat testily, "I don't have a clue, since my wing didn't operate there. Our targets were only in Laos and in North Vietnam."

I tried to explain the difference and must have sounded patronizing. One angry individual interrupted, asking, "If that's the case, why don't we just pull out of the whole thing?"

I was shocked at his inference. It wouldn't be the last jolt of my day. I tried to be reasonable. "Well, sir, if we do that, we'll lose the rest of Laos, then South Vietnam, then Cambodia. . . ."

"Oh, so you believe in the domino theory?"

"I've never heard the expression before, but it certainly sounds reasonably accurate. Yes, it's my personal belief that's what will happen." It dawned on me that the situation had escalated far beyond any interest these hard-bitten members of the Fourth Estate might have had in me personally. I knew I was being asked to comment on issues far above and beyond my level of competence.

Before I could backpedal any further, the same cynic almost snarled, "Well, Colonel Olds, how do you think we should end it?"

"That's easy!" I shouted back. *"Win it!"*

I don't remember much of the rest of the interview. When it ended I found myself back in the Pentagon standing in front of a three-star general's desk. He was a fine gentleman from the West Point class of 1942 who had the odious job of public relations officer for the air force. We knew each other only by reputation, but it's fair to say there was a bit of "ring knocking" going on in his decent treatment of me. My insubordinate behavior with LBJ and the press could have had serious disciplinary consequences. He very patiently explained that I couldn't say things like that. "Like what, sir?" I asked. "Like, 'Win it!'" he replied.

So far, it hadn't been my day. I figured I might as well just keep up the negative momentum as far as my air force career was concerned. "Sir, if I am asked that question again, just what am I supposed to say?" The general gave me some pointers on tact and diplomacy in dealing with the press and public. I respected the man but his words went right over my head. I thanked God I was just a peon and didn't have to deal with Washington bullshit on a daily basis.

Afterward, I was taken over to the Capitol to meet several congressmen, all of whom seemed surprisingly sympathetic and understanding. I wasn't aware of any more major boo-boos on my part and enjoyed myself in those foreign surroundings. John Stennis, a Mississippi Democrat and chairman of the Senate Preparedness Committee, was particularly friendly. He praised my mustache and asked if I wanted a drink. I eagerly replied, "Yes, sir!" The offered drink was Coca-Cola. I hoped my disappointment didn't show. South Carolina Democrat L. Mendel Rivers, chairman of the House Armed Services Committee, also said, "Looks good. Keep it." The well was dry in that office, too.

So ended the first day of my homecoming leave. The next morning I'd see what Mr. Rostow had in store for me. It was time to go home. The car took me back past the demonstrators. They glared in at me. I glared back at them. It was a good thing I wasn't walking.

When we approached the house just after dusk, my anxiety about Ella choked out all thoughts about the president, the Pentagon, and the press. My family were waiting for me, at least two of them with open arms. What could I do but be grateful for the love of my daughters and the dog? Everything else would work out. It had to. I was too tired to think of anything else.

The girls bounced around me like puppies when I came through the door. Something smelled wonderful. Roast beef and Yorkshire pudding? Great! Ella was in the living room, drink in hand. I joined her and poured one for myself. Chris and Susie stayed nearby, I thought somewhat protectively. Ella made a comment about me being late and dinner probably being ruined, but I ignored it and asked my girls how school was going. The two of them chattered happily as we trailed into the dining room. As much as I would have preferred a casual dinner of macaroni and meat loaf with the family in the TV den, I accepted my homecoming as a special event.

Ella had set the long dining table with white linen, our best silver, crystal, china, and tall silver candelabras, with a crystal vase of tall white flowers in the middle. We took our normal places and I sat down to a soup of some sort. It looked like squash. Was it supposed to be cold or was it deliberately not warmed up? Looking down the table, I couldn't see Ella over the tall flowers and knew that was deliberate. OK, fine. Chris was on my left, Susie on my right, and both were watching me as Ella went on and on about some symphony tickets we had and whose box we'd be sitting in. Her voice droned in my head as I turned my concentration to the soup. Just lift the spoon, Robin, nice and slow, all the way up, control the shaking hand. Concentrate, damn it! The soup started trembling out of the spoon just above the bowl. By the time it reached my mouth, it had all spilled out. OK, try it again, this time more slowly, get a big spoonful, take a deep breath, lift carefully. I controlled the shaking of my right hand until about halfway up. The soup spilled out again. I ducked my head to slurp it up but got more on my mustache than in my mouth. God, I was exhausted. This was awful. I put the spoon gently down on the plate, wiped my mouth, and looked up. Chris was watching me closely. I looked back at her. She smiled at me and whispered, "It's OK, Daddy, the roast beef will be easier." I'd hoped she hadn't noticed.

Somehow we made it through the rest of dinner, and the girls went upstairs to finish homework. I took a glass of scotch into the den and stood looking at my desk. My briefcase was on my chair. The routine of years had been picking up little trinkets for the children and hiding them in the small drawers of the rolltop desk. When Chris and Susie were very little they'd sit on my lap after a trip, opening the drawers one by one to find treasures. Now both were too big for that, but the gifts would still happen. I sipped my scotch and unpacked little jade bracelets, Thai rings, small silk bags, miniature books, all neatly wrapped and tied with ribbon. I recalled how my hands shook when preparing the packages. Was I really that war-weary? Yes.

After a while when the house was quiet around me, I went into our bedroom. Illuminated by light from the open bathroom, Ella was already a dark shape under the covers. I undressed, put my uniform over a chair, pulled on pajama bottoms, and went into the bathroom. It was a mess. Trash and dirty towels littered the floor; her makeup case contents were scattered over the counter into the sink. Pill bottles lay everywhere. What the hell was this? I went over to Ella's side of the bed, sat down, and put my hand on her back, asking if she was all right. She flinched away, forcing through gritted teeth, "Don't touch me." She smelled of gin. "Just go away, Robin. Go! You're taking us away from home again. You're a selfish bastard. Everything I've done for you doesn't matter! Go away, leave me alone!" She rolled over and pushed me away. The lamp on the nightstand crashed to the floor.

I jumped up. "Stop! Just stop it!"

Ella stumbled out of bed wildly and launched at me, hitting my chest with her fists, screaming, "Bastard, bastard, BASTARD!" I grabbed her wrists and held her flailing arms. She twisted and jerked, cursing me. I wrestled her back onto the bed and held her still.

"Shhh, shh, Ella. It's OK. It will all be OK." I tried to calm her. She mumbled incoherently and then slowly stopped struggling. I pulled my head back and looked at her. Her eyes were closed and her face was turned away. What a sad homecoming.

I walked out of the room and stood out in the hall for a moment, looking up the stairs. My poor daughters; I knew they had heard the fight. Over the years they had learned to stay hidden, pretending the next morning that nothing had happened but avoiding their mother's angry hangover. All was quiet upstairs. I turned to go into the living room. I poured myself a scotch. Down the hall I heard the bedroom door being slammed and locked.

I went to the door. From the other side she screamed, "Go away, just go away!" I leaned my head against the door and tears welled up. So this was how it was going to be. I had left my men for this. I had left the sweetness of Ruby for this. Why? In God's name, why? I stumbled down the stairs to the family recreation room, found the sofa in a corner, sank down at one end, and buried my head in a pillow. I shivered uncontrollably. The totality of the past year's bottled emotions took over. SAMs streaked by my vision; I saw and heard black flak, orange missile bursts, small-arms fire, the roar of engines, voices of men, "MiGs at six o'clock. Break! Break!" I curled into a ball and pulled the pillow over my face.

Suddenly, gently, a hand on my shoulder. "Daddy? Daddy?"

Oh God, no. Chris sat down beside me and put her arm around me. "Daddy, you're shaking so hard. What's wrong? Please tell me." She drew a blanket over my shoulders. "Please, Daddy, don't cry. Don't cry."

I took a deep breath. My heart broke as I whispered sadly to my fifteen-year old child, "Your mother won't let me in our bedroom." Chris was quiet but her arm tightened around me. We sat silently. I forced my breathing to settle down, grateful for the warmth.

After a few moments, my little girl said, "Daddy, I think you should leave Mother. Susie and I will go with you anywhere you want to go." I was stunned by the grown-up, matter-of-fact voice. What had this child endured for the past year?

"I can't do that. I just can't do that. We all have to stay together."

"Well, just please take us with you. I don't want to stay in Washington. We don't want to stay with Mother. We want to go to Colorado with you. I was so afraid you'd die in Vietnam. I went outside every night and looked at the sky knowing it was daytime where you were. I couldn't imagine what you were doing. What was it like?"

I don't remember what I told her. We talked quietly for several minutes. I grew sleepy and leaned toward the arm of the sofa. "Thank you, Chris, honey. I'm going to go to sleep now. I'll be fine. See you in the morning."

She hugged me tightly. "I love you, Daddy. I'm glad you're home. Go to sleep now." Then she stood up and pulled the blanket over me as I stretched out. Sleep was fitful, filled with nightmares. Christ, what a homecoming.

In the morning I retrieved my uniform by going through the unlocked patio door to the bedroom. Ella was sound asleep, an ashtray full of cigarettes on the bed, an empty glass marked by lipstick on its side on the carpet. She would sleep for hours. I hastily showered and shaved. God, I looked like shit. The girls were in the kitchen having breakfast before school. Susie handed me a piece of toast and a plate of scrambled eggs. I hugged the girls before heading outside.

An official car stood waiting for me in front of the house. We drove to the White House. I felt increasing apprehension at the prospect of meeting Rostow. Surely a man in his position had far more important things to do than waste his time on a troublesome fighter pilot who had mouthed off to the president. Maybe I'd be able to just mumble an apology and be dismissed; more likely, I'd sit and take my ass chewing first.

Mr. Rostow certainly seemed cordial. He shook my hand, nodded toward a chair, and asked how I liked my coffee. There was a moment of awkward silence as we looked at each other. Then he chuckled. "I imagine we're both wondering why you're here, Colonel. Just what did you say to the boss to have him set up this meeting?"

Oh boy, the ball was in my court. Surely the man knew why I was there, maybe had even been given a transcript of my outburst. My fleeting image of official Washington waiting in the neutral corner wasn't at all reassuring. Well, I'd asked for it. "Sir, I seem to have rather stupidly taken issue with the president's explanation of what we're doing in Southeast Asia."

"What did he say to you?"

"Sir, he told me we were there to keep the North Vietnamese away from the South Vietnamese so the South Vietnamese could exercise their own form of democracy. That's as close as I can recall his exact words."

"And what did you find so objectionable about that?"

I gulped. Just how deep was I going to dig myself into the hole? "Sir, there's nothing wrong with that objective, only the way we're going about it. We are not destroying the enemy's will or determination. You know I don't appreciate all the nuances of global politics and the subtleties of international relations, but to me and many of my friends, it's simple. The North is implacable. Those people have fully demonstrated their intentions. They are fighting a war to gain control of the whole of Vietnam. If it is our goal to stop them, then we must destroy their ability to fight, not just deter them, and to do that we must deny access to the harbor at Haiphong, destroy the bridges along the Chinese border, the ones we haven't been allowed to hit, bottle up their troops in South Vietnam, wipe out their supply dumps and sanctuaries in Cambodia, and level their seat of government in Hanoi."

Rostow was floored. "You mean mine the harbors? That's an act of war! That'll bring down the Chinese. We don't want another Korea, Colonel!"

"Sir, with all due respect, I can't believe the Chinese will react—"

"But they're fellow Communists."

"Please, sir, hear me out. I don't think communism means a thing to the Indochinese, or even very much to the Chinese. It's a form of legalized control used to impose the will of the few on the many. What do tribesmen in the mountains and farmers in the rice paddies anywhere in South or North Vietnam gain by communism? For that matter, what do any of the common people gain? The Southeast Asians have existed for centuries controlled and ruled by despots in one form or another. Do you recall the legend of the two Vietnamese princesses who got together an army and drove the Chinese out of their country, and that wasn't for the first time? That was five or six centuries ago. The Vietnamese, the Chinese, the Koreans, and the Japanese have all hated one another for hundreds of years. I'll wager they will for centuries to come."

Rostow didn't respond to my little history lesson but brought the discussion back to the present. We spent a good deal of time arguing the pros and cons of more direct action against the North. He was deeply concerned that anything more than we were already doing would broaden the conflict beyond control. I knew I was in way over my head and kept thinking there had to be more going on deep down: agreements, understandings, international protocols, linkages, domestic politics I couldn't possibly understand. I only wanted to get the hell out of there and hoped Rostow would forgive me for taking up his time. He finally shook my hand and wished me well.

On October 5 a cartoon appeared in a New Orleans newspaper, then was copied in a few papers around the country. It showed me holding smelling salts under the nose of a fainting figure labeled "Official Vietnam Line" held up by LBJ. The caption on the drawing read, "It's Simple—The Way to End the War Is to Win It!" Later, the artist would send me the original drawing, and it served well over the years to remind me of my chronic infection with the malady known as foot-in-mouth disease. This is a particularly virulent infection leaving the zealous, but sometimes misguided, warrior with many scars and bruises. A sadder, hopefully wiser, fighter pilot slowly learned to (mostly) leave those things unto Washington that were Washington's.

The next three weeks were spent packing for the move, giving more interviews, and participating in more meetings at the Pentagon, including a full-scale debriefing in front of the Joint Chiefs. I kept my mustache just for that meeting, then shaved that night. I managed to get some time sailing alone on Chesapeake Bay. Ella went without speaking directly to me for several days but accompanied me to many social events and cocktail parties. Somehow, I was able to work around her to get things organized at the house. Chris and Susie moved their homework into my den and we spent cozy evenings together. Their fall semester was well under way. Since Ella wouldn't let them transfer into the public high school on base, it was arranged for the girls to become boarding students at Holton-Arms in Maryland until the house was settled at the Air Force Academy. They'd transfer to the Colorado Springs School for Girls after Christmas.

The last week of October I set out west, driving alone in my Jaguar Mark IV, which had been shipped from Bentwaters. Ella would follow in November with a driver in our Plymouth station wagon. I also had a little right-hand-drive Mini Cooper S being delivered to Denver by train. Ella finally relented sullenly to the move. She knew leaving D.C. was inevitable for the sake of our girls. She was without a doubt the most reluctant air force wife imaginable. Within the social structure of the military, her attitude and lack of support would doom any future chance of a highly visible post on the Joint Chiefs. I preferred to think of it as being saved from that fate. By the time I drove through Kansas into Colorado, my mind was clear and ready for the challenge ahead. Pikes Peak appeared in the distance, welcoming me to a place that would become home for the rest of my life.

21

★

The Academy

My arrival at the Air Force Academy wasn't as memorable as my chewing out when I first returned to West Point. Having recalled the experience, I was wearing a brand-new AF blue uniform; my hair was cut, my face was shaven, and my shoes were shined on October 30 when I drove through USAFA's north gate.

A wise person in the Pentagon had decided that my predecessor, Brigadier General "Ted" Seith, and I should overlap by two to three weeks. I didn't exactly agree with that. Maybe Ted didn't either, but we had played football together at West Point, so it wasn't a problem. I wanted to lurk about for a while, learn the base, get a feel for what went on behind the scenes at the academy. The setting was spectacular: dramatically austere glass-and-aluminum buildings spoke of newness, of difference, of being a symbol of the air force's eyes to the sky and the infinity of space beyond. The Chapel's unique roofline said it all: no ivy-covered walls here, no sir.

My office door was closed when I arrived. The secretary looked at me and shrugged her shoulders. At first glance inside, I saw the long paper sign on the back wall. In huge painted letters: FUCKING SHIT HOT! I quickly closed the door behind me. Someone had also put four red MiG stars on my chair. These were good signs. Would it be easier to fly this desk than an F-4?

The first day was spent being led around the base always accompanied by a junior officer. No way I'd be able to get away and explore on my own; too bad. It was easy to tell the place was pretty buttoned-up. It made me suspicious. A lot of hoopla was going on concurrent with my arrival building up to the homecoming football game against Army on November 4. It made it a bit easier to hide along the edges and watch. General Seith planned to introduce me to the Cadet Wing at a noon meal formation before the game. I chuckled as we entered Mitchell Hall between rows of cadets at attention wearing fake mustaches. Walking behind Ted I stared fiercely into the eyes of several cadets. These guys were already my kids. Above the banquet level on the staff tower he announced, "Gentlemen, it is my pleasure to introduce your new commandant of cadets, Colonel Robin Olds."

I stepped forward to the railing, looked at the four thousand mustachioed faces, controlled my urge to smile, and said sternly, "If you don't beat Army tomorrow you haven't got a hair on your asses! I didn't want this job, but as long as I'm here, I'll do my best to enjoy it. I'm sure we'll get along just fine!" And I gave the whole group a quick one-finger salute. That brought down the house. For the rest of my time at the academy, that middle-digit salute was a shared joke among us. Over the years people asked me why I did it. Hell, it just seemed the right thing to do at the time. I was a fighter pilot; they'd better get used to it.

I don't know how Seith kept up the pace. We must have gone to five or six parties that Friday night alone. He put in a fifteen- or twenty-minute appearance at each one. I couldn't believe it; this was my new duty? I accompanied him to the AF-Army game and it proved to be a real schizophrenic experience for me. I was rooting for USAFA of course, but the Black Knights brought back some great memories for this old tackle. I couldn't help silently cheering when Army edged AF 10–7 in a hard-fought battle. The Cadet Corps seemed a bit less involved in the game than I was. Where was the esprit de corps? Something was wrong.

Over the following days, I spent a lot of time in my office learning the responsibilities of the three main entities constituting the academy staff underneath the superintendent: The dean educated the cadets, the director of athletics challenged them physically, and the commandant tried his best to make officers out of them. I was to be responsible for all cadet activities related to discipline, military training, and daily routine outside the classroom. I also ran the personnel, supply, and operations functions to support the cadets. It sounded to me like I'd be a super-duper den mother and base commander.

What was amiss didn't take long to figure out. Ted tried to impress upon me what a bunch of bastards were in the faculty. His predecessors, Sewell, Strong, Stillman, and Sullivan (why did they all start with S?) had fought an ongoing battle with the dean of faculty, Brigadier General Robert F. McDermott. Old McD had been in place since the establishment of the academy in 1954. He became permanent dean of faculty in 1959. As head of all academic programs he had the military equivalent of tenure, which offered him absolute power to challenge traditions in military education. He had introduced about thirty academic majors to the Air Force Academy and brought a degree of flexibility to curriculum requirements, but his lock on the place created contention among the three domains of academics, the commandant, and athletics. The goals of the three different branches were not exactly mutually supportive, particularly considering the egos involved. Life on the various staffs had devolved into a possessive fight for time in the individual cadet's daily schedule. Each section of the triumvirate was trying to do its best to fulfill what it knew for a certainty was the most important phase in the development of these future officers. It was a mess.

Before departing, Ted gave me a stack of folders about three feet high to prove his point. They were staff studies I was supposed to read: detailed research on the time, motion, hours, and availability of a cadet, statistics on how many hours were spent in one department versus another. I agreed I would devote myself to these exhaustive reports but knew it was the furthest thing from my mind. These folks took themselves very seriously. I saw the academy as a shining silver jewel nestled up against the mountains, operating in its own little vacuum, seething in the juices of ivory tower academia. The whole thrust of the academy was to give kids a college degree. They'd had twelve Rhodes scholars over the years, a remarkable achievement, but how much did that contribute to the United States Air Force? I wasn't mocking the academic side, just seriously worried about the balance and the product. When Ted left my office, I called in the secretary and asked her to file those documents as valuable records of the early development of the academy. Then I called the dean to make an appointment for a courtesy call. I banked on the fact that we'd been cadets at West Point a year apart.

McDermott's office was bigger and better appointed than the one I occupied.

I grinned, thinking how much that must have eaten at my predecessors. Well, I wasn't going to fight the dean; it was obviously a lost cause to begin with, and I don't like fighting lost causes, no matter how much I believe in the loser's side. McD was clearly in the driver's seat. Fighting him would only upset everyone: the faculty, the cadets, and poor old Superintendent Moorman, who had to buffer the whole mess. Fighting was illogical and nonproductive. Lick 'em or join 'em.

After preliminaries I came right out and said to McD, "Look, I haven't any intention of arguing and fighting over cadet time. We're in this together. I'll use what my guys have to the best of our ability, but I want and need your help." That got his attention. "Mac, I don't have time to make sure the cadets attend their classes each day. My staff is required to do that, but since it's your major concern, I expect your teachers to let me know if a kid skips class. I'll take care of the discipline end of it. That's for starters. Please understand, I consider it our mutual responsibility to graduate these cadets with the basic qualities, training, and drive our air force needs."

He agreed, we shook hands, and we never had any problems.

Despite the internal staff battle, it was immediately apparent that USAFA's military training was far superior to my cadet training at West Point. Hell, West Point in the 1940s was like summer camp in comparison! Oh yes, we'd gone on forced marches, fallen over rocks at night, crawled through some mud, shot Springfields loaded with blanks at one another, learned to drink beer, and had a wonderful time, but it bore no resemblance to the great training at the academy. What was all the fuss about?

Lieutenant General Thomas S. Moorman was a great guy. I admired and respected him enormously and we got along well. He had a little bit of a temper but he knew what he was doing. That gentleman had the big picture and had the best interests of the academy at heart well ahead of personal desires. He and his wife, "Miss Atha," anchored the whole place with their graciousness, in direct contrast to the rough demeanor I brought along. Well, after a year of combat I was still wound pretty tight. My gut told me to dial back my brash attitude, become civilized again, exercise prudence, get in the groove to make a good impression, but I just couldn't. Part of me kept wondering why I was commandant. The mantle did not sit easily. How this was going to play out was unknown, but I couldn't be anything other than who I was. There was also Ella. How would she take to this new environment?

To my surprise and relief, Ella liked it. I'd been commandant for only a few short weeks when we were invited to the supe's house for a large dinner party. The superintendent was quartered in a beautiful old home on acreage that had become government property when the air force first acquired the land. The large dining room had a table that could seat eighteen people. Our quarters were smaller but equally gracious, set back on a lawn under the trees. Both houses were the focal points for social events. This was the first of many such quasi-official occasions and attendance was not a matter of choice. I didn't resent these necessary gatherings; they were always interesting, the guests were fun, and Tom and Miss Atha were charming hosts. But my rough edges left a few splinters at that first party. I was like a frustrated gorilla tearing through a ladies' tea party. Ella, fortunately, was in her element as the center of attention as the commandant's wife. This seemed to bestow more social standing on her than the more nebulous position of wing commander's wife in the Officers' Wives Club at Bentwaters and temporarily made up for missing the high life of D.C.

The party started off on the wrong foot for me. Ella and I were set upon by a group of wives upset that we had enrolled our girls in a private school rather than Academy High. I told them it was none of their goddamned business and stormed away. That response might not have been fit for cultured society. Ella saved the day with her charm and social grace. She described the girls' prior schooling and her sincere desire to continue to provide her children with the best education. She charmed the group. There was polite laughter. I was rescued from a gaffe.

One of the supe's guests that night was a rather robust lady with an overpowering, booming voice. Regardless of whom she was talking to prior to dinner, everyone learned her passion in life was hunting. That meant *really* hunting, African safaris no less: elephants, rhinos, lions, impalas, gnus, you name it; she had shot it and had the record heads to prove it. The woman sat on my left at dinner, regaling me with endless details of barrel length, bore, shot weight, recoil padding, white hunter qualifications, and so forth, all for my edification and that of the whole group, whether we were interested or not. Finally sensing my bored bemusement, she turned directly to me and asked with scathing sarcasm, "You DO shoot, don't you?"

Knowing I had just fought over North Vietnam for a whole year, the other guests leaned forward in rapt attention for my response. I was aware of their interest and answered with studied politeness. "Only people, ma'am, only people." End of conversation.

Within a month of my arrival my two biggest challenges were clear. For starters, military training was working pretty well but discipline needed tightening. In my mind, firm discipline in military training is essential, whether for a jungle airstrip, in the trenches, in an aircraft, or at service academies. The system is designed to level the playing field. Kids came from all backgrounds: upper-crust East Coast families, cornfields of Nebraska, city slums, California beaches. All had been outstanding in high school to gain academy appointments, but they came with social attitudes intact. Doolie year was designed to neutralize that. When the hair gets cut, twenty extra pounds of baby fat melt off in Jack's Valley, and egos are stripped away on the playing field, everyone becomes naked. Personality and character show up. The whiners give up or sink to the bottom; the natural leaders rise through the ranks. It happens that way in any group, especially under the unique stresses of the military. Kids do that by learning to work together as a team; no man climbs an enemy hill by himself, and a pilot doesn't fly off alone without a team behind him. Military people have to operate as units, each member supporting the other with team spirit. Discipline to reach true teamwork is crucial—the MOST important part of being an officer.

Some people saw a paradox in the notion of a maverick fighter pilot instilling discipline in the Corps of Cadets. Many thought fighter pilots were probably the most unruly, undisciplined bunch of people in the military. Complete nonsense, of course. Every aspect of a fighter pilot's life demands strict discipline. Flying itself takes discipline. It is, in fact, both the end result of highly disciplined training and the constant application, through self-discipline, of the lessons of that training. I have a pet definition of discipline: It's what makes a person do the right and proper thing under many different circumstances. That doesn't mean by sheer instinct or innate ability, it means through knowledge gained by life experience, training, and learned judgment. If discipline were instinctive, I wouldn't be needed as commandant. To do the right thing from moment to moment, a person needs to analyze and judge a situation correctly, make the right decision for the proper course of action, and then take that action. All of these steps require discipline and training. It took discipline in Korea not to chase MiGs across the Yalu. It took discipline in Vietnam to break off a hot engagement when we got too close to China. It took discipline among the ground troops just to get the airplane airborne each day. Nothing is accomplished without team spirit and a focused work ethic. It's an acceptance of the gold standard, a set of rules you believe in and take an oath to obey.

It seemed to me that much of the day's society showed lack of discipline of any kind. Kids had grown away from society's standard and were trying to develop their own. If people had any standard at all it appeared to be based more on what was good, pleasant, or gratifying in the moment, rather than what was good for the whole. If laws need to be changed in a land where law is determined by a majority of the people, then laws need to be changed through an orderly, established procedure. That's democracy. Making up one's own laws creates chaos. Adherence to law brings rewards although adherence may sometimes be extremely difficult. Deviation from law usually brings punishment of some sort, yet compliance out of fear of punishment is weak. Compliance because of one's conviction or acceptance is true discipline. My job as COC was to lead a cadet back to his own essential core of "doing the right thing" through the discipline of military training. The concept was simple but my work was cut out for me.

Case in point: An AOC (air officer commanding) showed up flustered at my office one day reporting, "Boss, we've got a streaker at the noon meal formation and he's gotta be stopped!"

"What's a streaker?" I asked, knowing pretty well what the answer was.

"Some cadet is running naked through the ranks at noon meal formation with a bag over his head. We've tried but we can't catch him. It's making us look silly!"

I laughed at the image, thought for a moment, and told the AOC I would handle it. At a meeting later that day I explained to my staff, "OK, tomorrow I want an officer or NCO to appear in every exit off the Terrazzo when our streaker gets out there. You are just to stand there. No chasing. Mind you, no chasing! If he darts past you that's all right. I don't want to know who he is. Neither do you. That's not the point. Afterward I want the cadet wing commander and his cadet staff in my office at 4:00 P.M. sharp."

All went as planned the next day. I watched in amusement from my office window as our streaker tried to get back into barracks. I have to admit he was fast, perhaps inspired by the freezing November day. When I last saw him he was disappearing around the south side of the Chapel headed for the hillside woods. At four o'clock I welcomed a small group of defiant-looking cadets into my office. I shook hands with each of them and told them to sit.

"Gentlemen, I am certain all of you know the rules of the game at this stage of your lives. There is a vast difference between official responsibility and unofficial behavior. For instance, when you are at parade that's official.

When you are assigned guard duty that's official. As your commander I expect your response to an official responsibility to be totally trustworthy, to be something I can depend upon no matter what. To get to the point of this meeting, I am going to ask you a question after which I am going to leave. I don't want to hear your answer but I expect you to discuss the question for as long as you like. The office is yours." I looked at them sternly.

"My question: How can you stand at an official event such as the noon meal formation in front of the entire wing, knowing your acceptance of the verbal report from each squadron and each group stating all present and accounted for is an official affirmation meant to assure both you and me that all is in order, when you have every reason to know all is not in order?"

I left. End of streaker.

My other biggest challenge at the academy revolved around the honor system. Honor, to me, is a simple do or don't. USAFA had gone through some recent cheating scandals, which threw a sharp focus on the system of dealing with honor violations and demoralized the wing. At the academy our honor system seemed bogged down by specifics and nuances of meaning. It was treated like a court of law, which shocked me. At the Point, honor was simple; it wasn't thought over, it wasn't discussed, it wasn't codified, analyzed, beaten to the ground, or weakened by myriad interpretations. We just lived with it, accepted it; we didn't lie, didn't cheat, and didn't steal. Not lying meant you didn't make falsehoods, known falsehoods, deliberate falsehoods, or little white falsehoods. You didn't cheat on exams or in the classroom. You didn't steal. That just meant you didn't steal. Period.

Honor means to perform one's duty in an honorable fashion, to behave in a way that makes one a trusted agent of one's company. The standard of an honor code needs to be maintained, but violations committed for the good of the whole company (versus individual actions to further selfish personal gain) seemed to me simple to regulate. I ran into a brick wall with my commonsense notion versus the academy policy of automatically expelling a cadet for any honor code violation. Yes, the violator must be punished as an example to others, like the parachute episode in my Ubon trailer, but when a rule is broken for good reason, a good commander will wait until the uproar has died down. He will then take care of his subordinate privately without running it through a court of law.

The first violation on my watch was a doozy. The same enterprising fellows who had put the sign in my office and supplied the wing with fake mustaches were part of the "Rally" Committee, tasked to keep up morale. I had to hand it to them—they were an inventive bunch! Between the cheating scandals and the war going on in SEA for a number of years, the Cadet Wing was in an understandably deep funk. The kids thought their fate was to master academics, graduate, go to pilot training, then die in the war. Due to regular losses, the sports teams weren't inspiring, particularly in football. Alcohol for cadets of age was permitted in public places off campus, but on academy grounds it was verboten, so parties were a drag. Before one football game, that Rally Committee decided the morale of the wing needed boosting through a *beer* pep rally.

The committee head and a pal collected several hundred dollars from friends and made a deal with a local beer distributor to purchase two hundred cases of beer. Obligatory pep rallies were scheduled for Thursday night before Saturday games to show wing spirit. These guys checked a small flatbed truck out of the motor pool on Thursday afternoon, drove the truck to Colorado Springs, loaded the two hundred cases, drove the truck back to the Cadet Area, and parked it near the base of the Ramp. At 10:00 P.M., committee members assembled at the Ramp, dressed in cadet dark blue sweatsuits so they couldn't be seen. The truck was driven up the Ramp and slowly around the Terrazzo area while rally members unloaded and placed cases of beer in a long, continuous line on the ground. As 10:15 "Release from Quarters" bugle call sounded on the PA system, cadets drifted slowly out onto the Terrazzo without much enthusiasm. When a couple of them spotted the beer they ran back into dorms yelling, "There's beer! Get out here, there's beer!" A few diehard straight arrows tried to stop the runaway train, to no avail. Four thousand cadets had themselves one hell of a pep party that night. At the end, not one can of beer was left and the truck showed up in its parking place at the base of the Ramp.

Calls from squadron and group AOCs came to me by midnight. I knew I had a mess on my hands. By morning the AOCs were swarming to discover the perpetrators. By afternoon, Cadets H. K. Ownby and Wade Adams were planted in chairs in front of my desk with a phalanx of angry AOCs standing behind them. The AOC group blurted out the details of the plot, exclaiming they had the two kids on an honor violation for lying to the beer distributor about their identities. Ownby asked me to call the beer distributor myself and gave me the number. I picked up the phone and called, asking the man how much beer was purchased, how much was paid, what time it was picked up, and then who had bought the beer. I stared hard at the kids while the man answered my questions. Then I said, "Oh, I see. Well, thank you very much."

Addressing the AOCs, I reported, "He said they gave him the name of Nino Balducci." By this time at the academy I knew Nino Balducci was the fictitious cadet who had entered with the first class, of 1959, and got turned back every year. It was a standing joke that he was blamed for every cadet wrongdoing. The group AOCs, almost in unison, said, "You see, General, we've got them!"

"Yes," I responded, "it appears so." Then I looked hard at Ownby and Adams. "He also said the kids told him to give us the name of Nino Balducci if we asked. Then he was to tell us they told him it was a joke and to make sure he told us their real names, Ownby and Adams. I guess you don't 'got 'em.'"

To engineer a meaningful reaction to this very public infraction, those two faced a Commandant's Disciplinary Board and were punished with hundreds of tours to march, along with hundreds of hours of confinements. A few months later, I visited Ownby privately in his room. "Did you learn anything?" He answered, "Yes, sir." I turned to leave and said, "Good. You're relieved of the remainder of your punishment." I smiled at him, walked out the door, and delivered the same message to Adams. Enough was enough.

Over my three and a half years at the academy, I tried to change the honor system both individually and collectively. I tried in one-on-one conversations and in small group discussions on Saturday mornings when I'd bust in on training hour; I tried at my house in personal contact with the cadets; I tried through my office during Wednesday sessions; I tried at meetings with individual members of the Honor Committee; I tried throughout all the agony of trying the honor cases. It was an ultimately hopeless quest.

For many reasons, I had a love-hate relationship with my time as commandant. The tangled politics of the administrative system frustrated me no end, but I surely loved the cadets! Those kids were the cream of the crop, only a couple of bad apples in the bunch, and the Cadet Wing suppressed those quickly. It was rewarding to be around bright, eager young minds, to watch them grow as men and officers. I tried to hang out with the kids as much as possible. I loved their spirited high jinks and purposeful sense of fun. Pushing the boundaries of playfulness is the only way to live and work, in my opinion. Laughing adds lightness to even the most serious situation and one must not take oneself too seriously.

As a means of getting closer to them, Ella and I had groups over to the house in civilian dress for informal get-togethers. I think it helped having two teenage daughters around. We had lots of family slide-show nights (which horrified the girls to no end), barbecues, badminton tournaments, treasure hunts, croquet matches, and even formal dinners where table manners and proper etiquette were mandatory. Of special significance to me was hosting groups of first classmen from different squadrons for Friday spaghetti dinners. Several evenings ended with me narrating gun camera film from my P-51s and F-4s. The cadets paid rapt attention to those. On one such evening, a squadron group member showed up late in a flight suit an hour into the party. Turns out he had just had his first solo flight. I retrieved an old flight scarf from my dresser, tied it around his neck, and congratulating him with "Now you are a proper Wolf cub!" His squadron mates were understandably envious. Good. I wanted to push all of them to push one another. The cadets pushed me back with their endless shenanigans. I'm sure they thought the stern eye of the commandant was on them from his lofty perch as they marched or walked across the Terrazzo, but my observations were always tinged with a large amount of fatherly love. I was proud of them. I pulled for them. I sank or rose with them. They were my kids.

It wasn't long before the wing's mood seemed to shift into high gear. I did what I could to encourage it. For the senior class dining-in, I invited Chappie James from his new post as vice CO for the 33rd TFW at Eglin, suggesting he fly his F-4 over the academy to give the kids a show. Chappie had no idea I had "borrowed" an F-4 of my own to greet him. When I pounced on him at 1,000 feet, the ensuing dogfight was the damnedest thing the cadets had ever seen—that is, until another infamous flyby at the end of May.

To honor the academy and its many graduates serving in SEA, the air force sent a decommissioned F-105 to be placed on static display at the northeast corner of the Terrazzo. The F-105 was to be dedicated to the wing in a ceremony during noon-meal formation. Chairs were set up for attending dignitaries and a podium was placed next to the aircraft. The entire Cadet Wing was assembled in parade formation. Academy staff members stood close to the F-105. After speeches by General Moorman; Don Strait (head of Fairchild-Hiller the parent company of Republic Aviation, the builder of F-105s); General Gabe Disosway (by then TAC commander); and me, there would be a flyover of four F-105s from McConnell AFB.

The F-105s made their first pass in diamond formation in full burner and the entire Cadet Wing cheered. Then the F-105s swung around for a second pass and the leader separated to come in low again. As he approached from the east, I could see the rippling shock wave in front of him and thought, Oh shit! This time, there was absolutely no sound as he passed overhead. Two seconds later: kaboom! The sonic wave hit the Cadet Area. A roar went up from the cadets. Then boom! Huge windowpanes on Vandenberg Hall bulged in, then out, exploding in slow motion. All the forward-facing windows of the other buildings shattered in turn as the wave hit. Boom! Boom! BOOM! Glass flew, spectators scattered, dignitaries dove for any available cover, cadets yelled and ducked to the ground. Then came the ominous sound of shards raining down. Glass fell like a dumpload of gravel onto the top of Moorman's staff car parked below Vandenberg Hall. Glass rained on top of the static F-105. "Goddamn it to hell!" I roared. Chaos ensued. My ears were ringing. Moorman was shouting at me. Cadets scrambled up off the ground; many broke formation and ran for Vandenberg. I looked up and saw the remaining three aircraft pass safely high overhead. Thank God for that small blessing.

Cadet Wing Commander Ralph "Ed" Eberhart quickly called the wing to order and readied them to march through the broken glass into Mitchell Hall for the noon meal. As the first squadron approached the doors, personnel came running out, yelling, "Don't go in. Don't go in!" The first two to three squadrons rushed to the doors to see why. The shock wave had completely shattered the south glass wall of the dining hall, blasting shards back into the hall. Everything—the floor, tables, plates, glasses, and food—was covered with broken glass. There would be no lunch. Some upper-class cadets formed a barrier to keep others from entering. The cadet commanders ordered the troops to return to their rooms and check the damage.

Out on the Terrazzo, staff mobilized to call ambulances. Moorman was apoplectic. I wasn't far behind him. How many were hurt? It turned out fifteen. Most were superficial cuts. One officer was badly cut and was hauled off to the hospital. There would be hell to pay. I stormed back to my office to commence damage control. Moorman cornered Gabe Disosway in his staff car and set in on him about the damage to the academy, the press ramifications, injuries, congressional investigations, backlash from parents, bad impression on the cadets, on and on. Gabe reportedly grinned at Moorman and said, "Tommy, if I recall, you requested that flyby!"

The pilot of the F-105 claimed that "inaccurate instrument reading" had caused him to go supersonic. All four F-105s were impounded and inspected but no defects were found. The resulting investigation led by Moorman turned up a variety of reasons, including poor judgment by the pilot, poor planning procedures by the academy flyby staff, and broken fight regulations. The pilot was grounded. Some press attention occurred for two days in national newspapers and TV but quickly died down. Back at the Pentagon, Disosway, with only a few months left before he retired, filed the report in his bottom desk drawer. Months later, since the war was gobbling up F-105 pilots, the pilot returned to flight status. The academy graduated the Class of 1968 in a stadium infected by new spirit, electrified by the raw power all had witnessed. Over one thousand new lieutenants shook my hand with gusto, every one of them defiantly proud to be officers in the United States Air Force.

There was a brief respite in June before the next class of Doolies arrived, but no real break for those of us on staff. This assignment had even more paperwork to handle than all previous years put together, and it made me hungry to get back into the air. TAC HQ had forbidden me to fly as commandant and in my new rank as brigadier general. I would sneak up with the Doolies for their intro flights in T-33s occasionally, but I often found myself instructing them from the front seat to climb to safe altitude, airspeed, and heading, then letting them take over while I had a quick snooze. More than one cadet endured the sound of my snoring as they flew "alone" for the first time, proud as punch of themselves, embarrassed to wake me up. Hell, I'd be awake in an instant if the pitch of the engine or altitude changed! I knew that. They didn't.

To get in some real flying, I'd sneak down to San Diego and fly with the navy at Miramar. Damn—those guys were for real! It was dog-eat-dog, no pussyfooting around. Their air-to-air program was realistic and aggressive. They had their act together for training. If I didn't need to stay under the radar with admission of my flight time, I'd have been bugging TAC no end to ramp up our own training. But I managed to make a nuisance of myself in other ways.

People weren't learning that they shouldn't invite me to speak. Requests to attend civilian events poured in and I accepted as many as I could. One, more than any other, got me into a lot of trouble, slamming me back into the national news and getting my hands slapped by Congress. It was an address to the ROTC cadets at a midwestern university.

The place had been torn apart by a monthlong riot and feelings were at a fever pitch. My presence as a military man did not help matters. Except for a handful of ROTC cadets, the student body was seething with hostility. Many antiwar demonstrators attended my presentation. Their rage was an almost physical force. I understood their frustrations only too well and tried not to take the abuse being hurled my way as something personal. It wasn't easy. Waves of them rushed the stage shouting obscenities, wild-eyed, spittle flying. Campus police, aided by some ROTC kids, provided a meager barrier. I held my ground silently, staring at the crowd. When the clamor subsided I looked across the rows of faces and started my talk by telling them they were a bunch of amateurs who didn't know how to hate because they didn't know what it was they were supposed to hate. I suggested they listen to a pro. The war going on was indeed wrong, I told them. Wrong not because we were there, but because the people in Washington—Kennedy, Johnson, and particularly Robert S. McNamara—had never grasped the basic objective. The cost in human lives was a price paid for no stated reason. Men in Washington were playing at war with no understanding of its conduct and with little understanding of the emotional reaction by the American people to the seemingly pointless course of action.

"You want to talk about hate?" I lectured them. "Ha! We're going to leave Vietnam with our tail between our legs—nothing solved, nothing gained, the region left in chaos, the South Vietnamese, the Thais, the Cambodians, and all those fine people abandoned to their fate. This war is a waste. Mark my words; it will be an everlasting disgrace to our nation, a blundering inept prosecution of a situation that from the very start demanded a positive course with positive, believable, attainable goals. A government owes that to its people; a government failing in that obligation must be held accountable by the people! You people need someone to hate, and it's so easy to hate the visible guys in uniform. We're what you see. Hell, we are just following direction from Washington! More than that, every one of us in uniform works for YOU, the American people. The way to end that damned war is to win it. A member of the South Vietnamese government told me, 'Our people will go with the strongest, they will believe in the toughest, they will follow the winner, so you've got to win!' I will tell you young Americans that thousands of lives have been lost because we've never heard one of you or your congressmen tell us to WIN it. Until you tell us to do that, we're doing the best damn job we can. We're watching our close friends and comrades die while you do your peace marches from the safety of America's streets and colleges. God help us all!"

When I stormed off the stage and angrily pushed my way through people pressing forward I thought, Christ, you bloody fool, Robin. You're going to get yourself killed by hippies. Not the way you want to go. Shut up, for God's sake!" The backlash from that speech hit the academy before I got back. Moorman was on damage control—again. What was I going to do in those public, civilian situations? Lie?

At home, I continued to struggle with my love-hate relationship; I loved the kids, hated the shackles of my job. It was frustrating to have less direct authority as a forty-seven-year-old brigadier general than I'd had as a twenty-two-year-old major. Was I making any progress? Was I making any difference? The only bright spot in the whole endeavor was the Cadet Wing. Their behavior constantly lifted my spirits. If they'd known how amusing they were I'd have made no progress at all.

Three years at USAFA passed in a blur. Classes entered; classes graduated. But my life at home followed predictably sad patterns. The girls were on the East Coast, Susie in the twelfth grade and Chris in college, returning only during semester breaks. Ella's interest in academy life waned and she started making noises about returning to D.C. My marriage was undoubtedly the saddest part of my life, causing me to feel enormously capable in half of my life but inept in the other. My determination to merge the two failed, and I envied men with stable marriages and supportive wives. Part of me knew that Ella had gotten a bad deal giving up her career and choosing her desire to be with me. When I was in the mood to acknowledge the reasons for her discomfort and she was in the mood to soften and be vulnerable, we'd have moments—sometimes days—of coming back together into the blaze of our original love. The girls reveled in those relaxed times, which naturally happened during vacations when they were home. Our favorite times were ski weekends in Vail or Steamboat Springs. There were many happy, even joyful days with my family, but toward the end of my tour Ella had slipped further into her routine of pills and alcohol. It was a losing battle. The situation had not improved when word came of my new assignment in early 1971. Damn, I couldn't believe it! Director of aerospace safety at Norton AFB in San Bernardino, California. Ella immediately insisted that we live in Los Angeles. I called the Pentagon and offered to give up my star to return to combat in SEA. No deal.

The country seemed to be unraveling by then due to the worsening Vietnam conflict. It was tearing everyone apart. A good portion of America was outraged, a middle section of the population couldn't have cared less, and the rest were vocal to the point of treason; the only problem was, against what were they treasonous? According to Washington, the conflict wasn't a war. Government answers were vague and misleading at best, pissing everybody off. Young guys were fleeing to Canada to avoid the draft; Jane Fucking Fonda was doing irreparable damage and would soon do more by taking her protest show to North Vietnam. People were growing more argumentative and angry. Vicious riots ensued, well orchestrated and financed by foreign interests. There were no positive stories in newspapers or TV about the courage, loyalty, and devotion to country of our fighting men. All we read about was the lunatic fringe. I couldn't help noticing that those who squawked the loudest had never been closer than 12,000 miles to North Vietnam. There was no good outcome in sight.

Worst of all, the generally rebellious attitude penetrated the military. Things were really bad in battle zones by 1971: Officers and NCOs were being fragged by their own men on patrols; troops were offered cheap drugs by the Vietcong and thousands of them took full advantage of it. The army had huge detention camps full of offenders who had become more than disciplinary problems; many were medical and mental cases. Many kids arrived in SEA angry, bringing the homeland unrest with them. It was a mess. But it was hard to totally blame the people. How could our elected officials be so blind to their responsibilities?

At the academy morale was high but the kids were understandably influenced by the real world around them. The theme song at every Arnold Hall dance was Eric Burdon and the Animals' "We Gotta Get Out of This Place!" Whether they meant the academy or the war was debatable. Late in January a package arrived from the Pentagon, containing a long briefing and a carousel of 35 mm slides on the subject of drugs and drug abuse. Every military commander was ordered to give the briefing to his troops, accompanied by the slide show. The instruction was explicit. I didn't like it one bit but I had one of my staff assemble as many cadets as possible at one time and set up the theater for the show. I pleaded stage fright and appointed some poor major to read the prepared script.

The theater was packed. The slide show commenced. I sat on the stage with some of my other officers, watching the reaction on the faces of individual cadets as best I could. Everything from feigned interest to utter boredom was apparent. The briefing major droned on and on. It was all I could do to keep from nodding off myself. Had I done so I would have joined the majority of the youngsters in the audience by the time the dissertation came to an end. Pentagon instructions specified that the commander would follow the briefing with a few words of his own.

"OK, men, I suspect most of you know more about this stuff than I do. But let's get a couple of things straight. Having anything to do with those drugs is against federal, state, and military law. If I catch any of you I'm not going to kick your butt out of here, I'm going to prefer formal court-martial charges. You face a military trial. Understood? Pass the word. Meantime, if you still want to get into trouble, drink booze."

I knew in my bones that defiance was a part of youth, and I hoped I wouldn't have to follow through on my threat. To make sure, I had a session with the local Office of Special Investigations representative, asking for his help. Sure enough, in February, the agent came back announcing he had the goods on five first classmen who were actually selling marijuana. I immediately drew up formal charges and forwarded them to the adjutant general's office for review. In due time the charges were returned marked, "Disapproved."

"For God's sake, why?" I raged.

The judge replied that my charges would not hold up in court because I had no "proximate cause" to enter and search a cadet's room. I couldn't believe what I was hearing. Ever since the foundation of military academies, cadets' rooms had been subject to inspection. This action flew in the face of all reason and time-honored tradition.

I made an appointment and went over to the supe's office. "General, are you going to support the JAG or your commandant?"

"The JAG," he replied.

"Sir, I told the wing I would enforce the law to the full extent of military authority. You have just cut my legs off at the hips. Any clout I possessed in the minds of the cadets has now been made laughable. I request you find my replacement at your earliest convenience."

It took a while to find the guy. When he came, I figuratively folded my tent and walked away.

Leaving the academy was bittersweet. As an old man I was honored to command that new breed of kids. I found them to be tough and fine, the most highly motivated and patriotic young men in America. They were dedicated, determined, and ambitious. They were the smartest kids I'd ever seen in my life. Hell, I thought there were some very worthy successors to all the heroes of my childhood and all the great men I'd served with throughout my career. If the guys in D.C. and in commands would just let these kids follow their innate instincts as pilots and leaders, the air force would be in great shape for the future. Time would prove me right.

22

★

IG and Out

The job description for director of aerospace safety at Norton AFB went something like this: "worldwide responsibility for the development and implementation of policies, standards, and procedures for programs in safety education, accident investigation and analysis, human factors research, and safety inspections to prevent and reduce accidents in air force activities." What a mouthful. Actually, the assignment was challenging and interesting. It was also frustrating and ultimately disappointing. The bright spots, as usual, were the great people that crossed my path. The bad spots, again as usual, were the not-so-great policies that affected the good people, including this crusty brigadier. I learned far more than I ever wanted to know about the AF's inner workings. Not a pleasant discovery.

San Bernardino was too far from Los Angeles to live in one place and operate out of another, so Ella had to move with me into base housing at Norton. It was a small but comfortable house. She wasn't happy, but at least she was close to her old Hollywood cronies. She threw herself into meeting old friends and decorating our home in her usual elegant style. The girls came and went during vacations from college, and our social life was entertaining. Once again, life seemed fairly stable on the home front. Norton was comfortable; the flight line was right outside my office, the golf course beckoned, and the O club scene was good, with a big pool crammed with kids and teenagers throughout the year. I was able to immerse myself in work.

Meetings, studying reports, and moving paperwork back and forth across my desk were inevitable parts of the daily job, but about every third week I got to do real work as an inspector general (IG) leading teams on UEIs (Unit Effectiveness Inspections). In the process I inevitably became an inspector of SAC. Right from the start, I made no bones about my eagerness to expose SAC systems that I thought smelled. I found that most of SAC was like rotten cheese: full of holes and hot air. There was a structure there but the experienced guys who had forged the structure were long gone, leaving behind a legacy of "do it by the book" to the point where people weren't thinking. People were literally lying to themselves on their records and reports, not even realizing they were doing it because the system made them.

SAC had been established by belligerent old General Curt LeMay and General Tommy Power, both pronuclear nutcases. Under their rules, if a wing commander messed up even a little bit he was canned and gone forever, so SAC fostered attitudes about how tough they were. What they really did was made a bunch of liars out of many wing commanders, DMs, and DOs. Guys at wing level were scared people. They would lie, cheat, steal, and deny— anything to make themselves look good.

I went on an inspection tour of the bomb wing at Mather AFB and directed the commander, "Show me a load-out. Use load team number three. How many load teams does it take for you to be C-1?"

He answered, "Three, sir."

Three load teams for an entire bomb wing? I was familiar with a fighter wing, where you had twelve load teams per squadron, thirty-six per base. Three load teams! This seemed unbelievable. So I said, "Okay, take load team number three and give me a load-out." The resulting Chinese fire drill was something to see because I knew something he didn't: Two NCOs out of load team three had transferred the previous Friday. I arrived Monday and they hadn't reacted to it. They didn't even know it! I demanded, "What the hell happens when you have an ORI [operational readiness inspection]?"

They said, "Usually we borrow load teams from Castle."

"You pass an ORI with borrowed load crews? For God's sake, that's not realistic!"

At another base, I asked a CO, "What's your jet engine test cell reject rate?" This guy, who was on the general's list, looked at me and answered, "Oh, my staff keeps track of details like that."

I said, "I sat at your standup this morning, Colonel; your major briefed you and he gave you some figures. Have you got any idea what he said, even sort of?"

"Yes, sir, it's around 25 percent, which is quite acceptable. These are old engines, you know, the old J-47s, and . . ." Blah, blah, blah.

"Well, that was close, Colonel, but I'll tell you what, either the major was lying to you or he is awfully dumb, because that figure isn't really close."

He said, "General, I don't see how you can say that. The major is a good man. He—"

"All right then, he's just dumb! He did not check his figures. Right now your test cell reject rate is running above 50 percent. If you don't believe me, let me show you how I know this, and let me show you why it is important and let me show you why it is happening."

As chief of safety and IG, I was very unhappy with SAC engine maintenance. I had been warning them, "You are going to have trouble, deep trouble, big trouble." But they were too smart. They thought they knew better. They did not listen to fighter pilots or to anybody else for that matter. They lost five B-52s that year, the most ever lost in one year. Four of them had jet-engine maintenance as the basic cause: one at McCoy, one out of U-Tapao, one that went off the end of the runway at Griffith, and one guy that flew out of Guam, did a rudder exercise stall from 36,000 feet all the way down to 6,000 feet, and punched out. Maintenance.

I told the colonel, "Let's get in your staff car and go out to your jet-engine test cell." A look came across his face and I thought, You sucker! He'd been there two years and he didn't know where the test cell was—not even the vaguest idea.

We went and I introduced him to his maintenance chief. I said, "Sarge, let me have those records," and I showed the commander. "Now, Colonel, here is your true reject rate. What does this mean to you? You are manned 130 percent in your jet-engine maintenance facility. The rest of the air force, outside of SAC, is manned about 75 or 80 percent in their jet-engine maintenance facility. You have all the people. Now, let's see why your maintenance is so lousy." So we went to a huge maintenance hangar and I continued, "Now, Colonel, I want you to walk from this wall down to that wall and by the time we get across this floor you're going to tell me what's wrong with your maintenance." Well, of course, he couldn't do it. I walked him back and forth a couple of times, finally saying, "Don't you see anything?"

He replied, "Nope."

"Show me a four-striper. Show me just one out here in this big repair setup." There weren't any. "Now, let's go find those 130 percent. You are about 200 percent manned on the top three NCO grades. Let's go find them." The few we found were sitting around in offices with their feet up. "Now, let's go over to the NCO club." It was about eleven o'clock in the morning. There they were. All the E-7s, E-8s, and E-9s were sitting around drinking beer and coffee. And he wondered what was wrong with his jet-engine maintenance! Hell, he didn't even know that anything WAS wrong. Now, that is ignorance. He was working in a system designed to promote this guy and to reward his ignorance.

When LeMay scared the hell out of his people, he made something out of them that I don't think was their true nature. He made them cringe and hide the truth. He made them say, "Yes, sir, yes, sir," becoming chronic liars protecting their own skins. Whom were these guys going to promote? Whom were they going to favor in their OER (Officer Effectiveness Report) system? It wouldn't be somebody better, or even someone similar to them. A man like that has to have somebody working for him that he can dominate, and he is invariably going to pick a lesser individual.

After about twenty years of this system the incest destroys the force. I had a bunch of really great friends in SAC, but a big group of guys were developed into people who were afraid to think for themselves. They damn near destroyed the air force in the process.

My favorite IG tour was to Southeast Asia in late summer 1971. I spent a lot of time talking to some fine young pilots frustrated by lack of action. LBJ had stopped the bombing in 1968 and advertised to the world that we were not really serious about the whole thing. Essentially, from a combat pilot's point of view, he said, "All you troops can die for our country, but we won't let you win for it." Still, the guys had to serve their tours and be ready for anything.

At Da Nang my team passed out the usual safety questionnaires to the troops. Living in Rocket City and flying Stormy FAC missions daily, one would need to be a supreme optimist to think about dying in an accident. One smart-ass captain (God love him) answered the question about flight safety hazards, "If I knew of one I would report it to our flight safety officer," and on his ground safety quiz, he cited "sleeping through rocket attacks" as a major hazard. Another cited "flying combat." The wing commander was less than thrilled with my out brief. He didn't think it was funny. The troops really got it from him later.

The one SAC, B-52 base I visited was U-Tapao. I had been to every fighter outfit in the theater beforehand. When I arrived at U-Tapao they told me, "You cannot inspect us, General. We are flying combat." I said, "Not so that anybody around here would notice. Let's get on with it."

What a lousy place! U-Tapao was so godawful that I made a point of briefing the SAC chief of staff at Offutt when I got back. His staff practically called me a liar. They sent a SAC team of their own over, followed my footsteps, and discounted everything I reported. In response I got the USAF IG to send a special team of experts over to review their report. They proved everything I said was right, and worse.

There were some damn fine pilots, some fine squadron commanders in the theater, and some old-timers who were on their third tours, but everybody languished because there was nothing to do but kill monkeys and snakes. The best part left was the flying. I sneaked in about twenty more missions and got two more counters. It was fun! I flew with every wing except the 8th at Ubon. That CO would not let me near his airplanes, something to do with my previous reputation. I flew out of Da Nang, Phu Cat, and Phan Rang; I flew out of Tan Son Nhut in an 0-2; I flew out of NKP (Nakhon Phanom) in OV-10s and got some great F-4 rides out of Korat and Udorn. I wouldn't fly with U-Tapao. For Christ's sake, who had that amount of time? It took them fifteen hours to brief and then the chaplain took thirty minutes, which I really thought was funny. He would get up and give them a little prayer for his combat troops. I wanted to puke. The closest any of those guys had been to real combat was walking under the wing of a B-52, where one of the bombs might fall off onto them. It was laughable. My attitude was slipping down the toilet.

At the staff level, I met some guys who were just not with it. When I flew out of Da Nang we took a half hour coming back from the target. We dropped twenty-four 500-pounders. I couldn't believe it! On nothing! Coming back we just flew formation up the coast. I asked the wing commander that night,

"What in the hell did we waste all that time for? We should have been practicing pod formations, SAM breaks, MiG calls, and stuff like that."

He said, "Oh, we don't do that stuff. That's dangerous. We might have an accident."

I asked, "What will you do if they send you north?"

He said, "Oh, we are not going up there." And I knew they couldn't because, the damn airplanes were not being maintained. I discovered that about 10 percent of the F-4s in the theater in 1971 could not fire an AIM-7. If you tried, the damn thing would not even come off the rails. All the 7-A launchers were horribly maladjusted. It was sad. The attitude that prevailed was "Don't bother us with that stuff. You know that's not what we're here for."

Back in June, the wings had been briefed on my coming visits. Udorn sent me an invitation to attend a dining-in. Of course an IG could not accept such an invitation—undue influence and all that. I declined but mentioned that if I happened to be in the O club during that time I'd stop in. It turned out I arrived on my birthday and wing CO Colonel Lyle Mann and 555th commander Joe "Red" Kittinger went all out! After my sorry reception at Ubon, they really rolled out the red carpet. All the bar girls were in long white dresses and leis, about seventy-five fighter pilots and backseaters showed up, and of course all the Udorn colonels. It was a gala reception. They told me a giant cake with a couple of girls inside was scheduled to show up. It never did. Something about two guys talking the girls out of the cake before it left the kitchen. Harrumph!

Red Kittinger was determined to give me another chance at getting number five. Colonel Mann warned him his career would be at stake if anything happened to my precious hide, but Red got me on a protective reaction mission scheduled for North Vietnam the next day. We'd be escorting a recce aircraft with the Triple Nickel's best instructor pilot in my backseat. I was elated! After refueling, the recce aircraft turned back (due to lack of hostile fire), so we trolled around over Hanoi. To my great disappointment, the North Vietnamese didn't send up any MiGs that day, an obvious relief for the Udorn CO. Same thing happened the next day. Oh well, I had a ball anyway.

Just like my days at Ubon, MiG killing was not the name of the game at this stage of the Vietnam "conflict." As wing commander, I had carried out all the frag orders issued by 7th. Our mission was to escort and bomb targets. That's what we did. The name of the game for me was to get all my guys in— the Thuds, too—get them on target quickly, bomb accurately, and get the hell out with everybody. Seventh Air Force finally realized that we had to do that my way, and we did. I made the MiGs come to me on those missions. I never had any trouble finding them—they found me—but MiGs were not the name of the game anymore. All SEA wings were still playing by these rules in 1971 but Udorn was the only wing that really knew how to go north if they had to, the only bunch showing any interest. Those guys really had their shit together. They were eager to go, really thinking and reading everything they could get their hands on. They slept it, dreamt it, ate it, lived it. Jesus, Red pumped me and pumped me for advice and tactics experience. I loved it.

At the end of that tour I had to ask myself a very serious question: How in the name of God could the Air Staff populate a combat theater with people who weren't interested in combat? How could they say we were combat ready when all they'd been doing for two years was dropping Ping-Pong balls on muddy trails? How could they accept a state of training where the boss might say, "Go north! Right now!" knowing his troops couldn't do it? How could they put wing commanders in there who were not fighter guys but a bunch of staff weenies who were filling the square to get their stars? How could they use combat this way and risk people's lives? It was bad, really bad, and to my mind, part of a bomber general's thinking.

I had to brief the chief on all this but of course I couldn't reveal the fact that I'd flown missions. Hell, as a general officer I wasn't supposed to fly at all, just be ferried from place to place. The IG was definitely not supposed to fly combat, for Christ's sake, yet that's how I knew that only Udorn was ready. After I gave General Ryan the IG safety part of my trip, I said, "Sir, there is something else I'd like to say. Fighter forces in Southeast Asia today cannot fight their way out of a wet paper bag. Not only that, there's nobody down in 7th Air Force who would know how to frag a Pack 6 mission."

The chief snorted, "What?" And his three-star DO chimed in with, "I don't know how you can say that! They are all C-1. Besides, what makes you think that we have to go back north?"

I answered heatedly, "General, a marine guarding the gate at the embassy in London in full-dress uniform is still capable of assaulting a bunker with an M-16 and grenades because that's what he's trained to do. He's just doing that grand tour for funsies, but he is basically a combat-ready soldier. Your troops in Southeast Asia are just guarding the embassy gate and they are not combat-ready troops. If we have to go back north we are going to lose our hat, ass, and spats, and the record will show that we did."

The record will also show that General Ryan at the time turned around after I left and demanded, "What is the matter with those goddamn fighter people over there? The navy is shooting down MiGs. The navy is doing good work. What is the matter with those goddamn AF fighter people?" Well, I had told him what was wrong and he chose not to do anything about it. What the hell did he want? Even when he was told he wouldn't listen. It galled me.

This went on through the end of 1971 and into spring of '72. At the end of March and beginning of April, the People's Army of Vietnam rolled a massive force across the demilitarized zone in what became known as the "Easter offensive." At first Washington's response was lackadaisical and confused, but Nixon finally ordered Operation Linebacker, a continuous bombing effort by the navy and USAF in May, to halt transportation of supplies and materials across the DMZ, prevent the total collapse of South Vietnam, and protect America's prestige for the scheduled summit meeting with Soviet premier Brezhnev.

At the time of the invasion, we had fewer than ten thousand U.S. troops remaining in South Vietnam, most of them scheduled to leave within the next six months. Our air power was less than half that of its peak strength in '68–'69. An immediate ramp-up scrambled almost two hundred F-4s, a squadron of F-105G Wild Weasels, and over one hundred B-52s back into action. Navy ships steamed in, on high alert. But despite all this, we started losing.

I took all I could. I went back to Washington and said, "I volunteer to go back. You can bust me to colonel. I want to take about twelve good guys with me and put them in Korat, Ubon, and Da Nang. We can get this show on the road. After that I'll come back home again. But God, let me do this because right now, it's a shambles." It took the Pentagon a week to decide whether or not they'd do that.

When they called back, my IG boss, General Ernest Hardin, offered, "Olds, we'll let you take an inspection team over. You can inspect missile maintenance." Oh God no. The final straw.

"General Hardin, sir, what you are telling me is that you want me to go over there and try to fight the 7th Air Force commander all by myself, with no help from the chief, no support from here at all. I'm supposed to go, sneak around, and do it all alone. You know I will fly. You want me to go up there and get killed and you guys won't even support me? Nuts to that!" I turned in my retirement papers. That was SAC leadership. It really hurt. It hurt a lot of fine people in far more ways than it hurt me.

Starting in May of '72, when Linebacker went into action, pilots sent north on MiG CAPs were also going up specifically to find MiGs. A disreputable navy lieutenant, whom I shall not dignify by naming, got his third, fourth, and fifth MiGs on the first day of Linebacker. USAF Captain Steve Ritchie, flying an F-4D with the Triple Nickel out of Udorn, got his fifth MiG in August. Some F-4Es by then had the top-secret "Combat Tree" system on board, giving them the ability to identify and locate MiGs when still beyond visual range, a far different circumstance from five years previously, when we knew fuck-all about which aircraft were MiGs. Ritchie was a brilliant pilot, despite his annoyingly cocky egotism, and he flew a hell of a lot more combat missions than I did. I wish I'd had him with me at Ubon. He was the right man in the right place at the right time to get magic number five, and he sure enjoyed the ace fuss. But Steve later admitted to me that he was helped along by the new detector stuff and the dedicated ground controllers he had, which was big of him. It doesn't downplay his achievement, but it sure made me wonder what the 8th could have done with that new gizmo.

Nixon's Watergate scandal erupted in June and Jane Fonda visited Hanoi in July, broadcasting her antiwar message via Hanoi radio. It was horrible to think our American POWs were being made to listen to her crap. Operation Linebacker ended in October, Nixon was re-elected in November, peace talks collapsed in Paris in December, and Linebacker Two started up a week before Christmas, inflicting the most intensive bombing campaign of the war. Nixon and Kissinger pressured the North Vietnamese to get back to peace talks and the South Vietnamese to accept the terms of the deal, and finally, on January 15, 1973, Nixon announced the end of offensive operations against North Vietnam. The Paris Peace Accords ending the conflict were signed January 27. Thank God, the POWs were released and started coming home in February. Saigon fell with a crash in 1975. It was a hell of a scramble getting our civilians and remaining military personnel out.

What an utter disgrace that war was, costing more than 58,000 American lives, let alone 230,000 from the Republic of Vietnam, more than 1 million North Vietnamese and Vietcong, and between 2 million and 4 million Vietnamese civilians! A bloody, pointless war from the start, made even worse by the way it was conducted. South Vietnam fell under Communist control, just as if we'd never been there. What a fucking waste.

It was the right time for this warrior to get out of Dodge, but no way I'd go quietly. I voiced my opinions in a speech to the Touchdown Club in New York soon after the end of the war. My remarks challenged the administration and

Congress to "play to win," like in a football game, the next time armed forces were committed to combat. "Win the goddamn thing!" I thundered. "It will save lives and be over with quickly!" All hell broke loose. The reaction and furor rolling off Capitol Hill were spectacular. Chappie James was, by then, director of public affairs in D.C. He and legislative liaison John Giraudo nearly had heart attacks fielding the complaints. Chappie phoned me at Norton and said, "Boss, why in heaven's name did you say that? It damned near made me turn white!" God bless him.

Thirty days before leaving office, I was required to file an official report with the IG, General Hardin, before sending it on to Ryan at the Pentagon. They requested my opinion on how to cut expenses in AF operations. It was like sending a starving man into a supermarket! Needless to say, my response started fires in several trash cans. I suggested they cut staff and functions across the board throughout the top echelons of the air force and the Department of Defense, break down the surgeon general's Pentagon empire, cut headquarters USAF manpower by 50 percent, realign functions on a priority basis, let subordinate headquarters follow suit, eliminate the Air University and AFDAS—go contract, eliminate SAC and TAC divisions and ANG groups, reduce the number of authorized AF general officers by one-third, reduce colonels by one-quarter, return disciplinary power and personnel records to commanders, eliminate MET, RIF one-fourth of System Command GS-12s and above, RIF one-half of Logistic Command GS-12s and above, eliminate VIMS, BLIMPS, BEAMS, etc., stop the B-1 buy (since SAC claimed to have won the war in eleven days by carpet bombing, just equip C-5s with MERs and TERs for future wars—save a packet!), give ICBMs to Army Coast Artillery Corps, and return the air force to a mission-oriented service, rather than the factory it had become. They'd get a hell of a lot more out of proud military people than from mill hands.

Finally, the last line of my report read, "Retire one tired Brigadier General, ranked seventh on the April '73 one-star list. He's of no use to you anymore." In case my intent wasn't perfectly clear, I started growing my mustache back that same day.

My last days in the IG office were a bittersweet end to my military service. Had I made any difference at all? Did any of it count for the air force and for the country I loved so much? The people I served with through good times and bad were undeniably what counted the most, but I couldn't help thinking I hadn't done enough, hadn't tried hard enough, hadn't given it my all. I was undeniably done. There was nothing more anybody would let me do. In the last two days at Norton, I managed to get in some good golf with friends and have a few laughs, but I was mentally exhausted. Final packing at the house was rushed and argumentative. Ella had lobbied hard for us to return to Washington, D.C., but I was worried about both of us back in that sewer. It was the last place we needed to be; the high life for her would have been the ultimate low life for me. There was no way to reach a happy compromise, so we decided the only short-term fix was to buy a house back in Colorado, live there for a while, see how it worked, and find out if we could make it when I was no longer a fighter pilot. We were both willing to try a clean new start in retirement.

On June 1, 1973, I retired from the United States Air Force exactly thirty years after graduating from West Point. The ceremony was simple and subdued. The next day we took off in a caravan of cars driving back across the country to the little ski town of Steamboat Springs. When the Rocky Mountains came into view once into Colorado, I knew I was finally home.

It was the home I would never leave.

23

★

Final Landing

My years of retirement didn't last very long. I didn't have much time to mope around. After the POWs came home the River Rats threw a whale of a party in Las Vegas. Over two thousand people attended. It was our first "official" reunion and showed me clearly I would never retire from being a fighter pilot. My talents were needed to lead the guys in song. The RRVA grew into a national organization, holding reunions in every corner of the country, usually not in the same place twice. For some reason hotels seemed not to welcome the River Rats back. Fighter pilots grow older but never grow up.

Regrettably, Ella and I didn't make it more than two years after we moved to the mountains. We divorced in 1976. She moved back to Los Angeles, and died from throat cancer on Memorial Day 1988. Our two girls were by her side. It was a sad end to our beautiful, passionate beginning. We had simply been too much for each other. Luckily I found love again and married Morgan Sellers Barnett in 1978. Morgan and I spent many happy years living in the quirkiest damned house on the top of a hill south of Steamboat Springs.

I rebuilt the roof and foundation of that house with my West Point engineering manual, Morgan bringing materials up ladders, then hauling trash down. We skied, golfed, and traveled endlessly to 8th TFW, 434th, and RAF squadron reunions, and even hosted a few of our own in Steamboat. Those were happy times. My old friend Benjamin Cassiday corralled us into his fighter-pilot ski group, Aspenosium, yet another annual get-together leaving devastation in its wake. This hale and hearty bunch still meets yearly and is now anchored safely here in Steamboat. God love 'em all. Save some powder for me, guys! Chappie James's heart gave out in 1978. I visited him in the hospital a week before he died. We held hands and reminisced about the good old days. When I left his room I said, "Good-bye my friend." Chappie replied "Good-bye, boss."

After years of my making speeches to captive USAF audiences at bases across the U.S, Europe, and Asia, Morgan convinced me to make an honest living by signing on with the Aviation Speakers Bureau. To my surprise, speaking engagements piled up around the world and I took off on a second career. It was a fun way to meet new people and rehash old ideas. I was amazed at how well I was tolerated. Speaking also drew me fully back into reliving the life I had loved. Sadly, as a result, my marriage to Morgan ended after fifteen years. Bless her for hanging on so long with this disreputable, incorrigible old fighter pilot.

My younger brother Stevan died in 1988, way too young. I miss him. And damn that Phil Combies for leaving us too early. Pardo picked me up in a Lear for Phil's funeral in San Antonio. J.B. was copilot. I think I slept. I don't remember. What's vaguely clear is that we stayed at Dick Swope's house. I called some cops "cocksuckers," and the fight was on! For some reason, only J.B. and Pardo got thrown in jail. They were always good wingmen.

Distinct honors came my way as time went on. I was inducted into the Collegiate Football Hall of Fame and later the National Aviation Hall of Fame. Lithographs were done of my aerial battles. My old Mustang, *SCAT VII*, was refurbished by Jim Shuttleworth. I got to fly her again in 1993. What a thrill! It was hell forcing myself through the bullshit of getting a civilian pilot's license though. I often wonder if that nice instructor ever got his pants clean. One of the saddest days of my life came when Jim went down in that P-51 ten years later. I was one of his pallbearers. What a terrible loss.

Several pilot buddies bootlegged flights for me in the latest "teen" fighters until we could no longer get away with it. I shall remain mum to protect their identities. How kids today can fly with computers is beyond me. No doubt about it, I was one lucky old seat-of-the-pants guy. My F-4, *SCAT XXVII*, was rescued out of Phantom oblivion and put on display at the Air Force Museum at Wright-Patterson. The dedication was a helluva party. At a Fighter Aces convention I came face-to-face with Luftwaffe ace Günther Rall, and in true fighter pilot fashion we became good friends.

Through the last thirty-four years I've made hundreds of speeches, told too many bad jokes, given innumerable interviews to relentless journalists, attended countless dining-ins, written dozens of articles, opened a few museums, been in a couple of remarkable television shows, sung endless fighter pilot songs, played much bad golf, carved a lot of wood, bashed my way through deep powder snow, and caught my share of trout and women. I have a beautiful granddaughter, Jennifer. My daughters are well. Flying is over but good friends fill my life. It's been one hell of a ride.

Now in the spring of 2007, I look out at my beloved Steamboat Mountain and watch the season's first thunderstorm form over its flanks. For years it was enough to ski, fish, camp, and golf in this paradise, but these days I long to fly up the face of that cloud. This tired old body of mine can barely get down the hall to the living room and it frustrates the hell out of me. It would be easier if I didn't have to drag this goddamned oxygen tank around. What the hell kind of deal is this? I sit at this moody computer every day willing my fingers to write but distracted by a game of solitaire. There are so many e-mails to answer and letters to write, I can't keep up with them anymore. I've got to organize my file cabinet. I keep trying to type, but the day gets away from me. My daughter tells me dinner is ready, reruns of *M*A*S*H* are on, it's time for more pills, and time for bed again.

Doctors tell me I am out of time, that I have congestive heart failure. What the hell do they know? I'm just getting old! There's too much left to do—trips to be made, people to see, crossword puzzles to finish, songs to be sung, stories to tell, memories to write. It's just not fair. I'm not through. Chris is living with me despite how many times I've told her not to: stubborn like her old man, that girl. She nags me to take my medicine, keep my oxygen on, eat her cooking; what's so wrong with frozen macaroni and cheese? There's some in the freezer . . . been there for years. People call with invitations to reunions, air shows, parties, golf tournaments, gatherings of Mustangs and fighter aces, Warbird meetings, more parties. I confess, I tell all of them I'll be there. Let me just get organized, finish what I'm doing, take a nap. I'll shower, shave, and pack tomorrow. I need to book a ticket, drive down to Denver. Where are my glasses? Oh shit, sitting on them again.

During naps and at night now, I dream about flying; it's always the same dream. I keep myself in it when I wake up . . . keep my eyes closed to keep the feeling of it going . . . each time it gets better, goes farther. I know where I want it to end. It always starts out in total darkness, total quiet. A point of light appears in the center of the black and ripples outward, spreading light and sound as it comes toward me. The light becomes bright white, then blue, and the noise a deep roar. I'm in my F-4, screaming up the side of that thundercloud in full afterburner. Sunlight fills my cockpit. I invert over the top, then dive back down into white. There is white all around, like fog. Altimeter and horizon spin. Am I up? Am I down? I know my Phantom will tell me. I let go of the stick. We glide gently through the white, still no sense of gravity, but I can feel the descent. I can hear the engine whine. We are floating . . . we must be close to base. Have I called ahead? No time. No time. My jet breaks out of the fog just over some trees. There's a gray runway ahead. Where am I? OK, line up, throttle back, on speed, we settle down beautifully, haven't lost my style. I taxi in to a deserted ramp. Where is everyone? I open my canopy, hear my engine spooling down. I take off my helmet, pop the lap belt, throw the shoulder harness back, undue the Koch fittings, stand up, and climb out. There's a ladder but where the hell is my crew? I put my hand gently on my aircraft as the engine ticks. She's cool to the touch. Then I step away.

Wait! There's a sound, singing! It's coming from an old hangar on the edge of the ramp. I walk toward it. I open a door and walk down the hall. I hear voices, laughter, breaking glass. I rub my face. Can it be? My mustache is back. I push quickly through another door and there they all are. Dear God in heaven, there they are. There's Phil behind the bar. There's Chappie. There's Tex. There's Hub. There's Leon, Tooey, Pappy, Jim, Stevan, so many familiar faces. I know I'm dreaming, but this is the dream I've wanted.

I yell to the group, "Olds Flight, checking in!"

The singing stops. They turn toward me, a chorus of welcoming voices, "Robin! Robin, you made it! You're here." A beer is shoved into my hand. Someone claps me on the back. Faces swarm around. I move down the bar toward an old piano. The piano player stands up and steps toward me. It's my father.

"Hello, Robbie." He grins. "Welcome home."

"Hello, Dad." I smile shyly. "I was a fighter pilot!"

"Yes, son. You still are. I'm proud of you." He sits back down at the piano and says, "Now teach me some of those new songs, will you?"

I laugh. "Sure thing, Dad. But first, let me show you something." I turn toward the group. "Hey guys, how about one more MiG sweep?"

There's a roar of approval, the sound of tables scraping back, the piano starting up, voices singing, pilots cheering. I gulp down my beer, slam the glass onto the bar, and link arms with my men. We sweep across the room with a great shout, tackling the unwary, leaving nothing standing in our wake. We turn to crowd around the piano.

We sing, we drink, we retell our warrior tales, and we laugh.

I have flown home.

Index

★